THE TAMING OF THE DEMONS

THE TAMING OF

the Demons

FROM THE EPIC OF GESAR OF LING

TRANSLATED BY

Jane Hawes,
David Shapiro &
Lama Chönam

Forewords by

His Holiness the Fourteenth Dalai Lama
and Dudjom Sangye Pema Shepa Rinpoche

SHAMBHALA

Shambhala Publications, Inc.
2129 13th Street
Boulder, Colorado 80302
www.shambhala.com

Cover art: © Rinjin Dorje Sherpa
Interior design: Lora Zorian

9 8 7 6 5 4 3 2 1

First Edition
Printed in the United States of America

♾ This edition is printed on acid-free paper that meets the
American National Standards Institute Z39.48 Standard.
♻ Shambhala Publications makes every effort to print on recycled paper.
For more information please visit www.shambhala.com.

Shambhala Publications is distributed worldwide by
Penguin Random House, Inc., and its subsidiaries.

LIBRARY OF CONGRESS CATALOGING-IN-PUBLICATION DATA

Names: Hawes, Jane, translator. | Shapiro, David, (Tibetan scholar)
translator. | Chonam, Lama, translator. | Bstan-'dzin-rgya-mtsho, Dalai
Lama XIV, 1935—author of foreword.
Title: The taming of the demons: from the Epic of Gesar of Ling /
translated by Jane Hawes, David Shapiro, and Lama Chönam; foreword by
His Holiness the Fourteenth Dalai Lama.
Other titles: Gesar. Volume 4. English.
Description: First edition. | Boulder : Shambhala, 2021.
Identifiers: LCCN 2021012507 | ISBN 9781611808964 (trade paperback)
Subjects: LCSH: Epic literature, Tibetan—Translations into English.
Classification: LCC PL3748.G4 E5 2021 | DDC 895/.41—dc23
LC record available at https://lccn.loc.gov/2021012507

CONTENTS

THE DALAI LAMA

THE EPIC *GESAR OF LING* IS A GREAT WORK drawn from centuries of oral tradition that combines cultural, literary, musical, and historical elements with Tibetan Buddhist values. The Gesar story is one of the Tibetan people's most popular epics, its stories being enacted and sung at festivals and on important ceremonial occasions.

Many ancient peoples have recited epics as a source of inspiration: the renowned *Mahābhārata* and *Rāmāyaṇa* in India, the *Hamzanama* in Persia, the *Iliad* and *Odyssey* in Greece, for example. Tales of the heroic feats of Gesar of Ling enjoy a similar status among the people of Tibet.

By making the epic of Gesar available in English, the translators are offering the modern reader a chance to experience the particular character of this Tibetan tradition that has brought hope and fortitude to many generations across the Tibetan-speaking world; we have sound reasons to be grateful to them.

AUGUST 14, 2012

HIS HOLINESS DUDJOM RINPOCHE

Sangye Pema Zhepa

Supreme Head of the Dudjom Tersar

༄༅། །སྟོན་ཆོ་མ་དྲུ་གུ་རུའི་སྐུ་འཕྲུལ་གར། །བདུད་འདུལ་སེང་ཆེན་རྒྱལ་པོའི་ མཐུ་བྱིན་གྱིས། །ལག་ལྟོགས་ལྷ་ སྐློའི་བདུད་དཔུང་པ་མཐར་སྤྱུད། །སངས་རྒྱས་ བསྟན་པའི་རྒྱལ་མཆན་དགུང་དུ་བསྒྲེངས། །ཁྱོགས་ལྡན་གསར་པའི་དགའ་ སྟོན་མགྲོན་དུ་བོས། །ཕུན་ཆོགས་སྡེ་བཞི་དཔྱིད་ཀྱི་མཎ་ཐང་བཞིན། །འཛམ་ གླིང་ཞི་བདེའི་བཀྲ་ཤིས་དཔལ་ཡོན་དེས། །གང་འདིར་བདག་ཆག་རྣམས་ལ་ བདེ་ལེགས་ཤོག། ཅེས་པའང་བླ་མ་ཆོས་དབྱིངས་རྣམ་རྒྱལ་མཆོག་གི་ངོར་བདུད་ འཇོམས་སྤྲུལ་མིང་པ་སངས་རྒྱས་པ་བཞད་པས་སྨོན་པ་དགོའོ།།

Previously, as the magical manifestation of Great Master
    [Padmasambhava],
You, Lion King Tamer of Māras [Gesar of Ling], through your
    blessings and power
Expelled the dark forces of the barbaric māras to the farthest shore,
Hoisted the victory banner of the Buddha's doctrine high in the
    firmament,
And heralded in a celebratory time, a new golden age
Of the four endowments, like summertime in full bloom.
May all those glorious qualities of auspicious peace and well-being in
    the world
Bring us all great happiness now and always.

Thus, at the request of Lama Chönam, I, the one named Dudjom Sangye Pema Shepa, offered this aspiration prayer.

Translated by Light of Berotsana Translation Group.

TRANSLATORS' INTRODUCTION

THIS TEXT NOW BEFORE YOU is the first English translation of *The Taming of the Demons*. This important saga delves into the full-bodied and bloodied nature of the story itself. The previously published first three volumes of the epic begin with Gesar's timely birth in this realm and the beginning of the process of the theme of reincarnation. This then leads to the story of his rambunctious early years—the famous horse race, eventual ascendancy to the throne of Ling, and marriage to his destined wife, the lovely *ḍākinī* Drukmo. The current text is the story that generally follows this telling of the birth and coronation of Gesar.[1] However, it should be noted that there are various aspects of the Gesar epic that remain controversial and are ongoing areas of scholarly research. Besides the chronology of the story itself, the actual length of the epic is open to some question, as is the somewhat varying content across different versions. In addition to the version that originated somewhere in the Golok region (situated between Amdo and Kham in northeastern Tibet), there are several others, including Mongolian, Persian, Indian, Ladakhi, Bhutanese, and Chinese versions. The Mongolian is likely the first written version, produced in 1716. The current text to which we will now turn has its own story to tell.

In contrast to the stories in the first three volumes, this is much more a martial story of battles won and strategies applied. It is a story that may appear gruesome at times, but as in all Gesar stories, the vanquishing and destruction of enemies is done with the full heart of compassion and with a view toward the eventual liberation of those who are vanquished.

This story of the taming of the demons is generally the one that chronologically follows Gesar's ascent to the throne and is the first in which he acts as a general and leader for the land of Ling. Identifying the land of Ling represents our first geographic challenge. If we look toward Kham and Amdo and review their mountains and valleys and the rivers that source within their borders, what we see is complex. Current Lingtsang most likely represents the final distillate of a far larger area of Ling, dismantled by the Mongols in the seventeenth century. The actual land of Ling in all probability spanned a far larger area, incorporating much of Kham and some of Amdo and likely centered around the area between them, now known as Golok.[2] The other major geographic challenge is with the land of Hor, which is the Tibetan word for Mongol and generally represents any area over which Mongolian tribes held sovereignty as well as, in particular, a much smaller area east of Ling and just east of the Yalong River (Nyak Chu). In later centuries, the Mongols controlled vast swaths of land north and west of Ling and the land of Hor, which then referred to a considerably different geographical area. However, there remain other areas in the story that we could not place with precision on a current map despite our efforts, though they are no doubt specific historical locations. The map we created for this volume is simply intended to give the reader a general sense of the places in which the action takes place.

Gesar of Ling is the national epic of Tibet. It is often heralded as the longest in the world's canon of great epics including *Gilgamesh*, *Beowulf*, the *Mahābhārata*, the *Iliad* and the *Odyssey*, and the great epics of Scandinavia and elsewhere, although there is some controversy about its actual length. Most often, it is reported as being one hundred and twenty volumes and twenty million words in length. Regardless of its length, it has great importance both within the world's canon and to the Tibetan people. Up until the eighteenth century, it was an oral tale, the first recorded written version being the Mongolian text referred to above. A commonly studied version was compiled as woodblocks or xylographs by a student of an esteemed Tibetan teacher of the late nineteenth century, Ju Mipham Rinpoche,[3] who had a lifelong interest in Gesar and wrote numerous Gesar practices and commentaries. Mipham Rinpoche's disciple Gyurme Thubten Jamyang Drakpa compiled the first three volumes of the Gesar epic, incorporating Mipham's supplications to each chapter of the third volume. This was the version used for the earlier translation of volumes 1–3 and published first as *The Epic of Gesar: His Magical Birth, Early Years, and Coronation as King* and then again as a retelling titled *Gesar of Ling: A Bardic Tale from the Snow Land of Tibet*. As the current volume follows chronologically from the first three volumes, a recap of the story thus far is in order. This recap, then, is in accordance with the previously published translations based on the woodblocks compiled at the end of the nineteenth century in Tibet.

A RECAP OF BOOK ONE: GESAR'S EARLY YEARS AND ASCENT TO THE THRONE

It is a dark and difficult time across the Tibetan Plateau and, in fact, throughout the grand expanse of Eurasia. It is the early tenth century, and in Tibet, a period of relative calm and unity has ended, giving way to warring and feuding clans and districts with life marked by famine and pestilence not dissimilar to the conditions throughout much of Europe. Buddhism was newly established in Tibet, and the great bodhisattva Avalokiteśvara, in his compassion, wished to alleviate the suffering of the land and people of Tibet. He went forthwith to the buddha Amitābha, and after some discussion, they came up with a plan whereby a celestial being would incarnate and attempt to lead the Tibetans from their misery, first by unifying the Tibetan clans and then by defeating the many enemies that bordered their troubled land. What is more, they decided to bring Padmasambhava into their plan to perform the many managerial functions that this grand scheme—and scheme it was—would require.

So it was that Döndrub (Gesar's name in the celestial realm) was sent to earth after a proper mother and father had been selected and after Döndrub had negotiated his requirements for human incarnation. With suitable fanfare, he was born in the land of Ling as a baby, initially named Joru, to Gokmo, a young woman who began life as a *nāga* princess and came to the human realm destined to be Gesar's mother. At the time of his birth, Joru was a fully developed three-year-old, versed in Buddhist scripture and philosophy and endowed with a captivating presence. However, among Joru's requirements for incarnation was that he be challenged by a wily and crafty enemy who tests him and keeps him sharp. It is his uncle Trothung who plays this role. He makes his first appearance shortly after Joru's birth, and Trothung, sensing the threat to his own preeminence, immediately makes plans to do away with the baby. Though thwarted in this and much of his subsequent conniving, he continues to be an important adversary in this story and the subsequent volumes of the epic.

Joru becomes a rather rowdy youth, with his bad behavior egged on by Padmasambhava and also by a very special and powerful sorceress, Aunt Manéné. It is all part of a larger plot that causes Gesar and his mother, Gokmo, to be banished as outcasts to the neighboring land of Ma. Because of a terrible, harsh winter snowstorm that Gesar produces with a bit of help, the Ling people are forced to appeal to Gesar's good heart when the land to which he was exiled turns out to be the only inhabitable land left during the prolonged period of snow and ice. Gesar grants territory in Ma to the people of Ling, and they settle until the winter storms pass. When they return to Ling, through Manéné's scheming, Joru plants the idea of a grand horse race in Trothung's mind. Although he is reluctant, Trothung is forced to invite Joru to the race. The stakes are high as it is agreed by the leaders and warriors of Ling that the winner would become the leader of Ling as well as acquire the wealth of Kyalo Tönpa, the wealthiest man of Ling, and the hand of Drukmo, his beautiful daughter.

After significant preparation—including obtaining for Joru his destined steed, Kyang Gö, which only Joru's mother and Drukmo had the wisdom and destiny to find—Joru enters the horse race. However, despite its importance for his mission, Joru appears quite lackadaisical, necessitating prompting from Manéné to buckle down and win. He does and ascends the throne, whereupon he takes his prophesied name, Gesar Norbu Dradül, and this chapter of his story comes to an end.

DETAILS REGARDING THE STRUCTURE OF THE WORK

The work is presented in a way that mirrors the style of the Tibetan. It is most suited to reading aloud and contains both prose and poetic songs. The narrative that reflects the bard's storytelling is given in prose format, and the songs that are sung by the many characters are given in verse. It should be noted that in Tibetan there is a strict meter to the songs, most often with seven or nine syllables to each line, and each song is sung in a melody specific to the character singing. In addition, Tibetan proverbs are expressed throughout, and we have distinguished them with italics.

We have attempted to simplify the Tibetan names and terms and added some markings to aid in pronunciation. In general, digraphs and trigraphs such as *th*, *tsh*, and *ph* are pronounced as aspirated consonants *t*, *ts*, and *p*. *Th* and *ph* are not the single sound of *th* as in *that* and *ph* as in *phone* that we are used to in English. The *u* sound is never pronounced as the *u* in *luck* but as the *oo* in *book*. For Sanskrit terms, such as *cakra*, the *c* sound is always pronounced as *ch*. In Tibetan, the digraph *ng* is pronounced as in the English *king*, and this sound may also be found at the beginning of a term or syllable, such as the *ngu* in the name Nang-ngu.

The glossaries, warrior chart, and basic genealogy chart are provided as a reference for names of major characters, places, and terms that recur throughout the epic. We hope that the map that we have created provides the reader a useful visual reference for the plot.

STYLE CHANGES FROM THE FIRST BOOK

Readers familiar with Light of Berotsana Translation Group's first book on Gesar's adventures, *The Epic of Gesar of Ling: Gesar's Magical Birth, Early Years, and Coronation as King* (translated by Robin Kornman, Sangye Khandro, and Lama Chönam), will notice a few technical changes to layout and style.

The first book includes English translations of proper nouns in square brackets. For the second book, these were changed to parentheses so as not to be confused with the use of the square bracket to indicate the translators' insertions. Also for ease of reading, while the verse in the first book was formulated such that the first word of each line is capitalized, the present work utilizes sentence-style capitalization. As the text was designed to be read aloud, it is hoped that this new format aids in the flow of reading so that the quick rollicking tone of the songs is not lost.

There have been a few minor changes in the Tibetan phonetic system as well. While the first book uses hyphens in Tibetan names and terms, this second book uses hyphens only for names that begin and end with the same digraph consonant, Ching-ngön and Nang-ngu. All other names with a double internal consonant are simplified to a single consonant for phonetic ease. For the present book, the abbreviation "Tib." is not used to indicate Tibetan language before phonetic Tibetan or Wylie transliteration. The abbreviation "Skt." to indicate a term is in Sanskrit language is only used to differentiate it from a Tibetan term listed together with it. While the first book phoneticizes the vowel *a* when followed by a silent or voiced suffix as *ei*, this book uses only *e*. For example, the name "Yelga Dzeiden" found in the first book appears in the second as "Yelga Dzeden." As for diacritics, both books utilize the umlaut for *u* and *o*, pronounced as in their German usage. The acute accented *é* (as in the word *cliché*) is used only when it stands alone as a final syllable with the exception of the name Manéné. The first book includes the final *d* suffix in phoneticized terms and names. Here, the *d* is retained in the place name Düd as a fixed form (as is also common practice with the term *chöd*), while all other final *d* consonants have been removed, treating it as a silent letter. As for Wylie transliteration, Tibetan proper nouns in Wylie are italicized and not capitalized in the first book. In the present work, they are capitalized and not italicized.

Acknowledgments

This work, like every trivial or weighty moment in life, is the result of many circumstances. At its root, as in all epic tales, is the timeless battle of good and evil that here became embodied in the story of Gesar of Ling in the eleventh century in eastern Tibet. Over the course of time, this rich story was infused with the maturing of Tibetan Buddhism, the eloquence of countless bards, the vastness and multiplicity of the Tibetan Plateau and its natural environment, the curiosity of numerous Western explorers, the interest of Ju Mipham Rinpoche, and the diligence of his students. Incorporating versions and influences said to span from Rome to Burma and from Mongolia to Bhutan, the epic grew and flourished. As Socrates argues in Plato's *Phaedrus*, the written word will corrupt the minds of humans, destroying their memories and limiting them to learning what is recorded on a page rather than using their minds and knowing a subject firsthand. It was such an orality that marked the Gesar epic. For nearly a thousand years, it was sung and told and retold, as though hammered until it shone like twenty-four-carat gold in the bright noonday sun. Then, it was carved into woodblocks, written on paper, or, more recently, recorded in voice by great bards such as Drakpa (1902–1986), who, for much of the twentieth century, was the most revered and respected of the bards in Tibet. As the millennium unfurled, the Gesar stories permeated Tibetan culture, which in turn poured out countless individuals versed in these tales.

Now, in the twenty-first century, we are the recipients of these great gifts as the rich Buddhist and nomadic culture of Tibet has streamed into the West. In the intertwining cadre of destinies, the opportunity arose to translate this volume of the Gesar epic, the story of the battle between Düd and Ling. For us, Chögyam Trungpa Rinpoche planted the seeds of this varietal garden with his vision of imparting the wisdom of Tibetan Buddhism and the Gesar icons to the West. His student Dr. Robin Kornman tilled that garden with the profuse flowering of his mind and the eventual but unfortunately posthumous publication with Lama Chönam and Sangye Khandro of the first three volumes of the epic. Integral and essential to both that publication and this current work is Lama Chöying Namgyal, known as Lama Chönam, whose boundless knowledge of the epic was nurtured in his native Golok and transplanted to these Western shores. After the publication of the first book in 2013, Jane Hawes and Lama Chönam began an early translation of the second, this current text. A full draft version was then produced and carefully reviewed with the assistance of David Shapiro.

The text that we worked from is titled *The Battle of Düd and Ling*.[4] It was compiled by Tendzin Phuntsok from narratives that had been collected by a committee of scholars and administrators. The foundation of their work was twofold: recordings of the song known as "The Taming of the Northern King Lutsen"[5] as it was sung by the illustrious bard Drakpa and the published story *The Taming of the Seven Wayward Siblings*,[6] which in turn had been sourced from two previous texts, *The Taming of the Māras*[7] and *A Chapter on the Māras*.[8] It should be noted, and not just in passing, that all Gesar translation and scholarship is indebted to the thousands of bards who for centuries have sung, performed, recorded, and thereby transmitted the rich majesty of this epic tale.

We owe a heartfelt debt to Lama Chönam for his selfless gift of time and his earnestness in transmitting his Golok heritage. He imparted teachings for even the most mundane of questions. Without the teachings of Chögyam Trungpa Rinpoche, our root guru, we would never have come to this path or have had even an atom's worth of understanding. The late Robin Kornman—a devoted Buddhist practitioner, literary scholar, and friend—showed us how expansive curiosity could be. In addition, we are honored and profoundly grateful to Kyabje Dudjom Yangsi Rinpoche for the blessing of his words and humbled by the foreword provided by His Holiness the Fourteenth Dalai Lama.

We are appreciative of the scholarship of George FitzHerbert, Samten Karmay, Geoffrey Samuel, Timothy Thurston, and others who have helped elucidate many aspects of the Gesar epic. Without the inspiration of Sangye Khandro, her lifelong devotion to the teachings of the Buddhadharma, and her skill in the Tibetan language that is the heart of the Light of Berotsana Translation Group, this work would not have seen the light of day. The cartography of Karl Ryavec was invaluable in placing much of an ancient geography on modern-day maps. We are also beholden to the resources of the Buddhist Digital Resource Center, Rangjung Yeshé Institute, and the innumerable scholars who have blazed the trail to make these platforms available. We are deeply grateful to Nikko Odiseos for his enthusiasm for this work, for the consummate skill of his staff at Shambhala Publications, and in particular to Anna Wolcott Johnson for her precision and clarity as copyeditor.

Deep in our hearts, we are hopeful that you find inspiration in this tale of Gesar's conquering of the *māra* king Lutsen and the vanquishing of innumerable demons along the way. The carnage portrayed in the tale, in fact, is considerable and likely difficult to readily reconcile with our own hopes and aspirations for a peaceful world. That compassion arises out of difficult times is something that we all experience. That obstacles arise that appear to be external yet stem from within us is perhaps less familiar to human experience. To be a genuine, selfless, truthful, and noble human being in this world, though difficult to achieve, is the worthiest of endeavors. We are fortunate that great noble ones such as Gesar of Ling chose to incarnate among us, bring out the good in this world, and vanquish the hordes of haughty gods-demons[9] that plague humanity—and that they demonstrate how to do this as ordinary human beings. We are reminded again and again—in this epic and elsewhere—that a belief in the limit of what we might achieve is bound to be our greatest obstacle. May *The Epic of Gesar* be an inspiration to all beings as they overcome suffering and obstacles in their own lives and aspire to develop a depth of compassion that embraces all beings.

JANE HAWES AND DAVID SHAPIRO
Winter 2020
Belmont, California

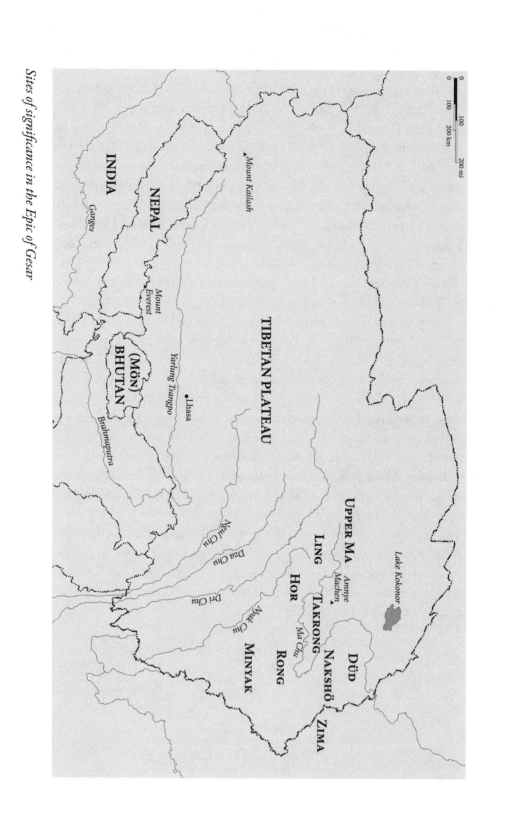

Sites of significance in the Epic of Gesar

VOLUME FOUR

The Taming of the Demons

CHAPTER ONE

Trothung, ever-fixated on Joru's political clout,
takes off, concealed valuables in hand.
He goes to Yutsé, the king of the Düd in the east, to seek
  asylum.
Together they plot to take the kingdom of Ling by force.

Now begins the epic tale of the battle of Düd and Ling. At this time in Ling, there are eminently virtuous tribes who are great in merit and morals, honored, and endowed with ever-increasing prosperity. In the upper lands,[1] the eight Serpa brothers and their troops, bearing golden pennants, are a great throng, numbering nine hundred. Likewise, residing downriver are the people of the four Mupa clans, stately as an ice-covered lake, and between are the six tribes of Ombu, scattered like seeds. Stretching to one side,[2] the district of Ga resembles a white silk victory banner held aloft, and to the other, the district of Dru reminds one of a maṇḍala arrayed with fresh barley grain. Settled in these districts are the Tau people, the eighteen great tribes of Takrong,[3] whose ruddy complexions evoke the rich color of golden armor.

The twelve myriarchies of Denma are like the sylvan subcontinents that frame the four great continents, and Tshazhang Denma himself and his nine wealthy tribes are as splendorous as the trees and greenery upon the earth. The six provinces of Guzi Achak are like a finely polished copper vessel brimming with fresh milk. Arching to one side are twelve myriarchies that sparkle like snow mountains beneath the morning sun, and to the other are twelve myriarchies massing like dark rain clouds over a forested gorge.

It is as though Upper Ma had matured to be the pride of the earth, teeming with well-fed sheep. The 920,000 inhabitants of Lower Ma are as dependable as notched arrows aligned in a quiver. The inner tribes—those most closely related to the leaders of Ling—are like the iridescent constellations in the heavens; their distant relations, the outer tribes, are like the majestic grasses of the meadows. These people are as grand as Mount Kailash and as innumerable as the stars in the sky. The Greater Lineage,[4] the excellent clan of Taktsang (The Tiger's Lair), flourishes like the six smiles[5] of a tiger in its prime.[6] Like a string of pearls, the Middle Lineage is as graceful as a white silk fringe,[7] and the Lesser Lineage is like a *garuḍa* with its beating wings outstretched, aching to fly. The gurus are akin to the sun and moon in the heavens, and the highest leaders to the kings of mountains. The fathers and uncles are the finest of Taktsang, their sons and nephews are like fresh bamboo shoots, and their daughters and nieces like flowers at the water's edge. The mothers and aunts are as implacable as silken ice upon a lake, and the citizens as robust as a bountiful harvest.

From their jeweled den, the clear and vivid sound of dragons is heard. Here, the melodious sound of the cuckoo resounds, and the evocative refrain of the lark reverberates. Within a palace in this treasured land, on an ornate lion throne sits King Gesar, the Lord Great Lion Sengchen himself. He is the destined deity of the world and the refuge and protector of the snow land of Tibet. He is the leader of Tramo Ling and the sovereign of Sengdruk Taktsé,[8] the one to subdue the evil forces of māras and the one who had come to be the holder of the wealth of Kyalo[9] and the ruler of its people.

As for Trothung, a ruler in the Greater Lineage of Takrong, he could think only of what he coveted: the royal seat of Ling, the beautiful Drukmo, and the riches of Kyalo. These thoughts so riddled his mind that he could not wrest himself free of them. Consumed by ambition, he called all the powerful, important leaders of Takrong to come before him, and after lavishing upon them an elaborate feast of food and drink, he paraded in a frightening costume and sang this song, "Harmin Hur."[10]

> OṂ MAṆI PADME HŪṂ
> Sing "Ala thala thala."
> "Thala" begins and
> "La la" gives the perfect pitch.[11]
> From the celestial palace of Meri Barwa (Blazing Mountain),
> the perfect encircling environment,[12]
> yidam Red Hayagrīva, think of me
> and look upon me with the gaze that reveals the teachings.

Please hear me as I call.
Do not turn away as I practice your *yidam* continually,
nor be feeble in your response, as I honor and rely upon you.
When the prophecy concerning Joru turned out to be false,[13]
my scheme failed
and I was without a deity or power.
If I can be so bold as to say so, it was Hayagrīva who had been
    deceptive,
and now he must support me unfailingly.
A man without authority has difficulty holding the throne.
To wit, here in this shady swath of land, in my fortress, Porok
    Nying Dzong (Raven Heart Fortress),
I, a chieftain lacking power, cannot remain.
If you do not recognize me,
I am Trothung, born as a manifestation of Red Hayagrīva.
I am the supreme king of my tribe, a leader in Tramo Ling.
My sons—unrivaled Takphen, Zikphen, great warriors,
Nyatsha, and Dongtsen Apel—the four of you, listen!
You four pillar chieftains, Yuthok,
Taktsha, Jachen, Khangné,
you twelve ruling generals,
Akhö Tharpa Zorna (Hooked-Nosed Tharpa) and the others,
nine who can run wherever they are sent
and three with great power in deliberation—all of you, listen!
While you were each caught up in parochial concerns,
your leader Chipön's dullard of a son—
his eldest, Lenpa Chögyal (Simpleminded Dharma King)—
went to the valley farmlands and was killed by a farm girl,
proving that he was untrained and much too young.
Now, Chipön is barely breathing, nearly a corpse.
And while he does nothing but poke up his thumbs like a
    beggar,
having taken it upon themselves to hunt down in revenge
    those who killed his son,
two of my own sons, Takphen and Zikphen—
commanding tiger and leopard[14] that they are—
took the women of those farmlands, along with its wealth,
as the blood price of revenge for that killing.

Not only that, there is still more.
An army of the fathers and sons of Takrong
descended on the country of Gok
to trounce its great magical king, Ralo Tönpa,[15]
with their prowess.
The princess Gokza was escorted from Gok
by us all, the soldiers of the Greater Lineage of Ling.
I led the six provinces of Ling,
but I never plundered, even though I had such great might.
Our words were our pledge
and what was spoken was written;
we agreed on each warrior's reward.
But soon, like fish drifting in a current, no one stuck to their
     promises.
And after that, born to that loathsome mother Gokza,
who came along but the ill-omened child Joru?
He and that fearless white-faced corpse of a boy, Gyatsha
     Zhalkar,
along with Denma, the great archer,
Rongtsha Marleb, and Nang-ngu Yutak,
all those young warriors, like tiger cubs asleep in their lair—
this bad time has their minds confused.
But they are united in their intentions,
and their only strategy is to cause me pain.
What is more, from the time that he was born,
Joru has done nothing but rustle livestock.
Knowing he was my nephew, I was tolerant,
but while I never argued against him,
his vulgar temperament became even harsher.
Eventually, all of my political power
and the wealth of Kyalo and his subjects were stolen away,
the prosperity treasure of Padmasambhava was plundered,
and the very core of Ling decayed.
The year before last, Kyalo
was debating about who would be seated with official rank.
It was pure nepotism that Gyatsha was elevated to the throne,
while one who was his equal, my son Takphen, was tossed aside.
Joru, who is neither human nor demon,

berated me ceaselessly, until I was struck down, ailing.
We are at a turning point; anything could happen.
I have pondered this, and at my very core
I am incensed, roused to revenge.
If I cannot command a single such furious battle,
I, Trothung, would rather die.
As in the ancient proverbs of Tibet:

If our stomachs cannot digest what we have eaten,
no matter that we have honey—its sweetness is an extravagance.
If our bodies are not warm,
no matter that we have silk brocade—its finery is immaterial.

If there is no profit to be had from political affairs,
no matter that the one in power is your nephew, that fact is
    moot.
That is the crux of the matter.
There are further examples:

Why speak of the stride of a horse
when it is the jockey's skill that gives free rein to its speed?
Why speak of the keenness of the cutting blade
when it is the warrior's swing that wields the blade?
Why speak of the swiftness of an arrow
when it is the archer's aim that finds the intended target?

Why speak of someone as courageous
when it is decisiveness that bears on events?
What counts is whether one is weakened or strengthened by
    challenges.
In fact, I, Uncle Trothung,
have a magical *torma* empowered with subjugating mantras
that can topple even Mount Meru.
I have powerful and wrathful mantras
able to bring down the sun and the moon.
By the mudra that summons the life force,[16]
I can reverse the flow of great rivers such that they climb steep
    hillsides,
and with the nine magical illusions

I can bind phenomenal existence in servitude.
Uniting fathers, sons, and all citizens,
I am equipped to rule both spiritual and worldly spheres.
This song is my decree,
and like drops of gold,
my words cannot be discounted.
Keep this in mind, you who are listening here.

Thus he sang. Takphen, Nyatsha, and others who were devoted to Gesar were quite troubled. Yet, although they were scornful of Trothung and his wife Sertsho (Golden Lake), they said nothing. Zikphen also had his qualms, but Dongtsen sided with Trothung. Akhö[17] Tharpa Zorna and others—some of the ministers who were less wise, as well as some of the servants—appeared to be delighted with Trothung's speech. The division leaders—Kazhi, Khanglé, Jachen, and so forth—felt unwaveringly that they would rather die than break their samaya to King Gesar; nonetheless, they too remained silent. Getting up his nerve, from his honored seat at the head of the right-hand row, Trothung's young son Takphen addressed the assembly—the fathers and uncles, chiefs and ministers—saying, "I may not appear sharp, but my inner qualities are astute. To my way of thinking, it is like this." And he offered this song.

OM MAṆI PADME HŪM
Sing "Ala thala thala."
"Thala" begins this song of Ling and
"La la" gives the perfect pitch.
From the palace on Glorious Copper-Colored Mountain,[18]
Lotus-Born Guru Padmasambhava,
surrounded by the vast ocean of the Three Roots[19]—
I supplicate you. Please look kindly upon me.
May your blessings enter my being.
Zodor, guardian spirits, and protector deities of Ling, watch
    over me.
May this aspiration be fulfilled.
This is the country of Ling in the land of Ma,
a divine pure land.
The valley to the right is as luxuriant as the smiles of a tiger.
Upon these six smiles, Takrong is situated;
accordingly, it is known as Takrong, the Tiger Valley.

The valley to the left resembles a leopard's fine coat of fur.
In the rosettes of the leopard's spots sits Zikrong, the Leopard
   Valley.
When the mighty *tsen*[20] were bound,
it was by two young boys, myself, Takphen, and my brother
   Zikphen.
This fortress here is Porok Nying Dzong,
the sacred space of sublime Hayagrīva,
and the leader is my father, Trothung, a manifestation of
   Hayagrīva.
Listen attentively to what I have to say.
My father's words, just spoken, hang in the air,
and although I do not ask him to take them back,
at this perilous time, neither can I remain silent.
Is it not just as in the proverbs?

The three months of summer yield the crops;
if they were to grow in winter, that would be a field of the gods.
But the seasons mandate the cycle from summer to winter,
and in this, the vegetation has no reason to lament.

Trothung has ruled over the six provinces of Ling;
if this were irrevocable, it could only be so by divine mandate.
But change is the nature of saṃsāra,
and, in this, Trothung has no reason to lament.
Chipön, Trothung, and Senglön—these three
are the sole fathers of a generation.
There is no distinction between fathers and uncles or
   between sons and nephews.
Whoever is up to the mark will be the sovereign of the
   kingdom.
There is no reason to trigger dispute through ambition and
   greed,
and no good comes of broadcasting spiteful rumors.
Gesar, the Masang[21] king,
is the magical manifestation of Orgyen Padma,
an emanation of the buddhas of the three times,
the pillar of virtue,

and the executioner of the evil māras.
In the eastern country of Ling,
he appeared as abruptly as mushrooms in a meadow,
born its sole heir, incomparable,
and from the moment of birth, endowed with magical powers.
The telling of his deeds is without end.
Throughout the valleys of Ling,
Gesar built thirty secure fortresses
and constructed Sengdruk Taktsé.[22]
In those days, although there was contention over the seat of
    the throne,
no one arose to challenge him,
as he had already been cured of the root of all disease[23]
and was without unwholesome thoughts.
He brought prosperity horses[24] down from the land of Zima
and distributed them to his kinsmen.
Even Trothung could already see the extent of Gesar's power.
Yet, there is still more.
According to the laws settled on by the arbiter of Ling,
the Düd king Lutsen's skull will be pierced by an arrow,
the Hor king Gurkar yoked around the neck,
and, along with the Jang king Sadam[25] and the Mön king
    Shingtri,
all the māras will be tamed.
Thus, prosperity will descend upon the eighteen minor
    kingdoms surrounding Ling.
All this is in accord with the command of King Gesar.
Who would have such power to tame, if not Gesar?
If he did not have power, how could he accomplish anything?
There is no point in warring over excrement
or value in spending riches to reap suffering.
Bringing misery to this life and the next is pointless.
Gesar should control the golden throne,
and his kinsmen should sit atop the sandalwood throne
with one mind, trusting one another,
a single white silken scarf bound to the path.
Trothung, if you have such power and magic, show yourself
    to the Düd,

and if you have such a mighty army, attack the enemy—
that is the way of this world.
Now, since last year's end,[26]
you have been ailing,
sometimes better, sometimes worse,
but unlikely to be cured.
Even so, that is no reason to detest Gesar.
It is senseless to bring ruin upon this life and the next.
Trothung, keep this in mind.

Trothung recoiled at these words. His face flushed and his eyes bulged, but he was afraid of his son Takphen and unable to utter a sound. At that moment, Dongtsen Apel sang this song.

> OṂ MAṆI PADME HŪṂ
> Sing "Ala thala thala."
> "Thala" begins and
> "La la" gives the perfect pitch.
> I call upon the Three Jewels; please think of me.
> Do not fail to assist me.
> We are here in the sparkling land of Ling.
> This imposing castle, Porok Nying Dzong,
> is the home of the fierce Trothung, my father.
> I am the one known as Dongtsen Apel,
> not celebrated for bravery
> but born to survive.
> Fathers and uncles, brothers and sons,
> leaders of the ruddy Tau people of Takrong,
> listen and consider carefully what has come of our actions.
> Chipön, devastated by the loss of his son,
> had come desperately begging to Trothung's household;
> we could not turn our backs
> and so sent out a brigade in revenge.
> The fierce battle that ensued
> harmed us as well as Gok.[27]
> We of Ling desired a son in payback but instead acquired a
>   daughter,
> one with a karmic connection to the leader, Senglön,

and the invincible Joru was born.
He, in due course, would undermine Trothung's position.
This stemmed directly from the damage to Gok and us.
Just as karma unfailingly ripens,
in the end our nemesis Gesar reaped the benefit
of what that gray-bearded Chipön had set in motion.
Chipön was inundated with disputes;
he swirled this troubled water, and from its midst
emerged the man who came to be known as Gesar.
This enemy arose directly on your watch, Trothung;
it is not important whether you were the father or the uncle.
According to the worldly proverbs of the people of ancient
    times:

It is no better being brought down[28] by those close to you than by
    strangers.
There is no lesser harm to your head smashed by a statue than a rock.
Food that has spoiled does you no good.

Spoken this way, we see the truth.
If there is no benefit in a governmental policy,
it is no worse made by your father than your uncle—
the result is the same.
The wrongdoings of Chipön
are infuriating and roil in my mind.
I cannot think of Chipön as my uncle
without becoming enraged.
I cannot think of Gesar as my king
without becoming incensed.
His horse Kyang Gö[29] is a fleet runner;
my own steed Yuja (Turquoise Bird) had hoped to challenge
    him in the race.
My dear father, King Trothung,
is the chief of all seven myriarchies of Takrong.
He is a manifestation of Red Hayagrīva
and a master of mantra and magic.
If I do not respect my father's authority,
how can others be expected to heed his words?

To go against him brings ruin to this life and the next.
Therefore, listen and value what he has said.
The matter of readying an army
to send forth warriors on horseback into great battle
is a matter for the leaders to undertake.
You, the Phunu, keep this in your hearts.

On hearing this, Trothung was as exuberant as a peacock listening to the summer thunder and he urged everyone to action. Akhö Tharpa Zorna, Guru's son Khergö (Solitary Vulture), Muktsen Nyobpa Lakring (Long-Armed Dark Demon), Nyiji's (Heavy Sun) son Lhündrub, Changmo's son Jemé (Traceless One), and so on, with voices low as a tigress' roar, pledged fealty.

All the while, Zikphen's mind had been churning with the thought that none of what had been said refuted the point that Gesar was in all respects the magical manifestation of bravery and that whether Trothung was a lama possessed of good qualities or not, he was still an ordinary human with a mind vulnerable to deception and confusion. Yet, for the time being, Zikphen held his tongue. By that time, Sertsho—disgusted by Trothung's very nature and that of their son Dongtsen and drawn by her unwavering faith in Gesar—wished nothing more than to be free of her husband Trothung. However, in front of everyone, making a pretense of reverence, she bent down, offered him *chang*, and sang.

> OṂ MAṆI PADME HŪṂ
> Sing "Ala thala thala."
> "Thala" begins.
> From the self-appearing celestial pure land,
> Queen Mother Vajravārāhī,
> surrounded by your retinue of mamos and ḍākinīs—
> I supplicate and yearn for you.
> Throughout this and all of my lifetimes, please do not be
>   apart from me.
> If you do not recognize this place,[30]
> it is Porok Nying Dzong,[31]
> the castle fortress of Trothung.
> It is the gathering place of the dear fathers and brothers,
> the great gathering place for dialogue.
> Here is the threshold of thoughts, both good and bad.
> I do not need to explain who I am—

I am Sertsho of the Den family
and the daughter of King Khara.
Now, my home is here with Trothung.
But I did not come here knocking my skull at the door like a
    beggar
or fighting off the guard dog like a stranger.
Rather, the leader of the Greater Lineage, Namkhé Sengzhal
    (Prince Sky-Lion Face),
and Trothung's private minister, Shemchok Rabsel (Supreme
    Knowledge),
along with seven servants, came to *my* door with
a herd of one hundred white *dzo* bearing one hundred boxes
    of tea,
bushy and freshly picked,
one hundred full-grown horned yak, and one hundred slabs
    of butter,
leather bags full of unspoiled fresh butter.
All this they brought to King Khara's doorstep
as a declaration of a boy's marriage proposal to a girl.
Yet, there was still more—
many fine-furred tiger skins
and a liter's weight of both gold and silver.
I was charmed with sweet tales to turn my head
and pressured with harsh ones threatening violence.
I was duped by your endless two-faced chatter
and led into marriage with you—
sent off with the well-wishes of my parents
with no say of my own.
You had not been able to hold on to any of the women of
    Ling
nor could you find yourself a bride from China.
It's not that you were not wealthy, dear chieftain,
but you never did have an inkling of Chinese customs.
The daughter of the Zikrong house, Bumtsho (One Hundred
    Thousand Lakes),
bore you a son, Zikphen, a silken rosette of a boy,[32]
and as a result, you then had two sons, Zikphen and Takphen.
But you had the ill luck to lose Bumtsho—

of course, dear Tro, you never really had the fortune to keep
    her.
And Lhadrön (Divine Torch), the daughter of Malu,
who had borne you the unrivaled warrior Takphen,
while you presumed she would come readily to your home,
had already slipped away to the chief of the Tapa Mitsho
    tribe.
The malicious lawsuits that ensued were on the verge of
    starting a great conflict
when Uncle King Chipön interceded,
adjudicating that Takphen belonged in Takrong[33] and not
    with his mother, Lhadrön.
Beyond that, Lhadrön's father never wanted you for a son-in-
    law.
That is how it transpired that she went to Mitsho,
though of course you received twenty-five times the usual
    reparation in payback.
Whatever you do, it all comes to trouble—
if I were to catalog it all, I could go on for days.
Chief Trothung,
these sons of yours, well-nigh namesakes of the tiger and
    leopard—
do not put them into the hands of the enemy, please just
    settle down.
Divine King Gesar—
do not make him your adversary; please just take it easy.
Chipön is like Mount Meru;
do not rattle him, just let him be.
Gesar is the destined king of the land of Tibet,
the one who will subdue the evil māras
and establish the teachings of virtue.
He is the sovereign of the six provinces of Ling.
Even if the entire world banded together, he could not be
    defeated.
Trothung, you have a mouth like hay dust.
Nothing of this life will remain;
in the end you will be certain to lose it all.
The incomparable King Gesar has already

set out a tiger-skin-covered sandalwood throne
where both uncles can sit as equals
and the three leaders of Upper and Lower Ling
can work alongside three of the sons of Takrong.
This is the way of his great kindness.
Unlike you, Gesar is not callous;
he is the lama buddha-bodhisattva.
May he hold me with his compassion as I go for refuge,
and may we be inseparable in this life and my lifetimes to
    come.
King Uncle Chipön
has knowledge and judgment that rise like the sun
and, like Mount Meru, he is unshakable.
When your three sons were small,
there was never a time he did not help your family.
These are the proverbs of the people of ancient Tibet:

Children who fail to obey their home
and return their parents' love with nothing but an evil eye—
their selfish skulking around the villages
only foreshadows that in the end they will become wandering
    beggars.
Tawdry ministers who fail to maintain the local villages
and come to despise others as nothing but rivals—
their fraternizing with thieves and robbers
only foreshadows that in the end they will lose everything.

The examples and the meaning are exactly the same.
You drag down your family name, peddling your reputation
    in the marketplace.
That you throw your plate at me
only foreshadows that someday, Trothung, you will go
    hungry.
Great people, sons and ministers of Takrong,
look here at the actions of Trothung—
even if he were to kill me, he would not repent.
You lamas and merchants had better think about this.
Dear brave Dongtsen,

you must give advice to your insane father,
running around all day like a fool, naked and crazy. . . .

Before she could finish, Trothung, affronted by Sertsho's sharp words and feeling that he had been unjustly shamed, with eyes rolled in anger, had thrown off his pocketed yellow robe and leapt to his feet. He had flung his silver plate, full of food, right at Sertsho's chest and was rushing at her with the sword that he had left leaning against a courtyard pillar. Zikphen at once grabbed his hand tightly, and a furious Nyatsha snatched the sword, sheathed the blade, and offered this short song.

OṂ MAṆI PADME HŪṂ
Sing "Ala thala thala."
"Thala" begins.
Divine assembly of *dralha* and *werma*,
please assist me.
As for us—father, mother, and me—
there is no question; everything is crystal clear.
Listen closely, Father Trothung.
The words of my dear, kind mother
are faultless golden droplets.
The master of Ling, divine son Gesar,
is the pillar of the gods who take delight in virtue,
the heart-son of a thousand buddhas,
and the one who subdues the demons and *rudras*.
His enlightened body is endowed with magic.
You know this, Chieftain Trothung,
yet you have hammered him with your hatred.
Even if that has escaped you, it is very clear to me.
The degree to which you have slandered his enlightened
    speech
cannot be measured—
it reaches beyond the heavens.
Your perverted views and confused mind
swirl like a dust storm
with not even a sesame seed's worth of value.
That is clear to everyone in Tramo Ling.
Uncle King Chipön
is the emanation of Berotsana,

17

the foremost support of Ling,
and the tether of all the kinsmen.
If we have Chipön, we have everything;
without him, we have nothing.
Look how you constantly clash with your rivals
and are continually pursued by misfortune.
You have a mean old monkey's treacherous air,
full of rage in the face of the bravery of your own family
and unable to return any kindness.
Do not look to your wife to answer for your evil.
No one should have to listen to your ranting.
Those like you who disgrace their ancestors—I wish them
     dead.
Today, I, Nyatsha, will kill you with this sword,
and the story will spread throughout Ling.
Tomorrow, I will invite Sengchen Gesar,
make hundreds of offerings of my most cherished
     wealth,
and you will be liberated.[34]
There is no path other than this.
These are not mere words—watch and see.

At this, Trothung became terrified even before the song's end. Without a second thought, Nyatsha unsheathed the sword and waved it around threateningly. Trothung slipped from Zikphen's grasp and into a small cave-like room and, without looking back, locked himself inside, closing the dark-red doors behind him. Dongtsen and Nyatsha, with opposing views regarding their father, Trothung, went at it with each other, shouting a few songs back and forth until Takphen and Zikphen, along with some of the other leaders, intervened to split them up before they came to blows. By nightfall, Nyatsha's scheming to kill Trothung had run out of steam. So, it was for many reasons that Sertsho and Nyatsha departed together for a secluded mountain retreat in Zikrong, leaving with seven attendants and fifteen mules weighted down with provisions. Takphen and Zikphen had only one desire—to meet with the lord of humans, Sengchen Gesar. Three days later, with five ministers and many mules loaded with supplies, they came to Gesar's castle Sengdruk Taktsé. But there, such harmony prevailed that they were loath to mention Trothung's treachery to Gesar. Of course, the omniscient Gesar was aware of all that had occurred and all that was planned, and furthermore, he knew that the time had come to tame the Seven Wayward Siblings. However, he too remained tight-lipped regarding his own plans.

Meanwhile, as the days wore on, Trothung was unable to settle down. Nightly, his dreams disturbed him, and he was consumed by the hatred that the deities had precipitated within him. His mind spun, questioning what he should do, and finally spewed out dozens of plans. He settled on some twenty-five of them and went on thinking, "If I go for safe haven to Hor, their butcher king, Shenpa, and Gyatsha, that little divine prince, the lot of them really, have such history[35] that for me it will come to no good. And as for Jang, I have no worthwhile connections there." Then, his mind turned toward the Zima Valley as a possible sanctuary. This was a place where Ling's powerful enemy, traitorous forces from the Mupa clan, were like the voice of the demon spirit Yama, lord of death. Here were those with human form as well as invisible demons: the Seven Wayward Siblings of Düd and their leader King Yutsé of Minyak, the one who had met his consort demoness by the roadside, had become a bandit, and was hence barred from returning to his homeland. There, in these lands overrun by demons, the villages swarmed with gangs of bandits. Those Mupa who had gone to Zima had become cunning through and through, and Trothung thought they were certain to be a powerful threat to Chipön. Trothung decided to divulge the details of his plans to his allies, and so he invited Dongtsen, Tharpa Zorna, Khergö, Muktsen Nyobpa Lakring, Lhündrub, Jemé, Ukmik, and a few others into his home to hear him out. Some of them had already been won over by the demons, but now because of the power of their previous negative karma, they were all in accord with Trothung's plans. To prepare, each then returned to their own homes where they worked with those they could trust, but from most everyone, they kept these plans a strict secret.

While all this scheming went on, Trothung's lesser advisors and attendants were waiting for him alongside a steep road on the slope of Lhamo Mountain. Finally, at pig-time[36] on the evening after the conclave, they had been joined by Trothung and Dongtsen. With thirty mules loaded with riches in tow and a loyal entourage filing behind, weapons in hand, Trothung and Dongtsen set out according to Trothung's plan. They had, in all, forty-three horses and seventy-one mules. It took five days and nights to reach the Zima Valley, a valley hemmed in by a jagged mountainside, a draped red curtain of rocky crags. In between its notched black peaks, the land resembled stretched human skin and was strewn with black boulders. There stood two demoness gatekeepers: one straddling a musk deer and the other, completely red, riding a black eagle. Their deafening voices called out, "Black-headed Tibetan earthworm! Black-headed Tibetan earthworm! Black-headed Tibetan earthworm!" Three times they called for Trothung to come quickly, and he and his ministers dismounted from their horses. With a trembling heart, Trothung said, "One hundred years long life to you ladies! You must not mistake friends for enemies. I am a kinsman, Akhu[37] Trothung of Ling. I have come to discuss an important undertaking with King Minyak Yutsé, my great and close childhood friend. I mean no harm. Great kind guardian protectors, I come in friendship with gifts of gold and silver."

When they heard this pompous so-called black-headed earthworm speak and refer to Ling, both guardians, Jama Jigo (Bat Head) and Jalak Derchu (Eagle Talon Beak), became suspicious that he was the enemy. That he came from Ling was not a good sign, so they decided that Jama Jigo would stay behind to protect the border and Jalak[38] Derchu would be the one to deliver a message to King Yutsé. Transforming herself into a black raven, she flew off. In the meantime, Jama Jigo manifested as a beautiful woman, and saying that she considered Trothung and his entourage her guests, she asked them to rest for a bit. Trothung and his ministers, with their horses and mules unloaded, sat down beside a great, notched rock to make some tea. After Trothung and Jigo traded a few songs back and forth, Trothung mesmerized her with mantra recitations and relaxed as his anger and fear dissipated.

The bard digresses to give background to the story: Trothung had come to a formidable land. It was rimmed with 108 smaller mountains and 13 great mountains,[39] each surrounded by a lake. Interspersed were grasslands and dense forests, and in the very center was a wall of red, iron-rich rock like that of Mount Meru. Within these red rocks was the broad and spacious cavern that was the gathering ground of the eight classes[40] of gods-demons. Although these were the sacred lands of the great deity Cakrasaṃvara, during this time they had fallen under the sway of the nonhuman gods-demons. During the lifetime of Chöphen Nakpo, an evil nāga named Jathül Nakpo (Black Rooster) had copulated with one of the *rākṣasas* of the nāga lands, and the child that was born was able to pass as a human and in turn became the mother of many māra family descendants. This nāga family accumulated abundant wealth and power and, furthermore, possessed the magical power of sharing in the mindstreams of the nonhuman gods-demons.

Four generations later, when Chipön had authority over Ling and Padmasambhava had come to glorious Samyé,[41] Lady Margyenma was born. Through her previous perverted aspirations, she had descended from the cannibal demon nāgas. Endowed with a strong mind and body, she was rather unambiguously named Yitrok Wangjema (Hypnotic Ruleress). She ruled by sucking blood and delighting in flesh, tramping around like a whore, and copulating with all the humans and gods-demons. From that state of utter defilement, at the pig-time hour, leading up to midnight, the seven *damsi*[42] of perverted aspirations simultaneously spawned seven black eggs. A fortnight later, they hatched, full-grown. They were born as six males: blue, black, red, green, yellow, and white; and a single female, red with coils of red hair. The blue one, the strongest of the males, was Lugön Tongthub Yamé (Unrivaled Nāga Protector Defeats One Thousand), a samaya-violator nāga vampire. Tongdü Lenmé (Unrivaled One Thousand Demons) was black, a samaya-violator demon. The red male was Tsenkya Bumthub (Pale Tsen Defeats One Hundred Thousand), the corrupt tsen. The green one, Shechen Yamé (Unrivaled Great Strength) was a defiled member of the Mu clan. The yellow one was Migö Yamé (Matchless Savage), the samaya-violator *gyalpo* spirit.[43] And finally, the white one, Shelé Lakring[44] (Crystal Long-Arm), was a *teurang*. All six males concealed their true identities, masquerading as human boys. The smallest of all was the crimson-red daughter named Trakrelma, Bloody Tress.[45] She was the queen of life and possessed all manner of powerful magical deceptions, magnetizing the three worlds. The story of these damsi will unfold, as their births in Düd had roused unhindered and relentless māra activity. Innumerable wild animals, fish of the rivers, and so forth were killed to be eaten, and these nonhuman spirits learned to cultivate the known earth and prosper from its annual harvest.

Meanwhile, the blue-complected King Yutsé of Minyak, that most eminent leader of the eastern Düd, had maintained sovereignty over the māra kingdom for some years. Although his two brothers, Metak Chökyi Wangchuk (Fire Tiger Powerful Lord of Dharma) and Chöpa Matshungpa (Actions of a Derogatory Misfit), had turned from their wicked ways, Yutsé decided to try to persuade the Hor king Gurkar, the northern Düd king Lutsen, and others to unite in conquering Tibet and plundering its resources. Therefore, he took thirteen of his own servants, fifty mule loads of the finest brocade, and treasures of gold, silver, and jewels, but as his caravan passed through Zichim and reached the border of Zi and Rong, Yutsé chanced upon the young Bloody Tress. Roused with energy, they delighted in singing songs back and forth. Yutsé was enthroned as the king of the degenerate eastern Düd and Bloody Tress became his consort. There inside that very same red rock cavern, the fearsome castle of Düd was erected and became Yutsé's royal seat. Outside the palace, beneath the rocky face of its cliff was Duktsho, a swirling poisonous lake that was the dwelling place of the life-force talisman of the gods-demons. At one time, hordes of māras dwelled there, and thrice their leaders, devoid of any virtue, had gone to raid Tramo Ling. It was the year of the warrior Gyatsha's birth to Gyaza and Senglön, and ten men led by Lhau Ösel (Divine Little Light) of the Mupa clan and no less than three hundred horses and yaks lost their lives. The Phunu, Chipön, and five ministers rallied in revenge, killing five Düd warriors and their leader, a Düd minister, Ngomar (Fierce Ruddy Face). Later on, fifteen Düd bandits led by

Tsenkya Bumthub came to Trothung's home and, true to form, Trothung gave away Chipön's location. Chipön went on a pilgrimage to Upper Tibet, and Trothung pointed out his vacant home to the robbers who plundered the homestead and rustled more than five hundred livestock. This was not the last of Trothung's deceits, as many years later, during the year of Gesar's birth, Trothung and Minyak Yutsé would meet again under cover of the dark skies of Ma and, again, Trothung, ever currying favor with the enemy, would ensure that more than three hundred livestock of Upper, Lower, and Middle Ling were herded away.

With that as background, we return to the story, where, within the hour, Jalak Derchu, now in the guise of a raven, was at King Yutsé's doorstep telling him that a man who claimed to have been his close childhood friend, known familiarly as "the black-headed earthworm of Tibet," had come with what he said was a very important matter. She said that she and Jama Jigo had decided that she, Jalak Derchu, would be the one to deliver this message and that Jama Jigo had stayed back to guard the narrow defile. Turning a deeper shade of blue, Minyak Yutsé pondered, "I guess that must be Trothung, the one who was said to have been the head of Ling but who has since been brought down from the throne of Takrong by his nephew Gesar, the son of that despicable Gok mother. That is what my spies have been telling me, and it must be true. I imagine there must be an important reason for Trothung to have come in person." After quizzing Jalak, he decided to go to meet with Trothung. He took along his most important minister, Tsenkya Bumthub, who was sure that he would recognize whether it was in fact Minyak's old friend Trothung. Minyak Yutsé was blueness itself all the way from his two turquoise braids and dazzling azure beard to his cobalt-blue armor and weapons. A poisonous dust cloud arose in his wake as he galloped off on his black horse, which could have been mistaken for a wild yak with wings of wind. Its saddle was made from the skulls of rākṣasas and rākṣasīs layered inside with fresh and dried cannibal skins and secured with a black snakeskin breastplate and blue snakeskin girth. Yutsé was nearly as tall as a pine tree, and as he rode high atop this saddle, the very foundation of the earth shifted and trembled. His minister Tsenkya was as red as a blood-painted torma and his armor and weapons were a deep scarlet. Blood spewed from his mouth as he heaved an uneasy sigh. His red horse galloped with wings of wind; dust rose up as he rode atop its acacia wood saddle, splendidly adorned with jewel-encrusted stirrups, a golden crupper and girth, turquoise halter, a golden bridle, and so forth. On his right shoulder rested his tiger-skin quiver tightly packed with arrows, and on his left, the leopard skin case where he kept his bow. A sword hung at his waist and a lance was strapped at his shoulder. Tied behind him was his leather breath-stealing bag. He brandished his snakeskin whip. A venomous fog arose from the monstrous sorcery of these mighty māras, eclipsing the sun. From within the darkness, they rode forth as suddenly as a lightning flash or meteor shower. In three hours, Yutsé and his minister had arrived at the narrow defile where the demoness Jama Jigo stood guard. Trothung rose when he saw them and, panting, fumbled to take a silk scarf out from his amulet box when Tsenkya offered this song in the melody of "Hara Hurthung."[46]

> As for this little song, sing "Ala thala."
> "Thulu ula" begins.
> The ruler of this world
> is the mighty Gulang Wangchuk.
> I call to him to be my support
> and to the sun and moon to be my refuge and protector.
> If you do not recognize this place,
> it is the junction of Zi and Rong,
> secured by a threefold succession of barriers.
> If you shout out its name, it is the scenic land known as Koḍ,
> hemmed in by jagged peaks and water,
> and with its protective belt of black rocks,
> it is inaccessible to those without six wings.
> Here, at the mouth of a single narrow defile,
> to the west is a perilous path strewn with human corpses
> penetrating a rugged, dense forest
> where two sisters are the sentries,
> the local guardian zodors of Koḍ.
> Their intense energy and power
> are the source of tempests of thunder and hail.
> They are both formless and with form.
> If you rely on them, they will be your protectors.
> If you do not recognize me,
> I am an earth cannibal, a child of the nāgas and māras,
> born from a red egg
> and called Marpo Tsenkya Bumthub,
> an offspring of the wild red tsen.
> I eat raw meat and drink blood.
> I am the breath-stealer of all the laypeople
> and friend to this blue man with his blue horse,
> the one who is the sun and moon of the azure firmament,
> the Mount Meru of this dense earth,

the jewel of the depths of the ocean—
the one known as King Minyak Yutsé.
He rivals the power of King Lutsen,
the skill of King Sadam,
and the eminence of King Gurkar.
He has surpassed all those considered to be his equal.
All who see him join with him; those who hear him are
    afraid.
This king has no equal.
That is the genuine meaning of these words.
But now you have come here, you little guest,
declaring yourself a friend
to King Minyak Yutsé
since childhood—a fine friend indeed,
and, not only that, you say you have come to call on him.
So, what is your story, your message?
Speak without cunning or deception,
it is best to be honest and sincere.
The plainspoken truth would make us happy.

If the east is vast, both the sun and moon can rise.
If the road is wide, it is easy to journey.
If speech is candid, it is easy to talk.

These words speak the truth.
There is no way to read between the lines spoken by a
    foreigner.
They tell stories, but the spirit of their words cannot be
    understood,
and, at their whim or will, they can pull the wool over our
    eyes.
A dishonest person can con his friends.
You, Uncle Trothung,
have a familiar face and many fine stories,
but in the long run, you will hoodwink us.
Uncle, your credentials are suspect . . .
Oops, did not mean to say that, just teasing!

This forbidding land is as uninviting as the jaws of the lord of
    death—
what is so important that you must journey here?
King Minyak Yutsé and his minister—
what is it that you have to say to us?
You, who was king of Tramo Ling—
how is it that you govern the masses?
That nephew Joru, the child of that despicable Gok mother—
where is that wandering beggar boy now?
How much has he done to benefit the districts and valleys?
What is he up to these days?
This is the song I have given in reply.
If you have not understood, there is no way to explain it.
May this song enter the hearts of those who have come here
    today.

Thus he sang, and King Yutsé and his minister both agreed that it was in fact Uncle Trothung who had ridden there on horseback. They made a show of reverence, bowing down and smiling insincerely; taking hold of his mount, they asked him to join them on a cushioned seat on the ground. Flattered, Trothung acted like an overexcited dog. He offered silks, measures of gold and silver, and, rolled up in five kinds of brocade, a precious water-purifying *ketaka* gem that had been given as an offering by the gods-demons to Dongra.[47] He thanked Yutsé and his minister profusely, saying, "How very gracious of you to have greeted me! Your time will be well spent; I have come with a matter of utmost importance." And he sang this song in his own melody.

Sing "Ala thala thala."
"Thala" begins and
"La la" gives the perfect pitch.
I supplicate the coemergent deities.
Please assist me
and help in this song of truth.
This land is unfamiliar to me.
I have heard about it only from afar,
yet, my friends, I feel it is my homeland.
You already know who I am—
I am called Uncle King Takrong or, simply, Trothung.

25

Long before Joru, the nephew of Gok, grew into such a man
and even before Gyatsha's birth in Ling,
there was no question that anyone but I would rule.
I—the one who subdues the wrathful enemy
and is the refuge of loving friends,
the one who established Ling
and is the worldly pillar of the Phunu.
Hundreds have looked to me for guidance.
The more we talk about these things, the more I feel
    defeated.
Chipön is the ocean that feeds these quarrels
and Joru is a demon wrapped in human skin. The two of
    them
are like hungry dogs and wolves; they are really quite a pair,
and Denma backs them with his support.
While honest men are thrown in jail,
praise comes to Joru, that liar of a boy.
He has put a halt to the hundreds of traveling merchants
and their leader Norbu Zangpo (Good Jewel).
He has stolen the wealth of those merchants
without earning any of it himself,
and he has plundered the granary of King Zahor of Den
and doled out the barley to bandits.
Not only that, but there is still more.
The Zima king's herd of horses
had been stolen by Joru,
but the charges fell wrongly upon me.
After a lot of talk back and forth, I was found innocent,
but the ill-gotten horses of the Zima king and ministers[48]
were distributed to those swindling men of Ling
and I was cut out of any share.
Not that I am destitute,
but, nonetheless, I wound up despised and disrespected.
Who could have done that except Joru?
Little by little, through his bad habits, he turns to evil,
urged on and supported by cunning men.
Beyond that, he has usurped the jeweled golden throne

by winning the horse race to become the lord of Kyalo's
    wealth.
In the inner circles of Sengdruk Taktsé,
he is said to be the king of Ling—
he proclaims this to everyone everywhere
and tramples over me.
My son Takphen is ailing,
Zikphen is well grounded,
but that tall one Nyatsha is inconsiderate
and discounts my words at every turn.
My good-looking son Dongtsen Apel
has unrivaled bravery and might.
It is foolish to think that there is but one person of courage.
His great horse Yuja, Turquoise Bird,
is the prosperity horse of Jambudvīpa.
As he gallops along the path of a bird in the sky,
there is no doubt he could take you from Tibet to China and
    back.
It is foolish to think that there is but one horse with speed.
Yutsé, I am hoping you will back me
and that we will find accord.
I have come expecting harmony.
As in the proverbs of the ancient Tibetans:

Doing business, arranging marriage, delighting in one's lover—these
    three
are done because they are deemed worthwhile.
The castle, its gate, and its latch—these three
are made because they are deemed secure.
Lovers, housemates, and friends—these three
are found because they are deemed sincere.

    Well then, King Yutsé and Minister Tsenkya,
    although I was born in Tramo Ling,
    I feel inclined toward the evil māras
    and plan to propagate the lineage of the Düd.
    Don't you think I want us all to benefit?
    I am still the feisty king of Takrong.

Even though I do not have dominion over all of Ling,
nonetheless, the family of Takrong holds the ancestral estate,
the district called Duktsho Khölma (Poisonous Boiling
    Lake).
All told, there are twelve myriarchies,
but they are made up of countless subsidiaries.
My wealth is unparalleled—
when I sit, it is on fine brocade cushions,
I have tea, liquor, and milk to drink,
I have bitter and sweet and honey to eat,
and nourishing meat, *thü*,[49] and butter.
Even so, I am not happy.
If I stayed there and fought, in truth, I would regret it,
since when it is over and done with, I will not have won.
How could I, when I am dependent on my sons,
and they cannot agree among themselves?
Nyatsha is a small matter,
But you, King Yutsé—
it has been years since we have seen each other.
You are bigger, and your face is radiant.
I was overwhelmed when I saw you.
Now, I have great hope of accomplishing what I came for.
And you, bandit chief, Minister Tsenkya,
look very healthy as well.
If this is not a dream, how joyous!
It is as wondrous as the sunrise
and the vanishing darkness of suffering.
Wrapped in an auspicious offering scarf
is the precious jewel, the ketaka gemstone.
One day I will explain the history of this jewel
that eclipses all the wealth of Ling.
Along with these measures of solid gold and silver,
it is my offering to you great men.
Take me in as your ally.
Support me through times of both good and bad fortune.
Eventually, I will have more to say.
I swear to Garab,[50] my words are not false or dishonest;
the truth will gradually come to light.

If my song was in any way confusing, the fault is mine.
If my words have been nonsense, please forgive me.
You two, without equal, keep this in your heart.

Thus he sang, and Yutsé thought as he listened, "These words spoken by Trothung are golden drops of truth. That wicked Joru has undertaken to destroy the world, and he has no intention of stopping until he has brought down my country of Düd. All the same, Trothung is the kind of leader who deliberately spills the secrets of internal matters and stirs up trouble with outsiders. He thinks it is he who has earned our friendship, when it is simply the benevolence of the māras. Look at him—so smug, and now tight-lipped but clearly smiling to himself." Then, Yutsé said to Trothung, "You have come from afar. Wonderful that you had no troubles along the way! It would be my pleasure to host you at the royal fortress. Whatever happens, good or bad, we will share. Little by little, we will discuss everything and come to a harmonious agreement." Delighted, Trothung rose to go. The two guardian demonesses appeared, carrying leather pouches bloated with blood and two dangling *drong* legs. Yutsé chewed them down to the bone, and Trothung and the ministers were awed at the astonishing power of this man, confident that he could defeat anyone. As they went, Tsenkya and Jigo cleared the narrow path of large boulders, rolling them to either side while leading their horses and mules. Trothung and his entourage followed behind Yutsé, and Jalak Derchu obliterated the path behind them with huge boulders so that anyone who came along would be unable to pass. The attendants who had traveled from Ling with Trothung had become quite frightened, but that night, they camped with Trothung and his ministers along the high mountain pass. King Yutsé and Tsenkya went on to their own fortress, and the two guardians returned to their posts as sentries of that narrow footpath. A few Düd ministers came to look after Trothung and the rest, and they settled down together as though they were one family, joined in the defilements of the māras.

Meanwhile, back in Takrong, Trothung's treasurer Bumga (One Hundred Thousand Happinesses) became distraught when he realized that Trothung had run off, and he sent sealed messages to Nyatsha and Sertsho as well as a messenger to Takphen and Zikphen, who had returned to their castle. The three sons immediately agreed that someone should go after Trothung and his ministers, and Zikphen and Nyatsha, accompanied by one hundred horsemen, went off in pursuit as avidly as hunting dogs chasing down a stag. But when they came to the border of Zima[51] and Ling, the north wind had blown away any trace of Trothung's journey. They found no footprints on the mountain passes, and the Zima road was deserted. With no idea what to do, after nine days, they took Sertsho's advice and Nyatsha, with five of the horsemen, went to confer with Gesar. He was led in and offered tea flavored with mustard butter. As Nyatsha presented a scarf to Gesar, he asked for Gesar's full attention as he explained his serious concerns. With the melody of Thala Demchung (Little Undulating Melody), he sang.

> OM MAṆI PADME HŪM
> Sing "Ala thala thala."
> "Thala" begins and
> "La la" gives the perfect pitch.
> Infallible refuge, Three Jewels, know me.
> May the Dharma teachings of the Buddha flourish.
> *Lha*, *lu*, and *nyen*, dralha, indispensable werma—
> I supplicate you and entreat you to assist me.
> May this world realm turn to the Dharma.
> Seated on your precious golden throne,
> just meeting you face to face closes the gate to rebirth in the
>   lower realms.
> Just hearing your voice removes obstacles in this very lifetime.
> The enlightened mind of the Buddha
> is the precious refuge in this life and those to come.
> With genuine heart, listen attentively to me.
> My father, the leader of Takrong,
> is without devotion to you.
> Though you are a buddha, he regards you as a mere human.
> He incites quarrels among the kinsmen
> and is disrespectful to his lifelong companions and, above all,
>   to my mother.
> He stirs up discord by conspiring with the enemy
> and taking advice from outsiders.
> A few days ago,
> he declared that there must be private discussions,
> and when his inner circle gathered,
> he said that we must become adversaries of King Gesar
> and fight against his allies,
> prepared with an army of men and horses.
> The four of us, we three brothers and mother Sertsho,
> and nearly all the leaders are of one mind—

we have talked with him endlessly, but Trothung does not
    listen.
He mistreats our mother,
and just as she cared for us, we sons have stood up for her.
When it became a physical fight,
the elders of the clan were forced to separate them.
Dongtsen followed after Trothung
along with Akhö Tharpa Zorna
and some of his more gullible personal attendants.
Before they fled with mules loaded with riches,
I had left with Sertsho for the secluded Zikrong Valley,
and my two brothers, Takphen and Zikphen, had come to see
    you.
When the message of Trothung's departure reached us, we all
    went in pursuit.
We looked carefully for footprints, repeatedly, and although
we scoured the mountainside, his tracks had vanished.
Zikphen and I, with one hundred horsemen,
returned after nine days
not knowing what else to do.
Sadly, it appears that Trothung, the Mazhi[52] chieftain,
has let the demonic damsi into his heart
and has become a living monster.
There is no telling what he will do.
He sits at the threshold between good and bad karma.
I am here requesting your advice about my own father—
something a good son would not generally deign to do.
However, respect for you as the king
and love for me as his son
are qualities my father surely does not have.
He has given over his heart and mind to the hostile enemy
and holds you up as his personal adversary.
His plans will surely go awry,
and his gold dust will end up squandered, as though tossed
    into a river.
It is essential that this not happen.
The best solution would be for him to retain a seat in the
    castle

but without power over others.
A mediocre solution is for him to live apart
with a goodly share of the wealth.
At worst, father and son will kill each other,
and the bad news will spread everywhere.
My supplication is not mere words.
As the proverbs of the ancient Tibetans state:

If you hide food from your mother, to whom can you give it?
If you keep secrets from your father, to whom can you tell them?
If you do not rely on the refuge of the guru, on whom will you rely?

That is not only what the proverbs say, but it is the truth
and, right now, an indication of how to act.
Your advice is like a gentle rainfall of *amṛta*
that quenches our thirst.
May your words be ones that satisfy.
If this song is confused, I confess any fault.
If this has been meaningless chatter, please forgive me.
Unrivaled king, keep this in your heart.

Thus, Nyatsha offered this song, and, showing great kindness to him as though applying a soothing balm, Gesar rested in the equanimity of deep *samādhi* and then offered this Dharma song of advice called "Quelling the Great Crowds through Splendor."

OṂ MAṆI PADME HŪṂ
Sing "Ala thala thala."
"Thala" begins and
"La la" gives the perfect pitch.
Within the palace of Glorious Copper-Colored Mountain
dwells Guru Padmasambhava,
surrounded by an ocean of *vidyādharas* and *siddhas*.
I supplicate from the state of non-wandering.
From your great bliss, immense heart, and wisdom intent,
blessings and siddhis fall like rain.
May this moisten the fertile soil of individual beings,
may the seeds of *bodhicitta* sprout,

may the petals blossom to benefit others,
and may the resultant three kāyas arise.
Here in this land of Ma, in Upper Ling,
is the fortress known as Sengdruk Taktsé.
I am King Gesar of Ling,
not so long ago named king
and principal ruler of the six provinces of Ling,
mandated by the gods to be the destined leader
and the one to quell the demons of the dark side.
Since I am the one entrusted with this aspiration,
my deeds and actions must follow.
Now, Nyatsha, endowed with bravery,
within your garuḍa egg, your six wings are fully developed,
within the tigress's womb your six smiles are fully displayed.
You, who are endowed with the precious qualities of a man,
have come here with such faith in me.
Unless your life is cut short,
you are bound to be a bedrock of Ling.
Do not have a heavy heart,
as, in my dream last night,
a Bengal tigress, as colorful as if adorned with flames
and with a retinue of wild bobcats and leopards,
stood on the peak of the richly forested mountain.
I dreamed that when the white lion tossed his turquoise
    mane,
that Bengal tiger leapt to the east,
slipping into the poisonous mountain shrouded in mist.
I dreamed that the Ling temple was obscured by darkness.
Afterward, the lha, lu, and nyen, along with
the gods and humans of Ling, lit a great fire,
and the poisonous mountain burned to the ground.
The tiger and leopard with their six smiles unharmed
returned as the retinue of the white lion's throne.
In the cinders were gold, silver, turquoise, coral, emeralds,
    and so forth.
I dreamed that untold jewels welled forth
and myriad visions arose.
If you analyze this dream, it is not inconsequential.

Regard Trothung as the Bengal tiger
and Dongtsen as the spotted leopard,
each with his own retinue of wild bobcats.
The rich forested mountain
is the spirit mountain of the mothers and sisters of Ling,
the personal mountain of Kyalo's family,
and the lion is my spirit.
That the lion tosses its turquoise mane
signifies that I am the victorious earth lord.
That the Bengal tigress leaps to the east
signifies that Trothung will join the māras.
That the eastern mountain is poisonous
signifies that the vicious māras have gone there,
and that the tiger disappeared into those poisonous
    mountains
signifies that Trothung has gone into their midst.
The mist that then rose from the mountain
signifies the exodus of the enemy dark forces, the Düd.
That the temple of Ling was obscured by darkness
signifies that the governance of Ling is endangered.
That the gods and humans of Ling ignited a great fire
signifies that the flames of victory will burn the dark side.
That the tiger and leopard have allegiance to the lion
signifies that Uncle Trothung and his sons
will return to me as allies.
The gems that welled forth from the ruins of the burnt forest
signify that we will reach the fortress of the precious treasure.
The dream, when analyzed, is excellent.
Trothung is a manifestation of Red Hayagrīva.
Even though he portrays himself as the great enemy,
he has not harmed life or limb.
His hatred toward me
signifies nothing other than his vow to the higher gods.[53]
He is the man who leads the enemy in.
Yet, I have no reason to think that he has broken samaya,
his sons have no reason to hate their father,
his subjects have no cause to reproach him,
the brave warriors have no cause to feel he has betrayed them,

and I hope Sertsho can find forgiveness in her heart.
Begin by being certain to cut all obstacles.
In my fortress shrine room, Yungdrung Kyilwa (Rest
    Unshakably),
first, offer a feast and fresh butter lamps
and make offerings to the supreme oath-bound *dharmapālas*.
Your preparations should be in accord with scripture,
and, before long, I will address you.
To the sons and to Sertsho who stayed behind,
I have given precious pearl necklaces,
one hundred pearls strung on each strand.
Although the gift is a mere token, it abounds in significance
as, just like the threaded string of pearls,
the divine lineage and the sons' lineage are not frayed.
May you keep utterly to samaya.
Nyatsha, keep this in your heart.

Thus, this unceasing *vajra dohā* was imparted to the joyous Nyatsha. He stood up quickly from his seat and bowed deeply to receive the dust of the venerable feet of Gesar on the crown of his head. Then, for the next three days, he stayed at the fortress discussing various matters with Gesar and his ministers. It turned out that Neuchung had had a dream in parallel with Gesar's, the meaning of which Gesar had accurately deciphered. Gesar returned with Nyatsha to Porok Nying Dzong, and as Nyatsha had understood both Gesar's explanation and how the same dream had come to Neuchung, he was able to rest contently and practiced earnestly.

CHAPTER TWO

Wangjema, Trothung, and Bloody Tress
come to Ling in order to destroy Gesar.
Manéné brings poisonous liquor to the Düd,
clouding their minds and subduing their life-force talismans.

LATER ON, TROTHUNG AND KING MINYAK YUTSÉ were conferring. The fearsome Yitrok Wangjema, the demoness tether of the samaya-violator māras, interrupted. Her hair was streaming up, her four craggy fangs were clenched, and her breasts were bound with a fine silken sash. She looked voracious and imposing as she swallowed down cup after cup of human and horse blood. Then she spoke, "You two just sitting here, this is what we must do." She began the demoness song with the low tones of "Am am."[1]

> Sing "Ona ala ona."
> "La la ona" begins and
> "Ona" gives the perfect pitch.
> Within your dark space of evil,
> life force of sentient beings of the three realms,
> bloody-eyed black nāga demon Trakmikma (Bloodshot
>   Eye)
> and your retinue of one hundred thousand demons of the
>   dark side—
> I call out and offer to you. Please assist me.
> If you do not recognize this place,

it is Drongnak Nying Dzong (Black Drong Heart Fortress),
the gathering place of the Düd king and ministers.
If you do not recognize me,
I am the earth rākṣasī, the evil mother
who bore the nāga demon Jathül Nakpo,[2]
the first in the stream of generations of māras,
the unbroken lineage of the hordes of māra demons.
I am the red woman called Yitrok Wangjema.
There is neither god nor human with power greater than
    mine.
I am without equal.
I relish fresh meat and blood
and harvest the breath of sentient beings.
I am the mother of the Seven Wayward Siblings,
more magical than Wangchuk,
more splendorous than the sun,
and firmer than Mount Meru.
Moreover, on top of that, I am invisible.
I am the powerful māra queen.
Bearded fellow of Ling, listen.
From now on, the story goes like this.
There is no reason to scorn the young lion cub;
he is the king of the wild beasts.
There is no reason to scorn the royal garuḍa chick;
he is the king of the feathered birds.
There is no reason to scorn me, the daughter of outcasts;
I am the queen of the vicious demon rākṣasas.
This is not conceit—it is the way it is.
You, Trothung, that black-headed earthworm from Ling,
since the day you were born
you have taken on the values of the evil māras,
leaving not a single evil deed undone.
The wealth and might of the māras
are the eyes and heart of the demons and rākṣasas of the dark
    side.
This aunt earth rākṣasī's throat song
is the life pillar of all samaya-violator demons.
That one of legendary might and power—

he has not so much as been seen since the moment he was
    born.[3]
Who else could do that?
In time, he will destroy our world.
It goes without saying, it is as obvious as if it were written on
    the palm of your hand.

As is said: *Neither enemies nor sparks hesitate.*

That is what the proverbs say, and it is the truth.
This time the spoils of victory will fall to me,
and it is up to you, Trothung, to be the leader.
Greatest King Yutsé, please stay in your homeland,
here, in the company of your powerful ministers.
My uncle, the cannibal nāga Belgo (Frog Head),
must see about mustering an army.
My youngest daughter, Bloody Tress,
can be counted on for support
and will relish the flesh and blood of humans and horses.
As for the magical sacks of vital energy—
the sacks of disease are bound in front of our saddles,
and the sacks of stolen breath are bound behind.
We fling weapon balls into the air,
running quickly and generating hatred.
In the daylight, we gaze from the mountain peaks
at the peopled valleys of the countryside below.
Tonight, in the pitch darkness,
Joru, Gyatsha, and Chipön are the three
who we will try our best to lasso
and lead forcibly to the māra lands.
This heroic feat
will rob them of their souls, longevity, and life force.
Their breath, stolen away into the breath-bag
and offered as a precious gift to the Düd king and his
    ministers,
will be enough to erode the tenets of Ling.
This advice and counsel is uppermost.
May such things be kept in your hearts.

As she sang, Trothung reflected, "Joru's power surpasses that of a thunderbolt, and his understanding outshines the sun, yet, today, it is clear that I must go with Wangjema. It has come to a head; I have no choice. Not to go implies cowardice, and, besides, I should go in order to point out the landmarks to the Düd, who otherwise will not know them. All I can do is hope for an opportunity to free myself through some kind of magic." Trothung held his head high and smiled, feigning bravery despite his trepidation and affecting cheerfulness that belied his misery, saying, "I agree with what you have just said, Madam Lady Queen. I am an expert in the lay of the land, and you are the one with power. How wonderful it would be if those three disaster-producing men of Ling could be delivered into our hands."

King Yutsé mulled things over and realized that Wangjema, concealing herself with various magical displays, had, by now, surreptitiously scouted out Ling. Moreover, as he knew without doubt that she was a life-force ruler, he said, "Trothung, Wangjema, and Bloody Tress are the three who should go to Tramo Ling." That decided, the three of them gathered for a meal and then Wangjema and Bloody Tress rode together on the single-eyed wheel of the queen of wind and, like the birds soaring in the heavens, never touched even a single cubit of earth. On the fronts of their saddles were the sacks of disease, and on the back of each saddle, those that held the stolen breath of life. Weapons encircled their bodies. They rode westward, with Trothung leaping alongside, toward the sacred land, the prosperous jeweled valley of Ma. There, in front of them, was the single beautifying ornament of the world, the mere sight of which brings benefit—the celestial palace of supreme bliss.[4] Sitting atop its golden turret was Gesar, the lord of this land, the sun of humanity, the torch of the teachings in the world, the destined deity of the black-headed Tibetans, and the one to quell the evil māras. He was accumulating feast offerings to the divine Three Roots when Manéné appeared from the midst of an expanse of the five lights. In a relaxed posture, with her small body dancing and swaying in the manner of a ḍākinī, she sang in a clear and melodious voice the song called "Unobstructed Prophecy."

> OṂ MAṆI PADME HŪṂ
> "Lu ala" gives the sky melody of the father lineage,
> "Thala" gives the earth melody of the mother lineage, and
> "La" gives the melody of coemergence.
> Its wisdom intent is the great expanse of *dharmakāya*.
> This is a song of unobstructed clarity.
> My voice intones the melody without constraint;
> what is expressed is without confusion.

This place is the realm of great bliss emptiness-appearance,
experienced undisturbed by obscurations,
the spontaneously present splendor of the pure realm.
In this impure world, it appears as an ordinary royal castle
set before the divine child, the Dharma king.
Of course, you recognize me,
Manéné Göcham Karmo, born as Gesar's dralha protector,
the mother deity who is the torch of clarity.
You, divine child Joru, have been given the name Gesar.
According to the proverbs of the ancient Tibetans:

A young colt only a few summer months old
cannot settle down. It is its time to run wild through fields far and
*   wide.*
Roaming the frontiers, the day will come
that it is famed as a great steed.

The leader Gesar, having attained the throne,
cannot relax. He has come to subdue the māras and rākṣasas.
By coming to tame the māras, he will receive the prosperity
    fortress
and be renowned as Dradül, tamer of enemies.
That is the essential meaning of these words.
East of here, the land of Zi
was the sacred dwelling place of supreme bliss.
But in its immense, verdant forest,
the nonhuman gods-demons have seized control.
Padmasambhava turned the wheel of Dharma in Tibet,
but, simultaneously, the perverted aspirations of the māras
    arose.
Since the teachings of the Buddha were being destroyed,
you, Gesar, have arrived to remedy the situation.
Wangjema, born into a lineage of evil,
had perverted views toward the Buddha's teachings
and aligned with the ten evil spirits.
She was of the lineage of nonhuman nāgas, rākṣasas, and
    māras,
a beautiful woman, a whore, a queen of great power

who consorted with humans and gods-demons,
giving birth to the māras that destroy the teachings of the
    Buddha.
Those Seven Wayward Siblings appeared in Düd,
bursting forth from their eggs.
They are not birds, nor feathered, yet they soar through space.
Their strength and magic are incomparable.
They must be tamed this year,
otherwise they will join the forces of the four māra kings,[5]
heaven and earth will convulse,
and if they unite with Garab Wangchuk,
they will obtain the power of life-force ironclad immortality.
You have the fortunate karmic fruition to tame them.
Although through taming them, you could bring them to
    well-being,
it may be difficult for them to have faith in you.
Hence, unless they are liberated through fierce, wrathful
    means,
the samaya-violator demons will be your undoing.
As for the crux of today's speech—
your paternal uncle, Trothung, who is an emanation of Red
    Hayagrīva,
through the aspiration prayers of the divine ones above,
at this moment, is helping you, even as he seems to be causing
    harm.
If he did not spoil your heartfelt feelings of love for him,
you would not know how to act.
Therefore, you are indebted to Trothung.
Now is the time to bring down the samaya-violators.
The teachings of the Buddha are unshakable.
Now is the time to collect the precious prosperity treasure;[6]
it is the time to push the nāgas and rākṣasas to the breaking
    point.
Actually, this very day,
the demoness Yitrok Wangjema
and her daughter Bloody Tress,
each simmering with magical power,
are coming full force to Tramo Ling,

here, to the very spot that Trothung pointed out.
Invisible and carried on wheels of wind,
they have singled out the various ancient Mupa tribes,
and their hatred of Gesar, Chipön, and Gyatsha
gnaws at them like an abscessed tooth.
But shielded by the vajra tent[7]
within the trichiliocosm as though enclosed in an amulet
    box,[8]
the men of the Lesser Lineage and their horses,
along with the zodor, dralha, and werma,
will capture the demoness Wangjema.
See if she makes good on her promises or not.
She has the key to the precious wealth treasury
and the weapon storehouse of the armies of nāgas and māras,
as well as the key to numerous magical manifestations.
If you fail to get ahold of these,
you will be unable to crush the Seven Wayward Siblings.
As for the heart blood of the demoness,
if it is not spilled into the lake of the demons,
the nāgas and the demons are sure to lend her a hand,
and it is possible that Bloody Tress could escape.
Do not kill Trothung. Let him go,
as maybe this will bring surprising karma.
This tiger-skin-clad dralha
will be disguised as Wangjema and sent out to the land of the
    māras.
When these wondrous deeds finally come to be,
the gods and humans will confer.
Do not be lazy, Great Being.
If there is any confusion in my song, please forgive me.
Divine son, keep this in your heart.

She sang, and, then and there, disappeared. Gesar made offerings in thanks
for her help. Ling, in general, and the Lesser Lineage, in particular, were unequivo-
cally protected as their three great leaders—Gesar, Chipön, and Gyatsha—rested
within the mind of samādhi and produced the vajra tent. By that same morn-
ing, between hare- and horse-time, the two demonesses—Wangjema and Bloody
Tress—and Trothung, accompanied by the magical emanations of the māras, had

arrived at the lowlands of Ling at the foothills of Magyal Pomra. They had almost reached its upper mountain pass, Traphu Dzamling, but the landmarks and settlements that Trothung was pointing out were concealed from the demonesses' view by the vajra tent that had been set up through Gesar's power. When the demonesses finally admitted that they could see only rainbows and rings of fire, Trothung blessed his invisibility wand, holding it as he recited one hundred reversal mantras of the Bönpo god Yungdrung Nakpo (Black Ageless One), scattering dust and pebbles. Suddenly, he was enveloped in dark clouds and a smattering of hailstones fell. Because Trothung's connection to Gesar was offset by the strength of his perverted view, a small rent was torn in the protection circle through which the two demonesses could now clearly see Ngülchu Trodzong (Ormolu Fortress), the iconic fortress of the warrior Gyatsha. The demonesses pressed on, but Trothung protested that he was too frightened to accompany them, saying, "Gyatsha, with his mighty power and great magic, will certainly be coming to threaten, torture, and kill all three of us. While I wait here, you two with your greater powers, you go . . . There is no one who could rival you."

Haughtily, both women agreed. They took the form of hideous rākṣasīs, permeated with the vapors of various diseases and towering in height, eighteen armspans tall with heads as many handspans wide, framed by hairlike coils of black serpents. Their breasts were flung over their shoulders and their fangs were clenched like bundles of daggers. Blood dripped from their mouths and their striped snakeskin sashes and bootstraps trailed behind. Clutching a single breath-bag containing the breath of each and every human, they rode on icy clouds. As though an earthquake had shaken its foundation, the gate of Ngülchu Trodzong abruptly opened and the gruesome beings entered.

Earlier that same day, Gyatsha's wife Rakza[9] had borne an extraordinary baby. However, Gyatsha had sensed turmoil in his newborn son's life and had decided to approach the great meditator Akhu Gomchen Tingmé (Profound Great Meditator) to request a divination and protection ceremonies for the child. With ten mules loaded with offering gifts, Gyatsha and four horsemen left for Gomchen's monastery where they stayed for several days, leaving the grandmother, Gyaza, and some attendants behind to look after Rakza and the baby. The dreadful demonesses arrived and the hearts of those who were left in the castle swelled with fear, with Rakza drowning out their screams and shouts, calling out, "Three Jewels and Gesar King of Ling, look to me!" Hearing this summoning shout, the room filled with light and the demonesses saw Gyaza Lhakar sitting with the small child on her lap. The infant was carried off by Bloody Tress, and Wangjema made off with Gyaza in the crook of her arm, like an eagle clutching a lamb.

Just then, as though a wind had stirred, the red dralha Nyentak Marpo came down astride his red horse, and the eighteen great valleys of Ma and Dza filled with armies. The golden *kulha*[10] Nyenchen Gedzo descended on a yellow horse, and the thirteen great hills[11] of Ma, the pathway of travelers, overflowed with soldiers. The area all around teemed with troops emanating from Tsukna Rinchen and the zodor Magyal Pomra. Gesar, elegantly uniformed with a warrior's three accoutrements [bow, arrow, and sword], emerged from samādhi. Hastily shouting out orders to his attendants, he tacked up his capable steed Kyang Gö and, leaving a cloud of dust behind, arrived to join the troops.

The demonesses reached these thirteen hills only to find them already crawling with armies. Bloody Tress did not have the nerve to engage in battle, and so disguised herself as a howling icy wind. As for the demoness Wangjema, she was roused to great courage, impelled forward by gale winds arising from the breath-bag. She confronted Gesar, saying, "Just like you, I could return as a renowned warrior of the land of Ling." But at that very moment, the dralha king Gesar swooped down on her like an eagle onto its prey.[12] He was awesome with the splendor of his threefold panoply, dazzling with glittering color and light, and surrounded by his retinue of dralha forces. Wangjema menaced her weapon balls toward Gesar, but no harm came to him; instead, flowers showered down, and resplendent rainbow light arose. She raised her arms in a motion of fierce pride and Gyaza dropped from her armpit. In answer, Gesar thrust his sword three times. With the first, the breath-bag split open, and Wangjema fell to the ground in the ensuing dust storm. With the second, the breath-bag again split open, this time emptying it of sentient beings and bestowing life essence to them. And then finally, Gesar struck Wangjema and she curled up, insensate, as the channels of her black magic dissolved. Gesar bound her with his lasso, called Khamsum (Three Worlds), as he sang.

> OṂ MAṆI PADME HŪṂ
> "Lu ala" is sung to the Three Jewels.
> "Thala" travels the winds and channels
> to cast down samaya-violators.
> Wrathful Padma Heruka,
> today enjoy flesh and blood by severing
> the family line of the violent she-māras.
> Lift their consciousnesses to the state[13] of nonreturners.
> May all the powerful dralha and werma
> drink the potent amṛta of this expression of gratitude,
> quell the doctrine of the māras and rākṣasas,

and extol the teachings of the forces of virtue.
The land at the base of the mountains is the divine valley of
   Ma,
the playground of *ḍākas* and ḍākinīs,
the land where they perform their dance of bliss
and sing their melody of happiness,
the land that brings delight to their faces.
If you do not recognize me,
I am the one known as powerful Joru,
the one who quells the evil māras and rākṣasas,
the one to establish the teachings of the virtuous Dharma.
If you have faith, I am the awakened guru.
If you have loathing, I am the razor that cuts life force.
Now, I have come upon you, the demoness,
in the divine upper valley of Ling.
Why have you extended your spirit-hand
toward me, the Mupa king of the azure firmament?
Why have you dared to position yourself as an adversary?
From the divine palace Ngülchu Trodzong,
the Dharma MAṆI mantra spontaneously resounds.
Why do evil demons come with such frightening suddenness?
Gyatsha's son, a child of stainless destiny,
why have you taken him away?
Right now, release him if you have him in your hand.
Vomit him up if you have devoured him.
If a day goes by that you fail to do this,
there are a hundred ways of killing you.
Your days on this earth are numbered.
What reason could you have for coming here?
The samaya-violators, those Seven Wayward Siblings,
and the main ministers of King Yutsé
have put their lot in with the thieves and robbers,
opting for lies and dishonesty.
Over and over, with white pointed fangs, you have fed on
   Ling,
leaving behind the sour taste of various quarrels.
This surely summons the lasso Khamsum.
When thrown, it can catch the icy winds;

when tied, it can encompass Mount Meru.
You seem to have great power and strength,
but look at your body—bound up like a ball of yarn.
If you have such power, fly away like a bird.
If you have such strength, burrow underground like a worm.
If you have the force of an army, gather it like hail.
If not, your thoughts of freedom are mere pride.
This exchange of words
marks the boundary between good and bad.[14]
Demoness, keep this in mind.

He sang these words as a command, yet no faith arose in the demoness. Saying that she would prepare a celebratory banquet, she asked him to sit down just as an enormous black serpent appeared from her gaping mouth. The sight of its gleaming head, along with its odor of venomous vapor, disoriented Gesar. Confused, he took a step back as the whole serpent emerged. From its mouth came many more serpents. Gesar was further distracted, and the demoness disguised herself as the wind and would have slipped away were it not for a descending storm of dralha and werma. She was caught by the tip of a dralha lasso. The werma and zodor emanated as great birds—magically, they appeared and devoured every last serpent. This was an undisputed triumph, since the first serpent to emerge was in fact a manifestation of the great Mahākāla Lekden Gyipa (Excellent Warrior). Now stricken with fear, the demoness began retching involuntarily. She vomited up the keys to the treasury with its manifold magical displays. Gesar recovered and began to interrogate the demoness, but, bolstered by her pride, she managed defiant silence. Gesar knew that, long ago, she was the one who had brought ruin as the demonic force behind the decay of Samyé Monastery,[15] and, since then, had roamed the bardo. Even now, she was intent on evil deeds, scrupulously disregarding all virtue and bringing the Seven Wayward Siblings into the world. In order to sever the continuity of this malice and establish her in the pure realm, Gesar arose in a wrathful form and gave rise to great compassion from within the expanse of the wisdom intent of emptiness. Stepping with his right foot on the sternum of the demoness, with his right hand he unsheathed a small white-handled crystal knife and, revealing the skillful means of view, meditation, and conduct, he sang a song of aspiration prayer without hesitation. From within that state of emptiness-compassion, he pierced the chest of the demoness who called out in pain, "A tsha, A tsha! It will be said that this blackheaded earthworm, this Tibetan, has killed me!" She died without another word. She had no inclination toward faith and although Gesar had tried urgently to lead her, she was unable to ascend to the pure realm. Instead, she took rebirth in the city of Dashara in Chamara, the southwest land of cannibal demons, as the daughter of their demon king Maruka.

Then, Gesar, the king of the dralha, cut out her heart. The heart's blood was entrusted to the Nyentak dralha siblings, and every bit of the flesh was set out in a feast offering to the dralha and werma—nothing remained. Gyaza gradually came back to life as Gesar purified her with cleansing water,[16] beguiling her soul.[17]

By the darkness of pig-time, Bloody Tress, still disguised as the icy wind, had returned to her homeland. Since she had actually swallowed the infant, in the future she would become a great obstacle to all children. *The bard gives an aside:* Indeed, seeing the consequence of broken samaya, it is imperative to realize that maintaining samaya should be more precious than one's own eye.

Although at the sight of the mountains and valleys massed with Gesar's troops in pursuit of Bloody Tress, Trothung had thought about disguising himself as a golden-eyed fish and swimming upriver back to the castle Porok Nying Dzong where his sons and wife were, he dared not proceed. He thought, instead, to mount his horse Phurba Nganak (Black-Tailed Jackal), but the horse had vanished, and it turned out to have been killed by the dralha and werma two days previously. Alarmingly, the two gatekeepers Jalak and Derchu approached. Trothung had told them many lies, but, nevertheless, he felt that they considered him an ally and so he explained to them that Joru had killed Wangjema, saying that at least she had died quickly. Suddenly ravenous, he gorged himself on flesh and blood given to him by the gatekeepers, rapidly becoming too muddled to say anything more. Meanwhile, Denma, Gadé, and Michung had caught up with Gesar. Although Gesar had killed the demoness and revived Gyaza, there was nothing to be done about their great sorrow for the loss of the little child, and, woefully, they trudged back to the fortress Sengdruk Taktsé.

The dralha sister Manéné, extracting the essence of the demoness Wangjema's heart blood from the crystal vase into which it had been placed, manifested as an imposter identical to her. Manéné enclosed the heart essence of that malicious demoness samaya-violator into a breath-bag, and, at that instant, like lightning, she displayed the great power of the dralha and werma in front of both gatekeepers who shuddered in fear, stammering with cries caught in their throats. Trothung saw Wangjema, unaware that she was an imposter, and embraced her as if he were happy to see her alive and inquired after her health. She snapped at him, "You spineless, cowardly fox cub! You have accomplished nothing—why are you here?" She flung sparks at Trothung three times, slapped him, and spit in his face three times, all for three secret reasons: since she was a dralha werma sister, the defilement of the māras was cleared with the sparks, the defilement of confusion with the slapping, and the defilement of eating unwholesome, filthy food was cleansed by her spitting. In this way, she endeavored to reel his mind away from evil.

Trothung, standing up from where he had fallen in a daze, miserable and very frightened, said, "Oh Queen, you should not act like that; I have trusted you. *Those who take refuge should not suffer. Those who borrow must not be stingy in pledging to repay a loan.* As is said in the proverbs—that is no way to act. *If I face the sun, is it not because I count on it to be warm? If my back is to the mountain, do I not hope to be secure? If I make friends with the rich, do I not wish for luxury? If I join with the kings, is it not for power?* Just as these illustrate, until now, I have never known how miserable and weak I could become." So saying, a fine mist of tears moistened his eyes. The Wangjema impersonator replied, "Whether or not I welcome you is not important; what matters is that you had no choice but to seek refuge in me. Not only did you come where it is forbidden, banging your head at the door and butting up against the dog, but the prowess you boasted of was all in your mind. Just yesterday, you bragged that you were some kind of warrior and then, right when the armies of Joru and Zikphen appeared, you vanished and could not be found. As for me, look here at this head—it is my reward for fighting." As she spoke, an apparition of a head materialized. It appeared to be his son Zikphen's head, and while Trothung sat gasping, his heart trembling, frozen by its glaring eye, the imposter Wangjema struck both guardian gatekeepers with fatal blows from the curved blade of her ax.

As Trothung was wondering how all this could have happened, the imposter Wangjema turned to him demanding to know if he was coming with her or not, dismissively adding, "If you decide to stay back, I will simply eat you." Trothung was trembling, greatly afraid and despairing that his plans had come to naught,[18] when a werma appeared in the form of a snow bear. The impersonator Wangjema told him to mount the bear, prodding him, and, again, giving him no choice. Panicking, he realized that in this kingdom, Wangjema was the one whose words held sway, and he wondered when she would devour him. It seemed that even Joru was unable to capture her. He thought to himself, "She is so ferocious that it is like: *Taking shelter in the water, your butt will freeze* or *pillowing your head on a fire, your skull will burn.* Asking for protection from these flesh-eating demons and māras is ultimately nothing but suicide. Not only that, she has slain my precious son Zikphen." The more he thought, the more ominous things seemed. He continued thinking about the truth of the old sayings: *If children's roughhousing gets out of hand, limbs will be broken. Unchecked careless talk will come between friends.* Moreover, he reflected on the joyful happiness and abundance of his home and on the words of Sertsho, Nyatsha, and Takphen, as well as others: "Repeatedly, I upended everything out of rivalry with Gesar, yet, he generously allowed me a position of high rank, and now I am in the difficult situation of being obliged to go back and face him." Full of second thoughts, he began silently reciting supplications to Gesar and to the dralha and werma. Finally, Trothung arrived at the fortress of the Seven Wayward Siblings with the imposter Wangjema who was looking as intimidating as ever. King Yutsé and his ministers had been in mourning since Bloody Tress had not returned, but they were overjoyed to see the apparent Wangjema, as they thought that she had been lost as well. They crowded around her as she opened the breath-bag and took out an intact fresh heart. With awesome splendor, as though she were a Hor warrior seated high atop a wrathful serpent throne, and with the comportment of someone who had done a hard day's work, she offered this song.

> For this little song, sing "Ala thala."
> "Thala ona au" begins and
> "Au" gives the perfect pitch.
> From the midst of the ocean of flesh and blood
> the demoness stares out from the body of a fierce woman
> surrounded by hundreds of thousands, a vast retinue.
> I am the woman who shouts out for your assistance.
> May I accomplish all wishes and extol victory.
> If you do not recognize this place,
> here at the border of the countries of Zi and Ling,
> in the homeland of the Seven Wayward Siblings,
> I am the sovereign demoness of the kingdom,
> the mistress of the skies and the earth,
> and of the humans and gods-demons dwelling there.
> Ruler of humankind, King Yutsé, listen.
> Each of you, listen!
> A few days ago
> I and the maiden Bloody Tress,
> with Trothung as the guide,[19]
> went on to the land of Ling.
> Young Bloody Tress and I—
> the very day we entered the fortress of Tramo Ling,
> it was a mark of our bravery that we carried off that woman
>   and the infant.
> As soon as we were heading back,

troops filled the mountain passes and valleys.
Bloody Tress disappeared without a trace
and Trothung was nowhere to be seen.
Abandoned and without an army,
I killed, slaughtered hundreds and hundreds, beyond count.
To look into the heart of the enemy shows courage.
Through my actions alone,
the highlands were piled with corpses
and the lowlands filled with blood.
That legendary Joru—
in a fight, how could he even be called a rival?
And the so-called Pathül warriors, famed from afar,
are no match for a woman like myself,
a murderous butcher who has slipped out of their hands.
As long as the Seven Siblings are in agreement,
we can definitely demolish Ling.
Dear Lutsen will relish that.
The doctrine of the evil māras is certain to be exalted.
Right now, the king is in his glory.
The Seven Wayward Siblings are savage in their bravery.
The dark side—with all its subjects, men, and horses—
      flourishes.
But unless we unite like a band of brave outlaws,
we will be like toothless women gathering in town.
Furthermore, I am a fierce, savage woman.
Look what I did just yesterday
and think carefully about what you see.
The king and ministers came first, one after another,
tripping over each other, flaunting their heroism.
I, the lady of the Düd, followed on their heels.
My uncle Dölpa Nakpo
I asked to muster a fierce army.
From the wicked nāgas and rākṣasas were sent
twenty-one thousand troops,
enough that we need not fear Ling.
That is the whole story.
The proverbs tell the way things are:

In the depths of the sandalwood forest,
the tiger is renowned for devouring the flesh of humans.
His reputation precedes him,
but up close, he is just a stray old mountain dog.
On the path of the unspoiled rocky ridge,
the drong is renowned for his untamed ways.
His fame precedes him from these high plateaus,
but up close, he is just a stray old yak.
On the path among the bamboo of the cultivated valley
in the south is the one renowned as Yeti.
It is said that he kills whatever he sees,
but when you come close, he is just a naked old man running
around.

From the country of Tramo Ling in the Ma Valley,
the one called Joru is renowned.
They say he annihilates whatever he sees,
but if you come close, he is just a little boy dressed up in
armor.
I am not just jabbering; this is the way things are.
The bravery of the Ling warriors is a myth.
It is said that they flay their enemies alive
and that they are undaunted by the dragons' ferocity.
But their feats are as illusory as a rainbow.
Do I speak the truth? Look and it will be clear.
Even I, a woman, was able to escape.
Joru, that nephew of Gok with such a dishonorable mother—
better to tame him before he becomes a man.

Better to snuff out the life of both sparks and enemies while they are
small.[20]

This is what is said in the proverbs, and it is certainly true.
As Joru gradually matures,[21]
there is no telling what will happen.
I could stay here in our homeland and be of some use.
There is no danger of losing our fortress or lands to the
enemy,

as they can be protected by the armies of nāgas and rākṣasas.
Or, I could leave to cut the enemy off at the border,
as I have obtained the deathless iron life force.
I am not bluffing.
If you think this sounds true, keep it in mind.
There is no reason for doubt.

Thus, this song of pretense arose from the depths of innermost, enduring, fearless confidence and was received through the force of karma. For the imposter Wangjema, it was the mark of warriorship and immeasurable triumph. Songs were sung in turn by each of the Wayward Siblings.[22]

As for Trothung, who since the previous day had renounced his ways, he could not say what should be done. Without having to be prodded, Dongtsen Apel, who had stayed behind with King Yutsé, sang a spontaneous song of the people and culture of Ling. Finally, from his throne of red coral, King Yutsé of Minyak offered this song called "Spirited Intense Short Words of the Warrior."

Sing "Ala."
"La lu ona" gives the perfect pitch.
Within the abyss of wrongdoing's dense fog,
from the immeasurable celestial divine realm,
to the sovereign king of māras, Garab Wangchuk,
with your retinue of innumerable māras,
I make offerings of human and horse blood.
I call upon you to give me strength and lead me forward.
Nine peaks of the eastern mountain[23] Minyak, know me.
Wherever I go, may the dralha support me.[24]
King of these turquoise mountain peaks, know me.
Brave warriors and capable horses, assist me.
This land is the gathering place of māras,
the hidden valley of robbers, bandits, and raiders.
Certainly, you recognize me.
My one lifetime has nearly become two,
two karmic circumstances in a single lifetime.
My birthplace is the narrow Minyak Gorge.
The one who is the guru of the holy Dharma[25]
I look to as if he were my own father.
The tactics of the robbers and hunters—

tales of these excite and delight him.
To the monks and secular leaders both,
I pledge a hundred, a thousand slaughters.
May I see clearly the face of Garab Wangchuk,
the constant guardian.
At the moment of greatest importance,
may he come by way of the *mu* cord,
and, welcoming him, may I be inseparable from the deity.
While this song tells all,
the meaning must be made clear.
Wangjema and Bloody Tress
are the ones rumored to be inherently capable;
their skillful awareness is unmistaken.
Joru is neither a human nor a demon;
there is no telling what he will do.
Before the week is out,
have a detailed discussion with the district military,
muster the troops with the king and ministers in front,
and that land of Ma in Tramo Ling
will see the true bravado of an army of heroes
as their Pathül warriors are rewarded with defeat.
As for that Joru with that dishonorable mother,
let us see whether he has bravery and magic.
As for Drukmo, the crowds of Kyalo part for her,
but we will see if she is all that lovely.
Those famously named Pathül warriors—
let us see about their strength and bravery.
Ling claims its wealth to be as abundant as that of the nāgas.
We will find out if this is true.
As for our incursions into foreign lands,
the king and ministers must construct a plan.
Cherished young Bloody Tress
must make a blood offering to Garab,
that of birds and animals,
and to the life-force talisman lake Duktsho Nakpo (Black
    Poisonous Lake)
she should offer blood of various kinds.
The three golden owl spirit siblings

must be sent to my brother Yu Ö (Turquoise Light)
to ask how to defeat the wrathful enemy
and, as the warriors are without backup,
request military assistance.
Be meticulous in doing just what I have said.
Not only that, King Lutsen
must be consulted.
Wangjema and Bloody Tress will stay back
while our troops make three raids on Ling.
Then, we will trumpet our success
and, afterward, gather for a joyful celebration,
making offerings to the divine spirits with dances of delight.
Trothung, the one who knows the layout of this valleyed
    land,
has arrived with his ministers.
They should be extended all hospitality.
When the Ling subjects are conquered,
Trothung will take his place as the leader.
This is my advice regarding who will go and who will stay.
Do not fail to keep this in mind.

Thus he sang. The gates to the storehouse with its abundance of food were opened and messengers were dispatched throughout the country with the news. Everyone, including Trothung and his ministers, gathered to enjoy an elaborate feast. That night, the imposter Wangjema mixed the heart blood of the highest she-māra [the real Wangjema, who had been killed] with nine poisonous substances, binding the mixture with garuḍa mantra recitations and scattering it into the māra Spirit Lake. Instantly, the flesh of the cannibal demon Dölpa Nakpo and that of all the evil nāgas who devour humans, as well as the flesh of the *makara* and the seven spirit fish of the māras, separated from their bones, dissolving into the water. Furthermore, Wangjema gave an offering of milk to all the violent barbarians who dwelled in the lake, thus depriving them of their protection.[26] Then, taking out the twenty keys [that she had obtained from the original Wangjema], the imposter Wangjema opened the door to the treasury containing the seven life-essence butter lamps, their blood and fat ablaze. She doused them with the same heart blood, and with a blistering sound, they were extinguished. Continuing on, she pulverized the single, huge black boulder that tethered the life-support of the nāgas, rākṣasas, and māras.

Then, from the released māra life essence arose a seven-headed frog with a body at least as big as that of a marmot, and, immediately, the imposter Wangjema saw that it must be destroyed and wondered how best it could be done. Of course, Gesar would be the ablest, but he was too far away even to ask. Next in line was Trothung who, as an emanation of Red Hayagrīva, would have the savvy. Accordingly, the imposter Wangjema took the seven-headed frog and shoved it into an iron box,[27] nailing it shut. King Yutsé and the Wayward Siblings had been poured an intoxicating quantity of chang that had been contaminated with the nine poisonous substances. Smoke trailed into the room from an incense censor burning the hairs of a dog, a coyote, and a man, all rabid. That night, poisoned and drunk with liquor, everyone slept insensibly. By dusk, ghoulishly dressed and carrying the iron box, as well as a leather flask filled with amṛta liquor, the imposter Wangjema had returned. Finding Trothung asleep, she shouted him awake and took a silk runner[28] from a fold in her *chuba*, unfurling it in front of him and indicating that he should step onto it. The moment he put his foot down, a hollow feeling, as though he had been flung up into the sky, arose in his chest. They came to a dark and solitary land, an uninhabited wilderness. There the imposter Wangjema illuminated the darkness with her wisdom fire and, placing the iron box on the ground, offered Trothung some chang and sang a song placing trust in him.

> Sing "Ona alu thalu."
> "Thalu ona la lu" begins and
> "La lu" gives to the demoness perfect pitch.
> I need all the gods and protectors;
> I entreat you to befriend me.
> May our endeavors[29] be praiseworthy.
> This valley is the hideout of robbers and bandits.
> There is no one in these lands who does not need our help.
> If you do not recognize me,
> I am the queen of the māras,
> the great power that devours the three worlds,
> the life force of sentient beings.
> There is nothing above me—
> that you understand already, Trothung.
> If there is any protection, it is through me.
> Listen, Trogyal chieftain.
> By drinking this chang,
> bravery is instilled into cowards.

It is the magical instrument of speech
and the key that opens the body's channels—
your reward for stepping on the silk runner.
Drink it until you are satisfied.
Inside this iron box
is my personal enemy,
ranked not with the virtuous deities
but with the evil māras,
with the one said to sever the aortas of anyone he sees.
With deadly poisonous breath,
his inherent nature is endowed with magic,
producing white-, yellow-, red-, blue-, green-, and black-
    headed serpents
spewing out poisonous mist.
Seeing them, one recoils with dread.
I fear that they may slink up into the sky
or slither deep into the earth.
This demon frog has been deaf to the virtuous Dharma
and seethes at the mention of the divine lama.
To you, Trothung, the bastion of mantra,
he comes now to seek refuge.
If you have a divine yidam, meditate on its clear appearance.
If you have a mantra, count up the recitations.
If there are magical illusory bodies, cast them out.
If there is samādhi, rest in equanimity.
When you tame this particular vicious enemy,
you may not tell others.
Each of us must accept that we stand on our own.
Whereas you should go to Upper Ling
to advise the king and ministers along the way,
I am to stay here in my native land
to hold the seat of the evil māras.
To this demoness who delights in flesh,
fresh meat is the most delectable.
To this demoness who delights in drinking blood,
warm blood tastes the sweetest.
Stay too long and I might yet make a meal of you . . .
Today, act like a man

and precious gold will reward your bravery.
Uncle of Ling, keep this in mind.

Thus she sang, bringing a jug of chang to Trothung who was terrified by this chilling song. Trembling, he downed the liquor. This divine amṛta unleashed his physical power and he blazed forth with bliss-luminosity. He discovered the inner confidence of fearlessness and remained in the generation and completion stages of the divine Hayagrīva Heruka and then, having entered into luminosity, he offered a song that exhorted and invoked the deities.

OṂ MAṆI PADME HŪṂ
As I sing, it is to the Three Jewels.
As the melody invokes, it calls out to the mindstream of bliss-
emptiness.
Divine Hayagrīva, I call only to you.
I call out for your support.
Please tame enemies and obstructing spirits.
Ageless primordial Shen god of the Bön,
your divine armies fill sky and earth.
In accord with your promise, subdue enemies and obstructing
spirits.
I call upon you.
Foremost guardian deity of Tramo Ling,
Dralha Nyentak, with your divine retinue of one hundred
thousand,
you, the great nyen, the friend who tames the enemy and
obstructing spirits,
please come now to assist me.
Annihilate the dreaded enemy and obstructing spirits.
Brahmā, with your divine retinue of one hundred thousand,
I call upon you to assist me.
Nyenchen Kulha, with your divine retinue of one hundred
thousand,
come this very day to assist me.
Those of the side of virtue, the local spirit protectors of the
teachings,
surrounded by the oath-bound dharmapālas,
I call upon you to assist me.

Annihilate the bitter enemies and harm-doers.

Divine assembly of wisdom ḍākinīs, remain.

Kleśas, the embodiment of the five poisons,

revealed as the enemies and obstructing spirits, those who
   cause harm—

slice them to bits with your primordial wisdom sword.

Lead their consciousnesses to the realm of great bliss

and offer their corpses to the deities.

Do not let smoke rise into the sky,

do not let purple[30] disease clouds swirl.

Trample the hateful enemy underfoot.

This very day, divine Three Roots, do not waver.

May I attain the mark of courage.

Thus his song ended and, just as the dralha sister imposter Wangjema cracked open the iron box, Trothung unsheathed a formidable blade.[31] He closed his eyes, and with a mind inseparable from his visualization of Hayagrīva, he slashed the life-support talisman frog again and again, nine times in all, cutting it to pieces as he performed *phowa*. Once more, Wangjema gathered the frog flesh and blood into the iron box without letting even a drop seep out. Through dark magic,[32] the life-support of the Wayward Siblings was completely tamed.

Then, the imposter Wangjema, with a slightly unveiled look, gave Trothung a handful of gold, saying, "This gold is a reward for killing the frog-serpent. But of course, no place is free of frogs and serpents. And rather than demonstrating bravery and magical power, you stood trembling with your eyes tightly shut, afraid even to look. Such a useless man should return home. It was a joke, letting you kill the frog-serpent, and it would be better not to speak of it as it will only expose your flaws. As for myself, I will keep quiet. Now, let's get you off to bed." *The bard interjects:* The imposter Wangjema is pleased with how the affair has turned out, although her happiness is undermined by the fact that she is still in the māra country.

Now, just as before, Trothung placed his feet on the unfurled silk runner and, just as before, he closed his eyes and instantly found himself back in bed. He thought, "No matter how much the king and ministers respect and like me, it is the demoness Wangjema who has the greatest powers[33] of magic. It looks as though Zikphen might in fact actually have been killed, and [though it pales in comparison], although I arrived here only yesterday, already she has humiliated me. Not only did she assault me, but she made me ride on that terrifying bear and, tonight, even though there was nothing to kill but the frog-serpent, I lost my composure because of her ruse that made it appear as though there were great enemies and obstructing spirits. In no time, this demoness will surely strike, beat, and kill me." Struck by the bleakness of his situation, once again, he recalled the simple joy and happiness of his homeland. He fell asleep supplicating the gods and protectors of Ling. The following day dawned with the Düd king and ministers so stupefied by the rabid incense smoke that had overcome their life-support that they were unable to do anything but enjoy idle merrymaking, struggle to gather up their army, and tally their armor and weapons.

CHAPTER THREE

Before Yutsé was able to draw up an army,
Gesar's troops came to the hidden valley
and the Seven Pathül warriors clashed with Yutsé's military
  spies.
Trothung, two-faced as a *ḍamaru*, returned to Ling.

GYATSHA HAD LEFT HIS CASTLE—Ngülchu Trodzong in Ling—and gone to request prayers for his newborn son from Akhu Gomchen Tingmé, bringing him an offering of ten ingots each of gold and silver. Gomchen Tingmé spoke, "Your son is the human richness of all the gods and humans of Ling. He has come as an emanation inseparable from the dralha Nyentak to be the leader of chieftains, but it is difficult for such a being to remain given the malevolence of you samaya-violators. However, now, under the rule of Gesar of the lineage of Mukpo Dong—who himself is the magical emanation of the three protectors[1] and the prophesied king of the six tribes of Ling—the time has naturally come for your son, a prince naturally surrounded by dralha, to be born. He will be Gesar's heart-son, the one who quells the hateful enemy, and the solid life pillar[2] that prevents the collapse of Ling. He will be surrounded by all the werma and will come forth as a conquering hero." These were the words that Gomchen spoke as the stainless promise of the vajra command-prophecy.

Gyatsha's own thoughts were on his increasingly turbulent dreams, but he realized that there was no point in dwelling on them and that what would happen was unavoidable, so he simply replied, "Yes, sir," and continued on to Gesar's castle, Sengdruk Taktsé, where he was met with the news that his son and Gyaza had been taken away by the demonesses. Enraged, Gyatsha vowed to amass an army and wage war. (*The bard inserts:* They sang several songs back and forth, but so as not to bore you, I have not included them.) Gesar went on to explain[3] that, just as Manéné had foretold, she, the tiger-skin-clad dralha sister, had disguised herself as the demoness Wangjema. Gyatsha, in particular—and Darphen, Gadé, and the rest of the warriors—took to heart what Gesar had said.

A week later, at the daybreak hour of the ox, Manéné was riding a white lioness and leading her companion blue buffalo. Her topknot swayed with its ornament of the five buddha families, a ḍamaru hung loosely at her side, a necklace of bone ornaments clattered around her neck, and the silk ribbons of her crown fluttered. Her hands sounded a skull ḍamaru and rang a silver bell. Around her, the sweet smell of incense spiraled, and rainbows and rays of light swirled. She was so exquisite that one could not have enough of seeing her. She appeared vividly in the space above as a thirteen-year-old brimming with youth. Her voice was as melodious as a flute and she gave three recitations of the MAṆI mantra, followed by a song of prophecy. In his heart, Gesar understood every detail, and he made a maṇḍala offering in gratitude. Manéné gradually faded away like a rainbow.

Then, as day dawned, Darphen and Denma, the warriors, and others were called inside, and to everyone's great delight, the story of the prophecy was told. The rulers of Ling, each with an entourage of their hundred best horsemen, simultaneously sent messengers to broadcast that on the ninth day there would be a gathering at the Tea Fortress, Jadzong.[4] The news spread throughout Ling and soon was well known to everyone, and on the ninth day, as smoothly as a polished knife is drawn from its sheath, nearly five thousand troops, warriors of awesome splendor, came forward parading before Gesar and scores of tents were pitched beyond the fortress. Offering presentation scarves to Gesar, the Phunu were then seated by rank on cushions arranged in the assembly hall. After a splendid feast, Gesar—with lustrous, radiant clarity brighter than the full conch moon—addressed the brave army of Phunu. Relaying the prophecy that Manéné had bestowed, he sang the melodious song, "Quelling the Great Crowds through Splendor."

> OṂ MAṆI PADME HŪṂ
> Sing "Ala thala thala."
> "Thala" begins and
> "La la" gives the perfect pitch.
> From the immeasurable space of the crown *cakra*,
> embodiment of the Three Jewels and Three Roots,
> glorious root guru,

I supplicate from my heart center.
From the expanse of your enlightened mind, please confer
    blessings.
May the sentient beings of the three realms dwell in the
    Dharma.
This is the country of Ling in the kingdom of Ma,
the place of both worldly and monastic disciplines,
and I am the one known as King Gesar of Ling,
entrusted by both gods and humans
to dispel the dark ignorance of the mind.
Uncle Chipön,[5] listen!
Gyatsha Zhalkar of Bumpa,
Nyibum Daryak of Serpa,
Pathül warriors, Takphen and Zikphen, listen—
to listen means to grasp the meaning.
As for the unmistaken prophecy of the gods,
these Seven Wayward Siblings of Düd
are the samaya-violating demons of perverted aspirations,
the spawn of the tsen, the māras, the vicious cannibal nāgas,
the *mu* spirits, the *gyalpo teurang*,
and the *dritsen gongpo*.[6]
These [six] progeny pose as animate beings, sons made of
    flesh and blood.
But there are those with power over this wicked artifice.
Akhu Gomchen Tingmé,
on behalf of the thirteen senior lamas of Ling,
has requested protection from the army guard
since these [lamas] are the teachers of the stages of
    meditation and recitation
according to the clearly written ancient texts
and are the eldest of three hundred monks and subjects.
Respecting them and sustaining them with whatever they
    need,
thus, the Mupa are the ones to serve them unerringly.
King Yutsé of Minyak
is the one I, Gesar, must vanquish.
As for the vicious nāga in the guise of a human child,
the nāga lord known as Lugön Tongthub Yamé—

one of his own color, an entirely blue man with a blue horse,
the principal warrior Denma should be the one to place an
    arrow in his forehead.
As for the samaya-violator māra in the guise of a human,
known as Tongdü Lenmé—
one of his own color, a man entirely black[7] with a black horse,
Chökyong Gadé must be the one to tame him.
As for the degenerate tsen in the guise of a human,
the red tsen called Tsenkya Bumthub—
one of his own color, a man in red with a red horse,
Chief Zikphen must be the one to tame him.
As for the samaya-violator mu in the guise of a human,
known as Shechen Yamé—
one of his own color, a man in green with a green horse,
Nang-ngu Yutak is said to be the one destined to tame him.
As for the samaya-violator gongpo in the guise of a human
named Migö Yamé—
one of his own color, a man in yellow with a yellow horse,
Sengtak Adom is said to be the one destined to tame him.
As for the emanation of the evil teurang in the guise of a
    human,
the one known as Shelé Lakring—
one of his own color, a entirely white man with a white horse,
the unrivaled warrior Gyatsha Zhalu is said to be the one
    destined to tame him.
Furthermore, as for the one thousand māra armies,
those hordes of wild savages with no fear of dying—
the Pathül are said to be their destined enemy.
The daughter Bloody Tress who stayed behind in her native
    land,
she who is the ruler of all life in the three realms—
it is difficult for corporeal humans to contend with her.
It is the dralha Nyentak who will bind her,
and I will be the one to vanquish her.
The tiger-skin-clad sister dralha,
posing as Wangjema, the heart essence of the māras,
she whose stomping ground is the country of Düd—
hers to tame is the māra life-support talisman,

the bottomless black Spirit Lake
that is the submerged citadel of Dölpa Nakpo,
the great evil nāga who devours humans as fodder.
Every month as the moon waned, on the twenty-ninth day,[8]
each living being was forced to make an offering
to the crocodile-headed makara nāga demon
of one hundred horses and livestock
and with these choice offerings, a semblance of peace was
     maintained.
Not only that, the seven māra spirit fish
each had to be fed a hundred million little fish,
the sight of which was unbearable.
Therefore, for the māra life-support talismans,
the heart blood of the actual demoness was prepared,
mixed with the nine poisonous substances,
and annealed through the subjugating garuḍa mantra.
It was hurled into the barbarian abode of Spirit Lake
to annihilate the talismans so that not even their names
     remain.
Furthermore, since this lake was the dwelling place of evil forces,
milk was poured into it, turning it to the side of virtue
by removing the protectors of the māras.
Deep within the innermost storehouse
was the life-span essence of the samaya-violators:
those seven butter lamps of blood and fat
were annihilated with the heart blood of the demoness,[9]
she who was the tether of the nāgas, rākṣasas, and māras.
Then, from one of nine black boulders, the one that was the
     life-support
fell to the disguised Wangjema to splinter with a pickax.
Within this boulder, the life-supports of the Seven Wayward
     Siblings,
their souls, life spans, and life forces, all three
dwelled as a frog body with seven serpent heads
that only a human could tame.
Trothung is the emanation of Hayagrīva
and was the one with adequate skill to be entrusted to liberate
     those seven.

Most propitious is the worth that has come
from our achievements during this waxing moon fortnight.
Yet, as for the Düd king and his ministers,
residing in their hidden valley—
for three years we have struggled to revenge their raids.
Therefore, the tiger-skin-clad sister posing as the demoness,
with her many powers of deception
will no doubt send the māra bandit army here to Ling.
The nineteenth day of this month will be the time for battle.
The Pathül warriors should not wait here at Namtri Barma in
     Lower Zi;
they must capture that hidden valley in the turquoise
     mountains.
After the hateful enemies are decimated,
precious treasure and prosperity will rain down
and the eight classes will become allies.
The land will be emptied of evil humans and māras
and become a sacred land.
That is the prophecy.
There is no need to busy yourselves setting up an
     encampment;
the Pathül warriors can masquerade as skilled bandits.
There is no need to work on improving discipline;
the Phunu are already a supreme arrow against the enemy.
There is no need to ready the horse to race;
the supreme steed is already chomping at the bit.
It is unnecessary to wear three layers of armor;
there is the protection of the vajra tent.
There is no need for spies or watchmen;
there is the unobstructed wisdom of the divine prophecy.
The king and the others have no need for support;
virtuous guardian deities are with them.
There is no need to conscript an army;
volunteers have agreed to go.
This is the way of Tramo Ling.
Those who go forward are capable,
aspiring to the divine mandate.
The one who tried to turn the māra kingdom toward virtue

was the messenger of Padmasambhava,
the magical Trisong Detsen.
The Pathül are surely manifested mahāsiddhas.
There is no enemy that cannot be defeated.
Now, in front of the excellent supreme support,
uncles, mothers, and aunts, those who remain on native soil,
make worthy offerings of prostrations, circumambulate,
and dedicate excellent aspirations.
Without a doubt, within a month or two,
if you have understood this song, there will be heartfelt
    celebration.
If you have not understood, there is no point to my words.
Pathül and Phunu, keep this in mind.

While everyone commended Gesar's vajra song, King Chipön was think-ing, "In *The Mother Chronicles*, that small red leather-bound volume of ancient prophecy that Trothung safeguards, it states that within this maṇḍala of the jewel of supreme bliss,[10] the father lineage is of lions and the mother lineage of nāgas."[11] Then, he spoke: "In due course, the snow lion [Gesar] will be fully matured with its turquoise mane in full bloom, its skills perfected, and will be sovereign over the eastern snow[12] mountain land of Ma. The Bengal tiger [Trothung] will slip into the eastern mountain forest. Waves from the poisonous Lake Duktsho will wash in and flood those woodlands. But in due time, when the great garuḍa [another epithet for Gesar] soars in space, the vicious māras will be reduced to nothing, and the seven great heart jewels of the treasure fortress will be revealed. If the torch of method and wisdom is not ignited, there is the danger [that Gesar] will fall to the depths of that poisonous lake. But if he opens the southern gate of the red rock cavern, the four-fanged black jackal [Yutsé] will be defeated, and the sorrel yak [Lutsen] of the north will be lassoed and nurtured. The citizens will blossom like colorful flowers. Thus is the prophecy; it will not be long until it comes about. Do not dismiss this out of hand." He had spoken from a roaring tiger seat atop a sandalwood throne. Distinguished in appearance and smiling, he continued, "Gesar, all of you ministers, and Uncle Trothung, listen for a moment," as he offered this song called "Long Slow Gentle Melody."

OṂ MAṆI PADME HŪṂ
Sing "Ala thala."
"Thala" begins and

"La" gives the perfect pitch.
Buddha, Dharma, and Saṅgha—
these we supplicate to lead us to the path of liberation.
This land of Ma is rich in virtue,
a glorious enclosure of happiness and bliss.
I am your old Uncle Chipön,
ancient as the known world
and the divine elder of the three sacred generations,
the main support of Ling
and the tether uniting the Phunu.
I am the paternal uncle of the Masang king Gesar
and the elder who discerns good and evil.
Without exaggeration, that is the way people speak of me.
You, seated upon the golden throne,
beneath a peacock-feathered parasol,
the emanation body of the buddhas of the three times,
great one who quells the evil māras,
divine heir, Gesar of Ling—
you have the countenance of a divine child,
you possess all the major and minor marks,
and your forehead is adorned with the syllable ĀH.
Dralha assemble like swirling sparks from a blazing fire,
werma gather like showering sparks from flint on stone.
Unrivaled precious Dharma king,
listen attentively.
In the right-hand row from your seat atop a conch throne,
Gyatsha of the Bumpa family, listen.
Upper, Middle, and Lower Ling, these three,
three great chieftains of Ling, listen.
Two sons of the Greater Lineage of Takrong, listen.
Darphen of the Dukgi clan, listen.
Denma, Pala, Gadé, you three,
and all the Phunu and Pathül seated here, listen.
Listen to what is said; it is the command of the king.
The prophecy is like drops of gold,
a genuine jewel, precise and flawless.
In the heavens is the conjunction of the sun, moon, and stars;
it is time to dispel the darkness.

The earth abounds with crops and greenery;
it is time to banish the poverty of sentient beings.
Between heaven and earth, kings, ministers, and subjects
    gather;
it is time to vanquish the evil māras.
In the prophecy of *The Mother Chronicles*,
within this jeweled maṇḍala of supreme bliss,
the father lineage is of lions and the mother lineage is of
    nāgas.
When the snow lion has matured to his full power
and is luxuriant with a turquoise mane,
he will be sovereign of the eastern snow mountain Magyal
    Pomra.
The tiger will enter the eastern mountain forest,
its woodlands will be inundated by the waters of the
    poisonous lake,
and when the great garuḍa soars in the heavens,
the divine gate of the red rock cavern will open,
the four-fanged black jackal will be defeated,
and the sorrel yak will be domesticated.
At this time, the citizens will blossom like multicolored
    flowers.
Those are the many prophecies.
Do not scoff at them.
King Yutsé of Minyak
is an enemy of the teachings of the Buddhadharma.
He ranks as one among the four great māras
and is the son of the chief māra Garab Wangchuk.
You can be certain he has much magical power.
The samaya-violator Seven Wayward Siblings,
through the perverted aspirations of the rudras
and the eight classes of spirits, were disguised as children
and are the stalwart allies of the nāga Dölpa Nakpo.
These intangible beings bring obstacles and grave danger.
Those in the thirty monasteries of Ling must each recite the
    Kangyur,
each household must recite the *One Hundred Thousand
Prajñāpāramitā Verses,*

and every person must recite the Vajrakīlaya mantra as
    exorcism.
It is most important to quash the samaya-violator demons.
On auspicious days, make offerings to the gods.
Each village should hoist prayer flags.
I have filled a small cup with gold dust
as a support to Dharma practice.
With the immediate compassion of the excellent Three Jewels
and the great blessings of the Three Roots,
without doubt, obstacles will be averted.
If the divine and human assemblies do not join together,
it will be difficult to attain the crucial victory.
There is no denying that those of valor
must not take this lightly.
As in the past, the fortress guards will stay back,
scouts will be posted outside,
and great forces[13] will be aligned with the warriors.
Only after all this is done will we understand what to do.

Divine prophecy and seasonal rains—
until they gleam upon the green earth,
save for the divine cuckoo bird and the nightingale,
it is difficult for creatures to intuit their approach.
Divine prophecy and warriors' arrows—
until they reverberate, striking the target,
save for the brave warriors with their twitching thumbs,
it is difficult for anyone to intuit their approach.
Divine prophecy and Yama's lasso—
until they wrap around your neck,
apart from the divine ones with the higher perceptions,
it is difficult for beings of the six realms to intuit their approach.

This is not mere foreboding; it is literally the way things are.
Perhaps the king and ministers should think this over.
Generally, in accord with the prophecy,
carry uncorrupted[14] precepts upon the crown of your head
and hold excellent faith and devotion in your heart.
As you earnestly embrace this,

may a harmonious society be established,
may the teachings of the Buddha flourish,
and may evil forces wane.
If my song has caused confusion, the fault is mine.
If my words have bewildered, I beg forgiveness.
King and ministers, keep this in mind.

Thus he sang, and his song was well received by all as true and honest. Then, Chipön prepared thirty gold brick offerings to the Mupa Sky King Gesar, the warriors each made a suitable offering and, in accord with Chipön's appeal, the patrons presented more than sixty bricks of silver. Those who stayed behind, the lamas and monks, fathers and uncles, mothers and aunts, regardless of rank, high or low, together with natives and foreigners, all pledged to practice the daily *sādhanas* diligently until the prophecy was fulfilled. A joyful celebration ensued, but three days later, Neuchung had an ominous dream that portrayed the weakness of the Ombu and Muchang ministers. She relayed this to Gesar and those ministers—Anu Paseng and Rinchen Darlu—were commanded to stay behind.

The bard interjects: Each of these ministers sang a song or two about how much they wanted to come along, but I left these out, thinking that they might be boring.

Then, on the thirteenth day of that month, the troops and leaders gathered. The Ling military standard bearer, the one who was the core of its one hundred thousand troops, the hammer of the enemy, Denma, was a man so blue—armored with nine types of blue weapons and mounted on a blue steed—that it appeared as though a turquoise dragon had risen from a crystal blue lake. Then, descending like a thunderbolt, came the unsurpassed warrior, Gyatsha Zhalu Karpo, the butcher of the hateful enemy. White-robed, riding a white horse, and armed with white weapons, he looked like Brahmā going to war. With his nine courageous dralha guardians concealed in the crook of his arm,[15] he led the army column. In its center was Gesar. His face caught one's attention as would the luminous full moon. Luxuriant eyebrows sparkled above his piercing eyes, and his teeth shone like a conch garland between his deep vermillion lips. His wisdom eye was vibrant and his hair, dark and shimmering. Dralha and werma gathered like clouds. Equipped with the armor and weapons of the dralha, as though he were Indra preparing for battle, Gesar was so resplendent that it was difficult to gaze upon him. Manifesting the power to magnetize and overpower the three worlds through his splendor, he rode upon Kyang Gö, the formidable mount tacked with the accoutrements of a great steed.

Likewise, blazing with the power of awesome brilliance, like tigers and leopards roaming the mountains or wild yak herds at the far reaches of the rocky path, the Thirty Mighty Warriors and the Phunu led their own troops and together with Gesar, departed for war. With the horses' murmuring neighs and the pounding of their great hooves, the clamoring[16] of the men's armor and the billowing of the victory banners, with a great roaring din—they departed. Drukmo, an emanation of White Tārā, and Neuchung both offered chang to the king, ministers, and Phunu and escorted them to the interior of Lhamo Mountain in Ma. Those who were staying behind bowed and offered *khatas*. In return, the king and ministers bestowed scarves to both Drukmo and Neuchung and touched foreheads with them, not bearing to part, and to all those who had come to see them off, even the lamas and monks of Ling, they offered auspicious scarves filled with the wealth of gold and silver as a symbol of their connection. There were celebrations and auspicious aspiration prayers and, with peace and reverence in their hearts, the householders returned to their homeland of Ling.

By that time, the rulers, lamas, and monks of Ling had spent five nights at the Zima mountain pass Namtri Barma. It was near the pristine Ma River valley—bordered by Zima above, with the kingdom of Zichim to one side and Limibal[17] beyond—and was the main thoroughfare traversed by a steady stream of merchants. In this remote valley were the thirteen great hills, arranged like a row of feast offering objects, and interspersed between them like golden trays were broad grassy meadows. Altogether, this was a powerful and sacred land across which were the encampment tents of the divine gurus. The sounds of the Dharma reverberated continuously from within them. Behind them was the main activity tent where Gesar and his ministers convened, and beyond were the formidable military barracks with the great army's main staging tent. A noisy din issued from the encampment. Herds of horses, cared for by the army, roamed the mountain meadows. The divine ones and the gurus practiced diligently, without wavering, according to the prophecy of the mother ḍākinīs. The protecting vajra tent was continuously present through the ceaseless practice of the three great lamas, Akhu Gomchen Tingmé among them,[18] and others, abiding in samādhi, such that no harm could be inflicted by samaya-violators.

As for the country of hostile māras, at that time, it was led by bandits and raiders. Their king with his seven ministers had conscripted an army of more than eleven hundred fearless volunteers. On the eighth day, they were gathered near the māra castle, where they had gone carrying offerings of flesh and blood to all their talismans: the barbarian forested mountain of devastation, Dölpa Nakri Ngampa, the black poisonous māra lake, Duktsho Nakpo, and so forth. But from the peak of the māra soul mountain Lari Nakpo (Black Soul Mountain), hedonistic asura gods sent down three red lightning bolts and violent hail, killing five of the māra troops and three of their horses. A vixen yelped: a bad omen. The lake became opaque with dense rainbow light and instinctively a little nāga bird chirped a warning. The white-turbaned nāgas said, "We have heard the sound of what is coming but have turned to the side of virtue—take away your flesh and blood offerings."

Great trepidation arose in the Düd king and ministers as now none of the nāgas, neither the barbarian outcaste nāgas, nor the human-eating nāgas, nor the crocodile-headed ones, nor the monstrous fish spirits, and so on, could now be seen in this lake, their accustomed dwelling place.[19] The māra king and ministers froze, stopping the army in its tracks. Realizing that the Düd army had been delayed by the lha, lu, and nyen, the dralha and werma instantly appeared in the form of the nāga beings that had vanished. The sight was overwhelming—there were countless nāgas, even more savage than before. They were vivid and shimmering and could be seen frolicking with delight, enjoying the offerings of flesh and blood. Perceiving this meld of good and evil, the Düd king and ministers returned with their troops to their fortress. The imposter Wangjema had left, saying she was going to proffer an army of her bosom nāga friends, and, in an instant, she reappeared at the fortress, carrying an entire army miraculously materialized in a single box. From within it came many sounds—those of rushing water, echoing thunder, and the rumbling of rocks, as well as human voices clearly heard in many tongues, spoken and sung. The Düd king and ministers questioned that so many troops could be contained in one place, and the Wangjema imposter offered this song in order to allay their doubts.

> For this little song, sing "Alu thalu."
> "Thalu" begins and
> "La lu" gives the perfect pitch.
> From the midst of this swirling ocean of flesh and blood,
> may my protecting spirits think of me, the demoness.
> Nurture me and be as inseparable as a collar on clothing.
> I offer flesh and blood
> and all my spoils to the lofty heavens.
> Within this kingdom may faultless stability be established.
> This is the land of the barbarian māras
> who eat raw meat and drink fresh blood,
> who take joy in killing and delight in thievery.
> This is a place endowed with prosperity.
> No one needs to be told who I am—

I am the mother of the māra lands
and its assembled gods and humans.
There is no need to explain; this is known to all.
Listen, unrivaled King Yutsé and ministers,
the chronicles of my life are a national treasure.
This morning, unhindered, I traversed the spirit lands.[20]
Where, as is their custom, the nonhuman gods-demons
display the wrathful power of the eight classes
and the magical meld of good and evil.
For you king and ministers, this has caused great worry,
yet the finest minds are free from any fear.
In the evening, I went to the chthonic nāga lands
where my Uncle Belgo gave advice for my journey and
     conduct
and excellent counsel on gaining victory.
As a support, I borrowed a wrathful box of illusion;
this very box is said to have room for the world in its entirety.
But humans are not at liberty to see it;
it is the heart treasure of Dölpa Nakpo.
There is an army corps of ninety thousand within it:
men white as conch, with horses,
armor and helmets, the threefold panoply, white as conch;
men of turquoise, with turquoise horses,
uniformed with turquoise helmets and armor;
men of coral, wearing coral coats of mail,
uniformed with coral helmets and armor;
men of gold, with golden horses,
uniformed with golden armor and helmets;
men of silver, with silver horses,
uniformed with silver armor and helmets;
men of copper, with copper horses,
uniformed with copper armor and helmets;
and men of iron, with iron horses,
uniformed with iron armor and helmets—
each[21] warrior a hero in his own way.
Even a mountain lofty as Mount Meru can be hurled far away;
even an ocean can be guzzled in a mouthful.

The world as it exists can be turned upside down.
The might of each of these men is unassailable.
Gradually, these very important matters will be clarified.
This ancient decree is a golden design—
the future holds no chance of reversal.
Just as when you—the king, ministers, and bandits—leave
    your native land,
there is no chance that your country will fall to the enemy.
You are consummate warriors—
the world itself could not defeat you,
let alone that miserable lowly Ling.
I will not worry while you are away,
and you do not need to be concerned about me.
Before a month has passed,
just as a vulture returns to its rocky crag,
you will find your way back home,
and afterward we will see what has come of the situation.[22]
Best would be to have plundered the kingdom of Ling,
second best would be to have deprived them of wealth and
    power,
and only as a last resort, to have beheaded the Pathül
    warriors.
These exploits will surely become legendary—
watch and see.
I have your purpose in mind.
Although outwardly we differ,
inwardly our natures are identical.
Why make distinctions?
Trothung is the guide who knows the way,
Garab Wangchuk will be quick to assist us,
the nāga demon Dölpa Nakpo is our greatest support,
King Yutsé has such lofty charisma,
the great vicious ministers such courage and skill,
and the Düd army has the power of more than a thousand
    thunderbolts.
It is preposterous to say that we could not defeat the enemy.
King and ministers, keep this song in mind.

As she spoke, Yutsé and his ministers were emboldened and, without a doubt or a second thought, they realized that they must act to ensure their legacy. That next day at first light, they were again on their way. The fearsome blue nāga protector, Lugön Tongthub Yamé, with a red pennant adorning his helmet, his blue horse, blue armor and weapons, and Nakpo Tongdü Lenmé astride his black horse, with a dark-red braid of hair beneath his helmet and an iron coat of mail, led the army, prepared for action. Since they knew the lay of the land, Trothung and his five ministers were just behind, accompanied by Dongtsen, Khergö the son of Guru, and so forth. King Minyak Yutsé, Tsenkya Bumthub, and Migö Yamé—their very natures that of the inexhaustible magic of formidable courage, each with their armor and weapons and mounted on swift horses—took up the middle of the marching line. Bringing up the rear astride his white horse was Shelé Lakring, blazing forth with an expression like that of a snow lion with a lavish turquoise mane. With this entourage, the māra bandits set out eastward toward Ling, picturing themselves as the glorious legacy of Tibet. That night, they camped along the Zi mountain pass, Namtri Barma.

That next morning, they came to the post of the two demoness-sentries, Jigo and Jalak, in the Zima Valley, but no one came to greet them. The king and ministers were growing uneasy, but just then, Manéné flew down. Now she was disguised as the two very same demonesses, one riding upon a jackal and the other on a musk deer. Then she sang several spontaneous songs, humbling herself to the Düd king and ministers, but I, the bard, left these out, thinking that they might be boring. She offered to quench their thirst, slyly bringing the king and ministers poisonous liquor tainted with various impure substances. After imbibing, they simply could not soldier on.

In the end, they made camp for the night just below the Zi mountain pass[23] and from there marched on, unimpeded, for three days. Gesar had alerted his troops that the Düd king and ministers were approaching, closer and closer, and the Ling warriors swelled with wholehearted courage for battle: Gyatsha, Denma, Darphen, Zikphen, Nyatsha, Nyibum,[24] and Gadé were the seven of unfettered bravery and awesome splendor. Each had ten capable ministers and trained horses chomping at the bit. With dralha and werma gathered like clouds above them, and the deities and the gurus blessing and protecting them, those Seven Super Warriors had departed immediately and were lying in wait along that very mountain pass, Namtri Barma. That night, the māra king and ministers had ominous dreams, and the following morning, when they convened, Shelé Lakring rolled the magical dice of the teurang, divining that a great enemy would come. They set up camp just below the cannibal demon rock overhanging the lower meadowlands. The three inner māra ministers,

Lugön Tongthub, Shelé Lakring, and Migö Yamé, decided that they would scout ahead, led by Trothung's son, Dongtsen Apel, who knew the lay of the land.

Trothung was thinking to himself, "I must go along; if I stay behind it will be disastrous. The past three nights, I have dreamed that I was welcomed by the many gods and humans of Ling. The kings and ministers of Ling will surely see my dreams as divine prophecy. Furthermore, the Düd king and ministers are courageous, but as an army, they are disorganized. As for myself, at this moment I am inferior even to the commoners, having been discredited by Wangjema who exposed my hidden flaws and humiliated me, and moreover, I have left my ministers and my mules loaded with riches behind in Düd. But there is nothing to be done about that now, since there are māra kings and demons living there, and it goes without saying that Gesar must be the one to tame them. But when that time comes, I fully expect that those ministers and riches will once again be mine." At that point he spoke aloud, "Gentleman, there is always trouble sending young, unexperienced men on a scouting mission. After all, there are men of superior, mediocre, and lesser ability. Lesser men set off to spy but, like pigs, they do not notice what is right in front of them, and like mules,[25] they never notice what is behind them. They bolt up without realizing that they need to stay hidden, and the moment they spy the enemy, they themselves are exposed and fall right into enemy hands. Mediocre men can be sent to scout ahead, but they are like wolves, concerned with what is ahead and, like mongooses, with what is chasing them. They patrol all through the ridges and valleys; however, as soon as they see the enemy, they themselves are spotted and become confused about what to do. When superior men set off spying, like the sun rising over the mountains, they see everything ahead and, like the rising moon, everything behind. They safeguard with the clear mind of both the sun and moon. They sleep cloaked in the darkness of the hillside, spying between the rocks and trees.[26] They sight the enemy before they themselves are seen, succeeding in obtaining the spoils. This is what is said, and it is true. I am an old man with great experience and, when my sons go, I must go with them, since the danger is great regardless of whether they encounter the Ling army or bandits, but it is particularly great if they meet Joru and his kin, who despise me. I, this old man, would find it unbearable not to go."

Lugön argued, "Our horses are fast enough to overtake the birds of the skies. There is no chance your horse can keep pace." Trothung laughingly replied, "Why are you scouts in such a hurry in the first place? Besides, my own horse can keep up with both Yuja and Kyang Gö, and they are clearly the fastest horses in the kingdom. It is impossible that my horse will lag behind yours!" The māra king and ministers, swollen with pride in the unrivaled speed of their own magical horses, hid their irritation and said, "Well then, let's go if we're going!"

Now that it was decided that Trothung would come along, they had something to eat and drink. Their swift horses were saddled and bridled and packed with all the necessary provisions. Arrayed with the threefold panoply, each uniformed according to his personal color, as swiftly as birds in flight, at the sheep-time of the afternoon,[27] they came to Namtri Barma, and there in the midst of a meadow were the Pathül warriors, waiting. When the Pathül saw the three māra scouts and Dongtsen, one after another hurtling on the path toward Ling, they were enraged and sprung into action, as excited as hunting dogs catching sight of a stag. Dongtsen had been the first to spot the Pathül, his Ling kinsmen, and he was immediately overcome with shame and particularly fearful of Gyatsha. His voice trembled as he called out to his māra companions, "Look! Over there, at those seven men on horseback! Think about it! They *must* be the Pathül warriors of Ling. Encountering them this way—here in this wilderness, without an army—we are finished! No good can come of this. We should retreat, and quickly." Fainthearted, Trothung had lagged out of sight, but the shrewd māra ministers were lifelong skilled warriors, and they were greatly affronted by Dongtsen's words. Wordlessly, they tensed their muscles and pulsed their thumbs, ready to shoot. They lowered their helmets and tightened the leather straps of their armor, geared up their weapons and ran full tilt at the Ling warriors. Gyatsha sprang forth, as intense and formidable as hail and thunderbolts. He held back the reins of his stallion Gaja Sokar to keep it from a nearly full, fierce gallop, and offered this warrior song.

> OṂ MAṆI PADME HŪṂ
> Sing "Ala thala thala."
> "Thala" begins and
> "La la" gives the perfect pitch.
> From the dwelling place of the crystal clear sky,
> great divine Brahmā with a retinue of a hundred thousand
> gods,
> I call to you to look upon us with your omniscience.
> Hoist the virtuous teachings to the heavens.
> If you do not recognize this place,
> it is the borderland of Zima Valley,
> at the edge of Tramo Ling.
> This is the mountain pass in Dokham, known as Namtri
> Barma.
> If you do not recognize me,
> I am from the country of Tramo Ling in the kingdom of Ma.

I am Gyatsha Zhalu of the Bumpa clan.
You four horsemen over there across the riverbank—
where are you going in such a rush?
What homeland have you left behind?
Attended by Lugön, your man all of blue, with his horse and
      pennants,
your own horse Yuja as fast as a bird on the wing—
if I am right, you must be Dongtsen Apel,
a heartless, spineless little louse
with that shameless two-faced hypocrite Trothung for a father.
All of Ling knows your story without wasting breath asking.
I never thought you would turn out like this.
You, the collective trash bin of Tramo Ling,
do not run off, come back;
I can assure you a position in Takrong.
I will not strike you with this steely sword
and risk violating the command of the highest gods.
Little by little, you will see the truth of these words.
But if you still think it is possible to walk away from all this,
a sharp prick of my sword will convince you otherwise.
Without more songs, just come,
and there will be no hard feelings.
You other three, listen to this song.
As for Ling, the jeweled land of the east,
have you noticed any evil demons trampling over it?
This is the divine pure land,
do you know of any incarnate māras running around?
Here in this spiritual seat of the noble arhats,
have you seen any heretic māras camped here?
Some months past,
the demoness came to Upper Ling,
and although she intended to take it as spoils,
Gesar, the divine ruler,
instead led her to the path of liberation.
Today, you three māra ministers have arrived.
You are hounded by calamity
and misfortune lies ahead.
You got what you asked for.

Goats spend their lives roaming the mountain ridges,
their dexterity foreshadowing their slaughter.
Fish spend their lives chasing after morsels in the water,
their undulating movement foreshadowing their capture.
Musk deer spend their lives rubbing their tails on trees,
their scent foreshadowing that they will be hunted down.

> You māras have spent your lives as the bandits of these
>   northern grassy plains,
> but now nothing good will come of being here.
> We seven men and horses of Ling,
> given that both past and present disputes
> are of such gravity, have come this great distance.
> If I may say so, this must all come to a resolution.
> If you cherish your lives, bow down and prostrate;
> otherwise, do not think I am inclined to free you.
> If you have understood this song, give an answer.
> If you have not, there is no way to explain it.
> Three horsemen, keep this in mind.

Hearing such a song, the three māra warrior-scouts raged. From within this blazing anger, the magical teurang lineage son, Shelé Lakring, displayed himself as three separate but identical selves, haughtily grasped his sword handle, and sang this song of great fury.

> Sing "Una alu thalu."
> "Thalu una" begins and
> "La lu" gives the perfect pitch.
> From the celestial palace of formless beings,
> three ancestral teurang fathers—white, black, multicolored—
>   know me.
> Do not tip the scales of worldly affairs.
> May the warriors' plunder be placed in my hands.
> Mother Thokmo Nayakma (Sharp Lightning Successful
>   Point),
> quell the enemy, cut out their hearts.
> These lands are the great plains of valor
> where men can profess bravery

and stallions can cavort and race.
If you do not recognize me,
in this demon land of bandits—
its secluded territory inaccessible but for a narrow defile,
a mighty stronghold of twisted ravines—
as one of seven siblings,
I burst forth from an egg,
one of six sons of equal strength.
Our seven lake-born horses, all equally swift,
could gallop to China and return in a single day.
I am called Karpo Shelé Lakring,
the magical son of the white teurang.
I am called "Shelé" after my father lineage
and distinguished as "Lakring"
for my arms that are long enough to reach far into the
      valleys
while I seize a bird from the sky
and bend down from the lofty peak of Mount Meru
to gather precious gems from the ocean floor.
Those are the reasons I have the name Lakring.
Seven men, bandits of Ling, listen—
especially you, Gyatsha, wholly white and straddling a white
      horse,
you, with your bold talk vying with the dragons' roar
and professing to be some celebrated warrior,
a hero of the miserable Ling crooks.
You think you will be the consummate bandit,
but along the arching sword strokes of our father warriors,
your gushing blood is a sign that your life force is spent.
You have uttered only insults,
telling me to give up if I cherish my life,
but I say it is you who must surrender,
and I will spare your life.
The king and ministers journey behind me,
eastward, toward the Ma kingdom of Ling.
There, that famous man they call Joru—
let us see if he is a miraculous hero or not.

That renowned Tea Fortress, Jakhar—
let us see if it is unassailable or not.
The legendary woman Drukmo—
we will see if she is a beauty or not.
As for that band of thieves known as the Pathül warriors of
    Ling,
we will see just how brave and mighty they are.
And as for that place of celebrated prosperity—
we will see about its riches,
and not only look but carry them away.
My two companions are, first, this man in blue with the blue
    horse,
the son of Dölpa Nakpo,
the nāga protector Lugön Tongthub Yamé
riding his blue mount Luta,[28]
and second, this man, a golden banner held aloft,[29]
the lineage son of the gongpo king,
is Migö Yamé
on his golden-hoofed golden horse,
galloping effortlessly, never breaking pace.
We are the children of Yama,
and these are the working knives[30] of the lord of death
and the barren wastelands of the roaming dead.
It is unthinkable that we would fear your seven-man army;
we are a match for hundreds of thousands.
Your answer only serves to waste another day.
If you have understood, this song is sweet to your ears.
If not, I cannot explain further.
Horsemen, keep this in mind.

Thus he sang, and as he finished, he strode closer and closer until he pressed in on the enraged Pathül warriors. Fuming, Gyatsha considered his response. His bloodshot eyes, as piercing as the morning star, rolled in his head and his round, white face clouded over as he replied, "You evil samaya-violator māras, warrior sons, you are but eighteen years old and have time for talking and listening, as well as for fighting. Do not be in such a rush; listen as I speak." And he offered this short song while holding the handle of his invincible sword Yazi.

OṂ MAṆI PADME HŪṂ
Sing "Ala thala thala."
"Thala" begins and
"La la" gives the perfect pitch.
Gods, nāgas, and nyen, these three, hosts of dralha,
zodors, and werma, assist me.
May the supreme Three Jewels be my unwavering support.
May the journey of this courageous son be of value.
This land is the borderland of Zima Valley,
where the divine gods and māras contend
and where bravery is discerned from weakness.
I, Gyatsha Zhalu Karpo of the Bumpa clan,
am a man who lovingly protects the humble
and stands up to the enemy, the lord of death.
You three, the samaya-violator Lugön Tongthub,
the teurang magical emanation-son, Shelé Lakring,
and the *gyalgong* magical emanation-son, Migö Yamé—
though you were not invited, you were drawn here
through the energy and power of the divine oath-bound ones.
You find gathered here: the expert archer, Denma,[31]
the skilled lancer, Darphen,
the exemplary hero, Zikphen,
the epitome of might, Nyibum,
the one famed for strength, Gadé,
the brave warrior sent to battle, Nyatsha Aten,[32]
and the one who has attained the siddhi of weapons,
myself, the intrepid Gyatsha,
whose great sword will strike down Shelé.
Our lives are in one another's hands—
how sad for you.
Your flesh and blood will be fodder for birds and wolves
and your severed consciousnesses will wander the bardo.
You have no other road.
Keep this is mind.

When he had finished the song, Gyatsha and Shelé, fearless as drongs and fierce as lions, promptly leapt at one another, swords flying. Other than severed links of armor, at first no harm was done to either of them. But then, while Darphen charged from behind with his lance, from the right, Nyibum threw a white, sheep-sized stone, which landed right in the midst of Shelé and his men and horses, and in their place appeared a swirling pile of ashes. His magic destroyed, the threefold emanation that Shelé had manifested dissolved at once, while his horse was revived by the breath of the teurang, staggered to its feet, and ran off. At the same moment, Denma and Zikphen charged at Lugön. Denma threw three golden-notched arrows, one after another. The first one struck the mirror at Lugön's heart center,[33] shattering it. The second sheared off the feather pennant of his helmet. But yet, even though the third struck again straight at his heart center, the time had not yet come to tame the māras, and in the end, Denma was able to do nothing more than stun Lugön who, on the verge of blacking out, shot two poison arrows back at Denma. The first grazed his upper arm, scattering the scales of his armor. The second struck Denma's right breast but did not penetrate his body. Seeing that Denma was becoming faint from the poison, the divine gods rained down ablution water, and everything became crisp and clear. Zikphen mightily thrust his sword three times; sparks flew but he cut nothing. He unsheathed his knife, but from this melee, no winner emerged. Zikphen threw a lasso but to no avail, as while he snapped it back, rather than falling from his horse, the enemy simply cut the lasso rope.

Then, Denma sheathed his knife and, summoning his strength, shot a single arrow. Since he had been wounded in the left arm, as he released the arrow, it veered to the right. Realizing he was unable to make a straight shot, he hastily pulled back from the fight. Migö had run right at Nyatsha and Gadé, and the three, all on horseback, clashed with spears but no one prevailed. Then, they fought briefly with knives, but with no decisive winner. Gadé's anger rose as he sheathed his dagger and threw Migö from atop his horse. They both rolled to the ground, and Nyatsha threw a lasso around Migö's neck and dragged him. But there were so many formless beings present that the air was thick with the sparks of magical gyalgong spirits and the māra men and horses were able to sidle off. Prodded by Trothung, Dongtsen, who had been on the sidelines of the fighting, alighted from his horse and meekly offered a scarf of respect to the seven Ling warriors who had been pursuing the māras but who now, realizing that victory was not to be had on this day, had agreed to return home to report to Gesar.

Trothung was trailing behind, drained and shaken to the core from witnessing the daylong fight, when he saw the three māra warriors returning to their camp with the Pathül some distance behind, also leaving the battlefield. Terrified that he would be seen, he wedged himself in a rocky niche to hide just as the Pathül passed by. But Trothung's mount, Pharwa Ngakné (Jackal Black Mane), recognizing the horses and men of Ling, shed big tears and, with a deeply resonant neigh, headed toward the Pathül warriors. The warriors' horses recognized Trothung's steed and, in unison, sang a refrain of joyous neighing and snorting. The warriors realized that Trothung must be nearby and, when they asked the steed where his owner was, the steed looked backward, whinnying and disclosing Trothung's location. Unnerved, Trothung manifested as a dwarf and pressed himself deeper into the boulders. The warriors' horses crowded in, milling around and stamping their forelegs on the ground. Their neighing came to a crescendo, and Denma dismounted and peered into a hollow in the midst of the boulders. There, he saw Trothung, no bigger than a seven-year-old boy, with his eyes wide open and his beard quivering. Dumbfounded, Denma said, "Akhu the chieftain lives inside a rock cleft! So much can come of such a devious mind." And he offered this song, "Thala in Six Modulations."[34]

> OM MANI PADME HŪM
> Sing "Ala thala thala."
> "Thala" begins and
> "La la" gives the perfect pitch.
> Protectors, gurus, and yidams, the Three Jewels,
> we supplicate blessings from your heart
> and from the vast expanse of your enlightened mind.
> Please hold us inseparable from your compassion.
> If you do not recognize this place,
> Zima, Barma, and Rongma, these three
> form a boundary of Ling
> known as the mountain pass, Namtri Barma.
> Do you recognize me?
> From the swirling turquoise waters of the Den tribe,
> I am the steadfast warrior Denma the conqueror.
> My song is "Thala in Six Modulations."
> These immutable words are golden drops.
> Trothung, as the Takrong chieftain, you could assume a
>   cushioned seat;
> why would you stay in that old rock cleft?
> Why are you not singing "Hara," your personal song of
>   fearlessness,
> rather than holding your breath?
> Why did you not respond courageously
> rather than submissively sneaking into that rocky confine?
> Why are you not serving the royal army

rather than wandering alone, an unattended chieftain?
Why does your magical body not soar like a bird
but instead succumbs to misery, crouching[35] and trembling?
If you do not listen to the advice of friends and relatives,
when you are a wandering beggar, it will be too late.
As the proverbs of the ancient Tibetans say:

The restless horse stumbles, injuring its master.
An arrogant son brings disaster to his family.
A flirtatious woman harms only herself.
A scheming chieftain brings ruin upon his subjects.

That is what is said and it is the truth.
But there are still more proverbs:

When the divine master verges on wandering in saṃsāra,
sectarian quarrels of love and hate arise.
He will slander the monks
and, lacking heartfelt understanding of the Dharma, will fall further.
Novice traders start out in business only to return empty-handed
when they contend with more seasoned merchants.
They buy indiscriminately, ill-equipped to discern quality,
and wind up as wandering beggars.
A young girl breaks with her household,
being scornful of everyone but herself.
She looks around for any man she can find
and is left with nothing but her leaking breasts.

What the proverbs say is both true and fitting.
The white vulture that soars too high becomes dazed,
the musk deer that ranges too far falls from a cliff,
the tigress that leaps too high hurts her back,
and the minister who is too forceful invites dishonor.
A spoiled child is always looking for more,
too much fresh butter is bad for the liver,
one who is too familiar will be struck by the servant girl,
and a minister who is too entrenched will challenge the king.
Trothung, this is how it is; don't you understand?[36]

Your palace, the mighty Raven Heart Fortress—
there you could have sat on cushions of fine silk
dressed in lambskin-lined brocades
and dined on whatever you pleased.
Whatever you requested would have been provided.
With self-control you could have been the minister of a
    hundred thousand subjects.
Your lifelong companion Khara Sertsho
is wise, worthy, and stalwart,
your sons are like an entourage of tigers and leopards,
your ministers are like poison thorns embellishing you,
and your subjects are like a boiling poisonous lake and hold
    you in high esteem.
Why did you run off to the mountains; why did you not stay?
The heavenly Mupa King Gesar
is the heart-son of a thousand buddhas,
the incarnation of the protectors of the three families,
the emanation of Orgyen Padma,
the yoke upon the evil māras,
the man to establish the teachings of the side of virtue
and subjugate the eighteen great kingdoms.
He is the king of Jambudvīpa,
the one to bring well-being to all Tibetans.
Why do you act with such perverse hatred?
You banished Gokza to the lands of Lower Ma,
where her only shelter was the blue sky
and her only companions were the demon māras.
Her suffering was beyond words.
If one gets right down to it, you are to blame.
When the divine child Gesar was still very young,
you assaulted his body and belittled his words.
All of this is your doing—
think about it, Trothung!
Time and again, this bodhisattva Gesar has shown patience.
Through the affection of the fathers and uncles,
your seat remains in the front row,
and you are unassailable and firm
atop the sandalwood throne.

Moreover, since the agreement was that the winner of the
    horse race
would take the golden throne and the wealth of Kyalo,
Gesar did not act out of self-interest.
If you were a man who understood this,
you would think carefully about your past deeds
and, from now on, resolve to have some insight.
Come out of there right now!
To the Pathül and their leader Gyatsha,
apologize for deliberately going against them.
As long as you comport yourself like such a scoundrel,
you, far more than I, bear responsibility for all this discord.
Promise not to act like that in the future.
Your own sons, Zikphen and Nyatsha,
heart-sons of Tramo Ling,
have great love for King Gesar.
Now, for the sake of unity,
accept your place as one of the Phunu,
and until you stand before Gesar,
the Pathül warriors will withhold judgment.
Since we all exist through the great kindness of our parents,
not to return that kindness would diminish our merit.
Even the great chief Gadé has softened [toward you].
Perhaps I, Denma, have spoken out of turn,
but I have no hidden agenda.
Do not be afraid; come out of there.
If you have understood, my words are sweet to your ears.
If not, there is no way to explain it.
Trothung, keep this in mind.

Thus he sang, and Trothung summoned what little bravery he had and emerged from the rock crevice, still trembling but respectful to the Pathül. Although Denma's words did not exactly ring true to Gyatsha, Nyatsha, Darphen, and the rest, they went along with it. Then, Akhu Trothung sang this song.

OṂ MAṆI PADME HŪṂ
Sing "Ala thala thala."
"Thala" begins and[37]

"La la" gives the perfect pitch.
From the self-appearing divine realm,
nirmāṇakāya longevity vidyādhara,
along with the assembly of the bodhisattvas of the Bön
　　lineage,
please watch over me with compassion
and lead this sincere song.
If you do not recognize this place,
it is Namtri Barma in the land of Zi.
I am the Mazhi chieftain.
In my youth, I was renowned far and wide,
but I have grown frail, worse than a low-down dog.
Around the Mupa King Gesar in the heavens,
relatives gravitate as though they were the sun, moon, and
　　stars,
and Denma is like the radiant Milky Way.
Chipön sits nearby, surrounded by the Phunu,
like Mount Meru encircled by lesser mountains.
Reminiscent of climbing vines, sentient beings cling to Gesar,
and all of humankind relies upon him—
he is the ground of all of existence.
Now, Gyatsha of Bumpa
and all of you formidable warriors,
out of loving-kindness, listen to me.
Regarding Gesar, the divine son of Gokmo,
why would my heartfelt faith in him have weakened?
He is the destined deity of humankind,
the King Great Lion, and my own nephew.
There is no difference between sons and nephews;
blood is thick, not thin.
I was the one to set up this auspicious connection at the
　　outset
and it has been flawlessly accomplished.
I sponsored the eighteen great celebrations,
and Gesar obtained victory over all eighteen.
If I had not been chosen as the one to deceive him—
Gesar, an awakened one,
would never have displayed his wrathful side.

If I had not concentrated all my energy,
Gesar would never have stood a chance.
Without all my machinations,
Gesar would never be renowned in these three regions of
    Tibet.
Oops, I was not supposed to say that—just joking!
But what is the true meaning in all this?
When I held the Raven Heart Fortress,
yidam Red Hayagrīva came to me and prophesied, saying,
"Akhu, do not stay, but go;
go to the bandit country in the east.
There, Minyak Yutsé and the Seven Wayward Siblings
are bound together like dogs and wolves
and, as their shared evil karma plays out,
Ling will be destroyed.
Not only that, if, by year's end,
Lutsen, Sadam, Gurkar,
and Minyak Yutsé join forces,
the entire southern continent will not be able to defeat them."
Therefore, one day this year,
just as the wind drives the rain and dogs follow a scent,
through deception, I was the one to welcome our māra guests
    to Ling.
Sent forth from my homeland by the gods
and released like a feathered divination arrow,
I have struck the intended target.
This prophecy of my yidam—
to contradict it would bring disaster to this life and the next.
Realizing that, I cultivated sincere exertion and effort
and, not hazarding to lay bare my plan,
I went deep into the māra country with my ministers
to fulfill the divine prophecy.
I, my son Dongtsen, and Guru's son Khergö,
not only we three, but our servants and horses and mules
were sent to the bandit country, reduced to hostages.
There, King Yutsé of Minyak and his one thousand troops—
calling back and forth, working together—
were making their way toward Tramo Ling

and have now pitched an encampment below the far
    mountain pass.
Yutsé and his three strongest māra ministers
held me and my son, Dongtsen, against our will.
Back in their homeland, there are two demonesses,
    Wangjema and Bloody Tress,
with Dölpa's illusory army contained within a single box—
no other army is so extensive.
The geography of that māra homeland
I know like the back of my hand.
Well then, sirs, all you fine gentlemen of power,
there is no question that, without intending to, I have
    displeased you.
I am at fault for not laying this all out ahead of time.
I wholeheartedly take the blame for my mistakes.
I promise to get along with everyone from now on.
This little song is not just empty words.
All of you sitting here, keep this in your hearts.

None of the warriors listening to Trothung's song were certain whether or not there was such a prophecy, although Gesar *had* said that Trothung had been sent from a previous life in the divine realm in order to allow the enemy māras to infiltrate by bringing them into the inner circle as though they were friends.[38] Realizing now that Trothung's actions had in fact been deliberately intended to tame Yutsé and the Seven Wayward Siblings, Denma said, "As for Gesar, his wisdom shines brighter than the sun, his magical power is more forceful than lightning. He has bestowed great kindness in remaining and in clearly showing us his wisdom mind. We need no further explanation." Privately, Nyatsha and Zikphen were elated that Trothung had been exonerated, though they said not one word to their father.

Gesar and Chipön had assembled the warriors who had stayed behind, and when the seven Pathül arrived back at the Ling encampment, they relayed the details of the battle and the role that Trothung and Dongtsen had played. The warrior Denma was celebrated by all and received a medal of bravery for being wounded in combat. In order to be able to purify themselves of the defilements of the māras, Trothung and Dongtsen were sequestered in a tent pitched outside the military encampment. There they remained for a week. Gesar requested a prophecy from the eminent deities and, in accord with the teachings of the Three Jewels and Three Roots, aroused firm resolve to rest in samādhi.

CHAPTER FOUR

The lead sentries return and explain the situation.
Yutsé departs for the north along with his army.
Under cover of night, Lingites come to attack his
    encampment.
Of the Seven Siblings, Lugön and Migö are tamed.

By this time, the māra ministers, Lugön, Migö, and Shelé, had returned
to the Zima Valley and were gathered for a discussion with King Yutsé. The magical
teurang Shelé sang this song.

> Sing "Ala una la la."
> Sing the māra song "La la una."
> The melody is a familiar one.
> Within the castle Longchö Chenpo (Great Abundance)
> abides the king of māras, Garab Wangchuk.[1]
> In your presence, I pledge to slay hundreds and thousands.
> May the teachings of the dark side be firmly rooted.
> Come Namthel (Sky Seal), Barthel (Middle Sky Seal), Sathel
>   (Earth Seal)—teurang deities of the heavens, the middle
>   sky, and the earth.
> I call out with yearning, like a son to his father.
> I entreat your unwavering loving-kindness.
> Here between Zi and Rong
> is Drakmar, a land of cavernous red rocks far below the great
>   hills.

I am one of the Seven Wayward Siblings
known as Shelé Lakring,
long celebrated and renowned,
as I have done what I set out to do.
Well then, unrivaled māra king Yutsé
and fellow ministers, listen to this song,
which today is about espionage.
Trothung lagged behind, his whereabouts unknown,
as we four, three māra ministers and Dongtsen, departed
    hastily
for the borderland between Zima and Ling.
There, along the mountain pass Namtri Barma,
we encountered seven warriors,
and just like that, Trothung's son, Dongtsen,
identified those seven men and seven horses
as likely to be Ling's very own Pathül warriors
traveling the wilderness without their army.
Needless to say, Dongtsen thought a confrontation would
    come to no good
and put forth that our only chance would be to turn and run.
Furious[2] at his words,
I made up my mind then and there and attacked those seven.
Although I thought this would ensure our glory throughout
    the three realms,
they were neither vulnerable to the strike of our weapons
nor penetrated by our notched arrows.
Neither did our sharp spears wound them
nor the powers of our magic frighten them.
One after another the Pathül leapt on us,
pouncing like vultures on carrion.
Their swords flashed like red lightning
and the fighting was to the bitter end.
A golden-armored man mounted on a golden horse,
a man of great bravery, came forth
and, with all his might, threw a large boulder.
My horse and I were stunned and fell into the swirling dust
only to be revived by the breath of the teurang.
Although for the moment we were safe,

my magical horse was severely injured.
Whether he lives or dies remains to be seen.
Lugön's bravery was without measure—
when a man clad in white on a dazzling white horse
and a man all in blue on a pure blue horse
came like red lightning[3]
with lassos whipping as though they were darting black
    snakes,
Lugön sliced the lassos with his sharp sword blade.
They struck back and forth, battering each other with arrows.
In the end, no one escaped being wounded.
Then came a dark man with long, flowing black hair
mounted on a dark horse more awesome than a drong,
accompanied by a pale man riding a white horse
who looked as though he could be a son of the white teurang.
Both sides fought and fought but made no headway.
Caught in the lassos, warriors were wrestling,
but with neither side able to prevail, Gyatsha put a stop to the
    fighting.
Coming like the wind, we have returned to apprise you,
not knowing now whether we should stay or go.
That Takrong chieftain Trothung
has disturbed everything. No one knows whom to trust—
Trothung is everyone's case in point.
Should we leave and return to our homeland
to request troops from the country of Minyak,
or should we stay and secure this strategic valley?
However, this is a gathering place of evil,
not suitable for an encampment.
Instead, in the borderland far north of here
is a hidden valley, high in the turquoise mountains.
Perhaps that is where we should set up our military
    encampment.
We must be thorough in surveying the entire territory
and, if we go, be sure to cut off the enemy.
As for Gesar and his seven ministers,
we each have our individual protector deities
and the support of battalions of brave men against them.

In addition, not one of us is lacking in magic.
Let us not squander this opportunity.[4]
There are examples of this in the ancient proverbs.

We provide for our horse, thinking it a great stallion,
but if he does not run fast when it is of consequence,
then only from afar did he seem a great horse;
all the resources expended were of no value.
We lovingly cherish our sons and nephews,
but if they are of no help when we need them,
it is only from afar that they can be called family;
raising them so lovingly has come to naught.
The home that was so painstakingly built—
if it is not impervious to snow and rain,
you alone think yourself an expert craftsman;
there is nothing to what you strived to create.

All of us so-called great warrior ministers—
unless we rout the enemy bandits,
it is only our reputations that are mighty;
our great name and fame amount to nothing.
The proverbs and this situation are one and the same.
Today, these seven horsemen of Ling
say we have been the problem all along[5]
and claim that is why they are in our homeland.
Those men and horses are in perfect uniform
and, though they are without servants or supplies,
surely, they must have reinforcements somewhere.
What should we do? Please think about it, king and
    ministers.
If you have heard my song, please answer me.
Those gathered here, keep this in mind.

Thus he sang, and he and King Yutsé burned ceremonial incense, calling out to Garab Wangchuk and the three teurang. They waved fans of human skin and trumpeted loudly with human thighbones while the rest of the māra ministers called fervently to their personal protector deities. It was a time of convergence of such evil that the māra gods were unable to be held back, and they gathered like clouds and roused like wind in the heavens. The teurang Namthel Karpo came from among these māra gods, riding amid rainbow light on a white goat, and sang this song.

> So! So!
> Chö ya chö ya o o!
> O o! Wrathful and short is my song as my retinue naturally
>   gathers around me.
> O o! No kidding! This is the way the song is sung.
> O o! King Yutsé, how you and your ministers wander this
>   empty plain, without refuge.
> O o! Indeed, you are deceived and thwarted by the Ling
>   deities.
> I am the māra protector Namthel.
> If you remain here without seizing the throne,
> the deceitful gods of Ling will leave you in ruins.
> You should flee to the far north.
> Joru, the son of that wicked Gok mother,
> has already seized the hidden valley with his fierce army.
> Not only that, he has stolen your soul and destroyed your life
>   force.
> Our plans are spoiled.
> While my best advice is not to stay,
> the real reason to go north is that,
> at least in the lower borderlands of Zima,
> among its many uninhabited forested[6] valleys is Nakshö,[7]
> and within the red rocky cliffs of Drakmar that rise high
>   above them
> is Amnyé Bumthub, the ancestral spirit of the māras.
> There, you will find a black wolf disguised as a rust-brown
>   yak,[8]
> a medicine that revives the dead,
> and a powerful magic that could destroy the world.
> If you do not put your trust there,
> even with the strong backing of others, what you do will
>   come to nothing.
> But in that place you will find success.
> King Minyak Yutsé,
> you must bring down thirteen lightning bolts from space,

hurl the magical wind-sword wheels into the heavens,
and overturn the world with your might.
Each of the heirs of the evil māras
must come forth with their respective strengths,
and all the resources of magical illusion
I will bestow this very night,
broadcasting the magic of the wheel of burning substances
and the marvel of the high canyons and rivers
that protect our encampment.
Do not stay; steadily make your way north.
I will be your constant companion.
All you gathered here, keep this in mind.

Thus he spoke, and the teurang Namthel vanished from sight leaving behind the attainment substances, the magical wheel of blazing fire, and so forth, all of which he had placed right into the hands of the māra king Yutsé. After that, the king and ministers and the hordes of demon samaya-violators all agreed to proceed north. In the early morning of the next day, they were camped along Namtri Barma, whereupon King Minyak Yutsé transformed into a vulture and soared into the sky, searching in every direction for the enemy. Then, just as the māra gods had prophesied, beyond the remote mountain ranges, in the great sawtooth hills, Yutsé saw the Ling encampment clearly, and, at that same moment, the unambiguous knowledge that it was the māra king flying above arose in Gesar's enlightened mind. Gesar took up his bow Ragö Khyilchen (Great Coiled Wild Horn) and his arrow Shazen Drokhar (White-Winged Carnivore) and shot, filling the sky with flames and sending the wing feathers of the vulture scattering. But as the raptor fell to the ground, with the help of the māra gods, Yutsé escaped to his own encampment.

Later on, the Ling lamas performed a wrathful fire puja, unifying the generation and completion stages and summoning the untamed samaya-violator spirits, ritually incinerating them and burying their ashes as an offering to the patron gods. Early the next day, even before the morning star rose, even before the skim of ice dissolved into the river, Gesar, Gyatsha, Nang-ngu, Nyibum, Darphen, Denma, Sengtak, Gadé, Zikphen, Nyatsha, and Gyapön Bendé Marlu (Red Monk Leader of One Hundred),[9] each surrounded by ten of their best warriors, departed like the wind. Before even the faint light of dawn, they set off and, from all directions and without hesitation, descended on the māra encampment. Coming from the east, Nang-ngu, Nyibum, Denma, and Darphen, those four side by side, killed about forty Düd soldiers. But not to be outdone, three māras—Lugön, Tsenkya, and Shechen—leapt onto the Ling warriors. They gnashed their teeth and, with faces dark as those of rākṣasas, seethed with venomous anger and swirled their bloodshot eyes. Warriors arrayed themselves around Gyatsha and Denma, fifteen to the right and fifteen to the left. Denma was pushed to the brink and thought only of war. He confronted Lugön and said, "You unfortunate man of midnight blue, do not be in such a hurry to die. Listen to my song." He nocked his arrow and sang.

> OṂ MAṆI PADME HŪṂ
> Sing "Ala thala thala."
> "Thala" begins and
> "La la" gives the perfect pitch.
> Divine Ling and all the guardian deities,
> protect us unfailingly,
> deliver the arrow that strikes the samaya corruptor,
> and rein in the spread of the barbarian[10] teachings.
> If you do not recognize this place,
> it is the Zima mountain pass known as Namtri Barma,
> a land overrun with samaya-violators.
> If you do not recognize me,
> I am Denma the warrior of the Tshazhang clan.
> Just now, I have encountered you, a blue-complected man—
> no doubt the same one I met yesterday.
> You must be the samaya-violator Lugön.
> We find ourselves together, you and I.
> From among many, this must be our destiny,
> and I am delighted to meet you.
> All you evil samaya-violator bandits,
> for as long as memory serves,
> your demon hands have reached into Ling.
> When Chipön left home on a pilgrimage,
> you plundered the great wealth that he left behind.
> Later on, in broad daylight, you rustled a herd of our horses
> and, just the other day, you kidnapped Gyatsha's cherished
>   son.
> I am furious when I think of it.

If you eat too many grapes from the vine, you will be sick.
If you run your horse too fast, its hindquarters will cramp.

If you have a bad disposition, your family will come to despise you.
If you are too strict in your authority, you will be slain by your
  subjects.

That is what the proverbs say, and it is the truth.
Today, we vie with arrows to determine who is the genuine
  warrior.
When the target is hit,
it is just like lightning striking the cliffs.
What a pity for you.
Gesar and the hosts of dralha and werma
have cut the bloodline of the nāga Dölpa
and exalted the side of virtue.
Evil māra, keep this in mind.

Thus Denma sang, and he let loose his arrow. As Lugön was pondering the song and searching for a retort that would illustrate his own warriorship, the arrow filled the skies with the magical flames of the dralha and werma and struck Lugön right between his eyebrows, severing his skull. His skull[11] and helmet were tossed a short distance away, and his body dropped in a heap from his horse. Nang-ngu slaughtered and gutted the magical māra horse and its entrails fell into the dirt. All the warriors shouted "Ki! Ki! So! So!" Although his corpse lay on the ground, since Lugön embodied the nāga demons themselves, not only did he not stop breathing but he became a huge writhing and slithering black serpent. Gesar, equipped with the array of armor and weapons of the dralha and werma, mounted his steed Kyang Gö and instantly, as though it was mere mud underfoot, trampled the writhing serpent. Gesar performed bodhicitta aspiration prayers that the hosts of māras would not flourish.

The māras Tsenkya and Shechen, with heartfelt anguish and bursting with rage, not caring whether they lived or died, appeared brandishing swords. A long battle ensued, but although many thrusts of blades were exchanged, at first, no one was harmed. White and red horsemen, emanations of the enlightened minds of Gesar and Nyentak, came to support the Pathül warriors. They struck them many times with swords and spears, and with their bodies wounded and their bones broken, the māras began to think that they should flee. Coming from the north, Gyatsha, Sengtak, Zikphen, and Nyatsha—thunderous as roaring dragons shouting the war cry "Ki!"—leapt without hesitation into the māra military encampment, felling thirty soldiers. Their plumed helmets clattered as they rolled to the ground.

King Minyak Yutsé—so blue with his plaited turquoise hair and armed with blue weapons spewing poisonous vapor—rode in on his black horse Drong Durlung (Wild Yak Runs with the Wind), along with Tongdü and Migö, and Bethül Chidak Nakpo (Powerful Tamer of the Evil Death Lord).[12] They reared their horses in front of Gyatsha. Panting,[13] Yutsé sang this song.

> Sing "Alu una thalu.
> "Thalu una" begins and
> "Una la lu" gives the perfect pitch.
> From the deep, dark, colorless gloom,[14]
> one hundred thousand murderous flesh-eating māra kings,
> today, come to assist this demon king.
> Sharpen my drawn blades,
> cut the life force of the enemy and steal their breath away.
> White, black, and multicolored teurang, the three, please
>   look upon me.
> May our doctrine never wane.
> If you do not recognize this place,[15]
> it is the lower Zima Valley.
> If you do not recognize me,
> I am the powerful king of Minyak, here in the east,
> fearless among hundreds and hundreds of men,
> an exemplar of brave warriorship.
> That must be clear right now.
> You pretty boy dressed up in armor—
> Gyatsha, you have no courage.
> That is what is said, and it is the truth.
> You so-called Pathül warriors are just a bunch of devious
>   men.
> Up to this point,
> you have been respected by your subjects
> and kind parents have looked after you,
> but your spoiled, arrogant attitude rings false.
> A poor little leader in his own tiny town
> is brave only in his mind.
> He would not know a true warrior if he saw one.
> Now is your chance to demonstrate.
> I do not intend to draw out my bow,

disturb the rows of my notched arrows,
unsheathe my long gleaming spear,
or hold the handle of my sword Guzi.
Today, we will fight shoulder to shoulder to establish the true
    hero.
I will tackle you and throw you to the ground,
and the rocks of Ling will drink your blood.
The azure firmament will witness this spectacle,
and your last words will sink into the earth.
Unless I can single out which men to subjugate,
my kingly birth is of no consequence.

Thus he sang, and coming closer, just like a gust of wind Yutsé jumped from his horse onto Gyatsha, and Gyatsha, with no time to answer with a song, struck Yutsé three times with his sword Yazi. But as it was not Gyatsha's fate to be the one to overcome Yutsé, he was only capable of nicking his armor. Yutsé grabbed Gyatsha by his chest, but only briefly, as Gesar and the dralha Nyentak each grabbed an arm, pulling Yutsé off of Gyatsha and throwing him to the ground. Gyatsha jumped from his horse and kicked the demon king such that eighteen braided locks of his various-hued turquoise hair dropped out from beneath his white helmet, and Gyatsha ripped them out, scattering shades of blue everywhere. But the time had not yet come to tame the māra king, and Yutsé transformed into red light and escaped, although his horse was slain by Gyatsha's sword.

Migö had come from the right and was standing face to face with the warrior Sengtak, brandishing his magical spear over his head. Although he had struck Sengtak three times, Sengtak was protected by the vajra armor and, save for a bit of his mail scattering, was unharmed. Then, with a single swing of his sword, Sengtak shattered Migö's magical spear and said, "You worthless man born of evil, listen to this song!" When his song was over, he swung his sword and the dralha and werma directed the blade so that it severed Migö's torso from his left shoulder through to his right arm. He fell to the ground, but the lower part of his body was dragged by his horse as it ran through the encampment, kicking up dust and escaping. Not caring whether they lived or died, Bethül Chidak and Sokchö Tongthub (Cuts the Life Force of a Thousand), with many reinforcements, retaliated with arrows, swords, and spears. A lengthy battle ensued. Bethül Chidak threw his spear, killing the Ling warrior Norbu Payak (Precious Good Warrior), and immediately Nyatsha threw his sword at Bethül Chidak and two other māras—Tongthub Yenkün (Capable of One Thousand Thief) and Tselé Sumdu (Peak of the Three Times)—killing all three at once. All together, nearly fifty key soldiers were slain, and the māra military encampment was scattered to the four directions. The Ling warriors, feeling that enough was enough, withdrew from further fighting, and protected by Gesar's vajra tent, the Ling army started for home. But King Yutsé, along with four[16] of the samaya-breaker brothers and five elite warriors, was already in pursuit. The Pathül turned back to face King Yutsé as he raised his turquoise lasso overhead and, with his menacing form enveloped by a dense, rising fog, sang this song.

> Na o o! Sing "Una alu thalu."
> Na o o! "Thalu una" begins.
> Na o o! "La lu" gives the perfect pitch.
> O o! Coemergent divine māras, look upon me.
> Local deities dwelling here, look upon me.
> All guardian deities of the evil māras,
> be swift as the wind, do not tarry,
> assure that my lasso is deft.
> If you do not recognize this place,
> it is the hideaway of cowardly foxes,
> the land of snarling, wrathful warriors.
> If you do not recognize me,
> I am that intrepid warrior
> here to clash with my personal enemy, Ling.
> If you run, you will betray your manhood
> and become like a girl trapped toiling at her loom.
> Then again, facing the army,
> it looks as though this cherished son's good fortune is
>   exhausted,
> this savage's bamboo arrows, shattered.
> Undaunted, Rāhu roams.[17]
> The sorrel *kyang* brings up the rear.[18]
> Such a brazen young man so full of himself,
> circling on a young horse that chomps at the bit—
> it seems you must be Joru, that wicked mother's child.
> I am delighted to encounter you now;
> as you were summoned by the māra deities, I did not have to
>   wait.
> A smug young man
> brings on his own troubles;

ill-conceived ideas meet with chance and bring ruin.
Here, in the six provinces, a person like you is a burden upon
   their family.
If it weren't for you, they would both have a measure of
   happiness.
. Right now, I cannot imagine that you will stay alive.
These proverbs tell the way it really is:

The sun and moon fancy their light as radiantly clear,
yet the day they encounter Rāhula,
the very phrase "shimmering light" rings hollow.
The poisonous serpent thinks itself formidable,
yet the day it encounters the garuḍa of Mount Meru,
its fearsome body is devoid of venom.
The makara pictures itself voracious as it devours the bounty of the
   waters,
yet the day it encounters the little conch face to face,[19]
its great body loses its appetite.

Joru, you may be the destructor of beings,
   yet when you come up against King Yutsé,
   the fame and glory of your name will be empty.
Your celebrated horse Kyang Gö
   today races like a blazing fire,
   but we will see which horse comes in first.
The celebrated Gesar,
   right now, you are likened to a valiant king,
   but we will see whose helmet will be awarded the pennant.
Those illustrious Pathül warriors
   challenge my ruthless ministers,
   but we will see who is indomitable.
A single victory does not make a victor;
   we will see who prevails after many battles.
This turquoise lasso I hold in my hand
   is the heritage of the Minyak throne
   and the karmic wealth of the subterranean nāgas.
None of your sky-blue weapons can sever it.

If I throw it, it will even capture the winds of the azure
    firmament.
You will never get out of here alive.
If I can't bind you like a ball of yarn,
these words are meaningless chatter.
Just wait, mark my words.

Thus he sang, and he flung the turquoise lasso at Gesar. But since Gesar was resting in the samādhi of threefold emptiness—outwardly the heavens are emptiness, inwardly the mind itself is emptiness, and in between the continuity of channels is emptiness—even though Yutsé threw the lasso three more times, it was like trying to capture a rainbow. He dropped the lasso and was about to unsheathe his sharp sword when some of the Pathül warriors took out their spears and others brandished knives or nocked arrows and started to draw their bows. Just then, thirty emanations of the dralha Nyentak Marpo, each possessing warrior's accoutrements, and each thirty armspans in height,[20] majestic and awesome, came one after another carrying boulders the size of drongs, donkeys,[21] or yaks. They threw them with all their might, making a great clamor. Without any discussion, the māra king and ministers, with faltering courage, turned and fled and by virtue of their own individual magical powers, escaped some distance away. The five elite warriors perished, as, despite their great strength, they were ordinary men without magical powers. The Pathül warriors were regrouping to attack the māra encampment but Gesar felt that the battle had been won and that there was no reason to continue fighting. The warriors escorted Gesar to the Ling encampment to celebrate, shouting "Ki! So! Lha Gyal!"

CHAPTER FIVE

After Bloody Tress returned to the māra king Yutsé and
    ministers,
they delayed going north and prepared an illusory
    encampment.
Then, they started off for Ling together,
but Bloody Tress was liberated by Gesar and his troops.

THE MĀRA KING AND MINISTERS, distressed by their failure, had gathered in their encampment in an effort to hammer out what had gone wrong. From atop a seat of white-chested bearskin, Tongdü Lenmé sang this song of resolve.

Sing "Ona alu thalu."
"Thalu ona" begins and
"La lu" gives the perfect pitch.
Namthel Karpo, riding a pure white goat,
today look upon the king's strategy.
Barthel Trawo, riding a variegated goat,
be my refuge and protector.
Sathel Nakpo, riding a gray goat,
care for the plight of the citizens.
This land is the borderland of the Zima Valley.
Nakpo indicates that I am the son of the malicious māras
and, until today,
the name Tongdü referred to me as the killer of a thousand men,

and Lenmé to the fact that I was unassailable.
I was renowned throughout the land.
But today the situation has changed.
In the face of these foul Ling bandits,
my courage vanished like a rainbow in the sky.
I hurled my weapons in vain
against their boulders of meteoric iron
and threw my lasso to no avail
as though I had tried to harness the intangible wind.
Not just one or two men
but every last Pathül warrior was equipped with the threefold
    panoply.
Not just one or two horses
but all their horses had wings of wind.
Yesterday's unrivaled one,
known to all for his unmitigated strength,
was said to be just a herdsman,
but now he is not only one but thirty wild warriors
with bodies as massive as that of the one known as Lutsen.
I thought they were not real, a mere illusion,
but then those massive boulders struck
with such a forceful roaring din,
crushing our elite warriors and their horses.
Who can even the score?
I am not exaggerating the Pathül warriors' strength;
this is the way it is.
Right now, king, ministers,
and all convened, listen to my song.
In keeping with the previous divine prophecies of the
    protectors,
last night, plentiful food and an abundance of enjoyments
were spontaneously present, without effort—
great marvelous siddhi.
This is the faultless divine prophecy.
At the border of Lower Zima
is Nakshö with its many uninhabited valleys.
Although I cannot be certain,
I suspect we could arrive there within the week

if, starting out at daybreak tomorrow,
our troops go directly without delay.
King Yutsé and your minister Shelé,
you have both attained the power of magical illusion.
Therefore, collect all the implements you need
and manifest a mighty army hundreds of thousands strong
to accompany whatever actual forces we have.
Protect our encampment with magical burning substances.
March each and every day from sunrise to sunset.
Visit Amnyé Bumthub, the ancestral spirit of the māras.
Rely on him for a cure for death,
and ask him for the magical powers to destroy Jambudvīpa;
with that support, return home.
That is how you will decimate miserable Ling
and become its sovereign.
You do not need to be in a frenzy;
even if it were to take a year, we should be resolute.
Nothing good has come of what we have done so far.
The two brothers Lugön and Migö—
we never thought such an enemy could harm them,
but now we see that that was merely a dream.
Let us agree and undertake these matters.
All of you gathered here, keep this in mind.

Thus he sang, and the māra troops, roused and resolved, began readying the provisions provided by the māra deities. The previous night, the demoness Bloody Tress had had a troubling dream in which she was unable to subdue the Pathül warriors because the virtuous deities had intoxicated her such that she could not move. Therefore, she had called on Wangjema, not realizing she was an imposter, to request counsel about the advisability of going to check on the well-being of her own brothers and King Yutsé. The dralha Wangjema, seeing the situation clearly, had told her to go immediately, and Bloody Tress—frightening in appearance and inexhaustible with four legs of wind-wheels—rode away on her breath-bag like a wild storm cloud. At dusk a half day later, to the delight of Yutsé and his ministers, she had arrived at the māra military encampment.

Together, they had gathered inside to feast and make plans. Bloody Tress was so saddened to hear that Lugön and Migö had both been killed that she had fainted briefly but came to after they sprinkled her with water. The māra leaders

---

had recounted the divine prophecy and spelled out their decision-making. Bloody Tress, now irate and with overwhelming pride in her own ruthlessness, said, "Sit here, king and brothers. Listen to the prophecy-song of this she-demon, sung in the demoness's melody. O lu!"

> Na o o! Sing "Ona alu la lu."
> Na o o! The song begins with "Ona," and,
> na o o, "Ona" gives the perfect pitch of this māra song.
> To you in the abyss of the dark-red poisonous ocean,
> in the midst of the gloomy fog of disease,
> destroyer Trakmikma,
> I offer to and praise you, the coemergent deity.
> I, your daughter Bloody Tress, ask you to lead my song.
> Previously I was unfamiliar with this land
> that today is the gathering place of the king and ministers.
> I am the youngest, Bloody Tress,
> a woman of thirty-six[1] years of age
> who commands the life force of all sentient beings.
> Sit here, king and ministers.
> The magical wheel of burning substances—
> this is the time that it is needed.
> The watery ravine—
> now is the time to reveal its magic.
> Why should the encampment need guards
> when you, King Minyak Yutsé,
> are said to have accomplished Garab Wangchuk
> and can communicate with him directly?
> The play of various magical displays,
> even when it is not needed, is always there, swirling like dust.
> From space come magical wheels of lightning,
> from the azure firmament come magical wheels of wind-
>   swords,
> and from earth, the magical power to turn the world upside
>   down.

While you have power and freedom, use it.
Otherwise, it will be too late, and you will be dependent on others.

Why are you slipping so quietly back to your homeland?
The lot of you, all descendants of the malicious eastern māras:
Nakpo Tongdü Lenmé,
you have mastered the skill of catapult fire;
you must align with the nyen who is the māra king.
Do not lose your manhood, do something!
Marpo Tsenkya Bumthub,
you are the master of magical weapon-wheels;
you must align with the red tsen.
Do not lose your manhood; do something!
Shechen Drengyi Yamé,
it is said that your strength can fell an elephant;
you must align with the samaya-violator mu māras.
Do not lose your manhood; do something!
Karpo Shelé Lakring,
you are skilled with the magic of illusion;
you must align with the teurang emanation.
Do not lose your manhood, do something!
I, the youngest, the daughter Bloody Tress,
can bend down the heights of lofty mountain peaks,
drink the largest ocean in one gulp,
rival the radiance of the magnificent sun and moon,
and challenge the power of the majestic Gesar.
In the daytime, I am diligent in my pursuit of his destruction;
at night, I would not hesitate to steal his life force.
Until all my powers are expended,
I will not return to Nakshö.
Here are some examples:

The lion is haughty in the white snow mountains,
extending its claws as its full power blossoms;
but, if one day the glacier melts away,
what will become of the karmic destiny of the lioness?
The tiger is splendid in the forested mountains,
extending its claws as its fine fur grows in;
but, if one day the forests burn,
what will become of the karmic destiny of the tigress?

The golden fish are surrounded by pristine water,
their vigorous lives spent swimming its reaches;
but, if one day the waters are parched by the sun,
what will become of the karmic destiny of the golden fish?

The king and ministers threaten the enemy,
commanding the army they conscripted;
but, if one day the troops cannot stand firm,
what will become of the karmic destiny of their leaders?
A short time ago, two brothers lost their lives.
If you do not avenge their deaths,
wearing the threefold panoply is meaningless.
Is it true that you are planning to leave tomorrow?

Do not run like foxes with their tails between their legs.
I would rather hear that you died like striped tigers.

This is what is said, but it is also the truth.
All of you seated here, keep this in mind.

Thus she sang. The māras, who had previously planned to abide by the prophecy of their gods, instead delayed their departure in the face of the dreadful power of Bloody Tress, who in turn had naively been drawn in by the imposter Wangjema. And now, first they produced a magical wheel of burning substances and then a swirling lake several miles across to surround their encampment. Following that, a huge crevice formed and the fire became an inferno within which a mass of bird feathers, along with iron filings and copper powder, became an illusory army of troops with plumed helmets that immediately transformed into an army so perfect that it was indistinguishable from a physical army of seventy thousand troops. By daybreak, each warrior had roused their unique magical power and, in less than a fortnight, from upper space came a magical wheel of tongues of lightning; from middle space, a magical wheel of wind-swords; and on level ground, a pile of destructive catapults. Having all this in place, each made offerings to their personal māra patron god.

That same day, King Gesar, accompanied by the Pathül and Phunu, conferred with Uncle Chipön and all came to a harmonious consensus. Trothung and Dongtsen, who had been waiting, were finally invited into the staging tent and—following a cleansing ritual given by the deities and lamas, a fire ritual given by Gadé, and so forth—they were seated at the end of the back row on a single, thin cushion. The one who was the judge of the laws of Ling, Werma Lhadar,[2] the magical leader, the divine minister, sang this song of the essence of the teachings.

OṂ MAṆI PADME HŪṂ
Sing "Ala thala thala."
"Thala" begins and
"La la" gives the perfect pitch.
From the crown cakra of great bliss,
gracious root guru, look upon me.
May I be in your presence.
Dharmakāya Amitābha, know me.
Saṃbhogakāya Avalokiteśvara, know me.
Nirmāṇakāya Padmasambhava, know me.
This land is the crossroads of Zi, Ling, and Rong.
Moreover, you, the king and ministers, are in the presence of
   a great man.
This is the court of Dharma as well as of worldly laws.
If you do not recognize me,
I have been the judge from the inception of the six tribes of
   Ling,
the adjudicator of truth and falsehood, right and wrong,
the trustworthy judge of imperial rule,
the religious and secular rule that is the ornament of the
   world.
Of the eighteen royal families of Ling,
I am the judge, descended from the eighteen ministers of
   preceding generations.

The azure sky may have the vast view,
but the sun and moon have greater sway
over the sovereignty of the four great continents.
Mount Meru may have greater height,
but the seven golden mountains[3] have greater influence
over the sovereignty of the four great continents.

The king and ministers of Ling may have high rank,
but the judge has greater autonomy.
As for the silken cord of the monastic law of Dharma,

the judge is the one to tie its silken knot,
and, as for the golden yoke of the imperial rule,
the judge is the one to give it weight.
The well-being of the country is like bundled white silk,
and the judge is its adornment.
This is not conceit but simply the way it is.
Now, Mazhi Chieftain Trothung
and brave warrior Dongtsen Apel,
listen, my words could not be clearer.
As for the supreme ornament of all humans,
Gesar, the unrivaled king of the three worlds,
is the master of magic and understanding.
It is only out of arrogance that Akhu Trothung challenges
    him,
like a scrawny dog confronting a lion.
Just as the four-cubit human body portends its own decay,
the Takrong chieftain's claim to be king
portends the loss of his rank.
You scorn the truth of cause and effect,
yet your own victory brings great anguish to others.
As for the golden yoke of the imperial rule
and the statutes of its thirteen laws,
you have been careless and made mistakes in carrying them
    out.
To falsely claim innocence is the ninth,
and punishment is mandatory.
This is clear in the statutes of the law.
Have you learned anything, Trothung?
Confess these past deeds,
and from now on, accept whatever Gesar says,
promising to carry it out unfailingly.
He who is the gracious, kind, wish-fulfilling jewel—
even though he may display anger, he does not cling to it.
He has great love for all, including you, Uncle Trothung,
great compassion toward all parent sentient beings,
and in particular, great affection for all the children of
    Takrong.
This is clearly the message of Gesar's arrival.

Given the mountain wolf's vicious legacy,
he deserves the stone from a long, colorful slingshot.
Yet, it is not in the shepherd's nature to loose his stone
out of his kindly regard for the gods-demons and all of worldly
*   existence.*

Given the legacy of Trothung and Dongtsen,
they deserve to be expelled as evildoers.
Yet, it is not in Gesar's nature to do that
out of his kindly regard for the continuum of generations.
He is the sovereign of worldly and spiritual beings,
the source of refuge and lord of the maṇḍala.
To this sacred being,
bring one hundred pieces of silk of the five colors,
the thirteen kinds of tiger skins with excellent fur,
and various bricks of gold and silver to number one hundred.
Sovereign chieftain Trothung, you must come to confess with
    these offerings.
Then, to Gyatsha, the divine heir of the Bumpa clan,
and your two brothers Chipön and Senglön,
come with the thirteen kinds of leopard skins with excellent
    fur,
giving each one an equal portion
as the mark of warriors able to subdue the enemy.
You, Trothung, will return to your natural place
seated on the tiger skin of your sandalwood throne,
but the Takrong tribe will be led by your descendants.
Things will not go according to your view.
Make a *lhasang* offering at the peak of the sacred mountain,
a smoke offering to the nāgas at the summit of the nāga
    mountain,
and a special smoke offering to Magyal Pomra in the east.
As for the many charges that have come down according to
    the law,
once again, they are made light for you out of regard for your
    descendants.
In the future, take care to act prudently.
As for you, Dongtsen Apel—

When red fires blaze in the mountains,
why would one need more dry wood?
When great rivers are already swollen with water,
what need could there be for a heavy rain?
When there is already discord between countries,
why stir up further turmoil?

When Trothung is already so fractious,
why, Dongtsen, do you foster his treachery?
You are like a stupid ox ornamented with gold,
a conceited young man.
Oh, the unscrupulousness of humans!

Sunshine envelops the four continents,
and a torch brightens a home—both illuminate,
but though you fancy them the same, they are not.
The way they dispel the darkness differs.
The plaintive voice of the blue cuckoo
and the tinkling sound of the sparrow—both resonate,
but though you think their calls alike, they are not.
The timbre of their melodies differs.
The six-smiled tigress
and the little reddish-gray badger—both have fur,
but though you think their colors alike, they are not.
The pattern of their fiery red stripes is distinct.

A king such as Gesar with dominion over the world
and a chieftain such as Trothung who rules one corner of a
	country—
though you think their power commensurate, such is not so;
their power, wealth, and authority are poles apart.
Trothung, whether you will be exiled to a foreign land
or subjected to the rule of our law
falls to the kindness of your relatives.
You cannot be permitted to retain your assets and status.
From among the ancient and modern Bola tribes of the
	Takrong district,[4]
choose three hundred households

and, in particular, some of your personal wealth
to offer to the clan of King Chipön.
Look how your spitefulness has discredited you.
Whether those with ministerial rank have a lifetime of ill luck
    or good fortune,
regardless, they must be loyal to their citizens.
There is no difference between a father and an uncle;
any boy, grown into a fine young man, is like your own son,
and, whatever the status of the kingdom, it is in your hands.
Some things are over and done, others unfinished, and still
    others not yet begun.
We cannot be sure what will happen.
There is no one better than I to spell out the verdict.
The law transcends the heavens above;
it is more decisive than a plumb line
and more substantial than the solid earth.
The resolution of this case brings the tale of the goatskin-clad
    pauper and the golden-armored men to mind,
and, just as in that story, this matter should have been dealt
    with internally,
but now there is no way to rescind my just verdict.[5]
Those ministers who strayed to the māra lands,
whether or not this decision is taken to heart,
will be scrutinized with the precision of a geographer's survey.
If you have understood this song, its words are sweet to your
    ears.
If not, there is no way to explain it.
Finest Takrong father and sons, keep this in mind.

Everyone admonished Trothung to accept the judge's decree and, realizing he had no choice, Trothung signed a binding agreement. Then, in the presence of the deities and the guru, he made offerings of one hundred thousand feast accumulations and one thousand butter lamps to the divine Three Roots, black tea to the protectors, and so forth, and he gave five gold coins to each monk. As regarded Trothung, the minds of the deities and lamas were now at ease. Akhu Gomchen Tingmé and King Gesar had ordered that a powerful black magic torma be thrown against the evil King Yutsé and his ministers and that the Ling king and ministers would be the ones to properly carry this out. Nyatsha and Zikphen agreed that the verdict was fair and added that it would be best if Dongtsen became part of Chipön's tribe. Through all of this, the situation became one of an auspicious connection of merit and good fortune.

By these ancestral words of truth, for friends and enemies alike, all harmful activity was transformed and this *tendrel*[6] gave rise to supremely good fortune. Given all this, Gomchen Tingmé had already decided on throwing a black magic torma, but Trothung was inclined to bring down an amplifying maelstrom. His sons, ministers, and troops accompanied him to a solitary cove in the great hills of the Takrong Valley to go into retreat to accomplish this Bön monstrous torma. Now it happened that five days previously, Bloody Tress, arrogant and spiteful, and grief-stricken at the slaying of her brothers Lugön and Migö, had decided to set off alone to the Ling encampment. Since no one could dissuade her, King Yutsé and Shelé Lakring, their armies at hand, had promised support. As the three of them left on horseback, headed for Ling, the dralha Nyentak transformed into a golden honeybee and landed above Gesar's right ear, saying, "Listen closely. The evil damsi demoness Bloody Tress, the demon king Yutsé, and his minister Shelé Lakring, these three nonhuman damsi, are about to arrive here with their troops. If we cannot stop them from invading our encampment, just as a fire consumes a forest, this blunder may destroy Ling. Gesar, your emanations of one hundred tiger-skin-clad warriors, your bodyguards, the Three Ultimate Warriors—Falcon, Eagle, and Wolf—and the dralha army will come swiftly with force. The gods-demons will vie for power; sky and earth will clash like cymbals. Do not let your resolve weaken. I will bind the demoness, and you will tame her. Those divine gurus who will stay behind should attend to the vivid appearance of the wrathful guru and mantra recitation. Please, at once, tell everyone." Thus he requested, and the lha, lu, and nyen set out like a hailstorm to confront Yutsé, Bloody Tress, and Shelé.

The mind essence of the dralha king Gesar arose, and through the energy of windhorse, in the presence of Akhu Gomchen Tingmé and the other high lamas of Ling, he imparted the unsullied prophecy of the inseparable three awarenesses— deity, mantra, and the vivid presence of wrathful Padmasambhava.[7] Then, Gesar arrived, embodied and magnificently garbed with the armor and weapons of the dralha. The moment of seeing him was enough to quell the four enemies. The werma gathered naturally around him, and the dralha accompanied him like a shadow. Like Indra taking to battle, he rode his elegant mount Kyang Gö. Their bravery and magnificence overwhelming, Gesar and the warriors, Denma and Gadé, departed as if blown by the seven great winds of the eons,[8] their dralha flags tossing, each with a retinue of four attendants. But there, at a narrow gap in the lower Zi Valley, they encountered King Yutsé, Queen Bloody Tress, and Shelé Lakring and wedged them in like notched arrows. Immediately, from those three māras arose manifold emanations, each furious and with an inseparable but distinct retinue of ten warriors. Without interruption, one hundred warriors arose as an emanation of Gesar's body, speech, and mind, and from the lha, lu, and nyen, one hundred emanations sprung forth like a flood. Among those hundreds of emanations was Gesar, like Indra with flowing white robes, riding a white horse. He halted the steed by its reins and, grasping his knife handle, offered this song called "Crouching Pose of Quelling the Enemy."

> OM MAṆI PADME HŪM
> Sing "Lu ala," the song of the sky, the father tantra.
> Sing "Thala," the song of the earth, the mother tantra.
> Sing "La la," the song of coemergence.
> May the Three Jewels and Three Roots dwell upon the crown
>   of my head.
> Please support me in slaying the hosts of māras.
> Lha, lu, and nyen, this assembly of dralha—
> be the guardians of virtue.
> I entreat your unwavering buddha activity.
> Manifest the *rūpakāya* of your compassionate wrath
> and give thought to this activity of destroying
> the enemies of the teachings, personal enemies, and the
>   samaya-violators.
> Take their lives and drink their blood,
> render them nameless, crushed to dust.
> May their minds dissolve into dharmakāya.
> May they be the heirs of the *sugatas*.
> Are you listening, Yutsé, Bloody Tress, Shelé?
> Do you understand my song?
> These lands are a narrow defile;
> its topography subjugates māras.
> If you do not recognize me,
> I am the son of Brahmā,
> the grandson of Tsukna Rinchen, and as well,
> the spirit son of Nyen Gedzo.[9]
> I am the crown ornament of virtuous teachings,
> the one to bring happiness to sentient beings,
> the one to quell the evil samaya-violator māras

and sever their heads.
I was the one commended by the high gods,
and like a full-grown tree,
this spirit son has matured.
Here at the passage of such a narrow defile,
we did not have to wait to confront the enemy.
Without question,
we are delighted to have encountered you—
our mutual karma has ripened.
Although it is clear that our warriors are equally fierce,
one will be distinguished as the victor
and one horse will run fastest.
The redheaded cannibal rākṣasī maiden
is undoubtedly Bloody Tress,
a blazing mountain of hatred,
who can only be answered by a great river of compassion.
Her snarling teeth and bared breasts, the likes of her—
the splendor of monstrous wrath
will quell this vile demoness.
Māra King Yutsé,
you are full of pride but powerless,
cowardly as a fox cub.
Your bragging is as loud as a dragon's roar,
but what you have in hand is as evanescent as a rainbow.
How pitiful!
Against our forces
you require power to match the lha, lu, and nyen
and might to equal the lord of death.
You must be as invisible as the wind,
as swift as red lightning,
and in command of an army as inexhaustible as a rushing
    river.
You are a lowly beggar bandit;
in no way are you one of the noble ones.
You are an evil man, a bastard, and a thief;
in no way are you one of the brave warriors.
Until now, you have been a robber in the northern valley
and have never encountered a true warrior.

All you have done is kill the weak and plunder wealth.
Now is the ripening karma of your evil deeds;
you have only yourself to blame.
The way through the lofty heavens is barred
by the swirling razor-winds;
you cannot slip away through the middle sky realm,
as it is encircled by the sevenfold protection fence of
    samādhi,[10]
nor escape through the earthly domain,
as all the gods-demons of worldly existence are alert to your
    footsteps.
Escape is out of the question, even if you were beings without
    physical existence.
If you are brave, now is the time to show it;
if you have magic, now is the time to reveal it.
If it exists at all, you have it now;
if it doesn't, you have nothing.
Thinking you will be free today is just rubbish,
rubbish suitable for evil māras.
The Ling army warriors are here,
unwavering, even if the sky and earth were to collapse,
unfaltering, even if we face the lord of death.
We have the iron life force,
the power of deathlessness.
Ours is the sword that shatters the three-thousand-fold world
and cuts the corpse of ego-clinging.
Its blade severs the root of the family line.
The provenance of this sword is marvelous.
In time, this will all become evident,
but if it is clear to you right now, then surrender.
Good or bad, this is the song I offer in reply.
If you have understood, it is the tale of the warrior.
If not, there is no way to explain it.
All of you here, this is the way it is.

Thus he sang, and Bloody Tress exploded with anger, like a snake whipped with thorns. She was immense, and blood rained from her mouth, a thick mist of disease spewed from her nose, and the darkness of evil permeated the air around her. Through the power of the great magic of the māras, King Yutsé became equally fearsome. The mountainous earth quaked, and the sun became a reddish glow. As its light rays disappeared and the far side of the mountain plunged into darkness, the demoness revealed power great enough to destroy mountains, singing this song of awesome fury.

> Sing "Alu ona thala."
> "Ona" gives the melody.
> O once, o twice, o many times,
> o many times. As for the one dwelling on high,
> Garab Wangchuk, the great magic one,
> surrounded by hundreds of thousands of māra families,
> encircled by a million harmful obstructing spirits,
> you who can cut down the lives of sentient beings,
> today you must assist me, the youngest one.
> Please deliver courage into my hands.
> Offering the flesh and blood of the enemy,
> I promise to kill hundreds, thousands, tens of thousands.
> May our doctrine flourish.
> With no mistake, this is our homeland.
> If you do not recognize me,
> I am the nonhuman nāga rākṣasī daughter
> of the greatly powerful Wangjema
> who is united with the gods-demons of phenomenal
>   existence.
> She gave birth to each of the noble gods-demons.
> I burst from within my red egg, and now
> my might is famed throughout.
> I am the youngest, Bloody Tress,
> the foremost of the female māras,
> the one who controls the life force of sentient beings.
> Wretched ones of Ling, I am the damsi.
> The sacred Dharma is false; there is no logic.
> The Saṅgha is false; there is no protection.
> The Buddha is false; there is no view.
> Sentient beings are false; there is no cause and effect.
> Virtue and nonvirtue are false; there is neither renunciation
>   nor indulgence.

There is nothing to your clever words.
My blood boils at all this Buddhist talk.
In particular, you—wretched Ling son of Gokmo,
destitute, without food or wealth,
the wicked boy who is the ruin of many countries,
the troublemaker of miserable Ling,
the yoke upon the necks of our fathers and uncles—
for us, the evil māras, you are our nemesis.
Today, I am delighted to meet you.
With your fierce cavalry thrumming, *sha ra ra*,
your daunting courage scintillating, *tshub sé tshub*.
Your tongue's incessant clacking, *thak sé thak*[11]—
you profess to have a full-force army in front and behind,
the mustered forces of wretched Ling.
We, the māra king and queen, are ruthless
and, when you strut your military might,
we will annihilate you right then and there.
Look at both what I have and have not said—
wait just a moment and all will be clear.
Do not think you can outdo me with your armor and
    weapons.
If there is destruction, it will be Mount Meru that falls.
If there is cataclysm, it will be heaven and earth that implode.
If there is collision, it will be the sun and moon crashing like
    cymbals.
If there is chaos, it will be the depths of the oceans that churn.
If there is war, it will be fought against the sons of miserable
    Ling.
If there is hatred, it will be the teachings of the Buddha that
    are targeted.
If there is devastation, it will be the principles of Ling that are
    annihilated.
You may be our demonic enemy,
but we are the samaya-perverting destroyers of the teachings.
Both sides seem to be equally resolute.
I speak sincerely from my heart.
Divine protectors of the evil māras,
do not waver in your support,

and, inseparably as a body and its shadow, protect me.
Be the vicious demons that destroy the military strength
  arrayed here
and destroy all comfortable earthly dwelling places.
Keep this in your minds.

Thus she sang, but just as Bloody Tress and Yutsé set about destroying the mountains, Gesar visualized the mountains as Mount Meru with its unassailable iron core, and so they did not budge, let alone crumble. Instantly, beneath the seal of the principle wind energy[12] of his practice of nine-vase-breath meditation, Gesar brought Yutsé, Bloody Tress, and Shelé to his feet where, instantaneously, the three of them were thrown forcibly and lifted a league into the sky. They fell back to the ground, stunned and for a moment barely breathing but protected by the māra deities and cradled by Khyabpa Lakring, the nemesis of the Bön deity, Amnyé's wife Nyüljema (Bird Woman), nine-eyed Trakmikma, and the teurang U Werma, and others, until they revived. Garab Wangchuk and the dralha Nyentak confronted each other, and the lha, lu, and nyen fought with the black, white, and multicolored teurang. Each of the local deities and the zodor fought. The mountains shook with a deafening sound. Meteors and molten lava assailed the earth.

The three Pathül warriors were not certain what to do, but knew they had to act. Denma focused his attention on the māra deities, sending an arrow into the fog that was rising in front of him, Sengtak brandished his sword, and Gadé manifested as Padmasambhava, his body luminous, pointing a blazing threatening mudra in all directions. The māra deities were overcome and withdrew their support and vanished. Although the dralha king, Gesar, had intended to simultaneously liberate the three māra rulers, they had retreated nearby under the protection of the māra deities. But the dralha Nyentak, with the lha, lu, and nyen, lassoed Bloody Tress and carried her off like falcons snatching a little bird and with such magical energy that neither King Yutsé nor the minister Shelé had a clue where she had gone. The Pathül warriors, along with the dralha and werma, with their many weapons of war, rained down upon Yutsé and Shelé who nearly stumbled to the ground under the barrage of stones and knives. They tried to retaliate, shooting arrows until their quivers were empty. Full of disappointment, they escaped back to their military compound.

Bloody Tress was carried above the narrow defile to a plateau where the dark face of the shady side of the mountain and the sunny side, where the rivers ran, came together. There, Gesar and his ministers were assembled, and Nyentak Marpo instructed, "This demoness has such magical power that you Super Warriors and ministers must focus your samādhi and bind her firmly with the divine lasso. She is a savage rākṣasī, a samaya-violator demon incapable of developing true faith in the Dharma. Therefore, it is you who must liberate her with your enlightened wrathful activity." The Super Warriors threatened the demoness as she, with breasts bared beneath her shawl of human skin, hissed through her clenched teeth, "May I be the one to cut your life force and to destroy the teachings of the Buddhadharma!" She had no sooner spit out these words when Gesar, as Norbu Dradül (Jewel Enemy Tamer), manifesting as a wrathful wisdom deity, pressed his right foot onto her sternum. He held a small white-handled crystal knife, the symbolic hand emblem of Mañjuśrī, and, chanting Avalokiteśvara's aspiration prayer with tears of measureless compassion, focused his enlightened intention on all sentient beings. Through his wrathful activity, the demoness was liberated, and her body offered to all the deities. Her consciousness forcibly tried to eject, but, because of her deep-seated impiety, she took rebirth as the daughter of a cannibal in the village of Darika. Gradually, through the power of aspiration prayers, she became a suitable vessel able to be tamed by the great guru Vikramaśīla.[13]

Then, Gesar and the Three Ultimate Warriors—Falcon, Eagle, and Wolf—arrived at the Ling encampment at sheep-time of early afternoon and were welcomed with a reception. Those who had stayed behind—the local lamas and the great leaders, along with their attendants—were joyous and offered khatas and received blessings. Gesar sang of the warriors' good deeds in his signature melody "Quelling the Great Crowds through Splendor." And then, having seen the prophecy fulfilled through Gesar's power and omniscience, those assembled wondered if there were others with such skills.

Chipön realized that both Akhu Gomchen Tingmé and the diviner Kunshé Thikpo (All-Knowing Adept) must have insight into the situation but, as subordinates to King Gesar, they were not speaking up. Chipön prodded them, "We have heard Gesar's words, and now ask your counsel regarding the prophecy. In particular, when will our victory be at hand, have Yutsé and his ministers already brought harm to Ling, and when will their authority come to an end?" Gomchen Tingmé rested awhile in samādhi, and then, fully comprehending, he arose saying, "Sit here, king, ministers, and to all you friends and relatives I offer this song."

> OM MAṆI PADME HŪM
> Sing "Ala thala thala."
> "Thala" begins and
> "La la" gives the perfect pitch.
> Here is the clear prophecy
> that Chipön has requested.

He and I have equal understanding
and have received the three great empowerments—
    mahāmudrā, dzogchen, and madhyamaka—
and as Chipön is my benefactor,
I cannot refuse his sincere request.
Here comes a little song from this old man's mouth.
I have no omniscience; nevertheless, these sounds appear,
and, perhaps based on my own confused perceptions,
here is the song that arises from my heart.
There are one hundred dense forests
and within each there are poisonous sé trees.[14]
There are one hundred carnivores,
and among them are the so-called man-eating tigers.
There are one hundred so-called mighty demons,
and among them are the samaya-violators of perverted
    aspirations.
One particular evil damsi
was born a jealous rival of the Lotus-Born One
    Padmasambhava.
As for the king and his subjects, the translators and scholars,
    and the Dharma king,
this damsi had perverted views, reviled them all,
and expressly despised the teachings of the Secret
    Mantrayāna.
Not only that, she was one of the seven damsi siblings
who had died and were dwelling in the lowest hell realms
until they simultaneously took rebirth in the human realm.
There they arose as a community of raiders and bandits
with ever-increasing power,
and, in the end, they became an army of samaya-violator
    demons
arrogant enough to think that they would take over the
    world.
They enslaved and exploited all sentient beings.
The very biggest devoured the small ones.
All living beings were cursed with misery,
and the dying were led to the lowest hell realm.
Therefore, at the behest of the victorious ones, we tamed

Wangjema, the mother of the samaya-violator siblings,
and now the damsi daughter Bloody Tress,
who were so formidable.
This has brought us great joy.
Now, do not delay; it is time to subdue the miscreants,
time to disband the māra ranks
and lay waste to the quarrelsome and obstructing spirits.
They, the māra king and ministers,
the degenerate tsen, the māras, the teurang, the nāgas,
the mu spirits and the nonhumans, and all of the *preta*
    demons—
just as it is for humans, a field of protection is prophesied for
    them.
Their actual military camp is not that impressive,
but their invisible troops are their actual force
and will be powerful and imposing when they appear.
Not only that, outside of their encampment
is their illusory display of fire, water, and the precipitous
    abyss,
evident now as a treacherous narrow defile.
If even Kyang Gö cannot cross, let alone an ordinary horse,
and Gesar cannot pass, it is senseless for anyone to try.
But by Trothung's conjured torma,
the invisible and visible forces alike
will be incinerated and trampled underfoot.
This was all set in motion long ago,
and if you let it unfold, there will be certain victory,
but delaying will create obstacles.
Consider the māras' phantasmagoria:
first, magical wheels of lightning from space,
second, wind-swords from the heavens,
and third, catapults of destructive power from the earth.
Amassing the machinery of magic,
they work diligently day and night.
While they strive so mightily,
delaying even a week will make your struggle difficult.
To my way of thinking,
Trothung should hurl his sorcerous torma

the day after tomorrow,
and on the following day
the Masang king Gesar
with thirteen warriors at his side
should go on the offensive and invade the enemy
    encampment.
Since the māra army insisted on coming,
I imagine it has encircled the camp.
To prevent the māra king Yutsé from escaping,
Gadé must bind him as though he were a vulture.
If he were to escape,
he would be led to Amnyé Bumthub of the māras
by the gods-demons who protect and guide him
and we will have failed to subjugate him.
Rouse your energy, king of Ling and ministers;
gather your great steeds[15]
and you will be up to the task.
Pack up nourishing food,
for you do not know the length of your journey.
Vajrasattva and Trowo Metsek (a wrathful form of Vajrapāṇi)
are your meditational deities. Accumulate their mantra
    recitations.
I will keep you under my protection
under all circumstances and without wavering.
This regiment of Ling warriors
ought not fight with savage cruelty and hatred,
but rather, don the armor of compassion and loving-kindness,
draw out the curved blade of the sword of *prajñā*,
tirelessly battle the enraged army,
hoist the banner of the sacred Dharma,
and shout the victorious chant "Ki! Ki! So! So! Lha Gyal
    Lo!"
Then, the divine prophecy will materialize,
the māra Amnyé Bumthub will be tamed, and
great marvelous heart treasure will be revealed.
The māra bandits and thieves
will turn to virtue,
and all beings will live in prosperity.

This is the foremost legacy of the king and ministers of Ling.
Until all the world is brought to the Dharma,
the karma of Ling is unfulfilled.
This is the melodious song that arose from the mind of this
old meditator.
According to the ancient proverbs of Tibet:

Even before the sun lights the day,
fireflies illuminate the path.
Even along the banks of Lake Manasarovar,
lowly raindrops quench one's thirst.
Even in front of a beautiful peacock,
a red rooster flaunts the color of his wings.

Even in the presence of Gesar, the embodiment of
Vajradhara,
this old meditator gave the prophecy as requested.
If there is any confusion, the mistake is mine.
King, ministers, and companions, take this to heart.

Gesar gave Gomchen a handful of gold dust and coins, presented him with
the finest khata, and touched Gomchen's forehead to his own.

The diviner Kunshé Thikpo spread a single, white, square silk cloth on the
ground on top of which he elegantly arranged all the *mo* divination implements,
mirrors, and so forth. He sang, and Gesar presented him with five gold nuggets and
fifteen silver coins wrapped in a khata that was embroidered with the auspicious
symbols. The meaning of the divination was understood by all, and the day concluded with an exhortation that all the healing ceremonies be practiced diligently,
without distraction.

CHAPTER SIX

At the encampment of the māra king Yutsé and his ministers,
Nyentak manifests, disguised as the god of the māras and gives
    a false prophecy.
The camp is ransacked, but the māra king and ministers escape.
The supreme steed, Gesar's horse, explains how to destroy the
    enemy.

KING YUTSÉ AND HIS MINISTER SHELÉ returned to their encampment,
despondent over their many casualties and particularly brokenhearted over Bloody
Tress. They sat and drank a mix of liquor and blood to the point of drunkenness.
They went on to tell the story of what had happened, but it sounded preposterous to
the many ministers listening, who felt that it would have been impossible for them
to have survived an encounter with a being as powerful as Gesar. Later, when Shelé's
mind had cleared, he resolved to request the counsel of the māra deities, but while
he was making a great smoke offering of human and horse flesh and blood, from the
pure realm of the wisdom deities, Padmasambhava called upon the wisdom mind
of the dralha Nyentak who, in turn, flawlessly disguised as a māra deity, manifested
before Yutsé and his ministers. Enveloped in a dense fog of evil, he sang this short
song of prophecy.

> Na o o! Sing "Una alu thalu."
> Na o o! "Thalu ona" begins.
> Coemergent deity, please hold me dear.

Within this azure firmament
is this tent of dense darkness.
I do not need to explain who I am.
I am the divine chief protector of the king and minister,
the caretaker of their minds, whether good or evil,
and a sounding board
for those two—mighty King Yutsé
and his rogue of a minister.
Why look so troubled?[1]
Why torment yourselves with such misery?
Why dwell on such a stream of sorrows?
Here, listen to what I have to say.

There is a jewel in the head of a poisonous snake
that everyone knows to be a wish-fulfilling jewel.
Do not let your mind go there,
as once you do, you'll think of nothing else.

As for those brave ones who have faced Yama,[2]
who everyone knows to be courageous—
do not confront them,
as, once you do, you will have to kill them all.
The one of consummate skill and strength
was the very youngest Bloody Tress,
but here are the cowards who escaped like foxes—
these two, King Yutsé and his minister Shelé.
Bloody Tress fought evenly with the Ling warriors,
and there were no winners or losers,
as we, the māra gods, came to her aid.[3]
Just as Bloody Tress had wished,
we brought her to Amnyé Bumthub.
She supplicated him without holding back
and joyfully, with loving-kindness, he took her under
    his care.
Little by little, he will heal her,
giving her the iron pill of deathlessness
along with the medicine that reverses death.
All of this will be done within a week.

Not only that, Bloody Tress
has already decided to invite Amnyé Bumthub here
and has said that there must be a meal and proper seating
    ready.
You have eight days at most—don't procrastinate!
Take charge of the encampment
with each of you responsible for your own tasks.
Don't be lazy!

Jumping from one idea to the next
and chattering will get you nowhere.
So much coming and going leads to misfortune,
and endless scheming, to calamity.

Until Bloody Tress returns,
do not break camp.
As before, the magic of this camp is in its illusion
and, despite their strength, it is unthinkable that the Pathül
    can breach its perimeter.
The time for your army's departure will come, but for now
    you must delay.
Just as the predawn sky
gives way to daybreak and mist clears,
with the sunrise the time will come for our plan.
If you have understood this song, keep it in your hearts.
If not, there is no way to explain it.
All of you here, keep this in mind.

Thus, pretending to be the god of the māras, Nyentak had bestowed this prophecy, and the māra king and ministers rejoiced and offered him a drink of the best blood and liquor. Each prostrated according to their tradition. Gradually Nyentak's divine mirage disappeared. The king and ministers, those who were the life tree of the lawless māras, the disaster-producing demons of the obstructing spirits of samaya-violators, the ego-demon rudras of perverted views, and the enemies of the teachings of the Buddha were overjoyed as a magical wheel of lightning spread through space, a wheel of wind filled the middle sky, and a catapult materialized on the earth—actually not one but thirteen catapults. Those, along with the three-fold weapon-wheel made sixteen, and in no time, the stage was set with diligence, complete with the magical māra army as well as fire, water, the great abyss, and other magical implements.

At daybreak of the sixteenth day, through the protection circle produced by their lamas, the troops of Ling invoked all the wrathful deities—the eight classes of gods and spirits, the local guardians, the zodors—to come to aid the beloved teachings. They offered a goblet[4] and reminded the spirits of their samaya commitment. They invoked the wayward gods-demons of the dark side and set out various support substances.[5] Seeing such extraordinary pageantry, such magically entertaining and beguiling displays, the māra spirits became distracted, leaving the māras without their divine protection. By then, Trothung had completed his meditation retreat, thereby perfecting the cycle of approach, accomplishment, and activity. He had accomplished the activities of summoning, binding, slaying, and union. Wearing the majestic and terrifying mantra-adept black hat and robe, he arose from within a blazing fire as the actual form of the Bön primordial sage. Holding a massive black-magic torma, he offered this song of demand with the Bön cry "So! Ya! Yé Gyur!"[6]

OM MAṆI PADME HŪṂ
"So! Ya! Choya!"[7] is my short, intense song.
Ya! To the life force of Gulang Nakpo![8]
Tri! Ya! Triumph over the forms of the hostile enemies.
Dza! Bring them to ruin and annihilate them.
From the upper gate of clear and luminous space,
the 360 primal Bön deities,
each in a dreadful, wrathful form—
some with nine heads, some with three, some with one,
with three eyes, clenched teeth, and uttering a roaring sound,
fire blazing from their eyes and smoke pouring from their
    nostrils,
their mouths gaping open with tongues curled and teeth
    gnashing—
relish the flesh and blood of the enemies and obstructing
    spirits.
With either eighteen or six arms,
they hold various accoutrements and blazing weapons,
fighting, binding, slashing, beating, and so on,
their quick movements unchecked.
Choya! Come from space
to destroy the enemy castle and annihilate the army.

Act with the fierceness of destructive magic.
From the lightning tent of the azure firmament,
the Bön deity Mithung, mounted on a dragon
and clothed in blazing flames,
emits lightning great as the fire that ends the kalpa.
Countless likenesses, small wrathful emanations, swarm
    above,
those middle sky deities of Bön werma,
eleven million strong, ordered into action.
Thunderstorms descend upon the samaya-violators.
Now is the time to focus.
Wage war on the enemy and destroy the enemy castle.
May your awesome fierceness be my ally.
From the swirling dust storms on the earth,
all everlasting protectors of Bön,
arise in your fearsome forms.
Act with fierce, enlightened wrath; do not let your power
    wane.
Render nameless the enemy obstructing spirits, those who
    inflict harm.
Today, the black magic torma is mine to throw.
I, Trothung, am the wrathful Hayagrīva
and the Bön deity Taklha Mebar.
These hosts of samaya-violator bandits,
those who pervert the view of the secret mantra teachings
and eagerly succumb to the ten nonvirtues,
are enemies of the Buddha's teachings,
but, in particular, they hold animosity for Tramo Ling.
Gather the troops of the lha, lu, and nyen.
With this torma weapon-wheel
and various magical weapons, lead them to destroy the
    formidable māra army.
Sever the mu cord that descends from the heavens,
destroy the magical wheel of the azure firmament,
and do away with the support of the earth below,
cutting off escape in every direction.
Direct the magical torma at the king, the minister, and their
    companions.

Direct the magical torma at the māra encampment,
their main strategists, their guardian deities,
their allied forces and the swift horses beneath them.
Make sure they have no safe haven.
Precious Three Jewels and divine Three Roots,
demonstrate your inherent power.
Gesar—you, the one entrusted by the gods
and the certain yoke upon the evil māras—
assist in establishing the legacy of my kingdom.
The dralha and werma, possessors of powerful magic,
must now be my allies.
Let there be no safe haven for the enemy.
Look upon the gods and humans of Ling.
May the bravery of their warriors be synonymous with the
　　heavens,
and may the teachings of the Victorious One equal the lofty
　　azure firmament.
May the family line of their bitter enemies be severed at the
　　root,
their flesh and blood offered in reward,
and their consciousnesses led to the pure realm.
Go! Do not fail! Do not fail!

Having sung this inflammatory song, Trothung threw the torma at the enemy as he recited inciting mantras and visualized his yidam deity. A deafening rumble shook the earth and red flames flared, filling the skies. Guided by the dralha, werma, and divine protectors, the torma flashed like a thunderbolt without warning into the midst of the hosts of evil damsi. As a result, the māra magical wheels were powerless to bring down lightning and the māra catapults that had been so skillfully crafted collapsed in a heap. More than seven hundred māra troops were incinerated as though they were merely feathers catching fire. Not only that, half of the māras' horses were destroyed and nearly all the leaders fell unconscious. However, because Trothung, as a mark of his obeisance, had previously given the ketaka jewel to King Yutsé, the torma had power neither over Yutsé nor over the two hundred troops who were with him in the encampment's staging tent. On top of that, his torma was powerless over those very māras who had become his genuine disciples, despite the fact that he, Trothung, had had a change of heart and renounced them.[9]

At the moment that Trothung had raised his black magic torma, the warriors and leaders of Tramo Ling, together with Gesar, wielding the panoply of fierce weapons blessed by the gods and lamas, had offered smoke and amṛta in praise of the deities. There were seven thousand horsemen mounted on trained horses, eager to run. The troops were resplendent in radiant white armor, their billowing longevity-knot pennants shimmering as they went. Those who stayed behind, the two Ling uncles (Chipön and Senglön) supported by three thousand attendants, diligently offered refuge prayers.

Then, at the snake-time just before noon, the Ling army and Gesar with his ministers arrived at the māra encampment in the meadows on the edge of Namtri Barma at the border of Zi and Ling. Encircling the camp was a deep abyss of a thousand strata, inaccessible to all but the white vulture. At its core was a blazing ring of fire encircled by the waters of an ocean, inaccessible to all but the golden-eyed fish. The abyss was shrouded in darkness by poisonous vile-smelling vapor, and inaccessible even to the invisible gods-demons, let alone to any human. Their courage broken, the Pathül warriors and their troops were at a loss. They supplicated Gesar, wondering what could possibly be done.

By that time, the king of magical awakening, the wish-fulfilling jewel, the dralha king himself, Gesar, looking like Indra about to do battle with the asuras, was fully armed. He shimmered with rainbow light and, with a body adorned with the major marks, quelled the three worlds with splendor. The dralha darted like shooting stars, the werma danced like light rays, the Three Jewels gathered like clouds, and the dharmapālas swirled like a blizzard. Gesar rode his capable great steed Kyang Gö. Great feathers sprang from the steed's main channel, lesser feathers from his minor channels and from between the tips of his hairs. Through the genuine meaning of the wisdom intent of dharmakāya, he radiated light rays and rose into the middle sky. Gesar led with a heroic and brave heart, and his majestic presence was overwhelming. Singing the melody Dralhé Thokching Barma (Binding Lightning of the Dralha), Gesar and his horse flew like birds over the abyss, swam like geese through the water, and appeared as a dome of fire in the midst of the māra protection circle of flames. Gesar gazed back and performed dispersing ceremonies, scattering consecrated rice, flowers, and barley. The protector gods gathered like cloudbanks. The earth trembled and, simultaneously, the great magical display of the māras naturally subsided, as the land became a pleasant, quiet place.

Witnessing this, the Pathül warriors more than ever before saw Gesar and his horse as embodiments of the Buddha and were filled with devotion. Joyful and courageous, spurring their horses, they fell in line behind Gesar. Sounding the warrior's cry, the Ling army went forth like a swollen river.

Discovering their magical weapons destroyed by the black magic torma thunderbolt, the damsi army of the evil māras—those evil disaster-producing demons, enemies of the Buddha's teachings and of Tramo Ling—was distraught. Their three swift steeds with wind-swords that cut without touching as well as the magical wheel and its forge lay in ruins, and the bodies of most of the māra magicians were missing limbs or heads. The māra king and ministers understood that this was the sorcery of Ling and, dejected, they convened inside their main meeting tent and decided to return to their homeland fortress. Upon the heels of this decision, they heard shouts of "Ki! Ki!" and "So! So!" and saw that the Ling troops had crossed over the narrow defile and traversed the ring of fire and water. The māras realized that they were trapped, surrounded by the restive Ling army and the Pathül warriors. Shelé Lakring, the emanation of the degenerate teurang, came to scout out the army, clinging to a magical swift horse and brandishing a spear, not caring whether he would live or die, and headlong toward the army he rushed, thrusting his spear thrice at Gesar, but again it was as though he was stabbing a rainbow.

There to Gesar's right was the warrior Denma who at once took out a bow and arrow and, without a pause, launched a single arrow at the wheels of Shelé's horse. Two wheels skittered out from under the horse and Shelé fell to the ground. Magically another horse appeared and Shelé mounted, but as the dust settled, his keen sword Yazi Kartren (Sharp Invincible Little Star) in hand, Gyatsha Zhalkar astride his great steed Gyaja Sokar, looking like a white lion adorned with a turquoise mane, roared out this song.

> OṂ MAṆI PADME HŪṂ
> Sing "Ala thala thala."
> "Thala" begins and
> "La la" gives the perfect pitch.
> From the highest awakened state,
> eighty mahāsiddhas of India, look upon me.
> Divine protectors of Tramo Ling and
> dralha, werma, and zodors, look upon me.
> Annihilate the vindictive enemies!
> If you do not recognize this place,
> it is the borderland of Zi and Ling,
> the land leveled by the samaya-violators,
> the land wiped off the map by the disaster-producing demons.
> If you do not recognize me,
> I am the brother of great King Gesar,

Gyatsha Zhalkar of the Bumpa clan.
I rival hundreds of thousands of troops
and I am the heart blood of an army of tens of thousands.
Those are the facts.
Now encounter you, this samaya-violator son,
a man pretending to be what he is not,
a man in white with the courage of a fox.[10]
You must be Shelé Lakring.
Like a twitchy fox, you have jumped the gun.
It will do you no good. It is as absurd as pouncing on a
　　rainbow.
As for you māras seizing our country of Ling,
how could your demoness possibly bring us down?
You are pitiful.
According to the ancient Bön proverbs:

Merchants who yearn for wealth
must be astute at recognizing value.
Hard-up merchants are imprudent,
indiscriminately buying up whatever they see.
In the end, they return empty-handed.
Notorious bandits
need powerful reinforcements.
Ignorant bandits and thieves who are unaware of this,
recklessly steal the wealth of the chakravartin.
In the end, they find themselves surrendering to the chieftain.

This is what is said, and it is the truth.
The lord of death and the Dharma king Gesar alike
are majestic as they come to stand by your pillow;
they each come with messengers.[11]
Even a gale wind could not escape.
Even a bird with wings spread would be powerless to fly.
Even a magician would be helpless to display illusion.
Now, this day, your time is up;
it is time to think seriously.
Surrender to King Gesar,
trust in Tramo Ling,

take off your armor and weapons and prostrate respectfully,
and you will be spared.
Insist, if you must, on violence, but
I, the warrior Gyatsha, know no fear,
the keen blade of my invincible sword Yazi gleams, and
its little twinkle[12] can split even a rock-solid boulder.
But I don't have time to list all the qualities of a good sword;
the very sight of someone like you
brings my blood to a boil.
My arm muscles twitch, wishing to swing the sword.
There are many songs, but time is wasting.
Everything will become clear in the end.
Once you consider my words, you will understand.
If you don't, I can't explain them.
Samaya-violator demon minister Shéle, hold this in your mind.

Thus he sang, and Gyatsha waited for a response, not at all certain that this
was Shelé Lakring. Spitting mad, Shelé burst out, "You, Gyatsha of miserable Ling,
it is time to fight, but first take to heart my answer to your eloquence and soon
enough we will see how warriors fight!" Wielding the handle of his sharp, poison-
ous sword, seated sideways atop his magical horse, he sang this song of bravery.

Sing "Ona alu thalu."
"Thalu ona" begins and
"La lu" gives the perfect pitch.
I invoke the divine protector of the evil māras.
The teurang—white, black, and multicolored—know me,
and today, consider my situation.
Gyatsha, this land is just what you said—
the graveyard of Tramo Ling.
If you do not recognize me—
to a māra bandit mother
seven nonhuman gods-demons siblings
were born from eggs,
seven champions of the māra kingdom,
and sworn enemies of the forces of Ling.
I am the emanation-son of the depraved teurang.
The snow lion and I—we two

are delighted by foes and blizzards,
quelling through splendor all the carnivorous clawed beasts.
The white lioness is admired by all beings, but
you, a low-down dog disguised as a lion,
are an inferior man, lacking all courage.
Your empty words are carried off by the winds.
You said that I must bow down and prostrate
to evil Joru and his wicked mother
and that I must surrender my mind to Ling.
That will never happen; those words are an affront!
I have no fear when I see you.
Even if you were the lord of death, I would stand up to you.
Even if you were a rocky crag, my weapons would split you
    apart.
Even if you were the icy wind, I could outrun you.
Beyond what I can do, consider the māra king and ministers:
This man who upends earth and sky
is the hale and hardy King Yutsé.
The strong man who holds a mountain to his chest
is Shechen Drengyi Yamé, the green Wayward Sibling.
The man who can down the ocean in one gulp
is Marpo Tsenkya Bumthub, the red Wayward Sibling.
The one to annihilate the savage enemy
is Nakpo Tongdü Lenmé, the black Wayward Sibling.
Not only that, our superb warriors are the cream of the crop.
That is what will become clear.
Gyatsha, your words are hollow.
No doubt you have plenty of support, men, and horses,
but a man's bravery hinges on his own courage.

Why speak of the keenness of the steely weapon's blade?
Whether it cuts turns on the expertise of the warrior's throw.

Whether men and horses win or lose in war
depends on the strategy of the commanders.
As for your confused way of thinking,
it is pitiful.
You imagine me to be afraid of you.

You? I'm not even afraid of Gesar.
The minister, the warriors, such "fierce" tigers and leopards—
let them come right up to me.
I, this magical emanation, have no misgivings about my own
    courage.
This sword Duklé Ngarma (Fierce Poisonous Blade)
was not made by a skilled smith,
but rather the great Wangchuk Chenpo
gifted it to me.
As day dawns, it emits poisonous vapor,
as night falls, it blazes with firelight,
and it splits boulders to dam the flow of water—
I can't imagine that it won't slice you!
It seems you are a clever singer,
but when we see who wins, the meaning will be clear.
If you have understood my song, keep the words in mind.
If not, there is no way to explain them.
All of you here, keep this in mind.

Thus he sang, and with the last word of the song he pivoted on his magical horse, angrily charging toward Gyatsha. Now certain that it was Shelé Lakring, Gyatsha lunged and in the ensuing sword fight he was struck many times but stood firm. Finally, Gyatsha swung his sword Yazi once; it flashed, piercing Shelé from his left shoulder clear through to the other side of his chest and Shelé fell to the ground, still breathing, limbs flailing. The dralha king Gesar's steed Kyang Gö stomped on him and a moment later he breathed his last. Like the roar of an avalanche, Gyatsha shouted, "Ki! Ki! So! So!" The māra deities, realizing that they had been distracted by this mayhem, gathered a humanlike illusory army as allies: the magician Khergö Mikmar (Joking Red Eye) turned the magical weapon-wheel against the Pathül, and nine māra leaders were sent out, including Drongnak Razung (Black Drong Horn Holder), Tongthub Kherkyé (Born to Defeat a Thousand), Akhu Yenthub Pungring (Powerful Extensive Courage), and Garsa Dramring (Dance Near and Far). They shot a deluge of arrows, pelting and piercing the Pathül warriors in spite of their protection.

Then, the warrior Denma shot three arrows, and Garsa Dramring and Takgö Lenmé (Incomparable Warrior Wild Tiger) were both killed. One arrow struck but did not injure Khergö Mikmar. Khergö trembled with anger, setting the weapon-wheel in motion. With a shrill roar, it started toward Nyibum, Gadé, Nyatsha, and Nang-ngu; their horses startled and shied away and the seven soldiers standing behind them were killed. Gadé quickly dismounted and, with the help of the protector gods, threw a rock the size of a sheep, demolishing the weapon-wheel. Khergö, planning to throw his second weapon-wheel, confronted Gadé, but Gadé fought viciously, leaping onto Khergö. He grabbed his shoulders, kicked him to the ground, and with clenched fists beat him to death. The other Pathül warriors, howling like jackals, had raided the māra camp, killing more than one hundred troops.

Yet the māra apparitional troops were strong in number and it had been impossible to kill them all or even to distinguish them from the actual māra troops. For a fleeting instant, the Pathül warriors' sharp weapons dulled and the strength of their troops waned; the mu spirits, māras, and damsi, along with the king and ministers, saw a chance to escape. They were running in circles, trying to piece the wind-wheel and the iron-wheel back together when the Pathül warriors tore open the main tent of the māras, and in the end they were tamed. The dralha king Gesar sang a vajra dohā supplicating and invoking the deities and instantly before him, amid an expanse of blazing fire, appeared the Lord of Protectors, Black Mahākāla. He wore a helmet and armor fashioned from iron and led a divine army twenty-one thousand in number. In a flash, as though the dralha had struck them with a hammer, the entire apparitional māra army was demolished. From within samādhi, Gesar offered a pleasing feast to the gods and, like the stars at daybreak, the illusory māra encampment vanished altogether. King Yutsé, Tsenkya, Shechen, and Tongdü, the four remaining māra rulers, vowed that they would fight to the death. Subdued by the clamor of the Pathül army, they had no time to prepare the iron weapon-wheel, and simply mounted any horse they could catch. Enraged, Shechen, threatening as a tree bent by a howling wind, came right up to Zikphen, Nyatsha, and Werma Lhadar with his sword Drongö Lingchö (Severs a Wild Drong in a Twinkle) half unsheathed and shouting, "Miserable Lingites, before you offer gifts to your boy-warrior, listen. I'll tell you how things really are." He sang this short song.

Sing "Alu thalu."
"Thalu ona" begins and
"Ona" gives the perfect pitch.
So! So! I offer to the māra mu spirits
and to divine Garab Wangchuk.
If you do not recognize this place,
it is the borderland of the Zima Valley.
If you do not recognize me,
to the magical nonhuman mother

from the union of gods and barbarous demons, seven
    offspring disguised as children
were born from eggs.
In particular, I am the manifestation of the evil mu,[13]
known as Shechen Drengyi Yamé.
On the full moon day of the midwinter month,
as the nine signs of the māra calendar conjoin,
on the grassy plain Münpa Kyamo (Gray Darkness),
in the presence of the all-powerful demon Lutsen—
those named as māra kings met
for a great contest of strength and skill.
Nine iron beams were bound together—
the hand emblem of King Sadam;
when Lutsen could not lift it, it fell to me.
I clasped it to my chest and lifted it onto my shoulders,
erecting these beams as the pillars of Sharu Namdzong
    (Staghorn Sky Fortress).
Lutsen said he was pleased to see such a strong man,
and I received the name Shechen Drenmé (Unrivaled Great
    Strength).[14]
Denma, if you are here, come and face me,
the one revenging those who were killed.
Sengtak, if you are here, come face me;
I will answer you with my bravery.
Greatly famed warrior, Gyatsha,
if you are so famous, come here now.
Gesar, you the leader who holds the throne;
if you want to continue your reign, come out right now.
My steely sword is my greeting khata,
and my great strength is my offering gift.
This sword is the inherited treasure from the māra mu king
and was bestowed by my youthful cannibal mother.
It will destroy even the greatest mountain,
crumbling its solid rock.
How could it not slice all of you as well?
There will be piles upon piles of corpses,
a mountain of dead men.
The lower valleys will fill with blood;

the lakes and rivers will flow crimson.
Just wait, you will see the truth of what I have said.
You, horsemen who have come here, keep this in mind.

Before the song was finished, Chipön's son, the splendid and courageous ten-year-old Nang-ngu Yuyi Metok, who was the life-support of all the Pathül and the lineage son of capable warriors, had been thinking, "This man all of green must certainly be Shechen, the one who I have the prophesied karmic destiny to tame. But he has such strength that if the army and the other Pathül warriors were to meet up with him, they would be defeated and possibly lose their lives. It would be crazy for me to even get near to him, but perhaps I could defeat him with an arrow shot from a distance." Thus it was that a small boy—handsomely suited to the small horse upon which he sat—nocked his arrow, his steely armor and weapons glinting. Shechen crouched into a lunge, thinking, "Such a small boy so arrogant to think he can rival me! Nevertheless, for certain he will respond to my song. Let's see who he is and what he has to say. There's no need to clench more than a single fist." Relaxing, he let out a great, derisive laugh. At that moment, the boy set the golden-notched vulture-feathered arrow, given to him by Gesar, on his bow and said, "Hey you! Shechen! Māra minister! It seems from your bragging that there is no warrior like you in all of Jambudvīpa. I am still young and small but here to fight. Calm down and listen to my song. If you are such a fierce warrior, there will be plenty of time to fight." Saying this, he sang this song called "A Little Melody."

> OM MAŅI PADME HŪM
> Sing "Ala thala thala."
> "Thala" begins and
> "La la" gives the perfect pitch.
> I take refuge in the Three Jewels.
> Respectfully, I supplicate with body, speech, and mind.
> May the six classes of beings be happy.
> From the blazing celestial palace of the herukas,
> the subjugating and wrathful deity Padma Thötrengsal (Lotus
>   Skull Garland)[15]
> takes form,
> smashing the wayward damsi demons to dust.
> Divine protector of Tramo Ling,
> protector of the Great Being Gesar
> and my personal deity,

please do not fail me.
May I deliver an arrow to the heart of the enemy.
If you do not recognize this place—
it is Namtri Barma in the Zima Valley.
If you do not recognize me—
I am the beloved son of Chipön,
the younger cousin of King Gesar,
and a cherished son of Tramo Ling.
Here is my destined enemy
right in front of me. My heart fills with desire to fight.
I have this unspoiled, superior arrow;
don't you think I can hit the heart of the enemy?
Already, I should be called a hero.
Don't you think I can face you, Shechen?

I am the child of the garuḍa, the king of birds;
don't you think I can soar the azure firmament?
I am the cub of the white snow lion;
don't you think I can navigate a blizzard?
I am the cub of the striped Bengal tiger;
don't you think I can cross the sandalwood forest?

Roaming free, you were just a bunch of bandits and thieves,
but now your arrogance has set your spirits high.
Never have I met such a brazen man!
Here are some examples:

A young upstart yak calf from the herd—
has he not learned that grown yaks have horns?
His arrogance in fighting them
portends the goring of his belly.

You, the ostensible chieftain of the bandits and damsi,
have you not noticed the superior warriors?
Fighting with those who have the upper hand
portends your outright destruction.
Consider whether this is true or not.
It seems the glory of your name is fading, Shechen;
it is unimaginable that I fear you.

Deep in pristine water, the makara is threatening,
yet a newly hatched conch can bring its end.
In the heart of a sandalwood forest, the Bengal tiger is forbidding,
yet a small poison-tipped arrow can deliver its death.
These solid red rocks seem majestic,
yet a small lightning bolt can smash them to dust.

Your strength is not what it seems.
That this small boy will take your precious life
is the meaning of what you call my "empty words."
It is carved in stone;
my word is as good as gold.
The lord of Ling, King Gesar—
at the mere sight of him, one transcends the lower realms.
At the moment of death, be resolute in devotion,
and you will be spared falling to the lower realms.
I, Nang-ngu, am soon to shoot an arrow,
but this bow is formed of goat horn, too stiff for me to bend.
Although I am armored in warrior style,[16]
let's see if I measure up to the archer's task.
Although I can't properly pressure the golden-notched arrow
    with my thumb,
let's see if I can steady it upon the bowstring.
Let's see if I can target a single blade of grass.
How embarrassing for you, Shechen, if you even flinch—
of all my worst enemies, you will be the one known as a
    coward.
I have made up my mind not to back down
but to challenge you
to see who will be victorious.
With long thin lances, we will see who is the defter,
and with a swordfight, who is most skillful.
Finally, we will wrestle, clad in full armor, to see who is
    pinned.
Win or lose, the results lie within our previous karma.
Enough time singing,
today I will vanquish my enemy.
Divine protectors of Ling,

support and lead this arrow.
May it strike down the enemy.
You, here, keep this in mind.

Thus he sang, and while Shechen was reeling from the insolent words of this clever-talking little boy and thinking he would hurl him onto the rocks, Nang-ngu shot the arrow. It left the bow with speed, strength, and steadiness, the three quintessential qualities of an arrow, and with a roaring din and radiating light, the arrow tip was drawn up by the divine protectors and struck the heart of Shechen Yamé, strewing the fragments. Shechen fell from his horse like a tree toppled by the wind, and Nang-ngu swooped up Shechen's helmet, and holding it aloft he rode, roaring with the sound of a thousand dragons and crying "Ki! Ki! So! So!" Seeing this atrocity, thirty māra warriors led by King Yutsé and several ministers[17] rushed at Nang-ngu. At that moment, King Gesar was dwelling in samādhi, and he placed the Pathül warriors within the firm protection circle of the union of the three emptinesses: outwardly, the emptiness of space; inwardly, the empty nature of mind; and between, the empty nature of channels and winds. Gesar sent out many magical emanations of his body, speech, and mind, one to assist each Pathül warrior, while he as well as his emanation as Brahmā, both shielded with crystal armor, fought Yutsé with swords.

Gyatsha, Denma, and Gadé fought Tsenkya; Nyibum, Muchang (Rinchen Darlu), Paseng, Sengtak, and so on fought the rest of the strong māra warriors. The Pathül warriors ran at the samaya-violator damsi, fighting like a thousand ewes and lambs corralled in a pen. The damsi were magically protected by their personal māra gods. They struck swords, which glanced off each other with blue light, they threw spears, which descended like meteors, and there was a swirling blizzard of clattering arrows; for a while, it was a melee of all-out fighting. Here on the Ling side, Nyibum Daryak, the cherished son of Ombu, and from Takrong, the principal warrior Thokgö Pungring (Fierce Thunder Broad Shoulder), seven volunteer warriors in all, were lost to enemy weapons. Over on the māra side, Kazhi Lhündrub (Effortless Four Pillar) stabbed Yenthub Pungring (Able Broad Shoulder) with his long sword, Gyapön Marlu (Red Chieftain) killed Drongnak with his spear, Tharpa Gyaltsen (Liberation Powerful King) stabbed Tongthub Kherkyé (Defeats a Thousand Born Alone), and Zira Marpo (Red Spark) and Yengö Jemé (Traceless Power) both were killed sword-fighting with Nyatsha.

Gesar repeatedly thrust his sword at Yutsé but did not kill him, nor did Brahmā's sword cut him. Likewise, Yutsé's sword glinted off Gesar as though striking rocks. The māra Tsenkya and the three Pathül warriors fought on, but no one raised a sword in victory. Just as the nyen Gedzo Kulha bore down on Tsenkya with his sword, Tsenkya's bodyguard put the steely wind-sword Rekchö Chik (Cuts with One Slash) into his master's hand, but Tsenkya was driven back and Nyentak Marpo immediately snatched the wind-sword. Seeing that Tsenkya was without a sword, the Pathül sheathed their knives to begin fighting hand to hand, but Tsenkya ran off. Zikphen pursued him, advancing like a hunting dog tracking a deer. As soon as he came within reach, without so much as a short song, Zikphen thrust his spear Nakduk Chengar (Sharp Black Poisonous) at Tsenkya who was killed, pierced clear through his belly. He fell like a flag blown down by the wind.

The people of Ling shouted "Ki! Ki! So! So!" with the sounds avalanching from their mouths. Then, an utterly blue emanation of the nāga king Tsukna, together with an emanation of the zodor Magyal Pomra disguised as a perfect likeness of Trothung, confronted Tongdü Lenmé. Tongdü was fooled and, trembling with rage and without hesitation, bellowed out, "You the Takrong chieftain are a bag of lies, a poisonous pit of shameless duplicity that will be your ruin. Now, I have you cornered." Tongdü brandished his sword and rushed at both emanations, but to no avail. On the other hand, neither was Tongdü injured, as there was no karmic connection for either Tsukna or the zodor to tame him. But his sword was destroyed by Tsukna's razor-sharp water-sword and his courage broken. Tongdü retreated furtively, without either of the two emanations knowing where he had gone. While searching for him, they fortuitously ran into King Yutsé, but again, as destiny would have it, it was not his time to die. Yutsé produced three self-emanations, and the fight that ensued with the nāga and zodor went on until, soaked with sweat and gasping for air, all at once, the combatants collapsed with exhaustion. The māra gods whispered into the ear of King Yutsé, "Run! Right now!" and then with the help of Wangchuk Chenpo, the gods enveloped King Yutsé and his minister Tongdü in dark clouds of smoke. They found themselves ushered outside the Ling encampment, with Wangchuk Chenpo poised to guide them home with the mu cord, but the dralha and werma protectors of Ling cut the mu cord, inciting a great battle with Wangchuk Chenpo that was so violent that it climaxed in an earthquake. In the midst of the chaos of the trembling mountains and flashing lightning, the Ling deities were ultimately victorious. The māra king and minister were rescued by the māra god Khyabpa Lakring who had brought a black steed. They mounted it, ready to flee to their homeland, while from the middle sky, the māra gods urged them on, saying, "Run through the eastern lands and across the mountains of the north! Escape to the country of Achen in Hor!" As fast as the wind, they turned westward.

That dark cloud had spread, and Gesar and the Pathül warriors were vexed that Yutsé and his minister had escaped. Gesar reflected, "We surely should have tamed Yutsé, but he seemed invulnerable. Not only that, he had many magical emanations willing to exchange blows. Tongdü was equally brave and invincible, and now they have both vanished. On top of that, even though our Ling deities appeared in human form, they obtained no meaningful victory. I am starting to think that that dark cloud will turn out to be the magical lasso of the māra deities, and that they are all headed back to the māra country." Gadé, contemplating the same morass, thought, "Tongdü is my sworn enemy; that is the prophecy of the gods. But today I fought him face to face without winning, and now he has escaped. Not only that, I tried to make a mantra protection cord to bind him, but I became distracted and now I am completely disgraced." He was so despondent and distraught that he started to think about calling the Black Mahākāla to rescue him. The rest of the Pathül were bewildered, looking at each other and all around for some hint of what to do. At that moment, Amitābha appeared as Gesar's magical and omniscient steed Dorjé Kyang Gö, raising his front hooves in a dance, uttering a single neigh, and offering this song in the human tongue.

> So! So! Hé! Hé!
> From the blazing fire tent,[18]
> So! So! Hé! Hé!
> Wrathful Padmasambhava, Wangdrak Pema Drakpo Tsel,
>   Hé! Hé!
> I supplicate divine Hayagrīva to
> annihilate the maleficent horse-demons.
> I entreat you to protect all sentient creatures.
> This place is the hinterland of the Zi Valley.
> Here are the ruins of the samaya-violator encampment,
> the ground where damsi blood was spilled,
> where the māra forces were routed,
> and the bandits trounced.
> It is the burial ground of their corpses.
> Surely, you recognize me.
> Outwardly, I am a Gyiling steed;
> inwardly, I manifest the wisdom intent of the buddhas.
> I am the all-knowing king of horses,
> Kyang Gö, who is beyond duality.
> "Kyang" refers to my coloration as a wild ass—
> ruby-colored, the radiant red of Buddha Amitābha.
> "Gö" signifies that I am like a vulture soaring the skies,
> unflagging and tireless.

I am the mount of Lord Gesar,
who is the magical incarnation of the three protectors,
the embodiment of the victorious ones,
the noble being, the holder of the teachings,
and the adversary of rudras, the enemies of the teachings.
As for this battle between the gods and demons,
there is a time to come together and a time to withdraw.
Both victory and loss are possible;
life and death are in constant alternation.
You are the incomparable divine heir.
There is no reason for regret.
Today is fading,
dusk nears, and night will fall—
a time when māra warriors gain power.
Tonight, the māra king's life has been spared
and in accord with the māra prophecy,
they return to the land of Hor.
Tonight, on the ancient Zi grasslands,
the dralha and werma will be the sentries.
There is no need to worry that the māras will slip away into
    the skies;
the divine being Brahmā will stop them
with a roadblock of men and horses
and an entourage as countless as falling snowflakes.
There is no need to worry that the māras will slip away to the
    azure firmament;
the dralha Nyentak will stop them
with a roadblock of men and horses
and an entourage as turbulent as a swirling blizzard.
There is no need to worry that the māras will slip away
    beneath the earth;
the twenty-one thousand werma and
the nāga Tsukna Rinchen will act as the sentries,
with a roadblock of men and horses
and an entourage as infinite as the particles in a mound of
    gold dust.
The four great gatekeeper kings are at the four intermediate
    directions,

and each of the ten directions has a guardian.
The twelve *tenma* are the scouts,
and the nighttime sentinel is Manéné.
Today, although the māra king escaped to the north,
there is no reason for you to have regret, Gesar.
I, your steed Kyang Gö, will not be left in the dust.
The longer the race, the faster I go.
The strength of the dralha never wanes.
The farther the journey, the more wholehearted their resolve.
The blessings of the Three Jewels are unfailing,
and if we trust single-pointedly, they will hold us with
    compassion.
Tomorrow, while we will make but one journey, there is a
    second purpose.
The heretic priest Amnyé
has been practicing the māra Wangchuk for nine years,
yet he has not once opened his eyes.
But if he continues another twelve years,
he and Wangchuk will be of the same nature,
and certainly then, as he opens his eyes, he will incinerate the
    world.
Therefore, although it is not your main task, unless he is
    bound by a samaya oath,
the teachings will become distorted.
Hence, tomorrow you must accomplish this.
You most mighty Phunu warriors,
the corpse of the samaya-violator māras
must be buried, not scattered.
You must invite Akhu Gomchen Tingmé,
plunder the māra encampment,
and then journey on your way.
Gadé Chökyong Bernak
must mount the speedy colt Yuja[19]
and journey along with Gesar.
The destined enemy is certain to be tamed
and, doubtless, the fleeing fugitives will be apprehended.
We will spend this very night in our encampment,
a spot for an untroubled night's rest.

Along with liquor, nourishing food, and relic pills,
bring the ax that can split great mountain rocks,
the magical lasso that can grasp the sun and the moon,
and third, the supreme medicine that cures one hundred
    illnesses.
These three, by all means, must not be forgotten,
and at dawn tomorrow you must get ready to go.
I, Kyang Gö, will guide you
through the mountain pass and across the great steppe.
If we are not fast enough to stop the enemy,
it is proof that neither I nor Yuja are divine horses.
Just as ready as an arrow nocked on a bowstring,
the time has come for another meeting of the Ling gods and
    the māras.
Whatever happens, king and ministers, there is nothing more
    to ponder;
we will see if you can demonstrate your courage and skill.
There is no reason to agonize over today's outcome;
you will prevail
and the māra enemy forces will be cut at the root.
Tomorrow's undertaking will be child's play.
King Gesar, keep this in mind.

Thus he sang, and Gesar dismounted, saying, "You may be the horse beneath me, but, beyond that, you are the emanation of Buddha Amitābha, possessed of omniscience and magical power. I confess my ignorance, and, from now on, I will think of you as my advisor." Gesar touched his forehead to the horse's forelock. The Pathül warriors stood in awe of this steed that had voiced the prophecy in human language, and they prostrated and circumambulated.

Not a single samaya-violator bandit was in sight; they had vanished like dust into the thin mountain air. The Ling troops collected the gear left scattered by the māra army as they fled, and the bodies of the three samaya-violator brothers (Shechen, Khyergö, and Shelé) who had fallen in battle were brought on horseback for ritual burial.[20] The Ling troops, as though their victory over the māra enemy was complete, shouted "Ki! Ki! So! So! Lha Gyal!" As night fell, Gesar and the Pathül warriors returned to the encampment, with the troops filing in behind. Chipön, Trothung, and other leaders gathered at the headquarters. With great celebration, the smallest details of the battle were recounted.

CHAPTER SEVEN

Gesar and Gadé pursue the māra king and minister,
liberating them, and then depart for the north.
Amnyé Gompa burns in a fire.
Having accomplished their goal abroad, they return to Ling.

BEFORE DAWN THE NEXT DAY, the Pathül attendants brought tea and, without delay, readied the saddles, and packed up food, the relic pills and curing medicines, the magical lasso that seizes the sun and moon, and the rest of the gear. Gesar wore magnificent dralha armor and weapons. The warriors Gyatsha, Denma, and Trot-hung, wanting to go with him, each sang a short song of supplication. I, the bard, have left them out, as they were repetitious.

However, Gesar indicated that they should stay behind and that he would simply dispatch a message by arrow if there was any matter of importance. As the morning star rose, Gesar on horseback looked as fearsome as the great god Indra going to battle the asura demigods. With Gesar rode Gadé, impressively armored, clad all in black with his ebony hair cascading down his back. He was brilliant and fierce riding atop the colt Yuja. Those who stayed behind offered a lhasang and prostrated, their murmuring hum intoning prayers to the Three Jewels. The three seed syllables spontaneously appeared on the tips of the ruby-colored hairs of the divine horse Kyang Gö. A vortex of light spun around him like oil glistening on water, sparks whorled from his mane and tail, and his hoofprints left an imprint of a rightward-spiraling conch. The horse snorted, impatient to go, and his unobstructed omniscience was as clear as individual grains held in the palm of your hand. He turned toward the northwest and departed like a bird in flight.

As if he were a mythic eighteen-winged bird soaring with its broad wings spread, the swift colt Yuja raced to match the speed of his old rival Kyang Gö. Beyond the Zima marshlands and across the Zima mountain pass, like a scroll uncoiling, before long the two horsemen arrived, past the eighteen marshlands, at the backside of Magyal Pomra. They found themselves on a small road where there was a junction of three lakes. The sun was just rising. Kyang Gö indicated that this was where they should stop, and Gesar and Gadé dismounted. They were joined by the lha, lu, and nyen, the zodor Magyal Pomra, and a swirling snowstorm of dralha and werma. From the midst of one of the lakes arose a *nāginī* bearing platters of sumptuous food and all the earthly goods and pleasures of the nāgas, which she respectfully offered to those four divine ones, the two men and their two horses. Once again, songs were sung, but as they are repetitive, I, the bard, have not included them.

In the meantime, Yutsé and Tongdü, the māra king and minister, had crossed the Zima mountain pass Namtri Barma on horseback. Traversing the six sandy plains of Zima, by dusk they had arrived at the lowest part of mountain pass road in Zima, but the Ling gods had shrouded it beneath dark rain clouds so dense that the path forward was obscured. Anxiously, they sat on the side of the road sandwiching themselves between scattered boulders, hoping for daybreak and looking back, afraid that they were being followed. In this state, they spent a long and miserably uncomfortable night. When no one had come by first light, their mood lightened, and they crossed over to the other side of the pass to the desolate lands of the nomadic tribes at the edge of Zima. There, they promptly demanded food and drink. The people of these highland clans were frightened by their fierceness and brought meat and butter, which the māra king and minister packed into saddlebags. They rode off, crossing the Zi River, and effortlessly traversed the eighteen marshlands as they drove their horses up through its heavy and muddy wetlands to arrive at the boggy headwaters of the Ma River. There, as they rested and ate, Tongdü worried about the tracks left by their horses, but Yutsé was unconcerned, as he was carrying a deadly dagger. They swore to each other that they would never retreat or surrender and jumped back on their horses. Above them was the largest of three lakes, and below, the smallest, a milky white lake. They arrived at the banks of the third lake, shaped like a claw print, where Kyang Gö stood as the sentry. He stomped the ground, signaling Gesar that the enemy had arrived. Gadé recited a sealing mantra of liberation, preventing the enemy's escape. Then, Gesar and Gadé set out on horseback, going higher and higher as though they were being drawn upward. Now, the small white lake was even farther below them, but at the spring that fed the lakes, just like an arrow's notch catching the bow, they ran into Yutsé and Tongdü who said to each other, "Certainly these men are scouts for that miserable Ling Joru.

Whatever comes of this, good or bad, we must stand up to them." But then, what the māra king and minister saw were men and horses of all colors spreading across the plains, coming straight at them. Gadé erupted with shouts of "Ki! Ki! So! So!" The majesty of his strength was like that of a wild yak—even the lord of death would flee. He drew out his spear, advancing as he sang this song.

> OM MAŅI PADME HŪM
> Sing "Ala thala thala."
> "Thala" begins and
> "La la" gives the perfect pitch.
> Supreme glorious celestial heruka—
> I supplicate you for support.
> Please guide me to annihilate these harm-doer samaya-
>   violators.
> From the Cool Grove charnel ground,[1]
> all Mahākāla deities, know me.
> Today, cast down the fierce enemy.
> I offer a feast of meat and blood in return.
> May the precious teachings soar,
> and may all sentient beings be happy.
> If you do not recognize this place—
> this white mountain, shaped like a leaping snow lion,
> is Magyal Pomra.
> Its eighteen sunlit southern slopes
> face Tramo Ling.
> It is the divine guardian of Ling.
> Its eighteen shady northern ridges
> face the evil māras.
> It is the adversary of the māras.
> This mountain is encircled by lakes,
> each rimmed with flowers in great profusion.
> These are the eighteen marshlands of the Ma River watershed,
> strewn with lakes, both large and small.
> If you do not recognize me,
> in the land of Ling in the Ma River region,
> I am of the Ga tribe, both east and west.
> There in the Zi Valley, where ten thousand families of the Ga
>   and Dru clans live,

the Ga have ten thousand people and one hundred thousand
    horses,
and among the dwellings of those ten thousand
is my fortress, the great, Dru castle.
I am Dru Gadé Chökyong Bernak—
an emanation of Mahākāla,
the bodyguard of the divine heir Gesar,
and the adversary of the vindictive enemy.
In eastern Ling, the maṇḍala of the victorious ones,
my rank is that of *chökyong*, a Dharma protector.
Those are the facts.
Here, alongside me, is King Gesar.
One of faith sees him as an awakened guru
and as a man who established Dharma in the three worlds.
Yesterday, you thought you could escape to freedom,
but today, where is it that you are going to go?
We, Gesar and Gadé both,
will pursue you like a piercing icy wind,
and there will be nothing between you and the lord of
    death.
Daylight fades;
shadows and darkness approach.
The happiness and well-being of your homeland slip away.
Death and the bardo loom;
not only are they near, but right at hand.
First were the aspirations of your previous lifetimes,
then your striving to fulfill them,
and now their karmic ripening.
You reap what you have sown.
What good will come of fleeing like a cowardly fox?
If you are afraid, take refuge in Gesar,
offer all that you have—body, speech, and mind.
If you care for this life and the next, listen to this advice.
As is said in the ancient Tibetan proverbs:

As long as you have an appetite, drink the elixir of life;
when the time comes that you can no longer eat, it will be too late.
If you wish for happiness, take refuge in a leader;

when you are in trouble with the law, you will have lost your chance.
While you have a clear mind, meditate upon the guru;
when you die and fall to the hell realms, it will be too late for regret.

That is what is said, and it is the truth.
This is the crossroads of virtue and evil;
there is a thin line between good and bad.
This is a matter of life and death.
Is this clear? You must think it over.
You can insist on being daring warriors,
but I hold the poison-tipped spear
that is the weaponry of Mahākāla.
There is more I could say, but the spear is set to go!
You each must decide what is best for you.
If you understood my song, please reply.
If not, may there be a nail in your heart.
You, seated here, keep this in mind.

Because they were incarnate evil spirits and because the karmic connection between them and Gesar was so compelling, the māra king Yutsé and his minister Tongdü flew into a rage at Gadé's song. Tongdü drew out his spear and fearlessly lunged at Gadé as he shouted, "You miserable Ling king and minister! Acting so fierce, roaring like tigers . . . my words are the last you will ever hear." And he sang this song.

Sing "Alu thalu."
"Thalu ona" begins and
"La lu" gives the perfect pitch.
Here in this place of darkness,
where the mountains are formed from corpses
and the oceans are of swirling blood,
where the breath of all beings wafts like mist blown by the
    wind,
is the majestic māra Khyabpa Lakring
surrounded by one hundred thousand demon-lords of illness
    and life force.
I call out for you to come quickly.
Assist me in destroying this enemy.

We do not know the history of this land,
for today we step on it for the first time.
We are mighty men, fierce as tigers and leopards,
but this dusty desert will single out the true warrior.
You may not recognize me,
as my name is not bandied about casually.
I am the magical emanation-son of the evil māras,
the unrivaled Tongdü Lenmé.
When I entered my thirteenth year,
I went as a bandit to the eastern country of Hashang.[2]
There, I killed more than one thousand,
destroyed more than one hundred golden-roofed castles,
and stole away more than five hundred mules with silk-
    ribboned foreheads.
Therefore, I came to be called Lenmé, the unrivaled.
I have killed as many enemies as there are hairs on my head.
Those monks in their monasteries—I have killed more than
    three hundred of them;
just seeing red robes, I become enraged.
But still I am not satisfied.
Actually, I have gone with my mother and sister,
wandering the world over and taking lives.
This song tells those stories.
Listen! You two, miserable Ling king and minister,
you think yourselves capable, but you are mistaken.
Army boy, you and your horse will both be lost to us bandits.
My king is fit and healthy,
the māra kingdoms are united with each other,
wherever the king resides is his kingdom.
As for the degenerate Gesar, here with his minister,
I would rather die than take refuge in you.
I doubt your professed hell realms even exist.
Prove it to me right now.
Although you have an army, I too have an army;
there is no being chummy and negotiating.
We are alike, both cherished mother's sons.[3]
Although you have a spear, I too have a spear;
they are equally sharp.

The magic of the spear is in the skill of the one throwing it.
Enough of singing; it's hard on the ears.
We will see which of us is the fierce warrior.
What are you waiting for, you miserable Gadé?
Don't sneak off now that we are face to face.
Both of you, keep this in mind.

As soon as his song ended, Tongdü jumped up like a sudden gust of wind, thrice thrusting at Gadé with his spear, but since Gadé's magical protection stood firm, the spear was ineffective. However, Tongdü was strong enough that Gadé rocked from his saddle and nearly dropped from his horse. On the verge of becoming dazed by Tongdü's intensity, Gadé shuddered momentarily and then firmly rested in the vivid presence of the deity. Taking up his own spear, Gadé pierced Tongdü's chest clear through to his right shoulder blade. The samaya-violator, biting his lower lip in agony, toppled from his horse and fell lifeless upon the ground.

Meanwhile, King Gesar and King Yutsé nearly collided. The māra king recognized Gesar, and not taking time to utter a word, he fired off three arrows that fell harmlessly to the ground at Gesar's side, his compassionate enlightened body impervious to the poison arrows of blazing hatred. Thereupon, Yutsé took from his tiger-skin quiver the owl-feathered iron life-force arrow that had belonged to Garab Wangchuk. He nocked it, ready to shoot, and sang this short song.

Sing "Alu thalu."
"Thalu una" begins.
I sing "Una,"[4] and
"Thalu" is the call to the gods.
From the dome of the cloudy skies,
māra king, divine Garab Wangchuk
with your retinue of hundreds of thousands,
today come quickly to support
three māra generations, from my grandfather down to myself.
We have offered to you the first portion of flesh and blood,
from our hearts we have come to you for refuge.
If you have any blessings for us, then now is the time;
if not, then it is all over.
If you do not recognize this place,
it is the border of Zi, Hor, and Ling,
known as the eighteen[5] marshlands of Magyal Pomra.

I am Yutsé, the king.
I rank among the four great māras.
In the lineage of the brave ones,
    specifically, I am the enemy of Tramo Ling, and
generally, the enemy of the teachings of Buddhadharma.
Yet, I am still not satisfied.
You are the worst of the worst—
young man, such arrogance
will only lead to disaster. Such a pity!
Young horse, you must not be so eager to run.
The ancient Tibetan proverbs say:

Even fresh butter is hard on the liver if you overindulge.
A tigress can leap too far and break its back.
Even the great dragon can roar too loudly and fall into the lake.
No matter how brilliant, the sun and moon can be eclipsed by
    Rāhula.

That is what is said, and it is the truth.
A young horse's chomping at the bit
is an omen that he will dash his four hooves on the rocks.
A young man's bluster of bravery
is an omen that he will lose his life to the enemy.
E ma! What great irony this all is.
It riles me to think of it.
It has been bloodshed since the day you were born—
first, the māra king Tobden Nakpo (Full of Evil Power),
second, Takzhal Gyalpo (Tiger-Faced King) of Zima,
third, the tsen, that most fierce of the male māras,
fourth, the musk deer, the principal one of the female māras,
fifth, the three nonhuman sisters,
sixth, the fish-headed water demons—
all were slain, and now, all my siblings are slaughtered as well.
The carnage you have wrought is incalculable.
It is you who is the butcher of the māra people;
without you, we would be at peace.
You have turned those who respected you into enemies.
Today, I will shoot an arrow into your heart.

This divination arrow set into the bow
has been kept in a tiger-skin quiver;
it is the arrow of Garab Wangchuk, the life-spirit of the māras.
This iron arrow adorned with owl feathers
when loosed can demolish a great mountain,
and when it targets the sun and moon, they drop to the
    ground.
This arrow's feats are without measure.
If you are a corporeal being, it is inconceivable that you will
    get away.
If, like a rainbow, you are intangible, that marks you for victory.
If you have understood this song, take it to heart.
If not, there is no way to explain it.

Thus Yutsé sang, and with all his might, he shot the arrow. Expelling poison-ous vapor and whistling with inherent energy, the māra arrow came at Gesar, but Brahmā was there with his golden shield deflecting it such that the arrow swung wide and, instead, fell into the lake. Its poison caused the lake to boil over, and through the poisonous vapor, the sun appeared a dazzling crimson. Gesar thought, "There seems to be no peaceful resolution for all this as Yutsé is deaf to my words. I must subjugate him and, with dedication and aspiration prayers, lead him to his next life." Gesar manifested in wrathful form as a maroon man with turquoise eyebrows. Dralha spread like sparks flying, werma hummed like buzzing insects, and Gesar's divine eye was bloodshot, like a guiding star dawning over a mountain pass. With his thumb, he nocked the black iron arrow Phurbeb Shepa (Understands Ascent and Descent) in the bow Ragö Khyilchen. "You, Yutsé, with your gray ponytail, don't be in such a hurry to die! These are beneficial instructions for the coming days that you will wander the bardo. Listen here to my song. Every word I say is crucial." Thus saying, he roared out his song with the great power of a dralha.

OṂ MAṆI PADME HŪṂ
Sing "Ala thala thala."
"Thala" begins and
"La la" gives the perfect pitch.
From the Copper-Colored Mountain in Chamara,
embodiment of all the victorious ones, Padmasambhava,
when you oversaw the taming of the fortunate disciples of the
    snow land of Tibet,

you revealed the fivefold and eightfold manifestations[6]
that are your essential nature, Lotus-Born One.
I supplicate you to look upon us with compassion.
May you benefit all those who meet you.
Hosts of dralha, lha, lu, and nyen, and
werma and zodor—gather for this enlightened activity.
Slay the enemies of the teachings and take their heart blood,
and uplift all that is positive.
This is the land of the zodor Magyal Pomra.
Here, Yutsé, you and your minister fearfully sought an escape
but were thwarted and rounded up.
This is the land where stallions gallop at top speed,
while the less swift-footed collapse, exhausted.
Here, the power of the māra gods will be challenged,
and the slaughterhouse of the māra king's execution,
   constructed.
I have been known as Ling Gesar
since I reached the age of thirteen,
and I decree that today is your last.
I possess bravery and the six powers.
I have already slayed eighteen well-known māra kings,
killed countless ratlike creatures of perverted aspirations,
and annihilated the life-support talisman of the samaya-
   violator King Yutsé—
there is no limit to the tales I could tell you.
I am renowned throughout India and China,
and a mere few months ago,
I was enthroned as the sovereign of Ling in the land of Ma.
Now, I have met up with you samaya-violator māras,
the king, minister, and the seven damsi siblings,
and today, as I cut the enemy at its root,
the spoils will be the first of hundreds,
the start of excellent shared good fortune.
According to the ancient Tibetan proverbs:

If a family is cohesive, life is excellent.
If you rely on a guru, your mindstream will be tamed.
If your chieftain is of high status, your dominion will grow.

If the first bandit succeeds, those who follow do also.
If the beginning is marked by good luck, the goal will be
  accomplished.

Today, the auspicious connections are excellent.
Gradually, I will tame the māra king
and take his treasury of wealth,
leaving it as a legacy for sentient beings.
Distinguishing between the māras and the gods
hinges on whether at the root their minds are good or bad,
as well as whether their underlying aspiration is good or bad.
Ultimately, all sentient beings of the six classes,
without exception, have been your parents.
Moreover, although all beings wish pleasure, suffering arises.
As for the māras that harm beings,
it is of benefit to hold a benevolent attitude toward them.
That the gods will benefit humans—
pray that little by little this will happen.
The taking of life and the harms done by the māras
have at their root perverted aspirations;
such is the seed of māras and gods.
Since the day you were born,
you have robbed and killed so many beings.
Everyone has suffered under your tyranny.
You have laid the groundwork for unending heinous
  behavior.
It seems your malice knows no bounds.
The burden of your evil deeds grows more and more onerous.
You cannot expect your next life to be any different.
In view of that, I have resolved to sever your ties to the hell
  realms;
I, Gesar, the parent of the six classes of beings,
will act only for the benefit of others.
This was my promise when I dwelled in the celestial
  realm,
and I will work unfailingly
for the happiness of all the world.
Until this is assured, I will not rest.

However difficult the situation, I have no concern for my
    own life and limb.
Just as the bodhisattvas, the heirs of the victorious ones,
tirelessly work for the benefit of beings, so shall I exert myself.
Yutsé, you, the one of perverted aspirations—
if I let you live,
sentient beings will never enjoy bliss and happiness;
you are the enemy of all beings,
and I am not Gesar if I do not liberate you.
Here is how an arrow is shot:
the excellent bow is drawn into a semicircle,
and, like an eagle homing in on its prey,
the arrow flies, darting like lightning through the heavens and
dropping to its target like a meteor striking a rock.
Just as it sows the seeds of liberation and virtue in the land of
    Tibet,
your body is the seed that will be sown
as your accumulated ties to the lower realms
are severed by the wisdom sword.
This is not all just talk; it is what will happen.
In the bardo after death, maintain strong faith and devotion,
and I will lead you to the pure land.
If you have understood, hold this firmly in your heart.
If you have not, I cannot explain it.
Māra king, keep this in mind.

Thus Gesar sang, and he shot the arrow. Yutsé shifted in his saddle attempting to avoid the arrow, but it struck his heart center. Just like a butter lamp extinguished by the wind, the māra king, his face growing dark, fell from his horse. This bastion of the evil māras, the king of the damsi, the enemy of all sentient beings, the particular enemy of the teachings of the Buddha, this nonhuman māra demon with all his degeneracy, a rudra of perverted views, was killed. The gods and humans shouted "Ki! Ki! So! So!" as the news spread, and they raised the banner of victory over their enemies throughout the three worlds.

Then, Gesar took the turquoise hair that was Yutsé's mark of bravery[7] and buried Yutsé's body with his minister—head down, according to ritual. The ritual continued with ceremonial dancing upon this burial ground, and Gesar and his noble horse offered aspiration prayers that the māras would never again flourish.

It is said that, even today, if you look, in the marshlands of the Ma Valley, you can see a stupa formed from a large boulder bearing the footprints of a man and a horse.

Gesar and his minister Gadé both made dedication prayers and guided Yutsé with the phowa, and the continuity of Yutsé's evil deeds and perverted aspirations was severed. He took rebirth in the country of Minyak in Jang as Kara, a cherished son of the Greater Lineage, and, once again, he met Gesar and was able to be of useful service to him. The māra minister Tongdü took many different rebirths in ordinary human form, and when Gadé died and passed to the pure land, he saw a sign that Tongdü had traversed the paths and stages and was finally reborn in Akaniṣṭha. The sun rose with its vivid light shining forth and a great domed tent of rainbow light appeared above as an indication that the gods were pleased. In the intermediate state, the eight classes of gods and cannibal spirits delighted in virtue and showed their true forms, taking an oath to support the teachings and serve enlightened activity. From the lake below, there arose an inconceivable multitude of nāgas, circumambulating and prostrating.

From among these nāgas, right in front of King Gesar and his minister, appeared a great white nāga with five hooded snakeheads and the coiled lower body of a golden serpent. The nāga dismounted his Gyiling steed and held aloft a silk flag snapping in the howling wind, offering prostrations. He called out, "Kye ma! Refuge of all beings, endowed with magical powers—where is it that you come from, what are your plans, your name, and so on? Tell me everything. I am Upananda, one of the nāga kings, one with actual faith in the teachings of Śākyamuni. Although I firmly abide by the law of Dharma, it fell to me to cleanse these despoiled and polluted lower valley lands of Hor and Zima, and now my body is racked with pain and ridden with disease. With your knowledge, please bestow the proper medicine to relieve my suffering. Whatever you command, I will obey and be your servant." Then, King Gesar revealed himself in the body of Avalokiteśvara the Great Compassionate One and gave ablution water and the relic pills that cure one hundred diseases. He even bestowed ablution water to the mountains, plains, and lakes. Immediately, like dust swept from a mirror, Upananda's sores, stupor, and misery cleared, and the land returned to its pristine purity. The nāga king and those around him were delighted, and joyously offered the jewel Samphel (Wish-Fulfilling) to Gesar, and the jewel Serbeb (Flowing Gold) to Gadé. Then, for the benefit of all beings, Gesar, through a divination song to the whole entourage, gave the complete instructions of the three protectors.

The nāgas gave a great celebration to show their reverence and respect, and the next morning, led by the zodor Magyal Pomra, Gesar and his minister left on horseback at a flat-out gallop. They crossed into Nakshö, the forested valley that was so dark as to be shadowless, dividing Zima and the north country, and came to the bank of a lake in Lower Ma where the *menmo* dwelled. They dismounted, conversing with the menmo who asked them to stay and offered them nutritious food, relic pills, and brandy, which they drank without becoming intoxicated. Their thirst was quenched with the ḍākinīs' longevity wine and so forth, and the gods and humans all celebrated, their joy inconceivable. At that moment, the dark zodor mountain spirit of Drongri appeared on a black horse, along with Gyimtsé Trachok, a man in white with a white horse, to escort Gadé on his return to Ling.

The lake opened like a wide door to Gesar and his horse, and they entered without hesitation. An exquisite island stretched before them with lush grasslands overgrown with flowers and resonant with melodic birdsong. In its midst was a beautiful palace gilded with the seven precious jewels,[8] resplendent as Indra's celestial palace. Bidding Gesar to sit atop the jeweled throne draped in luxurious silk brocades, the tenma, various Yama goddesses, and one hundred thousand menmo danced, sang delightful songs, and offered delicious foods. The menmo supplicated, and Gesar gave teachings on the faults of saṃsāra and on karma and its result, and then performed a *gaṇacakra* of the sensory objects of enjoyment. Continuously for six days and nights, he turned the Dharma wheel, expounding on bodhicitta in the manner of the sovereign heruka, Īśvara, focusing on the enlightened wisdom intent of the forefathers.

Neighing once again, the steed Kyang Gö, an emanation of Amitābha, admonished Gesar that they must go and, as abruptly as an unexpected chill wind, they continued through Nakshö, the wooded lowlands along the shady side of the mountains, where a cannibal demoness concealed as a jackal waited at guard. An earthquake signaled the arrival of Gesar and his divine retinue. The jackal-demoness, at a loss to identify him, became panicky and reemerged in her own body, that of a hideous female rākṣasī, still standing guard. With the suddenness of a fierce wind, the dralha Nyentak and Gesar manifested as tigresses, took hold of the demoness, and with one mighty tug, ripped her body apart, killing and taming her.

Afterward, they crossed out of the valley and ascended a steep, snakelike rocky outcropping. At its summit, in the guise of an owl, was a teurang protectress pacing back and forth, trembling with dread and frightened as never before, on lookout for Gesar. But when she looked out atop the mountain's flat grassy plain, she misconstrued Gesar and Nyentak as two lovely maidens, wearing colorful silks and dangling turquoise earrings, playing dice and calling out the numbers as they rolled them.[9] The owl-protectress did not recognize who they really were, but she was drawn to them, almost involuntarily. Right then, as the two apparent maidens faced each other, they winked. At that same moment, Gesar threw his magical lasso Nyida Trülzhak and, like a bolt of lightning, roped the owl teurang Garwa Nakpo (Black Ironsmith)[10] around the neck and bound her like a ball of yarn. Offering up the life of the owl-protectress, Gesar asked Dorje Lekpa to watch over her as one of his devoted subjects.

Gesar traveled on, through the great valley of the Khrom River[11] and there, spying on him, sat a massive nine-headed frog. Gesar[12] disguised himself as formless red light and, as he came nearer, the nāga-demon frog noticed him and inflated his body to thrice the size of a yak-hair tent, damming the flow of the river and creating a lake. Just as the frog raised its heads out of the water, looking frantically in all directions, Gesar saw that the great god Brahmā had transformed into a fearsome garuḍa that lifted the frog-demon out of the water. In accord with the signs and prophecy of the menmo, Gesar struck the frog three times with his great ax Drakri Habshok (Rock Splitter), ejecting the frog's consciousness and offering its flesh and blood to the dralha and werma. There was an earthquake, and from his palace Draknak (Black Rock) within the māra fortress, Amnyé heard at a distance the deafening reverberations and saw a great flash of red light. Full of unending superstition, he became alarmed at these ominous signs. As he gazed out, fire blazed from his eyes, incinerating those in front of him—the māra heretic Jangpa Nakpo, the Hor warriors' doctor Chisöl Menpa, who possessed a death-reversing medicine, the magician from Zishang, the Bön black magician Kara Kenglok from Zhangzhung, and the black-magic guru meditator Tagyen Takzik of upper Takrong; all five of his main disciples went up in flames. As he looked out again, his black magic substances caught fire, and with a final look, Amnyé Gompa saw that his box of ancestral ritual implements was burning. [Though he stamped out the flames], he became unnerved at this ill-omened turn of events. While Amnyé was trying to fathom all of this, Gesar was invoking the enlightened mind of the glorious protector Mahākāla, Gönpo Maning,[13] from the Padma realm. Pretending to be who he was not, the Mahākāla took on the form of Amnyé's guru and protector Wangchuk Chenpo and appeared directly in front of Amnyé. As he was easily fooled, Amnyé believed that this was the wish-granting prophecy of the divine māras, and profound faith, devotion, and delight dawned in him.

Yet, as the nature of Amnyé's mind was to harbor misgivings, a nagging suspicion grew like a weed as to whether this was truly his personal protector standing in front of him, and he spoke aloud, "If you are Garab Wangchuk Chenpo, discern from the later tantras the black magic mantra wheel. Show me those profound teachings." In response, Gesar, disguised as the Black Mahākāla, revealed that mantra from the heretical external tantra, convincing Amnyé that he was now in the presence of his protector Wangchuk Chenpo and should practice in earnest.

Meanwhile, Gesar had turned his attention to hunting with his attendants for the māra life-force yak that was disguised within a herd of some thirteen drongs,[14] grazing freely. He was elated when he saw the herd, and, among them, the life-force drong, sorrel-colored and with a mature rack of horns. Fearlessly, it let out a low-ing sound and displayed its horns and swished its tail as a sign. Gesar shot a single arrow to its forehead and tamed the yak. Thereupon, as though it were growing dark, Amnyé's vision dimmed and he fainted momentarily. The gods and humans concurred that the māra Amnyé deserved to be burned, and the dralha and werma readied piles of red sandalwood. Amnyé's wife Nyüljema, who was a black vulture, had been spying from her nest in the rocks, and was snared by Gesar with his magi-cal lasso Nyida Trülzhak and wrested to the ground. Gesar—deep red, with the face of Shinjé and rolling bloodshot eyes, menacingly clacking his teeth—seized her wings and threatened her with a small white-hafted crystal knife as he held her bird neck tightly. She pleaded with him and offered the twenty keys to Amnyé's treasury. Gesar gave her the transmission of the refuge vow and revealed many magical dis-plays, and with deep devotion she promised to protect the teachings of the Buddha.

The dralha Nyentak, the Nyenchen Kulha, and Gesar suddenly emanated as three identical white snow lions. Amnyé's tigress gatekeeper roared, the earth shook, and the lions leapt at her. The lions and the tigress clawed at each other and the tigress was soon overpowered. That tigress, now near death and terrified beyond measure, being an emanation of Gulang, a manifestation of Wangchuk Chenpo, dissolved as suddenly as a wind drawn back to its source and Gesar—the treasure of humans, the heart-son of the lha, lu, and nyen, the sublime guide of beings— was seen for who he really was. Outwardly, he possessed the threefold panoply: the dralha flag waving, his helmet with a white pennant tossing, and armor shining with vivid white light. Inwardly, he was a buddha with unwavering realization, empty and luminous, as the actual realization of Samantabhadra. An ocean of dralha, werma, and dharmapālas surrounded him, swirling like snowflakes. Gesar struck at the stone door of Amnyé's palace three times with his great ax, and it opened imme-diately. Gesar and his horse, their retinues around them, entered easily and came right up to Amnyé who, although he had heard the rattling of the door as it opened, remained trusting in his divine protector.

The dralha and werma were preparing a pyre, but Gesar thought that although Amnyé would not be able to be liberated by faith, it would not be right to just burn him on the spot without explaining the Dharma. Gesar revealed his body as a divine maṇḍala. Amnyé kept his eyes tightly closed. Gesar flicked Amnyé's forehead three times with his thumb ring and called three times with, "Ya ona! Well then, Amnyé! Great meditator! If you do not train your mind in bodhicitta but act out of attachment and aversion, there will be no awakening, only hardship and struggle. Listen to my song and this will be clear." Saying this, he sang in the melody of "Warrior's Short Song of the Dralha."

OM MAṆI PADME HŪM
Sing "Ala" to invoke the Three Jewels.
"Thala" gives the melody that calls the enlightened mind of
   the Three Roots,
and "La la" is the buddha nature of one's own mind.
I sing a ceaseless song, devoid of confusion.
May this song be meaningful.
Here is the dark valley of the māras
and the palace of a heretic priest—
your castle, Amnyé.
If you do not recognize me,
I am the heir of divine Brahmā.
I have been commended by the buddhas of the three times
as the yoke upon the evil māras
and their executioner, sent from the god realm.
I have arrived here, in front of you, Amnyé.
Whether I come as an icy wind or as Joru—
how can a sentry thwart us?
I have mastery over the five elements;
there is no limit to my unobstructed[15] omniscience.
Holding to the path of bodhicitta,
I have attained the resultant enlightened mind.[16]
That's the truth of it.
Now, listen, you who professes to meditate,
heretic Amnyé nāga, listen!
As for the six classes of sentient beings,
without exception, they have each been our father and
   mother.
They have taken rebirth and wander in saṃsāra,
and although everyone desires bliss and happiness,
all wander in perpetual suffering through accumulated karma
rooted in selfishness and resulting in pain.

Taking life is the upshot of the five poisons.
Karmic obscurations accompany you like a shadow,
inseparable and in turn,
your charade of meditation brings only trouble to you
and misery and suffering to all beings.
All sentient beings, whether great, middling, or lowly,
cherish their lives in the same way,
desiring happiness
without understanding the causes and conditions [of
   suffering].
They are devoted to the worldly gods,
exerting themselves in accomplishing the deity Wangchuk
   Chenpo,
killing sentient beings and offering their flesh and blood,
jealous and competitive to the end.
But your intention to harm the teachings of the Buddha
and Ling itself
will not come to pass.
Instead, you should seek refuge in the Three Jewels
and meditate upon me as your root guru.
If you understand that you must aspire to traverse this path,
it is possible that I can escort you all the way to the pure land.
Examine the truth of the words of this song.
There is little to be had from staring with such hateful eyes.
Through my inherent qualities,
that raging bonfire of your pride and delusion
will be extinguished with the water of my love and
   compassion.
Being frantic and frenzied will not help you;
I have come already as the lord of death,
and at this juncture, there is no escape.
Abandon your many schemes, your many stratagems.
If you wish bliss, you must have faith and devotion;
if not, do not even think that today you can be liberated.
Now is the time to distinguish between gods and demons.
You will burn alive,
purifying the burden of your negative obscurations,
bringing you to a path beyond good and evil.

These are honest and steadfast words.
If you have understood this song, answer joyfully.
If not, I cannot explain it.
Amnyé, keep this in mind.

The moment the song ended, with sparks flying from his hateful eyes, Amnyé stood up and transformed into Gulang. Full only of loathing and fierce pride, he had neither devotion nor respect for Gesar. But he realized, given Gesar's retinue and his incredible magic and invulnerability, that a military battle would be in vain and that he must count on his own black magic skills. Immediately, Amnyé's evil heretic black magic power substances burst into flame. Amnyé readied to throw them at Gesar and said, "You, the greatly famed Joru, I have been hoping to meet you, and, today, here you are, summoned by the divine Gulang Wangchuk Chenpo! Now, you must listen to my song, and I will speak frankly.

> Sing in the rhythm of "Tripa tridu trizhung."[17]
> The melody is the Bön Zhangzhung.
> Divine one of the māras, Gulang Wangchuk,
> surrounded by your retinue of one hundred thousand
>   assassins,
> come here in a flash of red lightning
> and assist in rooting out the enemy.
> This place is the fortress of Amnyé,
> and I am the man Amnyé Bumthub
> in whom dwells the life force of the evil heretics.
> I am the guru respected by all,
> one and the same as the divine Gulang (Wangchuk Chenpo).
> I am the support-dagger of the evil māras,
> their son who has attained the deathless iron life force
> and possesses the cure that raises the dead.
> Within me dwells the life force of the chieftains, Gurkar,
>   Gurser, and Gurnak,
> the Zhangzhung sovereign, the ruler Lutsen,
> the kings Shingtri, Yutsé, Sadam,
> the Takrong and Zikrong kings, and King Khaché.
> I am the life-support talisman of all māra kingdoms.
> All who see me request refuge;
> I am a man above all others.

You, the evil-mothered boy Joru—
how can you be called one of dharmic virtue?
You have destroyed everything;
how are you deserving of my admiration and devotion?
You, this divine form who displays himself as a magical
    illusion—
any magic you have, I can match.
Whatever your skills, I am equally adept.
Without great power in this life,
how can you know what will be in the so-called next life?
This corporeal body will be eaten by dogs and birds;
for mind to exist in that body is futile.
Fundamentally, a human is just a human.
Bamboo cannot turn to cedar,
wild rice cannot produce a harvest of barley,
nor can a boulder ever equal the size of the earth upon which
    it lies.
To say the impossible is possible would be a lie.
No truth can be seen in it.
Repeating this story will just hurt your ears.
If you cherish your life, you should leave;
if not and you oppose me,
using these heretic sorcery substances,
like a lightning bolt
pulverizing the mountainous cliffs,
I will shred your body.
Or else, I cannot lay claim to black magic.
Not only that, I have human skin that, when I wave it like a flag,
gathers up the life force and longevity of sentient beings,
and, what's more, a sharp butcher knife
that cuts the rocky crags to pieces when it strikes.
It's a pity to use it on weaklings like you!
Do not stay here; as fast as you can—go back home.
If you threaten me,
mark my words; I swear I will exact revenge.
You should think carefully.
Keep the true meaning of this song in mind.

Thus he sang, and hoping that Gesar might back off, Amnyé stood tall, glaring with hostility. Gesar retorted, saying, "You must know I have come too far to turn around now!" Amnyé lost control and hurled his black magic substances at Gesar. Momentarily, they sparked with blazing fire; however, Gesar's body had already ripened with the samādhi of emptiness-luminosity, and he was invulnerable. Then, Amnyé gave three tosses of his black flag,[18] but it did nothing except blow the air around a bit, and even though he thrust Gesar thrice with his knife, he might as well have stabbed a rainbow. However, the fighting was intense enough that the lha, lu, and nyen and the tsen protectors had to pull back a bit. Yet, it was already clear to Amnyé that he would not be able to defeat Gesar, and he tried to escape. Just as Amnyé mounted a magical camel, Gesar clutched him by the neck, pulling him down and binding him with his lasso like a ball of yarn. Then, wrapping Amnyé's body in oiled cotton, he placed it on a log pyre in the dark recesses of Amnyé's meditation cave. Gesar, chanting genuine aspiration prayers, burned Amnyé with wisdom fire and, not letting the smoke escape, sealed the cave with molten rock. Inside, the heretic Amnyé called out in pain, burning, and was liberated.

Then, at dawn, after five days, Gesar with his dralha retinue returned to the forested lowlands where Amnyé's wife Nyüljema Nakmo had remained. Gesar asked her to open the door of the twenty wealth treasuries, and as he reached toward her with the keys that she had previously given to him, she revealed herself to be a beautiful woman. She washed her hands of any uncleanliness and, gathering the monks and subjects, struck the stone knocker of the door of the Prosperity Cave that lay beneath a rocky crag of the mountain. The door opened into a crystal chamber luminous with the light of the water-crystal moonstone. Coffers of stones, maroon and various other colors, stood inside, and as Gesar revealed them, he called out their actual names, and from his enlightened mind, he sang a song of their great provenance, explaining in detail just how they were the basis of all wealth and enjoyments. Then, he spoke: "Doubtless, here is a great treasure of jewels that could be an inexhaustible source of wealth for Ling, but it comes with such a mix of good and bad, can any benefit really come of it? All the talismans of the heretic māra lineage, dedicated to the body-support of Gulang (Wangchuk Chenpo), must be burned. However, Nyüljema Nakmo, abiding by her promise, has already received transmission and gone for refuge; her respect for me and her yearning to be a Buddhist are apparent, yet it is uncertain that she will maintain samaya in the future." He went on, saying, "But now, what should be done with this country, its citizens, and so forth?" He conveyed his intention to follow the advice of the prophecy that he had been given.

"You handsome ones, all of you material and nonmaterial beings, have offered your wealth with purest intention. I speak candidly that this brings a good result—you have a refuge and protector and can be without worry. There is a reward for you; that goes without saying. I will advise my attendants that the jewels themselves must remain boxed for awhile, but you may drink this divine nectar." He presented the skull cup, and the māra gods drank whatever amṛta was given and fell into a state of drunken bliss, resting there.

From the enlightened mindstream of the long-life deities, Gesar invoked his guide Manéné, and she sang a song directing a course of action.

> OṂ MAṆI PADME HŪṂ
> Sing "Ala" and sing out the six-syllable mantra.
> Small and bright, "Thala" calls out to the gods and
> "La la" gives the perfect pitch.
> The song calls out to the Three Jewels.
> In the heart of Nakshö,
> this dark cliff that resembles a black snake slithering uphill
> is the ancestral residence of the heretic Amnyé,
> and now it is the meeting place of the deities,
> the land where the wealth treasury was revealed.
> I am Aunt Manéné,
> the one Gesar turns to when he is perplexed—
> not a common occurrence, as he is all-knowing.
> However, when he asks, we discuss and I advise him,
> but it is as though I was telling the sun what to do at dawn.
> These crimson jewels of Jang
> hold the siddhis of cultivating the five grains.[19]
> And there are thirteen more jewels;
> consecrate them all, place them within the deity statues of the
>   Ling monasteries.
> The siddhis will come to every territory.
> The swords in the heavy metal box
> are the ancestral swords of many kingdoms;
> distribute them to all those of good name.
> The white box full of various clothes—
> Buddhists in Ling have no use for them;
> some of the chiefs of the tribes
> could receive them on a special occasion.

The father and sons of the Thoktri tribe, all four
will find it difficult to pledge themselves to you.
Send them far away to the land of *yakṣas*
and give them weapons so that they can settle there.
The five kinds of silks worn as clothing,
the turquoise and coral inner adornments of the meditation
    room,
a small wish-fulfilling cup,
the magical knife, skull cup, *phurba*, and flag of human skin—
give those to Amnyé's wife Nyüljema
and command her to be in the retinue of Palden Lhamo.[20]
Until the teachings of Śākyamuni are perfected,
she is entrusted as a dharmapāla.
Within the meditation cave there is still more—
countless implements of gold and silver, among other things;
designate all those for the budget to build monasteries.
All that there is of the black magic substances
will enrich Tramo Ling
and constitute the excellent legacy of Tibet.
The day after tomorrow in the early morning,
with the chief Gyatsha Bumpa Zhalkar
commanding one thousand horsemen,
will be the time to receive you, the king.
All together, we will flourish
as the ten virtues become law
and an excellent legacy is imparted.
You must quickly reunite at the encampment,
bringing all of your forces,
and the bandits and raiders must all return home.
We [dralha and werma] will help as your guides.
As for the great wealth of the seven precious jewels,
each and every one
is a guiding ḍākinī emanation.
Those of the wilderness monastery Norgön (Wealthy
    Hermitage) in Minyak,
who helped themselves to the buddha statues—
because of their perverted views, put them into a deep dark
    pit.

Those one thousand buddha statues of the finest gold,
the Amitāyus and Medicine Buddha [statues]
of excellent quality and full of blessings,
and the many volumes of the *Prajñāpāramitā Sūtra*—
bring them all to a clean place and sprinkle them with
　　consecrated water,
purify any negativity with the supreme offering of ten
　　thousand lamps,
and return those treasures to Nakshö as their share.
Even so, this will leave more wealth than you can imagine,
all to enrich Tramo Ling.
Kharngön (Ancient Castle) of the Mu clan must die by a
　　lightning bolt,
and Trothung's minister Akhö Tharpa Zorna,
although he has a divine body, has transgressed samaya,
as has his son Muktsen (Maroon Power). They are no
　　different
and must be punished by the gods for breaking their
　　promises,
dying painfully from blood poisoning.
All the others you must take back to Ling.
The lake here is dried up, the fortress destroyed; only
　　devastation remains.
Unite the Düd [Yutsé's subjects] with those of Nakshö
　　[Amnyé's subjects].
Give them sovereignty over the one thousand districts of the
　　borderlands.
Doing that will be the catalyst of enlightened activity
that will soon reach its peak.
At the Zima mountain pass Namtri Barma,
rendezvous at the encampment on the great hill.
Distribute wealth to all the tribes
and make an offering in gratitude to the deities who have
　　assisted you.
Make sure none feel slighted.
Finally, return to your homeland of Ling
to happily engage in dharmic activity
and enjoy your family.

Divine heir, take this to heart.
If my song has errors, I am at fault.
If this is idle chatter, please forgive me.
Unrivaled one, keep this in mind.

At this counsel, Gesar rejoiced and offered a drink of warrior's amṛta liquor to the dralha and werma. In turn, Gesar was offered amṛta, and the excellent interdependent connections were spontaneously present as his wisdom channels opened and his qualities and strength blossomed. The tantras of the heretics and the life-support talismans of the māras were put into the iron box and then into the fire puja. The box burned but emitted no smoke. Gesar manifested in wrathful form and, with a large ax, pulverized the māra support; the iron box and its contents were now a mass of burning embers as he visualized the waning of the māra gods' power. With the nāga king Tsukna Rinchen, Gesar dug a deep pit to bury the ashes, and with a stupa on top to suppress the substances, he concluded with aspiration prayers. All that had happened became an auspicious sign that the strength of Gulang was declining, and that of Ling's was ascending, impervious to harm.

Gesar placed many precious ornaments and his vajra[21] into Nyüljema's hands, asking her to be in the retinue of Palden Lhamo. The veil of samaya violations that had tarnished the wealth was washed away by the divine ablution water ceremonies and purified by the lhasang smoke. The places of meditation practice were cleansed of defilements and became the gathering places of the Three Roots. Then, through that power, the rocky cliffs and the surrounding lands were flooded with rainbow light, flowers fell like rain, and the sweet fragrance of smoke permeated the land.

Around dusk, the great minister Gadé and his attendants burst like a gust of wind into the Ling encampment to report that, with the help of the gods, the māra king Yutsé had been tamed. Gadé instructed that they should invite Gesar and that, furthermore, they should welcome him with an escort party. He offered a song as he carefully considered who should be in the riding party and, without reservation, settled on Gyatsha, Denma, the two brothers Zikphen and Nyatsha, together with the diviner, the doctor, and the astrologer.[22] They set off in the company of three thousand cavalry troops, and for eight days, they traveled on a path rife with jackals, coming to a black earth wilderness inhabited by herds of wild drongs. Gesar already knew that they were coming and, in advance, had sent three hundred lha, lu, and nyen to greet them. First, Denma[23] offered a song asking who they were, all the while recognizing that these were the sublime deities sent by Gesar, and he offered thanksgiving, focusing his mind on these deities. The dralha and werma and humans alike were joyful and delighted. The riding party journeyed together beyond Dranak Mountain where, in the midst of the plains, was Gesar's encampment and they were reunited with Gesar and his ministers. The sun of happiness dawned, and darkness was illuminated. Gesar and the Phunu discussed every facet and, satisfied, brought the country together, offering both material wealth as well as supporting the māra princess to be their queen.[24] At that, carefree, all rested in a state of delight.

During this time, the māra kingdom had become a divine land of virtue. The hundreds of robes of the heretic lamas had been given to the tribal chieftains and, not to be squandered, the wealth of those same lamas had been loaded onto mules and horses. The welcoming party of Ling citizens that Gadé had sent forth ten days earlier had, by this time, met up with Gesar and his ministers along the mountain pass Namtri Barma as they were heading back toward the Ling encampment at thirteen great hills, and, little by little, the wealth had been distributed to them. The native māra people were overwhelmed at the wealth that the heretic lamas had accumulated. For three days, the welcoming party, along with Gesar and his ministers, remained there in a state of bliss and happiness.

CHAPTER EIGHT

The bandit country was conquered and harmony, established.
Icons were taken from the deep pit of darkness.
A dralha was born to Gyatsha's Queen,
and Gesar and the Lingites performed birth celebrations.

GESAR DECLARED THAT HE WOULD GO ALONE, farther into the lawless māra borderlands. At morning light, he departed with his miraculous steed Kyang Gö, along with a retinue of lha, lu, and nyen, and, like vultures, they flew to Drongnak Nying Dzong, the castle that had been Yutsé's, in the heart of the māra kingdom. There, Gesar's dralha protectress, the imposter Wangjema, welcomed him with a lhasang and cleansing water, and Gesar was seated. As the fortress filled with his illusory display—an army and its threefold panoply of bows, arrows, and swords—the māra king's thirty indentured servants fled and escaped to the mountains. Some jumped, tumbling chaotically down from the rocky overhang to fill the valley with shouts warning of Gesar and his troops' arrival. At the same time, the Wangjema impersonation blew a thighbone trumpet,[1] struck a drum of human skin and gestured with a black ram's tail. Those māra subjects who were far away ran farther, those who were a bit closer took off like unleashed dogs, and those who were powerless to flee woefully beat their chests, nearly unable to breathe. Wangjema, sitting cross-legged on a cushion, addressed them in song.

> Sing "Una thalu."
> "Thalu una" begins.
> All guardian deities—protect me, this woman,

and watch over me with your loving eyes.
May whatever my mind imagines be accomplished.
May all these words come true.
Everyone knows the history of this land.
I am the ravishing Wangjema,
the very foundation of this kingdom.
Long ago, I lay with those eight classes of haughty spirits,
conceiving each of my children.
Our happiness was consummate,
but not embracing this good fortune, we came to despise
Ling.
Instigated by Trothung's cruel scheming and provocation
by which he arrogantly convinced King Yutsé to dispatch his
entire bandit army,
in a matter of a month, it was all over.
Everything came to ruin; no one was left, not even the king
or his minister.
The situation is dire.
Not only that, yesterday
Gesar came with his minister and troops, united in strength.
Descending like rain pouring from the highest heavens,
surging like an ocean overflowing its depths,
raging like a piercing icy wind, the army came,
filling our fortress to the rafters.[2]
I cannot defeat them; I will lose my life.
Taking refuge in Gesar will be of greater help than parents or
friends.
If you have devotion, it is possible to aspire to a more
successful rebirth.
All you subjects who live here in these lawless lands,
everyone cherishes their own life,
everyone is attached to the wealth they have amassed,
and everyone loves their friends in mutual affection.
Therefore, the threshold of good and bad is upon us.
Time is not long, but neither is it short; it is upon you like
the length of a spear.[3]
If you were smart, you would take refuge.
There is an intermediate path between the sky and the earth,

and if you wish happiness, surrender.
It is pointless to be spiteful and vindictive.
Since our own deceitfulness was at the root of this quarrel,
we should not regret our defeat.
Those who are leaving and those who are staying
are all agreed.
The dead have no reason to remain with the living—
a warrior who dies, dies knowing full well his situation,
and a stallion that dies, dies in that same circumstance.
And, likewise, the living should not cleave to the dead.
Our own strategy was mistaken. We have been careless,
and, furthermore, our mistakes have come back to haunt us.
We should be careful about our situation.
As stated in the ancient Tibetan proverbs:

Even a rock as hard as a vajra can be demolished.
Even the sun and moon are born and die,
and ordinary time is impermanent, nothing but change.

Think this over, and better your frame of mind.
I am the mother of these many fine children;
these sorrows have not fallen upon others, but upon me.
Don't lament what has happened; it is the result of past
   karma.
We should offer all our accumulated ancestral wealth—
from that most valuable, stored in the tiger-skin box,
down to the least valuable, the iron chain that restrains the
   dog at the doorway—
to the son with the power to protect and the merit to receive
   this fortune,
to Gesar, with his ministers.
Everyone—from mothers down to children,
all the citizens left here—should ask for their life force and
   bodies to be protected[4]
and willingly accept whatever he commands.
This is the plan we agreed upon.
It would be best to quickly offer prostrations.
This is what I, your mother, pledged long ago,

and since this very life is not yet coming to an end,
what has been set in motion cannot be changed.
All of you present here, keep this in mind.

Thus she sang, and nearly everyone realized that they could neither escape to
freedom nor win by fighting. Moreover, Wangjema had been so unusually pleasant
that everyone was taken in and, with a roaring din, shouted that Gesar was their
sole refuge. The Wangjema impersonation went to Gesar on the crowd's behalf, and,
thereby, they all joined his retinue as subjects.

Gesar manifested many emanations of his body, speech, and mind and mag-
netized the worldly gods-demons. All those of the side of virtue worthy of respect
were bound by oath and appointed as devoted local guardians. The hosts of vicious
nonhumans, nāgas, and cannibal demons were expelled to the hinterlands. The des-
ecrated mountains and rivers were restored. The shrines of many local gods and the
lake of Dölpa Nakpo were obliterated, while the lake of the nāga Migön Karpo
(White Mahākāla) swelled. Thirteen terma treasures were revealed, and once again,
the representation of Guru Rinpoche, the cup of Vairocana, Yeshé Tsogyal's ear-
ring, and the thirteen scrolls scripted with enlightened speech were buried back
and sealed with aspiration prayers so that in the future they could be revealed again.

All the wealth of the samaya-violator māras was distributed equally to the
citizens; they were saved from the fear of being destitute. Norgön, Amnyé's wealthy
hermitage in Minyak, was dismantled and its contents distributed: the fine one
thousand Sri Lankan golden buddha statues and the Amitāyus statue were offered
to the nearby Ba Valley in Kham, along with eight large molded Medicine Buddhas,[5]
the golden statues of the Barol lineage, sixteen arhat statues from finest gold, 108
thangka paintings, and close to one thousand volumes of sūtra and mantra of which
the principal one was the *Prajñāpāramitā*. The bandits who had been confined in
a dark hole were released and bathed with ablution water, and they chanted and
gave offerings. Trothung was accompanied by his faithful ministers[6] who were to be
groomed as leaders of Ling, and each were given all that they needed and wanted.
Three māra bandits[7] were established in bliss through being guided to the pure
land. Those who met [Gesar] were joyous, feeling that he was like a father to them.
Amnyé's fortress had been destroyed, and the enlightened activity of the gods was
established. It was the dralha protectress who had bid all this to happen, bringing
the householders together and apportioning the wealth to them, naturally accom-
plishing all these activities without obstacle. This is the great marvel of Ling Gesar.

Then, as he traveled on horseback with his attendants for a fortnight, through
the colorful valleys of Zima, Gesar bound the cannibal demons by oath, after which

he gave extensive aspiration prayers and blessings for the future of that place. He arrived at the Ling encampment in the great hills with the entire welcoming party, along with all the māras who had come from the other side of the mountain. Senglön the Muchang chieftain of Ling arrived with one hundred horsemen, and everyone was joyously happy.

Gesar and his principal advisor Chipön, along with other dignitaries, had lively discussions as to how to proceed based on the divine prophecy. The following day, they prepared a spectacular feast in the tent, gathering everyone, those from Ling as well as those not from Ling, and set out great bounty—treasures, wealth, valuables, and abundant food and drink. Finally, Gesar gave spiritual speeches as everyone cheered. He revealed the treasury of all enjoyments and wealth. Then, Nyima Bumthub of the Serpa clan, following Gesar's instructions, offered the pure golden shrine objects and then distributed a *khal*[8] of gold to the lamas. He offered thirteen small golden protector cups to the gods, and golden powder to Tesé, an earth lord spirit who took the gold and became manifest as an embodied earth lord. Fifty gold coins went to the king, twenty-five to each of the distinguished elders, twenty to the Pathül leaders, fifteen to the division leaders, five to each soldier, and some to each of the citizens. Even then, much wealth was left over.

Afterward, Gyatsha, Gadé, Zikphen, Denma, and others joined together to make extensive offerings, and this event ended happily and successfully. The dralha protectress, greatly pleased, received reward and fulfillment offerings from Gesar, and, once again, she vanished, dissolving into rainbow light, but the māra bandits perceived this as though Wangjema had died.[9] Drawing on this, to show the māras how to clear away suffering, King Gesar gave teachings on impermanence. Nortsho (Wealth Ocean) and his sons were named as leaders of the country and, with the māra citizens, went back to the cliffs of Nakshö. An elaborate weeklong celebration ensued, as everyone was delighted with all that had been accomplished. At the close, the Pathül offered khatas to Gesar before returning home.

Upon the evening that he was about to return to his castle, Gesar's elder half-brother Gyatsha had a dream of a ḍākinī clad in robes and accoutrements of white. She spoke to him: "With heartfelt intent, you must place a victory banner white as a conch atop your fortress. If you supplicate Gesar and Gomchen Tingmé, you will quickly accomplish this." Gyatsha asked her who she was, and she replied, "I am White Tārā who arose from the tears of the Noble One Avalokiteśvara. The Great Compassionate Arhat Chenrezik (Avalokiteśvara) is your practice yidam." At her words, the day dawned, and Gyatsha awoke and went searching for Gesar and Gomchen to tell them of his dream. Gomchen replied, "As for that, according to the previous prophecy, if you supplicate the Three Jewels, it is certain that the divine heir of the victory banner of the teachings will appear. That is the meaning of your dream. If you invoke the enlightened mindstream of the divine ones by preparing a puja and feast, this will come to be." Then, Gesar continued, "Just as Gomchen has advised, you must make countless feasts and offerings in the temple. Eat no meat and give alms to dogs and beggars. Supplicate the divine ones above to not deceive you. If you do that, then all will ripen without obstacle." Gesar gave Gyatsha a stainless single-knotted scarf, and Gomchen gave him an icon card and returned to his meditation cave. Gyatsha arrived at his own castle Ngülchu Fortress, setting out unimaginable feast offerings. He invited the thirteen gurus from the distant monastery in Den and accumulated one hundred thousand feasts through the sādhanas of Cakrasaṃvara and Vajrayoginī.

Later, on the twelfth day of the first month of winter, Gesar and Gomchen invoked the enlightened mindstream of Guru Rinpoche. Light rays of the five colors in the form of the syllable HRĪ entered into the heart of Padmasambhava. From the guru's heart, the light rays of the five colors radiated out to the victorious ones of the ten directions, and with their blessings, the light rays gathered back, dissolving into Padmasambhava.[10] Once again, the five lights emanated from Guru Rinpoche's heart and came to rest in Chöphen Barampa of the ranks of vidyādharas; his essence appeared as a completely white syllable AH. The vidyādharas and lamas consecrated the ritual and performed special occasion practices. The ḍakas, ḍakinīs, dralha, and werma banished the demonic forces and then left the human realm. At their castle Ngülchu Trodzong, Gyatsha and his wife Rakza conceived a child. Four months later, they understood that she was pregnant with a son, and they asked the monasteries to read the Kanjur from beginning to end and to accumulate one hundred thousand feasts through the sādhanas of Cakrasaṃvara and Vajrayoginī. Alms from the thirteen monastic treasuries were given to the poor. A longevity golden bridge[11] of 1,028 rocks was created and one hundred thousand colored *tsatsas* were made. Having done all this, Gyatsha returned to Gomchen and Gesar to request long-life blessings. They answered, "Overall, what you have done is good, and now it would be best that the birthplace be the sacred red mountain cave of the dralha. Rakza should be attended by her trustworthy cousin Neuchung and by [Trothung's daughter] Künga Yutsho Tsokyi (Joyous Turquoise Lake). Sherab Wangmo (Prajñā Queen) from the Dru clan, Chipön's daughter Yudrön, and Denma's daughter Dzedrön have been with them, waiting for the birth in that mountain solitude for a month." In the Dragon year,[12] on the twenty-ninth day of the late summer month [July], she labored gradually and was closely attended at every stage, given medicines and precious relic pills. At sunrise on the third day of first month of fall [August], she gave birth to a son. Flowers rained down as

Neuchung, who was an emanation of Green Tārā, swaddled the baby in a white silk khata and sang this song of aspiration.

> OṂ MAṆI PADME HŪṂ
> Sing "Ala thala thala."
> "Thala" begins.
> Sing "Ala" to invoke the Three Jewels.
> Sing "Thala" free of cares.
> From Tārā's buddhafield, the Eastern Paradise Arrayed in
>   Turquoise Petals,
> atop a resplendent conch throne,
> Jetsün White and Green Tārās, know me.
> This son is the prince of the divine Mukpo Dong,
> born as the ornament of eastern Ling.
> May the mere sight of him quell all with splendor.
> Today is an excellent time in the constellations:
> eight excellent astrologic events have converged at sunrise.
> This stainless white cloth
> that came from the silk clothing of Brahmā
> was given to me by King Gesar,
> and today, the child will wear it.
> May the power and strength of the divine Brahmā
> henceforth be gathered into him,
> and may the military prowess of Gesar,
> when it is this child's turn to lead the world,
> take firm root in him.
> Great kind mother ḍākinī,
> cleanse him with purifying ablution water.
> May his kāya not be encumbered by wrongdoing.
> May his enlightened speech be unceasing.
> May his enlightened mind abound in wisdom.
> Chipön is the central pillar of Ling,
> and Yudrön,[13] you, his daughter,
> must cut the umbilical cord,
> severing the rope of delusion.
> May he attain a divine vajra body.
> Take from the precious engraved amulet box
> the queen of siddhis' long-life nectar,

adding the blessing substances of the thirty gurus.
Gesar has opened the gate to the treasure of Sheldrak,
    containing
the longevity nectar of Padmasambhava
mixed with the supreme medicines that cure one hundred
    diseases.
I offer all these to you, divine child.
May your head long remain beneath that white helmet, and
    may your hair grow white.[14]
May your body endure in that white armor, able to subdue
    the enemy.
May you wear the threefold panoply and nurture the world.
All-renowned Dharma king,
may your strength be famed throughout the worldly
    kingdom.
From the treasure of King Gesar comes
milk from the divine nāga prosperity *dri*[15]
and the lioness of Magyal Pomra,
along with the relic pills and the powerful nectar of the
    mother ḍākinīs—
three of you will offer these substances
and, as the baby takes them in his mouth, request aspiration
    prayers.
As I, the ḍākinī, hold pure samaya,[16]
certainly the auspicious aspiration prayers will be
    accomplished.
May you enjoy the delicious taste of this divine nectar.
The long-life arrow with the ribbons of five colors placed in
    your hands—
may you be adorned with all it represents.
May you be able to hold the kingdom of your father and
    uncles.
May you repay the kindness of your mother.
May your radiance, brilliance, and glory
pervade everywhere like the dance of the sun's rays.
May your body be as majestic as Mount Meru,
your mind as profound as the greatest ocean,
your power as great as that of Indra.

May your wealth be like that of the nāga king,
and may it become as abundant as that of Vaiśravaṇa the God
    of Wealth.
You are the regent of Padmasambhava;
may you turn the three realms to the Dharma.
You are the descendant of the Mukpo Dong;
may you not sever the lineage of divine teachings.
May you be the pillar that settles the six provinces of Ling.
I, this little goddess Neuchung,
was born a woman, but with an exalted body,
reincarnated in Tārā's buddhafield.
The Lesser Lineage is like a golden box;
I have never broken samaya with it.
Therefore, may these aspiration prayers of mine be fulfilled.
As I, the ḍākinī, hold pure samaya with my Dharma sisters
    and brothers,
may the truth of my auspicious words be accomplished.

While Neuchung spoke these words, the baby's mother Rakza first cleansed him with pure ablution water, and Yudrön severed the umbilical cord. Neuchung prepared the wish-fulfilling longevity water and the medicinal pills that cure one hundred diseases. The milk of the nāga prosperity dri, the milk of the lioness, and the relic pills and the elixir of the ḍākinīs were offered to the baby by Dzedrön, Künga Yutsho, and Druza Sherab. They did not sing a song, but with the murmuring sound of bees humming, they offered aspiration prayers with confidence in the Three Jewels, wishing the newborn all good fortune. Through the power of perfect samaya of these spiritual friends with the wisdom exaltation ḍākinīs, their words came true: the boy had great authentic presence, enjoyments and abundance, freedom from illness, auspiciousness, and long life. Dralha and werma gathered rainbow clouds, rained down flowers, and consecrated barley in order to remove obstacles. The favorable tendrel of the flourishing of the Lesser Lineage was established.

For three weeks after the birth,[17] the women made joyful feast offerings. Then, Gyatsha with nine attendant horsemen rode with his newborn son to the high mountain meditation cave where they came before[18] Gomchen Tingmé, and, in order that the child would be impervious to the stains of samaya violations, Gyatsha requested the cleansing ritual and long-life empowerment. Gomchen gave the long-life empowerment titled White Tārā Wish-Fulfilling Wheel, saying: "According to ancient prophecy, this child will be the lineage son of Mukpo Dong and the king of the six provinces of Ling, the ally of King Gesar, a loving and reliable friend,[19] and the steady pillar uniting the people of Ling. His fame will reach throughout Jambudvīpa, the dralha will naturally surround him, and he will be the pinnacle of the werma. As a hero victorious and brave in battle, from now on he will be called Dralha Tsegyal (Victorious Mountain Peak Dralha)." He bestowed this name with a knotted scarf and a protection cord of the sublime ancestral ones, along with the lamas who were offering many material gifts and longevity empowerments. They returned to Gyatsha's castle and then went on to Gesar's fortress Sengdruk Taktsé to a boundless feast of food and gifts for the birth celebration of Lhasé Dralha, born as the son of the Mupa leader Gyatsha. Everyone was asked to come to the gathering place between the upper, lower, and middle valleys. Those of status as well as commoners came and gathered at the divine castle, each offering a khata to the sovereign Gesar and then sitting down to enjoy drinks of tea and chang. The moment Gyatsha was seated on the throne with his newborn son, the patriarch Chipön offered many great gifts and praises and, setting down a [Margyen] life and prosperity container,[20] sang a song of good fortune. Assuming his seat, Gesar himself gave the offerings that had been arranged by his inner ministers and then sang this fervent aspiration prayer.

> OṂ MAṆI PADME HŪṂ
> Sing "Ala thala."
> "Thala" begins and
> "La la" gives the melody.
> From the palace of the Glorious Copper-Colored Mountain,
> Lotus-Born One and the ocean of vidyādharas—
> I supplicate you to look upon me with compassion.
> May this song fulfill all aspiration prayers.
> Divine Brahmā, Nyen Gedzo,
> Tsukna Rinchen, and Magyal Pomra, with your one hundred
>   thousand attendants—
> today please come to assist me.
> May you help these fervent prayers become true.
> This land is the castle where the king and minister gather.
> Here is the palace where the spiritual and the worldly act in
>   concert.
> If you do not recognize me,
> while I was in my mother's womb unsullied by kleśas,
> before I was transferred into a human body,

I was the emanation of the protectors of the three families;
I was all the buddhas
and the regent of Orgyen Padma.
Now that I have obtained a human body,
I am the destined son of King Senglön,
the pillar of the Lesser Lineage,
and the king presiding over the rise of Ling.
My elder brother is Gyatsha Zhalkar.
He offered this gaṇacakra feast to the divine Three Roots
and recited the profound teachings of the Victorious One.
He honored the beggars with his generosity
and requested help from all the lamas
that the wishes for his son would be fulfilled.
This boy is the heart-son of the Three Jewels,
the essence and lineage holder of Chöphen Nakpo,
the supreme glory of the Lesser Lineage reaching the azure
    firmament,
flourishing, all-pervading as the rising sun and moon.
All wishes will be spontaneously accomplished.

The lioness has great power as does her cub.
The horned wild drong is awesome as is her calf.
The tiger has six smiles mirrored in its cubs.

Today, a great warrior is born to the Mukpo Dong;
the power to transform the temporal world is in the palm of
    his hand.
Nine different silk khatas
knotted into a longevity crossed vajra,
nine abiding ribbons
sway colorfully, tied as a protection-cord necklace,[21]
a Buddha statue of finest gold,
a statue of Tārā endowed with blessings,
a text of *The Sūtra of Excellent Eons*[22] scribed in gold ink, and
a special stupa monument representing the Buddha's
    auspicious descent from Tuṣita—
today all these are offered to you that you may remain firmly
    in this world.

That this divine kingdom of power and wealth
will gradually come under your authority as you mature
is my auspicious aspiration prayer.
Dralha Nyentak Marpo,
just as you protect me, Gesar,
may no obstructing spirits harm this boy Dralha Tsegyal.
Elder brother Dungkhyung Karpo, younger brother Ludrül
    Öchung,
sister Thalé Ökar,23
and Aunt Manéné,24
together with all the dralha and werma—
protect this boy, Dralha Tsegyal.
May the harmful obstructing spirits be dispelled.
May the great evil spirits not be allowed to kidnap him.
May the lesser evil spirits not be allowed to slip away with
    him.
May he not fall under the sway of the black magic of Bönpo
    and monks.25
May the gods and lamas grant their blessings.
May he obtain long life.
May he never be separated from the *yabyum* yidam
    Hayagrīva-Vajrayoginī.
May he accomplish the ordinary and extraordinary siddhis.
May he keep company with the oath-bound protectors.
May he have great authority and powers of communication.
May he be sustained by all the wealth deities.
May his wealth swell like the ocean.
May the dralha naturally surround him.
May he rule the three-thousand-fold world.
May the werma come to him effortlessly.
May he suppress with splendor all the kingdoms of the world.
May he be the yoke upon the necks of the hateful enemy.
And may the minds of the Phunu be able to rely upon him.
Just as I, Gesar, have acted with virtue,
may he quell the secular world in his own right
and be a king among kings.
May he be a sovereign leader
and the lord over those with the threefold panoply.

> May he be as exalted as the azure firmament
> and a pillar as abiding as the solid earth.
> May the country of Ling continue to flourish,
> its vigor ordained at this moment by the gods.
> May all this come true in his lifetime.
> May the mind of this world turn toward the Dharma.
> May happiness be abiding.
> Until I perfect the benefit of beings,
> may you, Tsegyal, live your life without obstacles
> and accomplish the aspirations of your elders
> and my own fervent prayers.
> May the divine Three Jewels attest to this.
> May these words be accomplished.

Thus he sang this dohā, bestowing protection and support and, although the baby was tiny, he was a divine manifestation and was able to hold the statue and the long-life khata. Everyone heard him laugh three times.

The Pathül warriors of Ling rejoiced, and the tendrel of joy and happiness was spontaneously present. Denma Jangtra, the emanation of Saraha, the pillar of the earth, the adversary of the spiteful enemy, the division leader of the army, who was indispensable to Ling, had already prepared many offerings and entrusted the seven coral-hatted ministers to present them, while he himself offered five various colored khatas to the sovereign Gesar. Then, holding three fine silk khatas and standing at the end of the row of those seated on a fine blue carpet, he sang[26] and then took his own place at the head of the right-hand row on a tiger-skin cushion.

Similarly, all the ministers of repute of the six provinces made feast offerings commensurate with the importance of the occasion and after five days, in keeping with their stature, celebrated the close of the event by donating nine stallions, seven dzo, six cakes of each of five Chinese teas, and a threefold set of the finest swords. Dralha Tsegyal continued to be cherished, and, while his attendants[27] cleansed, fed, and suckled him, the gods, nāgas, dralha, and so forth protected him. Because of that, when he was just a month old, he was bigger than a three-year-old, could walk, and was strong and endowed with many auspicious signs.

CHAPTER NINE

In accord with Manéné's predictions, Gesar
spoke of the fact that he would go alone to the north.
Drukmo did not think that he should go,
but Chipön clarified the reasons.

THEN, ON THE NINETEENTH DAY of the middle month of summer of the
Tiger year,[1] as daylight was fading, the peak of the mountain wore a golden hat,
and the lake below was struck with golden drops. Constellations appeared in mul-
titudes across the vast Tibetan sky, but even before the Pleiades rose in the east,
from the domed rainbow sphere of the highest reaches of the thirteen heavens[2]
came Manéné mounted on a white lioness. She led a white buffalo, and a turquoise
dragon followed behind. In her right hand she held a long-life vase, and with her
left she scattered consecrated grain as she crooned a dohā. One hundred thousand
ḍākinīs surrounded her as she came, the divine castle was enveloped by the roaring
sound of the turquoise dragon, flowers rained down, and the snow lion displayed
its turquoise mane. From that dome of rainbow light, Manéné came, saying, "Ya
a! All-powerful, enlightened King Gesar! Do not sleep; get up and listen! There
are many things I have to tell you. In the proverbs of the ancient people of Tibet,
it is said that: *Just as a fox cannot help but howl until it collapses when a demoness
slaps its face, and a dog cannot help but bark when there is a burglar beating down
the door,* Manéné cannot help but come! At the urging of the divine dharmapālas
and guardian spirits, I, your little sweetie auntie, have come. Please listen carefully
to this song."

Sing "Ala thala thala."
"Thala" begins.
The song unfolds in three parts.
Today, I invoke the gods.
From your dwelling place, the sacred palace of dharmadhātu,
Vajravārāhī of the mother lineage, know me.
Assist me without wavering.
From Tārā's buddhafield,
from the palace of Akaniṣṭha,
from a seat atop a lofty golden throne,
revered White and Blue Tārās, all of you—
listen without distraction to this motherly song.
From the dharmakāya pure realm of great bliss,
from atop your golden peacock throne,[3]
supreme king Amitābha,
please grant your blessings of compassion.
If you do not recognize this place,
it is the maṇḍala of divine Ling in the east,
the celestial realm of Vajravārāhī.
In the very center of the world
is the land of Ma, this land of supreme joy,
and here rises the castle Sengdruk Taktsé.
It is the land where the tigers, lions, dragons, the three, pose
    majestically;
thus, the castle is named Sengdruk Taktsé.
This is the divine palace that sustains happiness,
the divine dharmakāya, *saṃbhogakāya*, nirmāṇakāya.
Here dwell the objects of refuge, the buddhas of the three times.
Of course, you recognize me.
Near the border of India
at the sacred Asura Cave,[4]
I am the one known as the great mother
from the highest reaches of the thirteen heavens,
Ama Manéné Karmo.
If you do not recognize this song,
it is the pure song of Manéné.
I do not sing this song casually, just anywhere, anytime.
It is for a special occasion, not an everyday melody.

However, today I have no choice but to sing it,
as it is crucial given the current circumstances.
Please awaken; do not sleep!
I will give you some examples:

When the chieftain sleeps, the laws of the land slumber.
When fathers and uncles sleep, no words leave their mouths.
When warriors sleep, the enemy lies at the door.
When women and daughters sleep, homes suffer.
When a baby sleeps too much, games wither away.
Fathers who sleep have no good qualities.
Rocks and stones that lie motionless fuse together.
Sandalwood trees topple when roots decay.

What is happening is no different than these words.
Today, my dear one, listen to me.
Now, you are fifteen years old.
Boys of fifteen have reached manhood;
they understand the intricacies of the salt trade.
Girls of fifteen have reached womanhood;
they have perfected the skill of churning butter.
A man begins as a small boy
but becomes a fierce warrior quelling the four enemies with
    splendor.
A horse begins as a small foal
but becomes a spirited horse journeying the four continents.
Likewise, you must not remain here.
Among the upper regions of the eight mountain ranges of the
    north
dwells Lutsen, the demon king of māras.
He is not like other great māras;
rather, he has taken rebirth as the evil death lord.
Human flesh, horse flesh, dog flesh for one,
and human blood, horse blood, dog blood for another—
that māra demon will be swift to both flesh and blood.
Before midday, he will go to westward to India.
There, he will go on a killing rampage in the monasteries,
slaughtering the golden-hatted lamas.

Nine hundred of those dressed in Dharma robes will be killed,
and the villagers dwelling there
will be devoured by that demon.
Before nightfall, he will go eastward to China.
There, he will slay the judicial officials,
killing those with feathered black hats.
Nine hundred of those dressed in silk brocade will be killed.
All the inhabitants of China
will be devoured by that demon.
During the daytime, he will roam the four regions of Central
    Tibet,
spreading storms over the three thousand worlds.
Fear will grip every district.
He will devour one hundred men while they are walking up,
he will devour one hundred women while they are walking
    down,
and he won't be able to resist devouring small children.
First, to the west in Beré is the best sheep fortress,[5]
second, in between in Balpö is the middling sheep fortress,
and third, east in Amdo is the lesser sheep fortress[6]—
all have corrals for both goats and sheep.
He flung slaughtered he-goats to the right
and she-goats to the left.
Hundreds of sheep were thrown aside.
He will snack on hundreds of sheep,
he will chomp down on hundreds of rams
and hundreds of ewes
and pop many baby lambs into his mouth—
still he will be hungry for meat and thirsting for drink!
Like all māras of the north, he is a horned demon
with a single horn eighteen armspans in length;
the females have a single copper horn[7]
that is eighteen armspans in length.
His head is as awesome as a cliff
and coiled with a white poisonous snake.
His torso is countless armspans in length
and coiled with a black poisonous snake.
It is as though nāga demons escaped to the snow mountains.[8]

Since he looks like a flesh-eating savage tsen,
Lutsen became his name.[9]
There are three brother nāga demons:
the eldest is called Chakchung Gyalpo (Small Iron Gyalpo
    Spirit),
the youngest, Mukchung Gyalpo (Small Maroon Gyalpo
    Spirit),
and the middle one is Achung Gyalpo (Small Ah Gyalpo
    Spirit).
Now, it is time to subdue these three.
Lutsen is the demon that was known as Achung
and this year he will be sixty-nine years old.
If they are not subdued immediately when the nines come
    together,[10]
then the chance will be lost.
Today, my dear Gesar,
you must not stay—but go, and go quickly.
At the Crystal Cave Sheldrak,[11]
reveal the nine weapons and armor of the dralha;
reveal your nine body armors.
Now is the time for you to display your true self.
First, eighteen ancestral treasure chests,
second, the twelve volumes of the *Prajñāpāramitā*[12]—
their revelation will be an auspicious connection.
From the dharmic land[13] of India,
from dharmadhātu, the supreme steed
Kyang Gö, the all-knowing steed,
is presently a few years old.
Now, he can run like the wind
without his hooves touching the ground
and soar[14] like a bird
untouched by the currents of the wind.
Both Gesar and his horse have magical channels and winds
and, today, must head north to subdue the māras.
Gesar, on your journey north,
the lha, lu, and nyen will be your allies
and, along with the great god Brahmā
and his divine army of eight billion,

even now they are setting out.
The Nyenchen Kulha Gedzo,
with an army of 990,000,
even now is setting out.
The nāga king Tsukna Rinchen
with a nāga army of thousands, hundreds of thousands—
even now is setting out for the upper lands of the north.
And I, being both your dralha sister Manéné Göcham Karmo
as well as your fierce mother Drubpé Namné Karmo,[15]
with my retinue of hundreds of thousands of mother ḍākinīs
will depart with you.
A retinue of eighteen warrior dralha
and an entourage of dharmapālas will accompany you.
Among the upper regions of the eight mountain ranges of the
     north,
in the east was built the fortress
of nine stories, Shazen Chakri Tsegu (Nine-Storied Demon
     Iron Enclosure),
to the south was built the fortress
Sharu Rimpa Namdzong (Flesh- and Bone-Layered Sky
     Fortress),
to the west was built the fortress
Düla Drongra Mukdzong (Māra Spirit Horned Drong
     Maroon Fortress),
and to the north was built the fortress
of nine stories, Dükhar Shomo (Shomo Māra Castle).
The central fortress
is the castle Thönpo Jagö Pungri (High Vulture Peak),
the palace of Akyi Meza Bumdrön (Lady of One Hundred
     Thousand Torches from Akyi).[16]
Like a cuckoo awaiting the rain,
she waits for you, Sengchen, to come
and will assist you in bringing down the demon of the north.
Ninety-nine days from now,
you must shoot the demon in the forehead with an arrow.
Little by little, you will figure out the best plan.
Supreme Being Gesar, keep this in mind.
If you did not understand, I cannot sing again.

Thus she finished her song, and Manéné vanished like a rainbow. Gesar was a little reluctant but nevertheless thought that he should abide by the celestial prophecy, and, at dawn, he went to the highest rooftop of the divine castle and beat the massive official governmental drum with a din that pervaded the eighteen kingdoms and sounded the conch trumpet with a prolonged call that broadcast throughout the land. Flags were hoisted, and a gong reverberated. Messengers and messages were sent out to tell everyone to assemble, and as soon as everyone was gathered, Gesar's father Senglön, his mother Gokza, his wife Drukmo, and his cousin Neuchung presented themselves. Drukmo spoke to Gesar, "Last night, a great sound arose from the empty heavens. That this great sound reverberated from the dharmakāya—is it true that this a good sign? Or is it bad? Either way, I have some things to tell you." Then, she offered chang from the gilded copper bowl followed by tea from the silver-plated copper bowl and finally yogurt from the conch-covered copper bowl, asking Gesar what magical signs and predictions had come to him.

Gesar had in fact received many divine prophecies. Chipön, the four division leaders, and the ministers of the Greater, Lesser, and Middle Lineages each settled into a seat according to rank, and King Gesar sang this vajra warrior's song of the way the prophecy had arisen.

> Sing "Ala thala thala."
> "Thala" begins.
> The song unfolds in three parts.
> It is time to call upon the Buddha.
> From the celestial maṇḍala,
> Bhagavan of the Five [Buddha] Families, know me.
> Please come to assist this brave warrior.
> Manifest from your seat in dharmic India.
> Bhagavan Śākyamuni, know me.
> Please come now to assist me.
> From the pinnacle of the red Jokhang Temple in Lhasa,
> Jowo Śākyamuni, know me.
> Please establish the sentient beings of the six realms in bliss.
> Please watch over them. Avert their fall to the hell realms.
> From Tārā's buddhafield, Paradise Arrayed in Turquoise
>   Petals,
> seated upon your resplendent conch seat,
> from its towering roof of gold,
> revered Green and White Tārās,

today please watch over the affairs of the warriors.
If you do not recognize this place,
it is the pure land of Ling in the east,
and within these lovely hillsides of Ma sits the plain Takthang
    Tramo (Colorful Tiger Plain),
whose colors resemble the taut skin of a living tigress.
If you do not recognize me,
from the Turquoise Valley of Lower Ma,[17]
I am the little minister called King Joru,
and even before I turned thirteen years old,
I knew how to establish Ling
and fought for its sovereign throne.
The stories of my birth are famed throughout the world.
Then, at the age of thirteen,
I opened the marvelous treasure gate to the Crystal Cave
    Sheldrak.
First, the divine prosperity of the world
and second, the wish-fulfilling armor and weapons of the
    dralha—
these treasures are incalculable
and are the inner essence[18] of this divine fortress.
Weary of a year of fighting, the enemy wished respite,
but just suddenly today,
the prophecy of the highest gods appeared,
and it is like these examples:
on the pinnacle of Mount Meru,
the day the great garuḍa bird settles on its nest,
a poisonous black snake arrives to welcome it,
and the great garuḍa has no choice but to fly away.
On the pinnacle of the lofty white mountains,
the day the snow lion makes its way on the snowy slopes,
the turquoise dragon threatens with an angry roar,
and the snow lion is compelled to answer.
The day the small gray mountain drong
roams the rock-strewn pastures,
it is startled by a snow leopard crouching between the rocks,
and the little drong is pushed to act fierce.
In the marshlands and alpine meadows,

as the great stags graze,
hunting dogs appear in pursuit,
and the stags are forced to run over ridge after ridge.
Across the great meadowlands,
wherever the small kyang graze,
nonhuman spirits, gods-demons, load them up to ride,
and the small kyang have no choice but to bolt.
As the raging tiger of the sandalwood forest
roams its southern jungle fortress,
the hunter comes with a nocked arrow,
and the tiger has no choice but to be strong.
In the great swirling ocean,
when the golden fish play,
a powerful iron hook comes to snare them,
and the golden fish cannot help but be agitated.
I, this young minister of Ling,
as the intricacies of the divination naturally revolve
and as the Dharma teachings of the divine masters are
    accomplished,
will bring to bear the prophecy of the highest gods.
The day before yesterday, wise Brahmā,
Nyenchen Kulha Gedzo,
and the nāga king Tsukna Rinchen
put forth the many prophecies
directing that I not stay but, instead, go to tame the northern
    lands.
Last night at sunset on the great nineteenth day,
when over there it was still light out
and over here it was still light out,[19]
Manéné brought down the prophecy.
High in the lands of the north, among the eight mountains
    ranges,
the demon Lutsen will have come to slaughter humans.
The earth and sky will be shrouded by the vapor of māras,
human blood will rain down from above
and, as though a blizzard filled the sky, minds will swirl with
    confusion,
and below, the vast plains will be strewn with flesh and bones.

Realizing all this, I must go north.
That demon of the north, Lutsen,
is a man of sixty-nine
and this is the year an arrow will pierce his skull.
What has been prophesied will come to pass.
I, Gesar, am compelled to be fierce,
and the warriors of Ling are duty bound to assemble.
With no choice but to tame the northern māras,
I cannot stay but must go north.
Ninety-nine days from now,
I will shoot the māra demon with an arrow
and bring his betrothed Meza back with me.
Isn't this how it is, Pathül warriors?
Did you understand, Chipön?
Did you hear, Drukmo?
Are you pleased, my kind mother and father?
Please take this to heart.
If you did not understand, I cannot repeat my song.

After they heard Gesar's song, the Lingites sat silently looking at each other. Drukmo's face shone full as the waxing moon when, as suddenly as storm clouds raining onto dark barren rocks, she burst into this song of emptiness.

Sing "Ala thala thala."
"Thala" begins.
Today, I call out to the gods.
From the buddhafield of the supreme dwelling place,
mother of transcendent knowledge, Prajñāpāramitā, know
    me.
Please bestow the blessings of your compassion.
From the buddhafield of Akaniṣṭha,
mother lineage five ḍākinīs, know me.
Khachöma, please assist me.
From the palace of dharmadhātu throughout the three times,
Vajrayoginī, know me.
Today, consider my situation.
If you do not recognize this place,
it is the thousand-pillared reception hall.

If you do not recognize me,
in a past life
I was White Tārā,
a ḍākinī unlike any other.
If you do not recognize this song,
it is Drukmo's melodic and piercing song, "Six
    Reverberations."
From the home of Kyalo, I came to be Gesar's wife.
For a year, I have stayed in this royal castle,
yet I still have no seat.
Throughout your youth,
before you reached the age of thirteen,
your hair was disheveled,
its matted ends dangling like yak hair,
a cushion for lice and their eggs.
Snot dripped, smearing your face
and hanging down to your chest.
On one hand, you were blackish like a crow,
and then again, pale yellowish like an owl.
The way you were, Joru,
and how you looked—
it all added up to wretched misery.
I certainly suffered,
and Neuchung suffered along with me.
Then, last year,
when you reached the age of thirteen
and your body had accrued the six marks of bravery,
you opened the door to the treasure cave Sheldrak.
The day that the Ling Pathül competed in the horse race,
you revealed your true appearance
to be like that of the full conch moon.
Like sunbeams striking the snowy mountains,
it was marvelous to all who saw it
and in delight we gathered, as now the king's castle was yours.
Now you say that you received a divine prophecy
directing you to go to the upper land of the north.
Are you certain of this divine prophecy?
Are you sure it is not a false prophecy?

Could it be that you are just going after that deceitful
    woman?
High in the north are the eight mountain ranges
ruled by the demon King Lutsen.
In keeping with previous karma, he must be tamed,
just as a needle picks out a thorn.
There is a time to shoot an arrow:
age-old is the advice that
acting rashly bears no fruit.
A young warrior who leaps impulsively into the enemy's
    mouth
will be defeated and must retreat.
Suppose that happens, how mortifying!
Chieftain Joru slips away into the north—
is it really to tame the māra demon?
More likely you are after that girl,
Trishok Meza Bumdrön of the north.
That daughter of the Akyi family of Ling
is as arrogant as if she imagined herself the sky
with the azure firmament as her hat
and white clouds for a chin strap.
Her boasting rolls off her tongue like boulders down a
    mountainside.
Everything she says is lies and deceit.
The whole world knows it.
You, the king supposedly going to tame the north,
in fact, are just pursuing Meza.
Aren't you ashamed, Gesar?
Aren't you disgraced, Joru?
If you say you are going to the north,
then for sure I, Drukmo, will go with you
even if it is my karma to die there.
Just as it says in the proverbs:

On a flat, grassy alpine meadow
are many stags and does, grazing.
The stags are wont to roam the high mountain peaks,
the fawns to run between,

and the does to follow along the lowland foothills.
Bird families are wont to soar the heavens.
The father birds soar to the heights,
the young chicks use the power of their developing wings,
and the mother birds soar below, ready to catch them.

Gesar, you say you plan to leave,
just you and your horse,
but I am not letting you go so easily.
I will come with you
and bring Neuchung along.
The great Ling people and the Pathül warriors gathered here
are frightened by your song. Yet there is still more:
Gesar, think about what you are doing—
first, the great mother consort Queen Gokza,
second, the great father consort King Senglön,
third, four great and wise men of Ling,
fourth, your wife Drukmo, and Neuchung—
you think it is so easy to walk away.
Do you think it is so easy to do what you want?
Chieftain Joru, keep what I have told you in mind.
This maiden will not repeat her song.

Thus the song was finished, and Gesar's father Senglön and his mother Gokza sat silently, not knowing what to say. The thirty Pathül warriors that had converged on Takthang Tromo resplendent in rainbow-hued armor had taken their respective seats with Senglön and Gesar. Those in the right-hand row were like the rising sun, those in the left-hand row like the waxing moon, those in the rows between were strewn like stars, and the last row strung like flowers. King Gesar sat atop a precious blazing golden throne as though he were the full moon rising, presiding over the sky. All the maidens of Ling, smiling, offered tea and chang to the contentment of all who sat there. Seated across from Gesar on the white conch seat of his turquoise throne, Gyatsha Zhalkar offered this song.

Sing "Ala thala thala."
"Thala" begins.
The song unfolds in three parts.
Now, today, I call out to the gods.

From the dwelling place, the palace of the excellent victorious
    one,
Conqueror Vairocana, know me.
From the maṇḍala of the secret gathering,
great and mighty deity, know me.
There are no gods higher than you to supplicate.
If you do not recognize this place,
it is Takthang Tromo, the Colorful Tiger Plain of the hills
    of Ma.
It resembles the stretched-out skin of a living tiger.
This assembly hall of one thousand pillars
encloses 1,022 buddhas.
The 108 great doors
encircle the one hundred peaceful and wrathful deities.
This assembly of deities is the excellent connection.
From the ninety of high rank,
from atop this white conch seat,
if you do not recognize a person like me,
from the iconic fortress Ngülchu Trodzong,
I am the steadfast warrior Gyatsha Zhalu of Bumpa.
To the subjects of the southern continent,
I am a man difficult to defeat.
There are many who imagined defeating me,
but to find someone capable was difficult.
If you do not recognize this song,
it is one of the Six Melodies of Purity.[20]
High ones, listen from the forested mountain;
low ones, listen from the sylvan riverbanks.
When you listen, perk up your ears.
When you look, open your eyes wide.
From your jeweled throne,
powerful noble being, listen to me.
Sent down by the gods, you no longer dwell in the higher
    realms.
In turn, we warriors left our homelands to gather here,
and drawn by our presence, soldiers came,
arriving speedily on horseback.
Now is the time to join forces and act together.

There is no benefit to just sitting around.
A coward who flexes his muscles
just shows his own weakness;
a horse that trots without a trained gait
brings on public ridicule.
Hoping an unbroken horse can race
may get you to the plain of Achen
but not across the high mountain pass.
The young man who talks big
can put some things over on brainless men,
but those schemes will not stand in the court of law.
Don't you think so, King Gesar?
Noble being, King Sengchen,
you said that you received a divine prophecy
stating that you can go it alone,
with only your horse
and a single sword drawn.
That is a lot of loud boasting.
Even those who did not see it with their own eyes
heard about it from a distance.
Demon Lutsen Gyalpo
has strength said to be unrivaled,
with eyeteeth made of steel
and lower teeth of copper.
In the morning, he devours one hundred children,
at midday one hundred men,
and at night one hundred women,
humming while he chews.
He has filled the three thousand worlds with blood
and heaped the lower valleys with corpses.
I heard that his eyeteeth are as sharp as butcher's knives
and his māra horn is unsurpassed.
His larger horn is massive,
said to have the strength of solid iron.
His lesser horn is still impressive,[21]
tensile as red copper.
That fearsome Yama lord of death, hero of the māras,
brave Joru of Ling, do you think he will buy your story?

You said that you are going to the north alone,
claiming that as the prophecy of the highest gods
and in accord with Meza's future.
If you look at it carefully, is it a divine prophecy?
Perhaps it is Meza's trickery
or an obstacle created by the māras.
You had better be sensible.
The problem is immense, but my point comes down to this:
if, as you are saying, you were to leave alone,
we warriors of Ling feel that we cannot stay behind.
Even if the signs are against us, we would go.
Here are some examples. Isn't this the way it is?
Every person has a name,
every stallion has a saddle,
every weapon has a handle,
and every chieftain has a minister and servants.
The right flank is in white, that of Bumpa,
fifty thousand able-bodied troops.
The left flank is in black, that of Takrong,
fifty thousand troops with black pennants.
The central great brigade, one after another,
fifty thousand troops with yellow pennants.
They have all volunteered, primed to tame the demons of the
    north.
The stage is set with the troops mustered,
the women in right and proper dress,
the horses perfectly saddled and tacked.
Astride his deep-brown Amdoan horse
is the chieftain himself with an entourage of ministers.
Citizens of Ling, keep this in mind.
Sovereign Sengchen Gesar, look upon us with your
    enlightened mind.
If my song has been at fault, please forgive me.
If my words bring confusion, I openly confess.

Thus he sang, and Gesar Norbu Dradül answered, "An excellent song, Gya-tsha. As you said, when the leaders escape, the servants are destined to escape, and, likewise, when the horses escape, their saddles come with them. But, Gyatsha, all

you eighteen excellent leaders of Ling, listen! I will elucidate the hazards of a north-
ward journey." So saying, he sang.

> Sing "Ala thala thala."
> "Thala" begins.
> The song unfolds in three parts.
> Right now, I call to the gods.
> Gods above, know me; Brahmā, know me.
> Gods of intermediate space, know me; Nyenchen Kulha,
>   know me.
> Gods below, know me; nāga king Tsukna, know me.
> Courageous dralha and werma assist me.
> Divine dharmapālas, lead my song.
> If you do not recognize this place,
> it is the great assembly hall of one thousand pillars, Kawa
>   Tongden.
> I am the man high atop a golden throne,
> the unrivaled Gesar Gyalpo.
> When we reached the new year,
> I turned fifteen,
> and the power of my six skills is fully developed.
> A bird with new wings and feathers
> all day soars the heights,
> unafraid of wind or cold.
> A young racing horse
> easily roams the plains with a grand gait,
> fearless on the high mountain pass.
> I, this bold young man,
> will flaunt my bravery to the māra clans.
> I have no fear of the four great māra demons.
> Today, Gyatsha, Chief Zhalu of Bumpa,
> I have several stories. Listen.
> There in the eight mountains deep in the north,
> the demon king Lutsen
> is not easily able to be defeated.
> One, I have sharp weapons that can cut flesh,
> two, a fast racing horse,
> three, an encampment of strong warriors around me,

but I have not yet faced the demon of the north.
On first approach to the north,
at the borderlands one glimpses the slate rocks[22]
and beyond, her stark, vast, red northern plains
where demons and cannibals assemble,
the gathering place of the thirteen types of teurang.
One is called Lungi Kyelwa Khadang (Wide-Open Sack of
    Wind).[23]
It will be difficult to cross this land
since high above its slate mountains
the frigid winds pierce like an arrow,
and to feel the warmth of the sun or a fire is out of the
    question.
A father's kindness is the fox-skin hat on one's head,
a mother's kindness is one's lambskin clothing—
but even with all of that, this plain is difficult to traverse.
On the steep right side of the mountain
is the lair of Khenpa Genmo,[24] the supreme mother of the
    teurang
and her 360 teurang children;
to face them all will be difficult.
Then, farther on
in the land known as the Red Plain of Māra,
is the slaughterhouse of the carnivorous māras.
Because those māra cannibals gorged and gorged,
the large plains are filled with human skulls
and the small plains with horse skulls.
This place is so full of bones,
there is nowhere to put your foot down.
Then, from there, going farther upward
is Lutsen's first sentry, a triad of
a raging tempest,
a blazing fire,
and a flooding rain.
There is no way to cross this land.
The earth lord is Acham Karmo.
When she comes down from the mountains,
she will be mounted on a lion with a turquoise mane,

making such a loud sound that the sky and the earth tremble.
She guides the cannibals and demons to assist her—
she who has as many manifestations as there are stars in the
    sky
and under as fine control as the stars arrayed in constellations
    in the firmament.
There is no passage for the living or the dead.
Can you imagine making this crossing, Gyatsha?
If you could, then you are a genuine warrior.
Could *you*, you fierce Ling warriors?
If so, without doubt,[25] you are true warriors.
Now, when you reach the higher lands,
there are the eighteen great plains of Chaknak (Black Iron).
Those eighteen plains
are the domain of poisonous snakes, white, black, and striped.
The path is blocked by these deadly snakes.
Even if you are in the farthest reaches of the sky, they will
    whip you down with their tails.
If you lie on the ocean floor, they will stir you from its depths.
If you are Mount Meru in the center, they will coil around
    you.
To tame the white and black snakes will be difficult.
Sharp weapons will not stab them.
Perfectly fragrant musk from musk deer will do no good.
In order to tame the poisonous snakes,
one needs the eighteen-winged great garuḍa
to soar like the razor-sharp wind—
the one with wings will be able to tame the poisonous snakes,
the one without, unable.
A bit farther on are
rocky cliffs of human skulls smashed together,
rocks made whenever human heads collide.
Heaven and earth have upended,
and the valleys reek with a repulsive stench.
Noxious vapor covers the four corners of the earth.
Diseases of all kinds—not one but hundreds—will arise.
Döns of all kinds—not one but hundreds—will occur,
great harm will come to humans.

The curing medicines will be useless,
and, even if the divine masters come, they will not be able to
    help.
There will be magical powers and strengths but no chance to
    use them.
How could the Ling Pathül survive there?
Then, crossing through the thick gloom and fog
by the low road joining the two upper valleys
are the eighteen cannibal lakes that never dry up.
From these eighteen murky swamps,
waves of molten lava reach into the skies
and a demon makara appears with its mouth wide open.
There will be no chance for men and horses to show off their
    bravery.
There will be no chance for the Pathül and their troops to
    show their muscle.
Their arrows will have no chance to sail through the skies.
Now, going higher,
the steppes to the right of the Zima lands
ascend as if the sky and earth became one,
with lightning shooting up from the earth
and flashing down from the sky.
Between them, the mountains have crumbled into a
    rockslide,
and, below, the land is flooded with rushing water.
What could the Pathül possibly do?
Next, the gatekeepers are
the seven sisters of the north.
Facing those seven sisters,
fancy women would have no chance to display their charms
nor brave men to show their valor.
The humble could not tell of virtues to come
nor the wealthy employ their riches.
From there, going farther,
one encounters the invincible gatekeeper,
she who was born among the *kuśa* grass
and has become master of the arrow
and holder of the arrow siddhis,

expert in all weaponry.
The one greater than one hundred warriors—
the gatekeeper of the māra king Lutsen—
is the incomparable Momen Atak (Atak Lhamo).
The sorrel yak and the iron sheep of the demon—
no one under the heavens has ever defeated them.
The māra demon's long-horned sorrel yak
has a horn on its right that reaches to the sky,
and its left pierces the earth.
His breath swirls like fog,
obscuring the earth in darkness.
His red tongue wags at the middle sky,
shaking even the sun and the moon.
Who will promise to tame the māra yak?
Who will hold the badge of victory?
The māra demon's sheep has iron hooves.
It is the life-force sheep of the one hundred teurang,[26]
the life-ruler of the human flesh-eating red māra,
and the life force of Lutsen Gyalpo in the north.
We must destroy the hooves of this demon sheep.
What can the people of Ling do in this situation?
There is one special shepherd
named Anu Sengtren (Lion Youth)[27]
who is clairvoyant
and very persuasive
and the heir to King Trimar of Rong.
What can you do when you meet a man like that?
Yet, there is still more; how could that be all?
Actually, there are many districts with visible māras—
twelve myriarchies, all told—
whose principal māra is Beu Natra (Spotted-Nose Calf).
The invisible māras have their own dwelling places—
thirteen myriarchies in total—
each with its own māra minister and each known by its
    colorful pennant.
The māra females are famed for their black noses,
and three māra males are known for their long fangs and
    limbs:[28]

first, Gyukpé Jakma Kangring (Long-Legged Grass Runner),
second, Dzinpé Chakyu Lakring (Long-Armed Iron Hook
    Grasper),
third, Nyinzé Chewa Ngaring (Long Sharp Fanged Heart-
    Eater)—
all three are made from stone.
But even enlisting the best of our warriors,
you will be unable to quell those māras or
Lutsen Gyalpo in particular;
there is no way to rival his power.
He can wear India as though it were his hat
and China like little shoes,
coming quickly to the four ranges of Central Tibet.
When he occupies all of Jambudvīpa,
a droning sound will pervade the three-thousand-fold world,
the corpses of humans and horses will become the
    mountains,
the rivers will run with their blood,
and little children will be the fodder of the māras.
How can you defend against the māra demons of the north?
It would be difficult even for a speedy horse like Gyaja.
Even though the sword Yazi is keen and sharp,
it will be hard for the warrior Gyatsha to make his mark.
There are no men brave enough to defeat these māras.
When I go to the dark land of the māras,
hidden will be the sun and moon.
The roads there are more treacherous than those of the hell
    realms.
For all one hundred visible beings, there are a thousand
    intangible beings
that I—this lowly son of that despicable Ling mother, a
    nephew of Gok—
have the magical power to emanate.
I have the name of that vile butcher,
and it is my destiny to meet him alone.
With pure intent I was sent to tame the māras;
I am not concerned about my own fate.
Don't these examples tell the way it is?

Stained by past karma, the hunter takes off for the mountain pass
setting a trap for the musk deer and antelope—
delighted when he sees the dappled deer,
and unhappy when he does not.
The karma of the fishermen spins out as they head out across the lake
dropping a line into the depths—
delighted when they see a golden-eyed fish,
and unhappy when they do not.

I, Gesar, have been sent by the highest gods
as the yoke upon the māras, demons, rākṣasas, and evil spirits.
I will be glad to tame Lutsen of the north
with an arrowshot to his skull.
Pathül, your assistance
will be of no help in taming the māra Lutsen.
If you thirty brethren insist on sticking with me
when I am face to face with the māra demon,
you will be a distraction as I aim my arrow.
No good will come of your youthful folly;
it is better if I go alone.
I will win Lutsen over with smooth talk,
and inveigle him with my powers of sorcery and magic.
Listen, chief of the Bumpa clan—
your valor, warrior Gyatsha,
will get you nowhere with the three māra brothers.
First, the eldest son Chakchung Gyalpo,
second, the youngest Mukchung Gyalpo,
third, the middle brother Achung Gyalpo—
these three māra sons are invincible.
The fact is that, among the Ling Pathül,
five high-ranking warriors are faced with an obstacle year.
You, Gyatsha, as well as Rongtsha
and Takrong Nyatsha Aten, those three,
Takrong Anu Takphen, four,
and fifth, the leader Anu Zikphen—
all five men are saddled with dice loaded against them.
When the Hor come to Ling,
the spoils will belong to the minister of Den.

You, Gyatsha, as one encumbered with obstacles,
take a single arrow from my tiger-skin quiver,
the best arrow from among ninety-nine.
This arrow eats flesh and drinks blood,
not unlike the demon Yama.
It is the best of my many arrows.
When it is shot, it returns to you;
when it is loosed, it whistles.
This arrow is protection for you, Gyatsha.
Where the river bend swirls dark blue
and a great avalanche fills the valley with earth,
a man, red as a tsen demon,
on a red mount,
a man just like the lord of death will come.
When a man like that appears,
that will be the time to loose this flesh-eating and blood-
    drinking arrow.
Gyatsha, keep this in mind.
Not only that, there is an arrow for each of the Pathül,
tied in the middle with a khata,
a silken-ribboned arrow that is an incomparable weapon of
    protection.
Chipön Rongtsha Tragen, for one,
Gokza Lhamo, second—
please check in your heart if this is right.
If you have understood, it is an ornament to your ears.
If not, there is no way to explain it.

Thus Gesar proclaimed in song, but the Ling Pathül were not convinced. The arrow that returned when released—his solid-gold, divine, clairvoyant, flesh-eating, blood-drinking arrow—Gesar rolled inside a red silk flag of Ling and gave to Gyatsha. He gave each of the thirty Pathül a divine arrow and then turned to Chipön and Gokza and spoke, "I am going[29] north, and will explain clearly why the Pathül warriors should not join me." Although it was true that everyone knew in their hearts that Gesar's strength was unrivaled, it seemed unreasonable for the ministers not to accompany their king. After all, the country of the north comprised twelve thousand visible māras and thirteen thousand invisible māras, and when the time came to fight, unless all the arrows and lances were gathered together, the opportunity could certainly be lost. All along, Chipön had been sitting at the head of the central row, on a spotted leopard-skin seat. He was a man with hair whiter than a conch and rather deep-blue eyes with sagging eyelids held open by a golden stick on the right and a silver stick on the left. The wrinkles on his upper face were upturned, and those around his mouth hung down, revealing little pearly teeth. And now his song to all the young warriors of Ling, "Long Slow Gentle Melody," was in regard to matters of culture and behavior.

> Sing "Ala thala thala."
> "Thala" begins.
> The song unfolds in three parts.
> Today, I call to the gods.
> From the pure land in the east,
> Bhagavan Vairocana, know me.
> From the perfect dwelling place of the buddhafield,
> Bhagavan Amitāyus, know me.
> Bestow the deathless siddhi.
> Bless me and do not be meager in your compassion.
> If you do not recognize this place,
> it is the land of eastern Ma in Ling.
> If you do not recognize this song,
> it is the iconic song called the "Long Slow Gentle Melody."[30]
> High ones, listen from the forested mountain;
> low ones, listen from the sylvan riverbanks.
> When you listen, perk up your ears.
> When you look, look with eyes wide open.
> Open your ears—I have several requests.
> The powerful supreme king said he would go alone,
> but you youths said
> a chief and minister are like a head and neck, never to be
>   separated.
> A chief and his people should depart together,
> just as both a saddle and bridle are integral to a horse.
> If the horse comes through, its saddle and bridle come
>   through;
> if the chief makes it, the ministers make it.
> All of that is true,
> but the actual story is like this, isn't it?

The powerful Sengchen will journey alone;
that is the command of the highest gods.
Within the elders' manuscripts
and the eighteen manuscripts of the ancient world
are tales like this of the māra demons.
In the eight mountains of the northern highlands,
the king of the māra demons
can manifest in one hundred visible forms and a thousand
    invisible forms;
he is a man endowed with power and magic.
When Jambudvīpa is occupied by the māra demon,
darkness will descend from deepest space
and the sun and moon will be obscured by the demon's
    breath.
Furthermore, Rāhula will retreat,
and the high gods will lose their rank.
The māra demon will control even the lowest hell realms.
This powerful great man, the demon king,
in a previous life
was born as Trarab Nakpo (Supreme Black Falcon).
Quicker than a lightning bolt, he severed lives,
his fangs were like a revolving weapon-wheel,
he ate flesh and drank blood like a vulture,
and cared not whether you were dead or alive.
He had no grasp of cause and effect, virtue or harm.
Regarding this demon king in the north,
there were many people, many hands, but to no avail.
They collected arrows and spears, but to no end.
Ling Pathül, you should not insist on going.
There is no way you will be able to face the northern demon.
As it is said,
the mighty Bengal tiger has sharp claws yet cannot climb a
    sandalwood tree.[31]
Just so, a young man has great bravery
but cannot rival the māra Lutsen.
Today, in brief, what I am saying is:
young warriors of Ling, prepare to see Gesar off.
The divisions of white hat-pennants, red hat-pennants,

and yellow hat-pennants, individually
must make excellent preparations and start on the journey,
going as far as eighteen days by horse.
Escort Gesar that far,
then pray for him
and return to your homeland.
Gesar will continue on and return alone.
When he comes back, he will have good news of his deeds.
You young warriors should remain in your homeland;
if you stay back, there will be no trouble.
There is more to this story and, gradually, it will unfold.
I, an old man, thinking now about
the past—the Ling country was oppressed by Hor,
the Lingites were helpless, obliged to compulsory service and
    taxes.
Since Joru's birth, Ling has flourished
as strong imperial rule and good customs have been
    established.
Joru went to the borderland of Hor and Ling,
spinning his long and colorful slingshot around his head,
saying he would divide Hor and Ling.
The division of those lands brought victory to Ling,
but, consequently, the young men of Hor are disgruntled,
and its maidens weighed down with sorrow, bent like juniper
    trees.
Furthermore, this set up an ongoing dispute.
If the Hor army comes to Ling,
it is prophesied that the spoils will go to Denma,
and that young [Gesar] will be his right-hand man.
No doubt, that is what was said,
but although it is the truth,
Gesar, you, with a mind endowed with the higher
    perceptions
and with clear and unobstructed super-knowledge,
must speak straightforwardly to all the Ling Pathül
about your journey.
Please don't hold back.
Isn't this the way of the proverbs of long, long ago?

If you keep secrets from your father, to whom can you tell them?
If you hide food from your mother, to whom can you give it?

> We, the four elders of Ling
> and the thirty warriors of Ling—
> since we are not clairvoyant,
> we grope in the darkness
> and count on you, Gesar, to tell us what is best.
> This silken white scarf from China
> wraps thirteen coins of gold;
> they are my offering gift to you.
> Although it is a mere token,
> with the silken scarf of pure intention and a heavy heart, I
>   have spoken.
> It is the tradition of Ling.
> Please accept this and take it to heart.

Gesar rested in the understanding of the truth of Chipön's song.

CHAPTER TEN

Gokza and Neuchung
once again try to persuade Drukmo.
Trothung insists that he will go with Gesar
and see what Gesar could really accomplish.

DRUKMO STOOD AND ONCE AGAIN made a completely pure offering to all the Ling warriors consisting of chang from a gilded kettle, tea from a silver-plated kettle, and yogurt from a conch-covered bowl. "Well, now then, Sengchen Gesar, you said you will not stay in Ling but will go to the upper lands of the north," she said, "Nor am I staying, but going to that wilderness as well." And Drukmo offered this resonant song,[1] "Six Reverberations."

> Sing "Ala thala thala."
> "Thala" begins.
> The song unfolds in three parts.
> May the three divine ones look upon me and grant their
>   blessings.
> From the Eastern Paradise Arrayed in Turquoise Petals,
> from the maṇḍala of Blazing Conch Petals,
> from a lofty throne of Golden Petals—
> motherly Jetsün Tārās, white, blue, and golden,
> today, come to assist this maiden, Drukmo.
> If you do not recognize this place,
> it is the divine maṇḍala of Ling,

the gathering ground Takthang Tramo,
the rows made up of ninety-nine venerable persons.
If you do not recognize me,
I am from the esteemed family of Kyalo,
the daughter of Kyalo Tönpa.
I am an eye-catching beauty,
the ravishing daughter Drukmo.
One hundred men have longed for me;
one hundred women have become jealous.
All of you here—ministers and subjects of Ling,
and, in particular, Norbu Dradül—turn your attention
    to me.
Listen! I have several concerns.

When the cuckoo birds come from Mön,[2]
they are unruffled, whether they land in mountains or valleys,
and sing their six-toned melody
perched atop the blue-green juniper trees.

It can be called a happy life, but it is the life of the divine
    cuckoo;
    it can be called a sad life, but it is the life of the divine cuckoo.
That kind of karma is simple: happy staying, happy going.
But for you, Gesar, the northward journey
will not be as easy as that.
These are the examples that are told, and isn't this the way
    that it is?
When the wild drong[3] roams the cliffs and alpine meadows,
the young dark brown yaks come along
following after the wild drong.
The little drong with their stubbly horns roam freely.
Their happiness hinges on the wild drong;
if they are sad, it is the doing of the wild drong.
Today, these ancient truths come to life.
I am not just blithely following you;
we share a life together.
Of course, I will come with you.
Will you be concerned for my happiness?

Will you care for me if I suffer?
Isn't this what the ancient proverbs say?

When a man falls in love with a woman,
it is like an arrow piercing the meadow;
when a woman falls in love with a man,
it is like grain scattered on rocks.[4]

If you go alone to the north,
this is the fate that may befall you.
Today, the crux of the matter is that
I am your life partner,
and therefore I will accompany you,
along with my horse.
In the eight mountains of the upper lands of the north,
even if we are eaten by the cannibal demons,
I will not grieve for this lifetime.
I have no regret whatsoever.
Gesar, keep this in mind.
My Ling girlfriends, it will not be long till we meet again.
If you have not understood, I cannot repeat this song.

Thus she sang. For the most part, the Ling citizens and warriors did not know what to say and sat silently looking at one another. Gesar offered that they could start out with him, but only he would make the full journey. The next day, the thirty young warriors were clad in armor of rainbow light and their steeds tacked with saddles golden as the sun. The horses were eager to run, neighing and stamping their hooves on the ground. Nearby Drukmo was saddling her excellent horse, Dromuk Dingshé (Roan Skilled Flyer). She was a divine maiden, clothed in lovely silks and turquoise garments.

Furthermore, Gesar's helmet, Mokchen Gyalwa (Great Victory Helmet), was surrounded by the lords of the three families and its garuḍa-feathered[5] top ornament, Khamsum Zilnön (Quells the Three Worlds with Splendor), was surrounded by 122 buddhas. His great armor, Zewa Bumdzom (One Hundred Thousand Precious Stones), was surrounded by the one hundred peaceful and wrathful deities, and the great shield,[6] Bakar Lebchen (Flat Piece of Linen), was surrounded by the dralha and werma protectors of the four continents. The tiger-skin quiver in his right hand was filled with the ninety-nine excellent arrows and the leopard-skin case in his left hand held the curve of his bow, Chokar Ragö. His sword, Tabpa Lenmé, was surrounded by a retinue of life-force-cutting dralha and his spear Khamsum Domé was adorned with the silk pendants, Yulé Namgyal (Victorious in Battle). Wearing armor swirling with rainbow light, he gathered and subdued all the gods-demons; all the various violent spirits that had arisen, he was naturally able to quell. Even the lord of death drew back. Not only that, on the supreme steed Kyang Gö was the saddle blanket Mewa Guyi (Design of Nine Astrological Signs) and the bridle Meri Khyilkhyil (Swirling Mountain of Fire), the saddle girth Karpo Gyangdrak (White Conch Proclaims) with a cinch Drukri Shenkor (Dragon Design),[7] the breast girth Lhadré Zilnön (Quells Gods-Demons with Splendor), and the crupper Tashi Yangkhyil (Auspicious All-Pervading Wealth). As for the golden saddle Rinchen Wangyal (Great Precious King of Power) itself, the front was like the rising sun and the back like the full moon. Many signs appeared; through the resplendence of all this, the four māras of the four directions were quelled. Neuchung elegantly served chang from a gilded kettle, tea from a silver-plated kettle, and yogurt from a conch-covered bowl while she sang this song of farewell.

> Sing "Ala thala thala."
> "Thala" begins.
> The song unfolds in three parts.
> From the buddhafield, the supreme divine dwelling place,
> Mother Prajñāpāramitā,
> with your retinue of hundreds of thousands of ḍākinīs
> and from the dharmakāya palace, the excellent dwelling place,
> Mother Vajravārāhī,
> with your retinue of hundreds of thousands of ḍākinīs—
> today, look upon this daughter's plans.
> If you do not recognize this place,
> they are the good hills of Takthang Tramo in Ma,
> where Gesar rides his mount.
> If you do not recognize me, this woman,
> I am the daughter of Ngolo Tönpa,
> known as the maiden Neuchung of Ngolo.
> Although I am not beautiful,
> I possess prophetic powers.
> In this world domain of Jambudvīpa,
> I am known for my strength and clairvoyance.
> If you do not recognize this song,

it is known as Neuchung's song, "Six Reverberations of the
    Lark."
I do not sing it just anywhere,
but today I offer it to you, Gesar.
When you were fifteen years old,
the divine ones told you there was no time to relax,
that you must obtain the supreme steed Kyang Gö.
You and your horse were not to sit around, but should go and
    face the enemy,
no matter how arduous.
As this would fulfill the words of the highest gods,
why would anyone resist such a journey?
Today, dawn to dusk,
I have but three things to say to you.
Once, as I slept, I dreamed of
lofty white clouds the size of sheep
and low black clouds just as big.
The clouds wished to battle.
At first, the black clouds came close to victory
and, in turn, the white clouds nearly won,
but in the end, red clouds gathered,
billowing between the black and white clouds.
The black clouds descended further,
the white clouds rose upward.
There, to their right,
the golden sun rose in my dream,
and sunlight spread over the southern continent.
On the right slope of the high snowy mountain peaks was
a snow lioness, white as a conch and with a turquoise mane,
and on the mountain pass, a youthful lion, its loins in a
    haughty pose.
I dreamed that the snow lioness let out a bellowing roar.
From the midst of the highest heavens,
a turquoise dragon thundered.
I dreamed that a blue dragoness roared
a ferocious roar of thunder and lightning.
If you examine this dream,
it is an omen that the māras will thwart

you, Gesar, when you go to the north
to face the enemy Lutsen.
Don't be careless; don't jump right in his face,
or it will be certain disaster—you will lose to the māra demon.
The white and black clouds battling
and the red cloud entering in alone
represent the maiden in the north.
Her body is rather fine.
Her skin is radiant as red coral.
She has the three eyes of clairvoyance,
lips of vermillion red,
and teeth lustrous, white as a conch.
Noble Gesar, she lusts after you.
When she offers you delicacies to eat,
I suggest you be careful, noble being.
From the lowlands of the eastern valley,
there is yet another woman unlike any other.
She displays ceaseless dralha energy.[8]
Her countenance is semi-wrathful.
Angrily, she grasps a bow and arrow,
gathering the obstructing spirits.
That woman, with all the major marks[9] will come to you,
Powerful noble being, requesting empowerment
with her ribboned arrow, lance, and sword
surrounding her as a threefold panoply.[10]
The wild sorrel drong of the north
has flaming horn tips
spreading a mass of fire.
Its breath is steamy,
its red tongue is like lightning,
and its four hooves stir up red dust as it runs.
Noble being, it will come right up to your face,
but no harm will come to either you or your horse.
The divine dralha will assist you,
as the woman marked with excellent signs [Atak Lhamo]
    empties her quiver,
felling huge black drongs
and innumerable small drongs.

Drong corpses will pile up like mountains,
and the blood of drongs will swirl like an ocean—
good fortune for vultures and dogs.
A woman will take the trophy,
confounding our expectations.
But then there will be some risk to you.
First, the māra Chewa Ngaring,
second, Jakma Kangring,
third, Chakyu Lakring[11]
those three are red butcher māras.
When these three come,
the red men on red horses, full of fury
from the plains, dressed like savage mighty tsen,
they will look just like Nyentak Marpo,
your protector,
the dralha who tames the butchers.
Furthermore, I have something important to say.
This, our homeland Tramo Ling,
is like white yogurt,[12]
but there is one man who is contentious, like red blood.
Outwardly, he is two-faced, like a ḍamaru.
Inwardly, like a bell-ringer, he takes both sides.
Secretly, he spreads tales everywhere,
two-faced as a large drum,
a poisonous two-tongued snake,
always stirring up trouble.
Don't you think so, Sengchen?
Isn't this the way things really are?
Today, we are at a juncture.
In my right hand is a gold-plated copper vessel of chang
that I prepared on a perfect stove
over a blazing fire,
setting out this kettle Tashi Khyilwa (Swirling
    Auspiciousness)
and pouring in fresh pure water, like nectar, and using
first, the father's barley from Ayak,
second, the mother's barley from Daryak,[13]
third, the storehouse of barley from Mulé,

fourth, the maternal uncle's barley from Phara,
fifth, the paternal aunt's barley from Drao,
sixth, the monks' barley from Darwa, and
seventh, the nuns' barley from Ngochung.
All this boiled for a week to make chang.
Then, I added white sugar wine from upper Nepal,
brown sugar wine from lower Nepal,
grape wine from Tshawarong,[14]
and white chang from our own homeland.
Chang fermented for a year—
I offer this strong, year-old chang from an excellent harvest.
Chang fermented for a month—
I offer many cups of this blended drink.[15]
Chang fermented overnight—
I offer potent overnight chang.
Chang fermented in a day—
I offer the day chang as vajra amṛta.
Please have three drinks[16] and your spirits will be uplifted,
your enlightened body will be even more radiant,
your mind will have the clarity that results from awareness
    mantra recitation.[17]
I also have wine for all the other Ling leaders and ministers.
The finest of teas is in the silver-plated copper vessel.
I will explain the origin of this tea.
It is from the five-peaked mountain Wutaishan in eastern
    China
and supremely compassionate Mañjuśrī,
divine Mañjuśrī, has blessed it.
The white tea leaves are from the sunny side of the mountain;
the black tea leaves are from the shady side.
It is the northern tea Metok Yangtsé (Flowering Prosperity)
    blended from
Jarab, the lama of tea,
Kandru, the king of tea,
Chenshel, the hero of tea,
Druthang, the mother and son[18] of tea,
Lhaja, the servant lady of tea,
Kotsha, the manservant of tea,

then, fresh clean water from the mountain stream,
northern white salt,
and fresh white butter,
all combined into Guzi tea,[19] butter tea well stirred.
Guzi tea from eastern China,
this very day I offer to you, noble being.
Drink three cups of tea and the enemy will capitulate,
the four enemies will be quelled by splendor,
and your renown will soar.
I also have tea for all the other Ling leaders and ministers.
I offer milk from the white conch-covered copper vessel.
First, the milk of the white snow lioness,
second, the milk of the turquoise dragoness,
third, the milk of the youthful dri,
fourth, the milk of the *gyatsha* cow,[20]
fifth, the milk of the white garuḍa dzo,
sixth, the milk of the white-muzzled buffalo,
seventh, the milk of the white prosperity sheep.
The first select portion of this rich milk,
today, I offer to you, noble being.
In particular, from this the best yogurt is cultured;
may you remain throughout eons like perfectly fermented
    yogurt.
May you deliver the arrow to the demon's skull
and turn the māra lands to the Dharma.
To all the divine protectors of the six classes of beings,
I offer the best of tea, chang, and milk.
I hold in my hands the treasure scarf,
a single piece of white silk
that was a farewell message khata for Brahmā,
but now signifies not a farewell but rather a reunion.
I pray that we are always together.
A single piece of yellow silk
that was a farewell message khata for Nyen Kulha,
but now signifies not a farewell but rather a reunion;
I pray that we are always together.
A single piece of blue silk
that was a farewell message khata for the nāga Tsukna,

but now signifies not a farewell but rather a reunion;
I pray that we are always together.
A single piece of red silk
that was a farewell message khata for the divine Nyentak,
but now signifies not a farewell but rather a reunion;
I pray that we are always together.
Furthermore, there is a singular marvelous silk
decorated with the eight auspicious symbols at each end,
the seven royal treasures of the universal monarch depicted in
    the middle,
and edged with a fringe of pearls
that was a farewell message khata for Sengchen,
but now signifies not a farewell but rather a reunion;
I pray for the great fortune that we will always be together.
White, red, blue, [green], yellow, the five silks
that were farewell message khatas for the horse Kyang Gö,
but now signify not a farewell but rather a reunion;
I pray that we are always together.
May all that I have prayed for be accomplished.
May there be good fortune and merit.
Powerful King Gesar, look upon me.
With your pearl-encrusted victory helmet Gyalwa Thögor,
surrounded by the red dralha Nyentak
and your armor Zewa Bumdzom,
I pray for the auspicious connection of your armor.
The special occasion robe Tsegö Mukpo (Maroon Longevity
    Robe) of the dralha
are the Dharma robes of one thousand buddhas
made from the hair of one hundred thousand ḍākinīs.
When you Noble Gesar go to the north,
divine yidams, ḍākinīs,
and dharmapālas, without exception, will go as your retinue.
I pray that all this comes together.
First, the excellent aspiration prayers of the parents,
second, the excellent teachings of the lamas,
third, the heartfelt advice of lifelong friends—
today may these three come together.
Noble being, keep this in mind.

Thus she sang, and all were greatly honored. They were savoring the tea and wine when Chipön announced that Gesar's departure was imminent. The Lingites roused themselves and diligently prepared to start out with him. The fathers and uncles and mothers and aunts were all elegantly attired and the young maidens beautifully dressed. The entourage of Pathül warriors was suited in armor, and as that day they were to set out on horseback, Sengcham Drukmo wore a precious necklace. She was luminously beautiful and was accompanied by Gokza Lhamo and Gyaza Lhakar. Gokza offered a song of prayer in the melody of ḍākinī code.

> Sing "Ala thala thala."
> "Thala" begins.
> This very day this song calls to the divine ones.
> From the pure land of Buddha Amoghasiddhi,
> Perfection of Wisdom, Mother Prajñāpāramitā,
> look upon me with your light rays of compassion.
> From your supreme dwelling place in Akaniṣṭha,
> Mother Jetsün, all White and Blue Tārās,
> today, come to assist this mother.
> If you do not recognize this place,
> it is the center of divine eastern Ling,
> the gathering ground of Takthang Tramo,
> the environment of happiness and bliss.
> If you do not recognize me,
> in a previous life,
> from the pure land of Buddha Amoghasiddhi
> I was the motherly Prajñāpāramitā, foremost of one hundred
> thousand ḍākinīs.
> In this life,
> I was born in the subterranean land of the nāgas
> and came up to the supreme land of Gok.
> A lake-born nāginī from the nāga palace,
> I became the queen of the Gok temple.
> Afterward, I came to Upper Ling,
> and now I am Gesar's mother Gokza Lhamo.
> If you do not recognize this song,
> it is the "Longevity Song of Six Modulations."
> I don't sing this song just anywhere,
> but today I have no choice.

Unrivaled Sengchen Gesar,
now that you are fifteen years old,
you are up against your first great enemy of the northern
    land
and are preparing to quell the māra demons.
You will go alone to that land
and shoot an arrow into the forehead of Lutsen
to fulfill the teachings of the divine Śākyamuni
and establish the six classes of samsaric sentient beings in
    bliss.
Powerful Gesar, you will accomplish buddha activity for the
    benefit of beings.
The sun of happiness will rise over this world realm.
There is nothing better than this.
Today, darling son,
listen. I have a few more things to say.
The divine horse Kyang Gö
is blessed with magical channels and winds.
With the heavens above and the earth below,
he is as fast as the wind in the skies between.
Among one hundred visible and one thousand invisible
    horses,
this steed is the one with magic.
Gesar of unrivaled power and strength
and the divine horse of incomparable magic,
together, will travel to the north.
The circumstances are ripe to crush the enemy.
You, this man and horse, are unrivaled.
According to the ancient Tibetan proverbs:

There on the right side of the white snow mountain peaks,
a conch-white snow lion develops a turquoise mane
and, from that day onward,
has no reason to fear the savage carnivorous beasts,
as that youthful lion has great presence.
On the pinnacle of Mount Meru,
the great garuḍa, king of birds, develops feathers and wings
and then soars the skies

with no reason to fear any other birds.
He is the garuḍa king of birds,
the one to conquer the poisonous snake.

In the eight mountains of the upper lands of the north
on the road toward those foreign lands,
there are forty-nine demon rākṣasas.
This year it is time to tame them.
Some must be liberated peacefully,
others tamed wrathfully.
For a safe journey on this path,
I call now to the gods
that no harm come to you astride your horse.
May the five families of the victorious ones protect you.
May Brahmā support you.
May the blanket between you and your horse be steady.
May Amitāyus watch over you with compassion.
May Nyenchen Khulha assist you.
May no harm come to the horse beneath you.
May the windhorse king Hayagrīva look upon you.
May the nāga king Tsukna aid you.
When you step onto the soil of the northern land,
at the outset, the best of the gatekeepers—
the cannibal Kyelwa Khadang,[21]
the lungs of the violent Düd[22]—
must be annihilated.
In the middle of Yama Thangchen (Great Slate Plains),
there are 360 teurang.
That sagely teurang woman is
the vital breath of the violent Düd,
vehemently opposed to the side of virtue.
It will not be easy to tame this woman
in her manifestation as a teurang.
It will require great skill;
noble being, you must bind the teurang by oath.
To the far side of the high rocky peaks,
the land is a narrow defile with mountains and rivers to either
  side.

There, you will come to red rocks that resemble a human
     head.
The upper rocks are like a jaw clenching down;
the lower rocks grind up as though they are chewing—
chewing and clenching constantly without a break.
Even a bird cannot pass between.
Even the icy wind cannot penetrate.
But when you and your horse meet with hardship,
you will be led by the divine ḍākinī of the wind,
the divine ḍākinī of the water,
and the divine ḍākinī of the sky.
These three will guide you
and you and your horse will arrive safely.
On the left side of the high snowy mountain
is the demoness Acham Karmo—
she who can cause heaven and earth to collide,
the one who can play the sun and moon like cymbals,
seize the constellations in her hands,
and quell the three worlds with splendor.
As a rule, there is no way to tame Acham.
However, Precious Gesar,
in order to turn her to the virtuous Dharma,
you must exchange songs of the five wisdoms with her
and change her mind through your power and magic.
Eventually, you will arrive at the central castle fortress[23]
in the eight mountain ranges of the upper lands of the north,
where there are as many as five great fortresses,
and in the central castle-fortress
is a cunning woman
greatly famed for her beauty.
With snowy skin and a rosy complexion,
her wisdom eye, red as blood,
and conch-white teeth,
she is an authentic beauty
who greets you with a smile
and an intelligent and thoughtful mind.
You must tell her your intentions.
Unless you act according to her advice,

there is no way to annihilate the life force of the māras
or to shoot the arrow into the evil demon's skull.
You must rely on this maiden
to swiftly accomplish enlightened activity for the benefit of
   sentient beings.
Only then will you be able to shoot the arrow
and, mounted on your horse, make a hasty return.
Take this path now without hesitating,
for if you delay, obstacles will arise.
As in my dream's portent,
I saw a pitch-black pot
filled with unclean foods.
I dreamed that you were offered these various foods
and were crippled and could not walk,
were mute and had no voice.
Five years passed and one day,
from the peak of the Glorious Copper-Colored Mountain,
from inside his dome of rainbow light,
nirmāṇakāya Padmasambhava
sent longevity nectar to you,
brought by three magical white birds.
These three birds[24] flew to the north
to offer you that deathless amṛta,
and I dreamed that your illness was cured.
Keep all of this in mind, Noble Gesar.
On that day [in my dream], you were restored to health.
Do not hesitate to wear your armor,
Zewa Bumdzom,[25] the great protection armor
possessing an outer retinue of dralha and werma,
a middle layer of dharmapālas and protectors,
and an inner core of gurus and yidams.
Upon this three-layered armor
I, your mother, fervently pray
that circumstances converge ensuring that this armor is
   impenetrable.
When the time comes to shoot an arrow into the demon's
   skull,
may no weapons harm your body.

May the bhagavans of the five families look upon you.
May you wear the white helmet
Mokchen Gyalwa
with its retinue of the protectors of the three families,
the pennant Khamsum Zilnön
with its retinue of dralha of complete victory,
and the shield Bakar Lebchen
with its retinue of the dralha and werma protectors of the
    four continents.
Today, this gathering of the hosts of dralha
is an excellent auspicious sign of connection.
The magnificence of the helmet indicates that
the accomplishment of excellent merit and deeds is assured.
You will shoot Lutsen,
armed with your excellent bow and arrow.
In the fine tiger-skin quiver on your right
are the best ninety-nine arrows.
Among them are ten arrows that can sing,
ten arrows able to return,
ten arrows able to understand human language,
ten arrows able to devour human flesh,
ten arrows able to drink human blood,
ten arrows able to destroy life force,
ten arrows able to guard the life center,
and ten arrows able to transfer consciousness.
The ninety-nine arrows
are the necklace arrows of the dharmapālas
and the longevity arrows of the Queen of Siddhis.
When the arrows fly upward toward the sky,
that will be a sign that the māras will be subdued
and that an arrow will be shot at the demon's head.
In the leopard-skin case on your left
is the bow Ragö Kyilwa,
the divine bent bow that unites the three worlds.
The thrumming roar that comes from the head of the bow
resembles the roar of the turquoise dragon,
the taut gonging sound from the bottom of the bow
sounds like the beating of a large metal gong,

the reverberation of the bowstring throughout the three
   worlds
is the sound of the māra consciousness transferring into basic
   space.
You will have accomplished this aspiration prayer
and annihilated the negative forces.
This sharp sword Tabpa Lenmé
with a retinue of dralha that quickly cut life force,
the lance Khamsum Zilnön
adorned with the flag Yulé Namgyal (Completely Victorious
   in Battle),
the pennant Gyaltsen Towo (Lofty Victory Banner)[26]
with its dralha silk swirling like a blizzard, *tsub tsub*—
all these indicate the gift obtained for Ling.
You have taken the benefit of beings to heart.
The māra land will turn to the sublime Dharma.
The māra consciousnesses will be led to the pure land.
Today, for you, my dear son,
there is wine in the gilded copper vessel on my right,
wine from the white rice of the abode of great divine Brahmā,
wine from the red rice of the great nyen Kulha,
wine from the blue rice of the nāga king Tsukna.
First, excellent father barley from Ayak,
second, refined mother barley from Daryak,
third, the storehouse of Mulé grain[27]—
the choice first portion of offering wine like nectar made
   from these three,
today I offer to you, Noble Gesar.
It is the longevity liquor of one hundred thousand ḍākinīs,
the amṛta of your loving mother.
Have three drinks to uplift your spirits.
You will suppress through splendor the enemy's head.
There is tea in the silver-plated copper vessel on my left.
From the dharmic land of India comes
Druthang, the fresh herbal tea flourishing, like the teachings
   of the Buddha;
this is the offering tea of the divine Śākyamuni.
From the middle of China, the secular land to the east, comes

Chenshel, the tea with the clarity of the fair and unbiased
   worldly laws;
this is the pure tea of divine Mañjuśrī.[28]
The merchant Norbu Zangpo (Excellent Jewel, a famous
   merchant)
together with his assistant Karma Tashi (Auspicious
   Constellation),
from ninety-nine excellent teas,
collected this tea, which is the nectar,
the best tea of China.
Today, I offer it to you, noble being.
Drink it and the enemy will surrender.
The enemies of the four directions will be subdued.
The white conch-covered copper kettle
holds the most excellent milk,
which symbolizes the world becoming firm and settled,
a sign that events have come together and fallen into place,
that your goals are as lofty as the sky,
and that you will accomplish buddha activity for the benefit
   of beings.
One, this aspiration prayer,
second, the path you will traverse,
third, the path by which beings will be liberated—
keep these three in mind, Noble Gesar.
Listen, Sengcham Drukmo.
The powerful Gesar and his horse—
escort them for some distance.
You will be angry if I say you cannot go,
but, young maiden, for you to fight so great an enemy[29]
is something that this world realm cannot abide.
Right now, for a woman to accompany Joru
is bound to make for trouble.
For this one time, it is necessary to be apart.
It is the karma of your previous lifetimes
that you have been born to be Gesar's wife;
may you spend your whole lifetime with him
in this joyous divine Tea Castle.
I pray that this may always be true.

First, the fathers and uncles of Upper Ling,
second, the Pathül warriors,
and third, the mothers and aunts
should come with you Drukmo, journeying eighteen days by
    horse
to see Gesar off.
Be sure to say excellent prayers when he continues on alone.
Once you return, you must guard the homeland.
Now, Sengchen Gesar, please listen
as I have three further concerns.
One day when the Hor army comes to Ling,
the burden of victory will fall to Denma.
But he and his horse alone,
how could they take on one hundred thousand Hor?
What soldiers would come to his aid?
One day when the Jang army comes to Ling,
the burden of winning or losing will fall to the son of Gyatsha.
But against the eighty Jang māras,
how will he be able to act alone?
Tell us what allies we can send as support.
When you, Gesar, leave for the north,
if other enemies of Ling arise,
which warrior will take them on?
In the end, what will happen?
You must tell us clearly what you foresee.
If you refuse,
    you will come to regret it.

One with the best mind knows what to do in advance.
Understanding the three times,
they are inherently able to go ahead according to plan.
One with a middling mind comes up with a strategy on impulse.
Acting without regard for the future,
they are shortsighted.
One with an inferior mind only recognizes in hindsight
when things have gone awry.
Many thoughts arise, all after the fact,
too late, bringing regret and misery.

You, Joru, you would never do that.
Please give clear advice
so that those who stay behind can relax.
Furthermore, those of you staying here, leaders and
    commoners, listen.
You should not act just according to your own ideas.

An arrogant man is short-tempered.
If he fights, he is asking for trouble.
He has a clever tongue,
but if he deceives an honest person,
no one will trust him.
Whatever you do, there has to be a limit.
A promiscuous woman who does not settle down,
in the end, finds herself alone.
A horse that runs without slowing down,
in the end, loses control.

These words are from the ancient proverbs.
If you have understood, keep this in mind, Ling.
If you have not understood, I cannot repeat it.

Thus the song was received, and while all the fathers and uncles, mothers and aunts, children and youths of Ling were praising Gokza's words, Trothung placed a beautiful copper-red saddle and bridle on his spirit horse Gugu Rokdzong (Bent Black).[30] He had a spirit helmet Namkha Khyungdzong (Sky Garuḍa Fortress) ornamented with a red silk, spirit armor Jaleng Marpo (Red Rainbow) adorned with a hem of precious coral, a spirit knife Yarla Khyenguk (Summons Uphill) with its handle of rabbit horn. The tiger-skin quiver on his right was full of spirit arrows Drodok Ngarma (Strong Feathered); the leopard-skin case on his left contained a spirit bow Wamin Yukchen (Curved Cow Horn). The hair on top of his head was unkempt, braided into many rigid, coiled scorpions down his back, and in front and on the left, braided into many rigid knots of crossed vajras. His beard was evenly divided and knotted several times, and resting on it was a golden mirror as big as a plate. "Today, I have several stories to tell you. Exalted King Gesar above and lowly servants below, all of you, listen to what I am saying!" And Trothung sang the song called "Roar of the Tigress."

"Ala thala thala."

"Thala" begins quickly.

Now, today, I call to the deity

from the pure land of Meri Barwa,

great deity Red Hayagrīva, know me.

Look upon me and come to assist me.

Crimson Taklha Mebar, know me.

Now, today, assist me.

If you do not recognize this place,

it is the eastern land of Ling; just to see it is to admire it.

If you do not recognize me,

before I took birth in this lowly body

struck with the poison arrow of saṃsāra

and sullied with the stain of habitual patterns,

I was Red Hayagrīva.

If you do not recognize my song,

it is Trolu's "Roar of the Tigress."

I do not sing it just anywhere,

but today I have no choice.

You said you must come to destroy the northern māras,

and that you will turn those savage ones to the Dharma.

You have said many things,

but I have some important key points:

the one to turn the evil māras toward the Dharma

could be the Lotus Born One or myself—

of the two of us, I am the one!

The one to lead beings from the hells in the next life

could be either Shinjé or myself, this Dharma king—

of the two of us, I am the one!

The one who always rides a red tiger

could be either the boy Joru or me—

of the two of us, I am the one!

The one who sits between the horns of a blue dragon

could be either the Bön lama or me—

of the two of us, I am the one!

The brave warrior hero of this worldly existence

living inside the fortress Porok Nying Dzong

is none other than Trothung the king.

The moment I came to this worldly existence, I was named a
    leader.
When I was three years old,
I wrestled the cannibal Khatsé Relwa
and threw him to the ground;
the cannibal Khatsé Relwa was conquered.
If I had not brought down the eastern cannibal fortress,
there is no way Ling could exist,
and if eastern Tramo Ling did not exist,
the Ling warriors could not have been born.
If the Ling Pathül were not born,
how could the Gesar exist?
Therefore, all of you Lingites, listen.
You all said that Joru, the nephew of Gok in Lower Ma,
is the unrivaled noble being Gesar.
You said he would be the one to shoot an arrow into the
    demon's forehead.
Do you really think he can do that?
If I lay out examples, it is like this:

If there is no snow on the high mountains,
how can water be replenished in the Turquoise Lake of Lower Ma?
If there is no water in the Turquoise Lake,
how can there be sandy shores?
If there is no sandy soil,
where would the sandalwood tree grow?
Without sandalwood trees,
where would the blue cuckoo land?
If the blue cuckoo could not land,
who would sing the melodious six reverberations?
If the melodious song of the six reverberations was not called out,
how could summer be divided from winter?[31]

Gesar the boy and Trogyal the chieftain,
just like those very examples, would not be set apart.
If I, Trothung, hadn't been born in Ling,
who would have conquered the cannibal fortress in the east?
There would be no place called Ling.

Today, Ling king and ministers,
the powerful noble being Gesar
and Takrong Uncle Trothung
will go together to the northern high lands.
We will see then who has signs of accomplishment;
we can compare who is an ordinary and tangible being and
    who is beyond that.
The boy Gesar needs a friend.

Young men showing off their muscles
find it hard when they encounter men of true strength.
Young horses champing at the bit
find it difficult to cross over the steep peaks.

I am an old man with both bravery and intelligence.

The person who speaks softly will prevail.
The horse that runs easily will win the race.
A knife honed slowly will become sharp.

Now, there must be someone to assist Gesar.
There is Chipön, but he is too old.
Also, for one, Kyalo Tönpa Gyaltsen,
second, Chief Achen of Serpa,
third, Shakya Guru of Ombu,
fourth, Weri Nyima Gyaltsen—
although these are four great men, they also are too old.
Although there are many Ling wild boys,
they are brave, but too young.
Actually, I think I am the one who should go,
as I am a man with both bravery and intelligence.
I am not staying, I am going;
I will be the ally of the boy Joru.

A brave man's duty is to drive out adversaries;
when enemies appear, he stands up to them.
A maiden's duty is to take care of the household;
when guests arrive, she attends to them.

I am going, not staying;
I am going to follow this great being, Gesar.
Ultimately, these events will unfold.
Those are my thoughts.
I confess any fault of this song; please accept my apology.
If any confusion has arisen from my words, please forgive me.

Thus Trothung sang, giving the Ling mothers and aunts and all the daughters a piece of white silk, and offered each a piece of gold. He said, "Until we meet again, be well! I will go to help Joru; there is no way that this wise old man is not going!" And he mounted his steed Gugu and together with Gesar, took to the road. Sengcham Drukmo and the thirty Pathül escorted Gesar, and on the eighteenth day of the horse ride, with grand pageantry,[32] they arrived all together at the northern great plain of Meri Barwa[33] and camped there.

CHAPTER ELEVEN

Thokna (Leads Lightning) protects the Ling warriors.
Gesar binds the teurang by oath.
Denma tells of future plans for Gesar.
Gesar explains how to act henceforth.

THE NEXT DAY, AS MERCURY ROSE AT DAWN, from the supreme celestial divine palace, beyond the domain of the razor-sharp wind, from the dome of both rainbows and clouds, Manéné, Queen of Longevity, manifested as a golden bee the size of a thumb. With a humming voice, neither too loud nor too low, she sang this melody of the channels and winds to the powerful Gesar.

Sing "Ala thala thala."
"Thala" begins.
The song unfolds in three parts.
This very day, I call to the deity.
Buddha, Dharma, and Saṅgha, the Three Jewels, the objects
    of refuge,
please grant your blessings.
If you do not recognize this place,
it is the northern great plain of Meri Barwa.
From the Dokham region of Ling to the east
have come the powerful, unrivaled King Gesar
and the thirty fiercest of their young men.
You, the leader, are surrounded by so many troops—

will such an entourage help you defeat the enemy?
Listen to this motherly song,
listen, noble being Döndrub.[1]
Tonight, long after the sun has set
and the morning star is rising in the sky,
at first light,
Noble Gesar, depart for the north
and do not delay along the way.
First, the women will sing many songs,
second, Trothung will tell many stories,
and third, there are many Ling Pathül following you.
These three will detain you.
The arrogant young woman Drukmo,
selfishly wanting to go with you to the enemy—
no one acts like that besides Drukmo,
so spoiled.
There is no benefit to her encountering enemy bandits.
You must listen to my motherly song.
It is just like these stories:

The white vulture with mature feathers and wings
shows off its power, soaring to the highest sky.
If it did not traverse the heights of the firmament,
it could not be called a white vulture.

You, the unrivaled Gesar, divine child,
if you did not go alone to tame the māras,
you could not be called Ling Gesar.
Importantly, all the invisible divine beings,
as well as the local protector spirits of Ling,
have come to assist you.
First, the warriors with a retinue of dralha and werma,
second, Brahmā, Nyen Khulha, and Tsukna,
and third, myself, Auntie Manéné Karmo
will stick to you like a shadow to a body,
inseparable as armor and weapons.
The Pathül and women of Ling must return home,
and you, Gesar, must go very soon

to the eight² mountains of the upper lands of the north.
The king of the demons—
the time has come to tame him.
Jangtri Meza Bumdrön
is now eighteen.
She has been waiting for you
like a cuckoo waits and waits for rain.
When one expects a guest from far away,
they make chang while they wait
and ask for a divination and stand watch.
Gesar, now I think it is time for you to leave.
The red tiger that lives in the forested mountain
is a carnivore; otherwise, it is not a Bengal tiger.
The white-muzzled kyang that lives in the alpine meadow
eats vegetation; otherwise it is just a lowly donkey.
You are the yoke upon the enemy;
if you do not quickly suppress the head of the enemy,
calling you Ling Gesar is nothing but empty words.
If you do not go soon
and Meza and Lutsen
consummate their relationship,
Lutsen will change Meza's mind,
the māra life force will become as indestructible as iron and,
    then,
even if you lived for a hundred years, you would not be able
    to tame him.
The beautiful maiden Meza Bumdrön
said she would wait for nine years for a good man,
for six years for a mediocre man,
and three years for a lesser man.
The king of the māra demons
said that he has been waiting just for Meza
as, when he found that in this lifetime, he inhabited a male
    body,
not to join with this young woman
would cause him great regret.
You, Divine Prince, please carefully consider all of this.
Today, dear son, come here.

Bow your head; I will confer empowerment.
Look into my face; I will offer nectar.
Tomorrow morning early, leave here
and when you reach the slate rock meadow, Yama Thangchen,
seven warriors will have gone to collect water.
They will not get water but will enter a bag of the cannibals
and not escape from inside this breath-bag
until finally I strike a lightning bolt
to free these seven Pathül men.
In the highlands of Yama Thangchen,
there is a teurang elder
and 360 teurang.
There, the one kyang with the exceptional gait
and the steeds of Ling grazing the pastures
will all be rounded up by the teurang
and hidden in caves,
with the divine Kyang Gö going first
and the others following like foals after their mother.
Now, listen, noble being Gesar,
You must go without delay after those stolen horses,
and if anyone asks, say that you came from the direction of
    Kongpo Draksum (Three Rock Ravine).
You must twist your hair around your head twice and put on
    a hat,
the hat should be made of brocade.
Wear a white chuba
with a collar adorned with Chinese beads.
Inside a bamboo container,[3]
put chang and old wheat and pork, these three:
first, the neck meat of a lifeless old pig,
second, liquor of cooked old barley,
and third, dough made from roasted old wheat.
Give all this to the old teurang as a gift
and deceive her with your clever words.
The northern king Lutsen—
work hard to do away with his life force.
First, he has blood-sucking grassland frogs,
second, bedbugs, fleas, and lice,

all blood-suckers as well.
These are the lifeblood of King Lutsen.
Put them inside an iron box
and annihilate all of them.
You must bind the teurang by oath,
rescue the divine horses,
and return those seven Pathül men to Ling.
Then, gradually, we will see the best strategy.
Keep all of this in mind, noble being Gesar.
If you have not understood, I cannot repeat it.

Thus she sang and vanished like a rainbow in the sky, and Gesar rejoiced
at this, the clear prophecy of Manéné. At dawn the next morning, while all the
minsters were eating their fill of breakfast, Gesar said, "Chipön Rongtsha Tragen,
Achen, the minister of Sertsha,[4] Michen Gyalwé Lhündrub, and Bumpé Tharwa
Bumlek (Liberation Elegance), all the supreme highest leaders of Ling, as well as
Bönser Könchok Jungné, Shakya Guru of Ombu, Tönpa Gyaltsen of Kyalo, Nyima
Gyaltsen of Karu, Tharpa Gyaltsen of Nakru, Nyima Gyaltsen of Weri, Chölu Dar-
phen, Rinchen Darlu of Muchang, it is best according to this supreme prophecy
that you return all together to the homeland," and he gave them many blessings of
ḍākinī amṛta and ribbons tied with longevity knots. These Pathül left one by one
while supplicating over and over with aspiration prayers.

The next day, Gesar departed with the remaining Pathül warriors and, like
a winding river, that night, they arrived at the northern great slate plain of Yama
Thangchen. The land was barren: no trees or water, nothing whatsoever except a few
sparse blades of grass were to be seen. Here, the sun rose like a heel, a flat disk emerg-
ing over its featureless horizon, and set as though dissolving into the earth; apart
from that, the skies were stark. The land was parched as a roasting pan, and while
they stood pondering a plan, the seven—Gyatsha, Zikphen, Nyatsha Aten, Rong-
tsha Lhadar, Nang-ngu, Takphen, Gadé—heard the sound of rushing water coming
from the east. Relieved, they ran carrying empty jugs, but when they came to the
source of the sound, they realized that the flowing water had the foul smell of urine.
"How can we drink that?" they said. "We had better go a little farther." At some dis-
tance, they saw dark rocks shimmering with what looked like water, but they soon
saw their mistake. Zikphen said what they were all thinking, "Nothing good is here.
The water is red and looks like blood!" The other six warriors had nothing to say.
At that moment, the cannibal Kyelwa Khadang, riding a two-razored wind-sword,
arrived. Reciting a mantra, he filled the sack with the consciousnesses of the seven

Pathül men as easily as sucking in air. He buried the sack beneath the rock mountain Khyungnak Bari (Blazing Black Garuḍa) while Gesar spoke to the warriors' corporeal forms,[5] "Looks like you did not find water. Stay here, and I will go up to the mountain peak and look around." He reached the highest peak and surveyed the land. In the meantime, Denma had gone hunting in Kardza Lungbar (Middle White Rock Valley), killing one of the six-year-old drong, and had been able to drag it down to Yama Thangchen where he found Drukmo, Michung, and Trothung wondering what they should do. Drukmo was saying to Trothung, "Uncle, you are very good at black magic mantras—can't you come up with one to help us find drinking water?"

Trothung took his crystal mala from his neck and recited the mantra HARMIN HURMIN. The great mount Kyang Gö came over by Drukmo and snorted three times, and with his left leg, stomped the ground three times. As soon as he had done that, from the nāga land below, pure clear water flowed as though the beautiful goddess of water had opened the womb of the earth. A sweet-smelling pond bubbled up from the flowing water, and they drank until their thirst was quenched. From high in the azure firmament with a loud crackling sound and a heavy treading noise, riding a wine-red he-goat of emptiness, Garwa Nakpo (Black Ironsmith)[6] arrived, clutching a load of red sandalwood. Drukmo said, "Let's split that wood and make a fire," and Trothung took out his spirit knife and cut the wood. Michung made a fire and sat down to make tea. Denma came dragging the drong he had killed and the four of them dressed and cooked the meat. They stoked the fire continuously with a black goat skin bellows and relaxed, enveloped in the swirling smoke.

Gesar, having surveyed the landscape from the mountain, had come nearly all the way back down. From the measureless castle of the clouds in the highest firmament, Manéné came, flanked underfoot by thirteen male dragons on her right and thirteen female dragons on her left. From the prosperity enclosure of the sky, as she was prophesied to do, she invoked her messenger, one of the eight classes of haughty ones, Thoknalak Zhongchan (Holding a Tray of Various Lightnings). True to his name, he held a blazing jeweled tray filled with thunderbolts. He offered this song.

> Sing "Ala thala thala."
> "Thala" begins.
> The song unfolds in three parts.
> This very day I call to the deity.
> From a seat in the enclosure of the heavens above,
> may all the buddhas who have attained the ten *bhūmis*
> today come to assist me.

From the pure realm of the precious gods,
motherly ḍākinīs of the Padma family in the west,
motherly ḍākinīs of the Vajra family in the east,
motherly ḍākinīs of the Ratna family in the south,
motherly ḍākinīs of the Karma family in the north,
motherly ḍākinīs of the Buddha family in the center,
and she who comes riding a lion, with thirteen male
dragons beneath her on the right
and thirteen female dragons on the left,
today, please assist me.
May the heavens be lit with thunderbolts,
may the middle sky be a hurricane of red lightning,
and may the lower sky be a barrage of hail.
May thunderbolts set off an avalanche,
demolishing the mountain to its rocky core;
the back side of the mountain will crumble,
the front side of the mountain will crumble,
the dense dark rock and the soft slate rock will turn to dust.
I, Thokna, will guide the lightning bolts
to pulverize the rocks.
Five families of motherly ḍākinīs, please assist me.
Today, please come to aid this brave man.
From your seat in the immeasurable castle of the highest
    heavens,
Manéné Namné Karmo,
soaring bareback on a lioness—
those seven authentic ministers of Ling,
today, when the breath-bag splits open,
will need protection.
Lord of Ling, Gesar, please come swiftly,
come like massing rain clouds,
come like rainfall, come like fire.
Come to protect the seven Pathül men.
When I send down lightning and thunderbolts,
there is a risk of injuring the warriors.
High gods above and Gesar, lord of Ling,
you have power to reverse this happenstance.
If you don't understand, I cannot repeat my song.

Thus he sang, and he brought down the thunderbolts. The back side of the mountain crumbled, the front side of the mountain crumbled, and the soft slate cliffs were reduced to dust that only dissipated after nearly a week. The cannibal Kyelwa Khadang was struck by hail and thunderbolts and atomized without a trace, but the breath-bag was not greatly damaged. Then, Thokna shot two lightning arrows, one after another, opening the bag and the seven ministers, their hair standing on end, eyes watering, teeth chattering, and noses dripping, exhaled and almost stopped breathing as they fell, gasping for air. Gesar manifested as a body of light rays more radiant than a thousand suns and invoked the protector Amitāyus. Gesar gave great blessings to the seven Pathül men along with long-life relic pills, touching his hands to theirs. He restored them, invoking long-life and life-force summoning rituals. The seven ministers prostrated to Amitāyus and Gesar and offered aspiration prayers. They all returned to the encampment where Denma had roasted the drong meat and was waiting; it was a meal of rejoicing. At that moment, Gadé stood up to offer a single white silk khata to Gesar and spoke: "Powerful King Gesar, if you were not in this world, not only would Lutsen not be tamed, but we would have perished here at the hands of the demon cannibal Kyelwa Khadang." Then, Gadé offered this song.

> Sing "Ala thala thala."
> "Thala" begins.
> The song unfolds in three parts.
> This very day, I call the deity.
> From the realm of the enclosure of the charnel ground grove,
> Dharma protector six-armed Mahākāla,
> today please come to assist me.
> From the Cool Grove charnel ground,
> charnel goddess Durtrö Dakmo, together with your
>   retinue—
> great dancers swaying, *shik sé shik*,
> ḍākinī dancers gasping, *heb sé heb*,
> and *pawo* dancers thrumming, *pung sé pung*,
> surrounded by hundreds of thousands of ḍākinīs—
> today, please come to assist this old man.
> If you do not recognize this place,
> it is Yama Thangchen,
> the land of the monotonous, flat horizon,
> where daybreak begins abruptly right at sunrise

and darkness falls precipitously at sunset.
I have never before seen such a place.
If you do not recognize me,
I am called Dru Gadé Chökyong Bernak.
I have the strength of a mad elephant and
the intense power of roiling molten metal.
My strength is unrivaled in all the world;
even the lord of death will yield to me.
This year, this day, no matter who,
the worst of anyone you could meet
is the māra cannibal Kyelwa Khadang,
riding with a breath-bag—
a fierce dust storm, *thul lu lu*,
black clouds filling the sky, *thul lu lu*,
black ash covering the earth, *thul lu lu*,
the oceans a black tempest, *thul lu lu*,
the slurs of evil men, *thul lu lu*,
the curses of evil women, *thul lu lu*.
Today, I have no choice but to sing this song of sorcery.
In this unfamiliar land of the north,
many difficult situations have arisen.
Over there, toward the red rocks to the east
I went, thinking I could get some water.
Unfortunately, at the same time a fierce wind arose,
plunging us into deep darkness.
We were trapped there,
as you know, Gesar.
Gadé, Gyatsha, Takphen, those three
famed throughout the world,
Rongtsha, Nyatsha, Nang-ngu, those three
famed throughout heaven and earth,
and that boy, the strong warrior Zikphen,
fearless in the face of power and magic—
these authentic seven warriors,
before they knew what had happened,
were caught inside a breath-bag.
It is farfetched to think that we can tame Lutsen
since our own lives were on the verge of being lost.

Encountering such enemy demons
is like climbing rocks without arms.
We should leave the north
and return to our homeland of Ling,
holding fast to our own country.
Here are some examples:
the cliff-dwelling white vulture soars the skies
thinking to cross the highest heavens,
but, there, he meets the razor wind
and wishes instead to stay clinging fiercely to the rocks.
Gyatsha, Rongtsha, and Nyatsha, and all the ministers
should go back to our homeland
and maintain our stronghold in Ling.
Noble being Gesar,
you will have been in the mountain ranges of the north
for ninety-nine days
before you shoot the arrow into the forehead of that
    quintessential māra,
but if you stay too long, there will be obstacles.
Precious divine jewel, powerful Sengchen,
there is hardly reason for me to speak, as you are omniscient,
yet this is a very pressing matter.
Listen, what I have to say is in earnest.
As they slept, first, Gokza's dream,
second, Drukmo's dream,
and third, the dream of Neuchung—
those dreams were not good dreams.
What Chipön said yesterday
might be true.
Once you have accomplished the benefit of beings,
please return quickly.
Divine Prince Gesar, keep this in mind.
If you have not understood, I cannot repeat my song.

Even before the song was finished, some of the Pathül were busy with preparations. Gesar said, "You don't need to be in such a rush; enjoy some tea and chang. Michung will go and take care of the horses." In the meantime, the teurang, Khenpa Genmo, had already seen the horses and said to her 360 teurang children, "There are some horses in the fields of Yama Thangchen, and, doubtless, they are horses from Ling. And surely that boy is Gesar, the Gok nephew from Ling, who has come north to fight his enemy, the demon king. Go quickly and herd every last one of their horses into the darkness."[7] When they were rounding up the horses, Kyang Gö went first, understanding that the time had come to tame the teurang children. The other horses followed like foals after mares, and the horses were all sealed into a rock mountain cave by the teurang children. There, without grass or water, they stood motionless, only occasionally switching their tails. Then, the great mount Kyang Gö circumambulated clockwise and at that moment many refuge deities such as Cakrasaṃvara and others appeared and dissolved back into the rocks; he turned counterclockwise three times, and the peaceful and wrathful deities and the Seven Ancestral Buddhas[8] instantly appeared from the rocks.

Unable to find the horses, Michung came rushing back, blurting out that he had searched everywhere. Breathlessly he asked, "Could they have gone up into the mountains?" Gesar already knew where they had gone and said, "All of you stay here in the tent. Unless I go, we will never get the horses back." Before dark he was ready, disguising himself in a white cotton chuba adorned with Chinese beads at the top. He had twisted his two braids down his back and donned a hat with a brim of rolled-up brocade. Inside the bamboo baskets he carried was burnt mature wheat, the meat of grown pigs, alcohol made from ripened barley, and so forth. Carrying all this, he came to the doorstep of the rock cave of the teurang. He rested there and some of the teurang children saw him and wondered who he was and went to tell Khenpa Gyenmo. She came and saw a boy standing in the doorway that she had never seen before, a boy like none other. She asked, "What land have you come from? Where are you going? Tell us your story and all about who you are," and sang this short, questioning song.

> Sing "Ala thala thala."
> "Thala" begins.
> The song unfolds in three parts.
> This very day I call to the deity.
> From the celestial castle of thirty-nine stories of thunderbolts,
> Namthel, Barthel, Sathel, teurangs of the sky, earth, and in
>   between,
> today come to assist me.
> If you do not recognize this place,
> it is the northern alpine meadow Yama Thangchen,
> and the rock mountain resembling an angry cannibal

known as the black crag of the cannibal Khadang.
If you do not recognize me,
I am the teurang Khenpa Gyenmo;
I have been alive for seven hundred years,
although I don't think of myself as old.
To explain my background—
months and years . . . long, long ago
in the time of the Buddha Dīpaṃkara,[9]
through the force of karma, I became a teurang
and was entrusted to protect Yama Thangchen.
Today, this very day,
I see men and horses hard at it—
first, horses fully tacked, with saddles and bridles,
second, men in uniform, their threefold panoply complete,
third, enemy flags flourishing, like a brash wind—
they have all arrived in the northern plains.
Where did all these men come from?
Where are they going?
These eight mountain ranges of the upper north
are not open for trespass.
Even though the great plain of Yama Thangchen is so flat,
horses are not free to run here;
wild horses cannot just come and flaunt their speed.
Even though I am old,
it is no place for your threefold panoply and your six skills;
a brave warrior cannot show off his troops here.
As for the reasons behind this—
the eight mountains of the upper north are ruled by
the powerful demon king,
lord of heaven and earth
and greatly famed in this world.
He can circle the heavens like lightning
and the earth as though it were his castle.
He can drink all the human and horse blood he likes,
and devour as much human and horse flesh as he desires;
it is his destiny to devour meat and drink blood.
I, Khenpa Genmo of Yama Thangchen,
am the demon's outer gatekeeper.

I never admit any wanderers,
but today, who are you who has meandered in?
What is your name, son?
What land have you come from?
What country are you going to?
Hide nothing! Tell me honestly!

A story and an arrow must be straight,
and the words and the bow bent to them.[10]

Otherwise, you are just asking for trouble.
If a great river wants to flow,
a strong dam cannot hold it back.
When a great man violates the law,
even if he is a high king, he cannot escape.
Think carefully about what you are doing.
You, warrior, keep this in mind.

The song was finished, and the boy said, "What you have said is true. Piece by piece, I will tell you my background. I came from upper Kongpo Draksum. My two brothers Chakchung and Mukchung[11] asked me to bring provisions and food for you. I am going on from here to see whether or not the Zhugadar Minister Chingngön (Ancient Felt)[12] and the warrior Atak Lhamo and the māra king Lutsen are well." Then, he sang this song of deceit to Khenpa Genmo.

Sing "Ala thala thala."
"Thala" begins.
The song unfolds in three parts.
This very day, I call the deities
not from nearby but from afar.
I call the Seven Siblings and the Bön god Taklha Mebar.
This place belongs to the one who accomplished the teurang
    life force.
I am the messenger of the māras of the dark side.
Namthel, Barthel, Sathel, teurangs of heaven, earth, and
    between,
today please come to assist me.
If you do not recognize this place,
it is at the foothills of the mountains of the upper north,

the great plain Yama Thangchen.
It is as round and flat as a roasting pan
and is therefore known as Yama (Slate).
Its dark crags look like the angry cannibal,
the rākṣasa gatekeeper Khadang.
You supreme mother who has accomplished the teurang,
this is my background:
I am from the white rock foothills of the Kongpo Valley.
High in this valley are four lakes:
first, Cannibal Red Lake in the northeast,
second, Great Spirit Lake in Gyaltsen,
third, Turquoise Lake in Beura,
fourth, Great Wood Lake in the upper valley.
Below these lakes are four valleys:
the first resembles the talons of the white falcon;
it is said to be the meditation place of Mañjuśrī.
The second is like a phurba raised to the skies;
it is said to be the meditation place of Vajrapāṇi.
The third is reminiscent of the mountain face of Falcon
    Fortress;
it is said to be the meditation place of Avalokiteśvara.
And the fourth is like a sheet of taut human skin;
it is said to be the domain of King Mukchung.
The māra castle built there is nine-storied,
and the warrior who lives within its walls
is the Zhugadar Minister Ching-ngön.
Khenpa Gyenmo, please listen closely.
This year I have come north,
and you don't seem to be yourself.
High on the plain Yama Thangchen,
horses' hooves thrum *tha la la*,
warriors brandish their threefold panoply *phar ra ra*,
the army commander unfurls the enemy flag *ur ru ru*—
yet you know nothing about them,
not where they came from, not where they are going.
That is a wretched state of affairs, don't you think?
Nevertheless, listen now.
First, an old pig has been slaughtered and butchered,

second, old wheat has been roasted and made into porridge,
and third, old barley has been boiled and fermented into
    liquor and chang.
These three gifts of wheat, barley, and pig—
I have a bit of each for you.
Chakchung, Mukchung, and I, Achung,
are brothers, your nephews.
I do not know what you should do;
nevertheless, I am the messenger bringing the news.

When a small spring comes up against an obstacle,
how can its water run freely?

Who will I come up against at the outset?
When I meet them, what should I say?
Are there answers to my questions?
What heart advice can you give?
Please answer my song.
If you do not understand, I cannot repeat my song.

Thus he sang, and then she said, "Boy, if you have come from the Kongpo Valley, you must know the lay of this land, its water and mountains. That is wonderful!" She invited him inside the rock cave where cooked and uncooked human flesh and blood and horse flesh and blood awaited him. When he turned his nose up at it, she offered rabbit yogurt, but this too he refused, saying, "Please sit and I will serve you some porridge made from the provisions I have brought: roasted old wheat, deep cuts of old pig meat, and liquor from old barley, and then we can talk." Since she thought she was his aunt, she sat down and drank the liquor, and soon enough she was drunk. She chattered on, "Listen to what I have to tell you. *Don't tell outsiders about private matters or drag outside rumors home.* Understand? Because I have secrets that only you should hear," and then she sang.

Sing "Ala thala thala."
"Thala" begins.
This very day I call to the divine ones.
Guardians of the teachings of Garab,
teurang—white, black, multihued—know me.
There are none above you to invoke.
If you do not recognize this place,

it is Yama Thangchen.
If you do not recognize me,
I am known as the long-legged female teurang of the north;[13]
my actual name is Khenpa Genmo.
Until today,
from the time of the māra king Trarab,[14]
all the way back to Yakṣa Nakpo,
I have been the earth-protector of these lands.
Here in these northern climes,
the demon Lutsen,
an emanation of the māra king Trarab Wangchuk,
is the king of the demon rākṣasas and pretas
and the charioteer of mortal beings.
To reach this land is difficult.
Listen now to this ruddy old woman Khenpa Genmo.
Look how far you have strayed—
why didn't you stay where you were happy?
What possessed you to come north?
What reasons can you give?
Now, my dear son,[15]
over these past several days
on Yama Thangchen,
lines of men and horses have been parading *khuk sé khuk*,
white and red helmet pennants have been fluttering *heb sé
    heb*,
and young men and women have banded together *rub sé rub*.
Desperate for a source of water,
warriors have been crisscrossing, scouring the land;
I guess they are the brave men of Ling.
On the highest rocky maroon cliffs
eleven steeds were milling about the pasture;
I guess they must be the horses of Ling.
That must be the wretched evil Joru[16] with them
headed north.
I guess he has designs on Meza.
Tell me, is that true or isn't it?
I sent some of the teurang children
to round up those eleven steeds,

and conceal them
inside a rock cave.
Among those grazing steeds
is one amazing horse
with the three colors of a wild kyang,
white, red, and gray—
the red of spreading flames,
a gray, light enough to clear darkness,
and a white radiant as a victory banner silk.
The kyang steed supports in three ways:
his shoulders hoist the army commander's war flag,
on his back rides the auspicious prosperity wheel,
and his torso hefts the seven royal treasures of a universal
	monarch.
As I think on it, that kyang steed
must be the fiendish horse of that wretched Joru.
Tell me if I speak the truth.
Today, those eleven steeds—is it better to kill them or leave
	them?
Is it better to give them back or hide them?
You must tell me.
And I have another incredible incident to divulge:
in a single instant a lightning bolt struck from the heavens,
destroying the fortress Drakmar—
do you know anything about that?
To go to the north
is not an easy journey.
The river valley is pitch dark,
closed in on all sides.
Forget about even a sliver of light, you will be groping in
	complete darkness.
No one will answer your calls.
And never mind about your weapons—you will be backed
	into a corner.
Then, farther on, coming to the highlands,
are the serrated red crags,
where the rocks bear down from above
and thrust up from below.

Like jaws, they clench together against your skull—
even if you were a bird, you could not fly away,
and even if you were a worm you could not find anywhere to
    crawl.
That is called the bite of the red rocks of Shinjé.
Now, as you continue northward,
that deep river gorge is the black river of death.
Its strong current roils into a great cascading waterfall,
while its weaker offshoots trickle downstream.
It is the life-force river of the māra Garab,
the sweat of the evil Trarab,
and the water of the evil spirits, curses, and diseases—
this one river is the water of all three.
Even one with the power of the lord of death cannot ford this
    river;
attempting a crossing is the same as dying and going to the
    hell realms.
Now, as you continue on,
on a seat atop the snowy heights of Mount Kailash,[17]
a white snow lion will appear showing off a turquoise mane.
The māra Acham Karmo
will come mounted on that lion,
singing a hundred melodies
difficult to counter.
Then, farther north,
you will come to the mud lake Damtsho of Shinjé,
where men and horses sink
and neither winged birds
nor the icy wind can escape.
You will be surrounded by male demons, female demons,
    dead demons, and relative demons—
there, these demons, cannibals, and evil spirits sing happy
    songs
and call you to your death.
Now, even farther north
is the long-horned brown māra yak.
Its right horn reaches the heavens
and its left pierces the earth.

The sky and earth churn,
violent, poisonous waves waft up from its horn tips,
lightning flashes from its tongue,
its tail switches like slow-moving southern clouds,
and its hooves spin like wheels of iron.
Despite their solidity, the rocks will be shattered
and not withstanding their size, the mountains will be
    destroyed.
It is difficult to plan an escape from the māra yak.
You will never get through all of that;
even I have never been any farther.
The king of the north, Lutsen,
they say is somewhat ill.
I heard that he was healing through the magic of the Mu,
but not that he was cured.
Keep this in mind.

Those were the teurang Genmo's words, and the boy feigned that he thought she had spoken the truth, exclaiming agreement and bidding her sleep, "Oh, yes! Now, slumber that I have served you such liquor and excellent meats. As for those eleven horses of that nasty Ling child Joru, keep them hidden. Although I wonder if there does exist such a horse of red, gray, and white."

Gesar went on, "I have heard that the infamous Ling child Joru is the worst kind of enemy. It would be best if we kept quiet!" The old woman saw the truth in this. "Yes," she replied, "But I am of two minds about what you have said . . . my hope was that you were the minister Ching-ngön, but I fear that you could be a magical emanation sent by the Ling child Joru. Whatever the case, I have these sixty keys, ten each of iron, conch, brass, copper, gold, and silver, and tonight you must keep them safe. Take particular care of this small iron box as I have already put Lutsen's life-force stones in it; you must be very vigilant!" she said. Gesar, still pretending to be the boy Achung, asked what kind of life-stones they were. She replied that inside the box there were various insects such as lice, fleas, flies, and so forth that ate the flesh of living humans and drank their warm blood. She advised that the only way to be rid of them was to burn them in a fire. The old woman was intoxicated and completely confused. Gesar immediately summoned the 360 teurang children and, straddling the neck of Khenpa Genmo, said, "Listen closely. In the morning I am the butcher; in the afternoon I am the guru who liberates. I am the messenger of a thousand buddhas, the wealthy lord of both China and Tibet, and the pillar between heaven and earth. So, if you have faith in the one who protects the side of virtue, the time has come for faith and confession. Today is your one chance, otherwise you will lose this, your cherished life." Then, Gesar offered this song.

Sing "Ala thala thala."
"Thala" begins.
The song is sung through the mindstream of bodhicitta
with the successive and distinctive melodies of the Buddha.[18]
Today, I call the deity.
Divine dharmakāya, saṃbhogakāya, nirmāṇakāya,
source of blessings, look upon me.
Brave dralha and werma, please assist me.
If you do not recognize this place,
it is the upper northern plain Yama Thangchen
enclosed within these dark rock outcroppings.
If you do not know me,
I come from Ling, the pure realm in the east,
my mother is Gokza
and I am the noble being of Ling, Joru.
My real name is Norbu Dradül.
If you do not recognize this song,
it is the heroic song that tames the enemy.
I do not sing it just anywhere,
but this very day I sing it to you.
You, the western māra teurang woman,
with your 360 children around you,
arose as the enemy of the Buddhadharma.
In the past, when Buddha Kāśyapa[19]
turned the Wheel of Dharma,
you supported the violent Trarab
and endeavored to abolish the teachings of virtue.
First, that māra Yakṣa Nakpo,
second, that māra Rudra Nakpo—
you are aware of the stories of these evil māras,
but I will explain them to you.
Suppose you listen to the song.
Listen. The story goes like this:
conch, gold, iron, brass, copper,

and silver keys, six kinds,
for the demon king of the north,
the gates of his soul, life force, and body,
those are the keys that protect all three.
But today they have come into Joru's hands,
denoting the time to shoot an arrow into the demon's
    skull
and for the north lands to turn to the Dharma.
Therefore, I came with my ministers.
We set up an encampment on Yama Thangchen,
letting our horses to roam the mountain pasture.
While the Ling steeds were grazing,
your bandits seized them in broad daylight
and hid them in a cave[20] among the dark rock outcroppings.
You arrogantly prattle on *ur ru ru*,
claiming that you will slaughter the Ling horses
and destroy Joru and his evil ways.
This is nothing but nonsense, Genmo.
Today, Ling Joru has arrived here in this land
and rides your neck.
Do you think the enemy is intimidated? Is that why you are
    not fighting?
Do you think the horses are already destroyed? Is that why
    you are not looking after them?
Do you think the fire has burned out? Is that why you are not
    extinguishing it?
That is no way to act.
Are you remorseful or merely trying to endure?
There is no way around it—your fortitude will be short-lived,
and in the end you will lose your life.
But if you have genuine remorse,
you must confess right now.
Request refuge in me as the Buddha
and I will spare your life.
You will become a guardian of the side of virtue
and be sealed into these red crags.
You will be a guardian of the teachings of the Buddha.
If that does not happen this very day,

you will lose your cherished life.
Genmo, think carefully what is best.
If you have not understood, I am not going to repeat my
song.

Thus he sang, and the old woman thought, "The ancient proverbs do say that at the time of death one must ask[21] the māras for help; that is certainly true." Then, she said, "Rather than death, I choose to do as you have said. I will be sealed in this red crag and generate sincere intention toward virtue and serve as a protector of the teachings of the Buddha." Gesar blessed Khenpa Genmo with the longevity vase, elegantly decorated with auspicious symbols, that he had received from Amitāyus, saying, "From today onward, eat no meat, drink no blood, take not another's life nor breath. Furthermore, as I have established you as the red tsen life-ruler of 10,900,000, you will assist the White Lotus King (Avalokiteśvara). Reside there as the retinue and circumambulate the 360 deities." Gesar placed a large buddha statue on Genmo's head and sealed her into the crag. Then, he herded the horses down, arriving at the Ling warrior encampment at daybreak, and returned each horse to its own warrior. Joyous and realizing that they surely would not have lasted without Gesar, with great devotion they offered him splendid food and drink, repeatedly requesting blessings with aspiration prayers.

After some time, Gesar spoke to the warriors, "There is no way you can go on any farther. The fact is that I bound the 360 teurang by oath, turned Genmo to the virtuous Dharma, and authorized her to be the red tsen lord of life force in the retinue of Avalokiteśvara. But even so, I don't know what will happen from here on out. I will tell you why you should not continue on with me." And Gesar proclaimed the vajra warrior's song, "Six Modulations," to the Pathül.

Sing "Ala thala thala."
"Thala" begins.
The song unfolds in three parts.
The start is majestic and stately,
mirroring the great Brahmā,
the middle is fast and lively,
reflecting that Nyenchen Kulha fills the space with his every
movement,
and the end reaches beyond the boundaries,
just as Tsukna's realm is distant.
This song is free from center and fringe

and calls out its unceasing melody.
If you do not recognize this place,
it is Yama Thangchen of the north,
the land where the grass blows in the wind,
where the thick grass sighs
and the thin grass whistles,
and together they sing a wailing song.
I never before saw such an eerie place.
If you do not recognize me,
I am Joru, the nephew of Gok.
Listen, warriors of Ling,
what is it you are thinking?
Yesterday, seven Pathül
went off in search of water.
They found none, but they wound up in a breath-bag
and buried beneath dark crags.
They came within an inch of their lives.
Guided by Manéné,
the serrated crags
and the mountain of gray slate and maroon clay
were struck by a lightning bolt.
The face of the mountain plummeted,
the back side collapsed,
and the rocks rained down as dust.
The leather breath-bag was ripped open,
saving the seven Pathül.
We had left our horses grazing,
and when they disappeared in front of our own eyes,
I had ventured after them.
Although our horses are said to be divine,
that did them no good,
as the teurang Genmo had them rounded up
and hidden in a dark rocky cave,
tormented by the lack of food and water.
Cleverly, I entered her castle
and took her in with my stories.
Ultimately, she was bound by oath,
and the 360 teurang bound to serve,

placed in middle ranks of assembly of eight classes.
You six warriors who have come[22] this far with me:
Gyatsha Dungda Karchung,
Kyalo Tönpa Gyaltsen,
Serpa Nyibum Daryak,
Denkhor Denma Jangtra,
Seng Adom Miyi Changki,
Chölu Buyi Darphen,
you must not stay, but return to Ling
and, there, defend what is yours.
Your journey home will be free of obstacles.
Knotted white silk longevity scarves,
those of the one hundred thousand ḍākinīs—
I have one for each warrior,
and I will supplicate the Three Jewels to protect you.
All this boils down to the main point that
as far as the future of Ling is concerned,
although the arrival of the enemy bandits is uncertain,
there is no reason for each to act alone.
First, let Rongtsha spell out the issues,
second, settle on a common goal,
and third, you warriors act in concert.
Do not forget all of this; keep it in mind.
Nyatsha, Nang-ngu, and Rongtsha are the youngest of
the group of young warriors of Ling.
We must look after them;
above all they must grow up happy.
In turn, I will continue northward.
It is as the proverbs say:

The white vulture lives on human flesh—
a gruesome life, it understands, but one set in motion long ago.
The blue mountain wolf roams remote lands[23]—
a life that gifts only suffering, but one set in motion long ago.

I was selected to expel the enemy,
a heavy burden but, long ago, set in motion
when the ancient gods sent me down as Joru.

Tomorrow, right at sunrise,
to everyone's surprise, the māra damsi will come.
Pathül, keep this in mind.
If you have not understood, I cannot repeat my song.

The warriors received the song with tears streaming down their faces and wept that they must take leave of their king. Denma Jangtra offered a white silk cloth to Gesar saying, "Your words are excellent. Since you have the higher perceptions, please continually watch over all of us as we return home. It is clear that we are not to accompany you; still, I have an important matter to mention." And he sang this song, "Six Reverberations of Thala."

Sing "Ala thala thala."
"Thala" begins.
The song unfolds in three parts.
From India, the earthly seat of dharmakāya,
on Vulture Peak Mountain,
I am the manifestation of Saraha.
Now, I have taken rebirth
in the upper country of Den
as a descendant of King Den Trokar.
With a matriarchal suffix to my name,[24]
I am called Denma Jangtra.
This song, if you don't know it, is Denma's song,
"Six Reverberations of Thala"—
a song not to be sung just anywhere,
but today there is no choice.
If you are happy, it is a marvelous song of tea and
    chang;
if sad, it is a song to restore your mind.
We, this entourage of Ling ministers,
have journeyed eighteen days on horseback
to escort Gesar
as far as Yama Thangchen.
But several obstacles have arisen.
Generally, ministers go with their king
on a quest to benefit others.
Here are examples from the proverbs:

The finest white garuḍa dzos are yoked,
roped together as they cross the land
to bring treasured grain to the clans of Tibet.

A king and ministers unite
to annihilate[25] the loathsome enemy
and bring harmony to the world realm.
But the situation in the north today
makes old customs outmoded,
and it seems we are fated to part ways with our king.
What I am saying is that
we are bound to follow our king's direction
and return to Ling.
When he takes his leave of us,
we should make prayers to be soon reunited.
Gesar the Great Lion
must go alone to the north.
This is the ancient edict of the gods,
your heartfelt objective, Sengchen Lama,
and vital to all sentient beings.
There is no better endeavor than this.
Today, as your minister, I request that
when you journey north
and come to their armed fortress,
first, do not fall prey to the evil māras
and, second, do not get taken in with longing for a beautiful
    woman.
As much as possible, think things through.
Watch out for a deceptive woman's words.
She may harbor both good and evil.
The clouds of the early night sky may be white,
but darken with night's advance
to bring down torrential rains.
One side of a woman's face may glow like the waxing moon
while the other swirls with dark gray clouds,
deceiving a young man.
There are proverbs like that:

Even a worthy man can be enticed by a woman's beauty—
there are many accounts of this.
Just so, gambling can seduce that same man—
the tales of this are legion.
And it goes without saying that liquor can beguile—
there is no one who does not know this.

In this world domain,
there are three downfalls of great men—
first is drinking,
second is gambling,
third is lust for beautiful women—
this is my heartfelt advice
and the prayer of the Pathül.
With this aspiration on our lips, we head for home.
Sengchen, keep this in your heart.
May our paths cross again and again.

Thus he sang, and the Ling Pathül sat there sighing, their eyes moist with tears, while Adom Sengtak[26] stood to present a treasured white silk khata to the king and sing this song of supplication and aspiration.

The song is "Ala thala thala."
"Thala" begins.
The song unfolds in three parts.
Today, I call to the gods
of the dharmakāya, saṃbhogakāya, and nirmāṇakāya.
Look upon me and grant your blessings.
Please be the guide of my song.
May the gods and lamas lead its start,
the ḍākinīs sustain the middle,
and the dharmapālas guard its end.
May the dralha and werma look upon me with kindness.
If you do not recognize this place,
it is Yama Thangchen of the north.
If you do not recognize me,
from the flaring edge of the iconic Vulture Nest Fortress,
I am the eminent steadfast warrior,

Darjé Khyungyal Sengtak.
I am Seng Adom Miyi Changki.[27]
If you do not recognize this song,
it is the very short song of the warrior Adom—
a song not to be sung just anywhere,
but today there is no choice.
Enlightened supreme king Gesar,
listen with your heart to my request.
That you must go alone to the north
you said was the prophecy of the gods
and the beckoning of the demon Lutsen.
Although we tried hard to understand,
we could not make sense of it.[28]
As in the oral traditions of old:

Where there is a leader, there are attendants.
Where there is a horse, there is a saddle.

But these are sayings from a time gone by.
I wonder why that is.
I have asked myself over and over.
It turns out that our way of escorting you
was just to follow along,
but today, here in the north,
we encountered much that we did not expect.
Many difficulties arose.
Forget about us being of help;
we have just caused you trouble.
Thinking on it, I know only regret.
The divine prophecy is faultless;
the king's command is without error.
We ministers did not understand the crux of the
    matter.
A man is riled up by a devious woman,
the earth is churned up by a crow,
and the country is riled up by evil māras.[29]
Here are examples from the proverbs:
isn't this what the proverbs say?

Though the sky is thick with mist,
its intention is not to create darkness
but, rather, blizzards of snow and rain
to welcome the seeds of spring.

Likewise, though Gesar goes for the purpose
of assailing the māra with an arrow,
his desire is to sow the Buddhadharma.
There is no endeavor more worthy.
The divine prophecy is excellent;
the king's command is strong.
Now, to act accordingly,
we must return to our own countries.
But we warriors, the lot of us,
after we return to our land
unaccompanied by you,
if enemies have appeared, how should we retaliate?
If we find friends, how should we repay their kindness?
How can we create a bond between ourselves and others?
Please give us your clear advice.
Noble being Sengchen Gesar,
as you journey on alone,
so that the māras will not hinder you,
we will offer prostrations
and pray no obstacles arise.

Thus he sang, and Gesar merely smiled, saying, "All that is true, and in due time I will gladly offer my advice." Then, Serpa Nyibum Daryak stood up holding a single white silk scarf with the finest turquoise knotted into its end as protection and, offering it to Gesar, sang this song.

Sing "Ala thala thala."
"Thala" begins.
The song unfolds in three parts.
May the gods and lamas lead its start,
the ḍākinīs sustain its middle,
and the dharmapālas guard the end.
May the dralha and werma look upon me with kindness.
May the vidyādharas and lamas support me.

If you do not recognize this place,
it is Yama Thangchen of the north.
If you do not recognize me,
as one of the eight Serpa brothers of Upper Ling,
and the general of the golden-helmeted ones,
I am called Serpa Nyibum Daryak:
Nyibum is one who hammers the enemy,
the Dharma minister of Sengchen Lama,
and the ally of Gyatsha Zhalkar.
Now, precious noble being,
for now, we must go our separate ways;
it seems this is karmic destiny.
Sengchen, leave quickly for the north lands.
We ministers are obliged to return to Ling.
Sengchen, as you go north,
first, may the māras create no obstacle.
And as we return to Ling,
second, we wish no trouble from the obstructing spirits.
As for the maṇḍala encompassing Ling,
thirdly, may its government not have declined.
We ask that all these be your blessings, Sengchen Lama.
Here are examples from the proverbs:

The snow lion on the crystalline mountain
promises this year to roam the slate crags[30]
so that the snow will not melt in the sun
and that the mountains will be still and stable.
The lion swears this will be so.
The wild drong on the snow-stippled ridges
promises this year to roam the grassy meadows
so that the rocky crags are not destroyed by thunderbolts
and that the valley will be still and stable.
The golden brown drong swears this will be so.
The red tiger of the sandalwood forest
promises this year to appear beside the riverbank
so that the forested mountain will not be consumed by fire,
and that the tiger cubs will develop their stripes.
The Bengal tiger swears this will be so.

Gesar the minister who resides in Ling
promises this year to go north
so that no bandit enemies appear in Ling,
and that Ling may be at peace.
Please swear that this will be so, Sengchen Gyalpo.
Today, as we part,
I offer this aspiration prayer
that Brahmā may be your refuge and protector,
and, so that no harm comes to the fine horse Kyang,
may Amitāyus be his refuge and protector.
May our aspiration prayers be fulfilled.
May the signs and auspicious connections come together.
May the king and ministers soon reunite.

Thus he sang, and Takrong Nyatsha Aten stood up and presented fifty gold coins wrapped in a white silk scarf, offering them to Gesar as he began this song of aspiration.

Sing "Ala thala thala."
"Thala" begins.
Today, I call the deity.
Divine dharmakāya, saṃbhogakāya, nirmāṇakāya, those three—
may the seat of the dharmakāya expand,
may the saṃbhogakāya be of benefit to beings,
and may the blessings of the nirmāṇakāya be great.
If you do not recognize this place,
it is Yama Thangchen in the north.
If you do not recognize me,
from the Raven Heart Fortress,
I am one of four warriors famed throughout the world,
Nyatsha Aten of Takrong,
the cousin of Gesar,
the compatriot of the leader Nang-ngu [the youngest son of
    Chipön].
Precious Gesar,
listen. I have several things to point out:
first, there are many divine prophecies,
second, you are fired up to go,

third, my father Trothung has many strategies,
and fourth, you have a wealth of advisors.
Without all of this, there would be disaster.
Your journey to the north lands
is for the benefit of beings
and to aid the teachings of the Buddha.
Now, as we part ways,
I have another request of you:
I, your cousin Nyatsha,
will turn eighteen this year,
and even though I am in the prime of my life,
it seems many obstacles await me.
I will tell you why.
The portents are adverse,
and all my dreams are ill-omened.
I dreamed of myself, a youth[31] traveling on a road
when demonic forces arose
and my legs would not move.
Then, in last night's dream,
as the sun moved through the heavens,
it was devoured by Rāhula
and the world enveloped in darkness.
As the conch moon roamed the skies,
it plummeted behind a mountain pass
and the constellations fell to the earth.
I am glad if this is but a dream,
but if it is an ill portent, that is bad.
Which is it—dream or omen?
I have thought it over and over
without understanding it
and, so, came to you for advice, Great Lion.
There is one more important matter:
prattling and rattling, rumors go on and on,
strained, drained, I pin my ears back to hear.
Sparring, warring—Hor and Ling will fight.
Tossed, lost—they say Nang-ngu will be lost.
Time and again, I heard them say it,
and I have thought about it over and over.

Soon, soon please be his refuge.
First, [if he dies,] please guide his way
and second, keep him from falling to the hell realms.
This is my request.
On this very day,
I offer a silk khata,
praying to meet you again.
Inside this jeweled amulet box
are three kinds of precious gems
offered so that we are swiftly reunited.

Thus he sang, and Gesar's face, hitherto clear as the full moon, clouded, dark as rain-soaked rocks, and he said, "If I think through your dream, it seems that Nang-ngu may well be lost in Hor. I will have Nyatsha bring the vajra protection armor and the longevity knot of the Queen of Siddhis, as well as relic hairs of one thousand buddhas. And I pray we will meet soon." As he sat down, Zikphen stood up and presented a white silk khata to Gesar. He offered his own song of aspiration, asking for blessings.

Sing "Ala thala thala."
"Thala" begins.
The song unfolds in three parts.
Today, I call the deities.
Dharmakāya, saṃbhogakāya, and nirmāṇakāya,
please look upon me and grant your blessings.
Omniscient ones, lead this man in song.
From your lotus seat upon the crown of my head,
gracious root guru, look upon me.
From the Dharma palace within my heart,
Dharmakāya Samantabhadra with consort, know me.
From the maṇḍala of the five buddhas in my body,
peaceful and wrathful supreme one hundred families, care for
    me.
I call to none other.
If you do not recognize this place,
here within the eight mountain ranges of the upper north
is the great plain Yama Thangchen.
If you do not recognize me,

from the vibrant districts of Takrong,
I am the steadfast warrior Anu Zikphen
famed throughout the world.
In times gone by,
a leader and his troops traveled as one.
King Sengchen,
before your birth in Upper Ling,
the leaders of its army
went to China
and invited Gyaza Lhakar to return;
Gyatsha was born to her.
They went to the farmlands
and invited Rongza Lhamo to return;
Rongtsha was born to her.
They went to the country of Gok
and invited Gokza Lhamo to return;
Gesar, you were born to her.
These three sons born to these great mothers—
Ling is indebted to them.
Always, until now,
however victory came about, it was that
first, the warriors went shoulder to shoulder,
second, the leaders and troops went as one,
and third, the lord and ministers went side by side.
We owe our good fortune to collaborations such as these.
But from now on,
Gesar must go it alone.
There is no way around this; it is the divine prophecy.
Talking more will change nothing.
Gesar goes to bring well-being to the north,
but suppose he never returns—
beyond the cycle of saṃsāra, what will be left for Ling?
Birds may feel most at home in the sky,
but suppose they never land—
what will become of their nests?
The tawny drong come to the pastures to graze,
but suppose they are not able to return—
what will become of the milieu of the rocks?

Since you have the omniscience of the buddhas,
please clear up our confusion.
I also had a bad dream:
water poured down from the snow mountain,
pitch-black water filled the valleys,
and, in my dream, a black-cloaked man[32] appeared.
I was hurled against the rocky crags
and propelled into Yama's prison,
covered with fresh red blood.
Without question, these are not good signs;
please help me discern their meaning.
This very day,
a khata from the amulet box,
in particular, an auspicious silk
adorned with a self-arising jewel and lotus design,
I place into your hands.
Precious king, Sengchen,
sublime among humans,
may your glory be unbounded
and may the northern demon be subjugated.
May the capable supreme steed Kyang Gö,
champion stallion of the horse race
with a gait that outpaces the swift flight of birds,
may the good fortune of Hayagrīva come to you.
Gesar, may your vajra body be completed by the threefold
    panoply.
May your armor be strong
and may you be victorious.
Gesar, take all this to heart.
Please forgive any fault in my song.

Thus he sang, and Gesar knew in his heart that what Zikphen and Nyatsha and the other ministers had said was true. In particular, he knew the young warriors faced great peril and he had heard it said before that the Hor army would descend upon Ling. His eyes welled with tears as he realized the urgency of going to the north and also of returning home quickly in order to shield the young warriors from danger. Just then, Akhu Trothung, quite beside himself, blurted out, "I[33] have something to say," but as he started to stand, Gesar said, "Akhu, please stay in your seat." Reminding the Pathül that he was adamant that they return home, Gesar sang this aspiration song.

> Sing "Ala thala thala."
> "Thala" begins.
> The song unfolds in three parts.
> The song of the father lineage is the song of emptiness like the sky.
> I pledge to sing the song of emptiness,
> like the lofty heavens, a song beyond center or fringe.
> The song of the mother lineage is a song of an overflowing river.
> I pledge to sing the song of overflowing,
> like a river, a song that flows unceasingly.
> The song of my own mindstream is the song of channels and
>   winds.
> I pledge to sing the song of magic,
> a song of unobstructed energy,
> a song of attaining mastery over channels and winds.
> My song is called "Quells the Great Crowd with Splendor."
> It is not sung just anywhere,
> but today I sing it to the young warriors of Ling.
> Listen, I have some things to tell you.
> Tomorrow, and the next day, and the next, those three—
> do not delay more than three days from now,
> the time has come for you young warriors to go to Ling.
> My regent Gyatsha Zhalu Karpo
> and Chieftain Akhu Trothung
> must be of one mind, with one goal—
> the common good and well-being of Ling.
> First of all, confer with each other,
> then discuss the issues with the ministers.
> Do not let self-interest undermine general welfare.
> Gyatsha, listen to me.
> When the bitter enemy comes to Ling,
> approach them with intelligence and wisdom.
> Do not act out of anger and jump into enemy hands;
> you, Uncle Trothung, are the expert at this.
> When you are back in your own country,
> don't be two-faced like a ḍamaru;

do your best to defend those who are young.
If, as it is said, the Hor army comes to Ling,
these five warriors should be dispatched:
Darphen, Gadé, Denma, Sengtak, and Nyibum[34]—
these five warriors have received medals of victory.
None but these five have had such great danger in their lives.
If, as is said, the Jang troops come to Ling,
the ones to oppose their demon-warriors[35] should be:
Gyatsha, Gadé, and Sengtak Adom.[36]
These three warriors should be dispatched.
Gyatsha, Yuyi Metok, Rongtsha, Takrong Nyatsha Aten, and
    Zikphen[37]—
these are the five men who can prevail in the face of danger.
Concerning the dream of Anu Zikphen
and that of cousin Nyatsha—
these dreams are not good but bad.
Not really dreams but omens
whose meaning will become evident.
You must be attentive and act carefully.
Water pours from the peak of the snow mountain,
as black water fills the mountain valleys.
If you think about it, it is the life-force water of the māras.
There is danger that Zikphen will drown.
You must be especially cautious by the water.
The conch moon and stars wander the heavens
and suddenly they fall to earth.
If you think about it, it is the māra lasso that was thrown.
Perhaps Nyatsha will be caught.
Do not leap thoughtlessly into the hands of the enemy.
The Hor minister Tongkor Drukdrak (Roaring Dragon
    Monarch)—
when he hurls his strong lasso,
even then, don't show off your bravery.
Better to carefully hold your own castle.
Now, I have still more to say.
In the land of the evil māras,
if no obstacles arise,
in exactly ninety-nine days,

it will be time to shoot an arrow into the demon's skull;
then, I will try to return without delay.
As for Meza Bumdrön,
she is not of the ilk to deceive me.
She is the emanation of Red Vajravārāhī,
who turns the wheel of Dharma for virtuous disciples.
Gradually, you will see this.

Before a flood, dam up the water;
before you mount a horse, check its saddle.

That is what is said, and it is the truth.
When events ripen,
all of this will become clear.
Today, young Ling warriors,
do not stay here, return to your own country.
First of all, the protection cord of one hundred thousand
    ḍākinīs,
second, the longevity pills of the Queen of Siddhis,
and third, relic hairs of one thousand buddhas—
these three blessings have been bestowed.
Supplicate the Three Jewels
to clear obstacles from this life,
to be led from the hell realms,
and to be born in a higher realm.
Pray that these three will come to pass.
Make many prostrations and offerings.
If you have understood, this is the teaching of your lama.
If you have not understood, I cannot repeat it.

Thus he sang, and all the young warriors of Ling openly praised Gesar. They promised to act in accord with these commands and went to saddle up their horses. Just then, Akhu Trothung confronted Gesar and said, "Precious nephew Gesar, I am your uncle, not just another minister, and I have come to escort you farther along, another three day's horse ride from here." He was so persistent that Gesar could not help but accept. Gesar, Drukmo, Trothung, and Michung watched as far as the eye could see while the warriors rode into the distance and one after another reined their horses and turned onto the road back to Ling.

CHAPTER TWELVE

Gesar and his three companions arrived at Jema Lachen
    (Sandy Mountain Pass).
They had no choice but to make a hearth with their knees.
When Drukmo asked the names of the Hor mountains,
Gesar said that soon enough, she would go to Hor.

THE NEXT DAY AT DAWN, GESAR, DRUKMO, TROTHUNG, and the young
Michung, traveling slowly on foot, arrived at the great northern plain of Meri Barwa.
There, mature falcons displayed the power of their full-grown wings, white vultures
fanned their wings, and the great garuḍa soared. That windswept land was known as
Jema Lachen. Brahmā sent snow that fell for three nights and days, stranding Gesar
and the other three without water, firewood, or hearthstones. Gesar went in search
of firewood and, at a recess in a rocky outcropping, came upon a broken-legged wolf
carrying a load of firewood that he dropped in front of Gesar. Gesar carried it down
and said cheerfully to Trothung, "There is nowhere to obtain hearthstones. As you
are the one with the mastery of black magic mantra, and I am the one with the major
marks of a siddha, we cannot sit here idly. Akhu, you must put out your two knees
and I will put out one knee; with our three knees, we will make a hearth and boil
tea." Akhu grumbled, "If you can put out just one knee, why can't I also put out only
one?" In the end, they each put out both knees[1] and were able to make a hearth.
They lit a fire and made tea.

    Gesar continued, "Now, we must also heat water for washing." But the fire
flamed up, and the water boiled over, scalding Gesar's knee. Gesar pulled his leg
away and the boiling water spilled onto Trothung's lap, burning his thighs and

crotch. He put ointment on his wounds and said black magic mantras, but to no avail. Despondent, he said, "Now, I have lost my chance to accompany you, and without my help it will be difficult for you to accomplish what you have set out to do. What if Meza offers you amnesia-inducing food and water?" Trothung offered this song to Gesar.

Sing "Ala thala thala."
"Thala" begins.
Invoke with OM MATRĪ MUYÉ SALÉ DU.
Liberate with AHKAR AMÉ DUTRI SOK.
Destroy with NAKPO SHIK MA MA YAK.[2]
Through black magic power, when I say HŪM, the demons
    die and with PHEṬ, they fall unconscious.
The sand blessed with this mantra severs anything it touches.
Now, I call the gods.
Bön longevity vidyādhara, know me.
Bön emanation Shenrab, know me.
Bön golden lamas all together,
today I entreat you to befriend me.
If you do not recognize this place,
it is the great northern plain of Meri Barwa,
the native land of māras and cannibals
and the stomping ground of the spirits of the dead.
If you do not recognize me,
from the impenetrable Dzama Abyss,
from the deep shade of the black *suru* bushes,[3]
from the iconic Raven Heart Fortress,
I am the Takrong chieftain Trothung,
the master of black magic and evil mantra.
I employ this power as I choose
and freely bring down[4] hailstorms.
This is who I am.
Today, you, noble being Gesar,
the emanation of the protectors of the three families
and the essence of Vajradhara,
when you encounter the evil māras,
do not be inattentive; be very careful.

May no harm come to you.
The maiden Meza comes from a bad family line,
and it is said that she is an expert at deception.
Do not be careless or have only your own pleasure in mind.
Drukmo and Michung
will escort you a bit farther;
they have offered to serve you.
I will not stay but will return to Ling
to protect the thirty young warriors.
Just as a hen would protect a golden egg
and, even though she wished to fly,
never abandon her eggs,
just so, I am up to the task.
Precious Gesar,
one, the mighty power of an elephant,
two, the bravery of the wild brown drong,
three, a roar like that of the turquoise dragon in the sky—
this year, may you reveal all three to the māra lands.
Among the 360 māra ministers
are four men of great power:
Changwa Lakring is one,
Chakchung and Mukchung make three,
and Yerkha Nanak is the fourth.
When you encounter these four demons,
in spite of your magic, it will be difficult.
To tame them, you will need the sand mantra,
as well as the sorcery of bringing unconsciousness and death.
The eight-syllable sand mantra is the black magic power,
which today I offer to you.
If you diligently recite the mantra syllables,
they will be of service to you when you reach the highlands of
    the north,
and you will be the one to receive the bounty.
A mala of countless precious pearls,
an incomparable garland,
I offer to you, Gesar.
This excellent turquoise,[5]

a mala of one hundred small turquoise beads,
I offer to you, Drukmo.
A single white silk khata
wrapping thirty gold coins,
I offer to you, eloquent Michung.
You, Michung,
must do whatever the king asks of you
and take great care of the supreme steed Kyang Gö.
You must become practiced in serving.
The invisible magical demon emanations
and those of the teurang—
guard against them.
Even if you gather up all of your bodily strength,
it is difficult to face them both;
even if you compose your mind and pluck up your courage,
it is difficult to face the cannibal demon spirits.
That is the reality of my experience.
Well then, precious Gesar,
until we meet again, be well,
and I hope that it will be soon.
Keep this in your heart.

Thus he sang, and Gesar said, "Yes, what you have said is true. There is no difference between a father and an uncle, nor between a mother and an aunt. Now, I offer to you Uncle Trothung this lance Darkar Tshomo (White Banner Ocean). When you travel on the mountain pass, use it as a walking stick; when you descend the mountain, it will support your legs. What's more, here is a golden swan's egg made from agate and a pearl egg given to me by Gomchen Tingmé; keep both of these within you, as there will come a time when you will need them." Both objects dissolved into Trothung, and he set off eastward toward Ling.

The next day as the sun rose over the eastern mountain peaks, Gesar and Drukmo, together with Michung, had reached the māra mountain Münpa Chutrik (Shrouded in Clouds). They stopped there to eat and drink, and Drukmo thought, "There is land wherever I look—India above, to the west, China below, to the east, and in between, the four regions of Central Tibet [Ütsang]. Not far away, I see white mountains, and red, black, and yellow mountains. I would like to go there." Excitedly, Drukmo said to Gesar, "Listen, don't you think this is a great idea?" She sang her song, "Melody in Six Reverberations."

Sing "Ala thala thala."
"Thala" begins.
The song unfolds in three parts.
Today, I call to the deities.
From the pure realm, the buddhafield of dharmakāya,
from the supreme realm of Akaniṣṭha,
goddess mother Vajrayoginī, look upon me with compassion.
Throughout the three times, from the buddhafield of
    dharmakāya,
maternal lineage Vajravārāhī,
omniscient one, come to assist me.
There is no one other than you to call.
If you do not recognize this place,
it is the māra mountain Münpa Chutrik
in the highlands of the north.
If you do not recognize me,
I am Sengcham Drukmo of Ling.
Up until today,
because of your many illusions, Gesar,
as well as my own arrogance,
I was mistaken in not wanting you.
I did not understand that you are a buddha,
I did not realize that your spiritual instructions were like
    nectar.
All of this thwarted the deepening of our karmic love.
I have given this a lot of thought.
It is said that a young man has a basket of tricks
and that a young woman is fickle.
Today, those sayings have collided with reality.
Gesar, at the age of thirteen,
you captured the divine horse Kyang Gö,
opened the door of the Crystal Cave Sheldrak
and won the horse race.
You have shown your true colors.
Your radiance pervades everywhere.
I realize what excellent karmic destiny is mine;
I realize what an excellent future is mine.
I trust in you.

Gesar, precious noble being,
undeniably, your body is Vajrapāṇi,
your mind is Avalokiteśvara,
and your speech is compassionate Mañjuśrī;
you are the emanation of the three protectors.
Please look upon me with loving-kindness.
I am your wife.
I offer you my body, speech, and mind.
This year, you will be in the north.
You say you will shoot an arrow into the skull of the northern
    demon.
A month ago, you started out from Ling,
and today, we have arrived at the peak of the māra mountain.
Listen, noble being,
see that mountain over there?
A mountain so white that it seems to be a torma,
so white it could be an offering torma painted with milk.
What is the name of that mountain?
Don't you think it is the divine mountain Gama in the Ma
    Valley?⁶
Those villages at the base of that mountain—
what are their names?
Who is their leader?
It would be joyful to go there;
if we went there, we could be happy.
Now, see that other mountain?
A mountain so red that it seems to be a torma,
so red it could be an offering torma painted with blood.
What is the name of that mountain?
Don't you think it is Magyal Pomra?⁷
Those villages at the base of that mountain—
what are their names?
Who is their leader?
It would be joyful to go there;
if we went there, we could be happy.
Now, look, over here.
A black mountain that seems to have black rocks tumbling
    down,

so black it looks as though it was draped in black silk.
What is the name of that mountain?
Don't you think it is Gadé Gyokri (Catapult Mountain)?[8]
Those villages at the base of that mountain—
what are their names?
Who is their leader?
It would be joyful to go there;
if we went there, we could be happy.
Now, look over there.
It is as though a golden drum was hoisted into the sky,
so golden that it looks to be draped in golden silk.
What is the name of that mountain?
Don't you think it is Gedzö Rimar (Golden-Red Mountain
   of Gedzo)?
Those villages at the base of that mountain—
what are their names?
Who is their leader?
It would be joyful to go there;
if we went there, we could be happy.
First, exciting thoughts have come to my mind,
second, I am singing very quickly,
third, this is all completely sincere—
whatever my thoughts, I have shared them with you, Gesar.
The crux of what I am saying is:
you are the embodiment of the Buddha, Dharma, and
   Saṅgha.
When you hold the seat of dharmakāya,
in order that you not stray from the nectar of oral
   instructions,
today the proper tendrel has arisen.
As the leader, you must uphold the letter of the law;
like sunshine, justice applies equally to all.
In order that corrupt leaders cannot wreak havoc,
today the proper tendrel has arisen.
When you point your sharp weapons at the demon,
Meza will be your ally.
In order that you and I not lose our samaya connection,
today the proper tendrel has arisen.

Having accumulated merit in previous lifetimes,
I am the one to be your wife.
If there is delicious food, we will share it;
if there is pure water, we will share it.
That you remain healthy
is my only wish.
Keep this in your heart.
Please forgive any faults in my song.
If there is confusion in my words, the fault is mine.

Thus she sang, and Gesar merely smiled and said, "Alas, Drukmo! For one thing, you are arrogant and selfish, and for another, yes, this land *is* breathtaking, and moreover, we may be able to regale ourselves with the names and descriptions of these mountain peaks—but all of this is only what has come from previous karma. Let us drink this rice wine given to me by Akhu Drenyé Gyalpo (Uncle King Fire Guide) who was my uncle in the celestial realm, and slowly I will tell you what I know." Michung and Drukmo, as well as Gesar, and even the horses drank their fill. After some time had passed, Gesar sang this song.

Sing "Ala thala thala."
"Thala" begins.
Today, I call to the deities.
Brahmā, from above, please look upon me.
Surrounded by your retinue of billions,
now today, please befriend me.
Nyenchen Kulha from the middle environs, please look upon
    me.
With the armies of nyen, your retinue of thousands,
now today, please befriend me.
Tsukna from below, please look upon me.
With your nāga army that, like an ocean, swirls around you,
now today, please befriend me.
There are no other deities to call.
If you do not recognize this place
of the eight mountains of the upper lands of the north,
it is the māra mountain Münpa Chutrik.
Sengcham Drukmo, you for one,
and especially Michung Khadé,

look at the sights.
Here in the highlands of the north,
the earth and sky are melded,
and pitch-black darkness obscures the path.
One is hounded by the winds of evil karma.
How can there be any joy or happiness?
Happiness can be found in your homeland;
going north, there is only misery to be had.
The hard fact is that here in Lutsen's motherland,
human blood rains down from above,
consciousnesses drift in the air, a swirling blizzard,
below, maggots crawl on rotting flesh,
and the vast plains are piled with bones.
The stench of death fills the air.
It is indistinguishable from Yama's storehouse,
this slaughterhouse of the demon māra.
That is the nature of the māra country.
You, Sengcham Drukmo, so arrogant and passionate,
look over there. Isn't that a sight!
If you do not know the name of the mountains there,
those mountains, I know their name,
those lands, I know how they are laid out.
Noble Lady Drukmo, soon enough it will be your desire to go
    to Hor;
the demon Gurkar and his evil karma will be tangled
with your own evil karma.

An old man's wrinkles cannot be erased:
there is no way to escape previous karma.

Negative circumstances, misfortune, and debts, these three
are not wished for but set out by karma.
Now, look. Isn't that a sight!
A mountain so white it seems to be a white torma,
white as milk.
If you do not know the name of that mountain,
it is Karpa Lutsé (White Warrior Peak Mountain), the eight-
    peaked mountain of Gurkar of Hor.

Someday, when you go there,
you will know the name of that mountain
and ask its spirit for refuge and protection.
Below that mountain
is the encampment of the white-helmeted troops.
You will be their queen,
with the uppermost seat.⁹
The qualities of Gama, the divine mountain in the Ma Valley,
and those of Karpa Lutsé of Gurkar of Hor
are not at all alike.
Now, look over there.
A red mountain so red that it seems to be a red torma,
painted with blood.
If you do not know the name of that mountain,
it is Chaklha Shalmar (Vermillion Divine Peak) of Shenpa,
    the butcher of Hor.
Someday, when you go there,
you will know the name of that mountain
and take refuge in the divine spirit there.
Below that mountain
is the encampment of the red-helmeted troops.
You will know the name of that mountain
and have the uppermost seat
as the queen.
Machen Pomra in the east
and Chaklha Shalmar of Shenpa
are not at all alike.
Now, look over here.
A black mountain that seems to have black rocks tumbling
    down,
as though it was draped in black silk.
If you do not know the name of that mountain,
it is Dzari Ngamchen (Awesome Rock Mountain) of Gurnak
    of Hor.
Someday, when you go there,
you will know the name of that mountain
and take refuge in the divine spirit there.
Below that mountain

is the encampment of the black-helmeted troops.
You will know the name of those districts
and have the uppermost seat
as the queen.
The peaks of Gyokri Mukpo of Gadé
and of Dzari Ngamchen of Gurnak of Hor
are not at all alike.
Now, look over there.
It is as though a golden drum was hoisted into the sky,
or a golden silk curtain draped.
If you do not know the name of that mountain,
it is Pangri Ngamchen (Awesome Meadow Mountain) of
    Gurser of Hor.
Below that mountain
is the encampment of the yellow-helmeted troops.
Someday, when you go there,
you will know the name of that mountain
and take refuge in the divine spirit there.
You will know the name of those districts
and have the uppermost seat
as the queen.
Pangri Ngamchen of Gurser of Hor
and Gedzo Mountain of Ling
are not at all alike.
The way each peak rises is unique.
This is the way the mountains and districts abide in Hor,
the domain of King Gurkar.[10]
Are you enjoying this pleasant conversation, Drukmo?
Is it bringing you happiness?
Today, the three of us
will go nowhere. We will remain at the camp,
and tomorrow at sunrise
we can decide how to journey.
Listen! It is just as the stories say.
In the eight mountain ranges of the upper north
brass- and copper-colored crags protrude like lips.
When we reach those crags
that even a strong wind cannot penetrate,

how could you possibly traverse them, Michung?
Then, farther on are the great marshlands of the north,
the swamp lake Damtsho and the blood lake Traktsho.
Men and horses have vanished, sinking within those lakes,
even a vulture cannot find a way to cross.
How could you possibly navigate these waters?
The point of all this is that
Michung, you cannot continue; please go back [to Ling].
Here are silks of the five colors;
someday you will need them.
Carry them with you.
If you understand that you must return, Michung, you are
    wise
as there you will be safe,
but if you wander about the north, you will meet only
    disaster.
Keep all this in mind, Michung.
If you have not understood, I am not going to repeat it.

Thus he sang, and Michung gave way to the many ideas swirling in his mind: his thoughts multiplied until he was completely muddled as to what to do. If he went to the north, he would likely die there, but to return to Ling was dreadfully far. As he boiled tea for their night's stay in the mountain pass, he was thinking that he must carry out Gesar's instructions. Gesar simply said, "Tomorrow right at dawn would be the most auspicious time for you to leave," and he gave Michung several *dütsi*[11] pills. Michung, with great faith and devotion to Gesar, offered aspiration prayers that no obstacles would arise on their journeys.

Sing "Ala thala thala."
"Thala" begins.
The song unfolds in three parts.
Today, I call to the gods.
To the deity who can gallop along the cliffs,
Siddha Thangtong Gyalpo,
and to the deity who can drive a dagger into a rock,
Master Padmasambhava.
Please look upon me and lead me in my song.
If you do not recognize this place,

296

it is the māra mountain Münpa Chutrik.
If you do not recognize me,
I am a young Tibetan man.
I am called Bötruk Michung (Small Tibetan Youth),
as when I was five years old
and had a small, weak body,
the four great ministers of Tibet
bartered for me with some curd
to which they had added congealed blood.[12]
Some said they got a good deal;
others said they lost out.
I did not understand what it was to win or lose,
but I went to Jowo Śākyamuni[13]
and offered prostrations.
On the way, several people called to me.
Some called me Bötruk,
some called me Michung,
and after that I went by the name Bötruk Michung.
When I reached the age of thirteen,
I went to Upper Ling
to be Gesar's butler.
With pure intention I accomplished excellent service.
I am just a little guy, Bötruk Michung.
I did not receive a large body,
but my skill in oratory is great enough.
From the blessing of my small, smiling lotus mouth
comes eloquence, fluent as a river.
With the turquoise blue handle of logic
come words, keen as the chopping of a Chinese sword.
Within myself,[14]
my speech masses with the power of southern clouds, swirling
    and turbulent.
The root tantra, explanatory tantra, and *upadeśa* tantra,
together with the subsequent tantra, the four medicine
    tantras,
dwell within me, memorized word for word.
I am the one who compounds the six medicinal herbs
and diagnoses diseases.

Today, Gesar has said I must return home.
Now, I, poor helpless Michung,
wish that when the other ministers,
including the Takrong minister Trothung,
headed back to Upper Ling,
I had gone with them.
Precious Sengchen Gesar,
as I return to my homeland,
may no obstacles arise.
May there be nothing that brings calamity.
Noble being, please look upon me with compassion;
I pray to you.
And for you, Noble Gesar and Drukmo,
that no obstacles arise on your journey,
I offer this aspiration prayer.
Today, on my return home,
will there be disaster along the road,
since you said that these silks of the five colors
I would need someday?
Sengchen and Drukmo,
I hope that we meet again soon.
Gesar, awakened one, keep this in your heart.
If there are mistakes in this song, the fault is mine.
If this has been but idle chatter, please forgive me.

Thus he sang, and although Gesar knew already that Michung would get lost in Hor, he said, "Michung, close your eyes and go. Nothing will go wrong." Michung just sat, skeptical, as Drukmo spoke to Gesar, "You said I have a bad karmic connection with Hor, yet I knew nothing about those mountains. Though you said that there could be happiness there, you also said that I would be entangled in my negative karma. Suppose everything that you said could go wrong does go wrong— who will come to help?" Drukmo took a small deep sky-blue turquoise bead from the loops of malas in her hair, wrapped it in a white khata, and offered it to Gesar. She sang this song.

Sing "Ala thala thala."
"Thala" begins.
Today, I call the deity.

From Tārā's buddhafield, the Eastern Paradise Arrayed in
    Turquoise Petals,
from the palace of Akaniṣṭha,
atop its exalted golden throne
on a resplendent conch seat,
Mother Jetsün Drölma, all White and Green Tārās,
look upon me with your light rays of compassion.
May the start of my song be excellent.
If you do not recognize this place,
it is the māra mountain Münpa Chutrik.
If you do not recognize me,
I am Sengcham Drukmo,
the best of all the maidens in the kingdom,
the ornament of the world.
Seeing me enchants one's mind.
I am the daughter of the gods.
If you do not recognize this song,
it is my piercing "Melody in Six Reverberations."
Precious Gesar,
first, please grant the blessing of your unsurpassed
    compassion,
second, please grant clarity,
third, please speak the Buddhadharma,
fourth, please show the courage that tames the four enemies.
May you be renowned throughout the continent.
Today, Noble Gesar, please listen to me.
That mountain so white that it seems to be a white torma,
you said was Karpa Lutsé, the eight-peaked mountain of
    Gurkar of Hor.
Yesterday it was far off, but now today here we are.
You said I would come to know the name of that mountain
and that I could request its refuge and protection.
You said I would be well seated
and would be the queen.
You spoke of my bad karma with Hor.
If, as you said, I will be taken there,
what good could come of that?
I want you to rush to my aid.

Say that none of this will happen.
If while I am returning home,
because of my bad karma I wander into the land of Hor,
then what should I do?
Just as the vulture is fond of its rocky nest
and that seems to be its destiny,
that I follow you
seems to be my destiny.
If today
you leave me behind,
I know not where my karma will lead.
Take the example of the high crags:
although the vulture is fond of its nest in the cliffs,
it cannot trust that the rock is indestructible.
It could shatter
and no one knows what could happen to the nest.
Take the example of the plunging river:
although the female fish depend on the water,
those blue waters cannot be trusted.
They rise and fall
and no one knows what could happen to the fish.
As for me,
Gesar, if as you say, my karma will bring me to Hor,
this golden amulet of method and wisdom[15]—
its upper half should be fastened around your neck
and the lower around my own.
When the time comes that the amulet is rejoined,
it will symbolize your return to me
and my trust in you.
I have a pair of golden bangles,
self-appearing lotus flowers—
one for your wrist Gesar,
and the other for mine.
When the pair of golden bangles is reunited,
it will symbolize your return to me
and my trust in you.
I have a set of rings,
a pair of lapis rings—

one worn on your finger, noble being,
and the other on mine.
When the rings come together,
it will symbolize your return to me
and my trust in you.
That is true—don't you agree?
If there are mistakes in this song, the fault is mine.
If this has been but idle chatter, please forgive me.

Thus she sang, and Gesar realized that unless it turned out that Drukmo ended up completely taken in by Gurkar the Hor demon king, what she had said was true. He promised that the ornaments will be reunited and said, "Drukmo, if you come to be lost in Hor, it is unfathomable that I would not come for you. How can you think that I would abandon you?" And he proclaimed the song "Ceaseless Self-Utterance of the Unobstructed Vajra," detailing the prophecy of how he would come to protect Drukmo in Hor. It seemed to Michung, who had sat silently listening, that although no good would come of going to Hor, even less would come of not following Gesar's command. Feeling sad, he stood and offered prostrations to Gesar, and slowly, with no choice but to start out on the road to return home, he left.

CHAPTER THIRTEEN

Michung loses his way in a snowstorm and ends up in Hor.
Gesar and his horse vanish like a rainbow.
Drukmo is escorted back to Ling by a wolf.
Gesar traverses the mud lake Damtsho in the north.

IT WAS GETTING TO BE EVENING AS Michung approached the mountain gorge Münpa Chuthung (Dark Drinking Water) in the north, but by the time he arrived, there was only inky darkness. There was no way he could travel on. The next day at first light[1] he awoke to find himself stranded by a blanket of snow that filled the valley. Meanwhile, the tireless Hor lamas, Amchö Guru (Ceremonial Guru) and Tonglok (Returns Empty-Handed) of Gyashi, had executed a mo divination, a prophecy, and an astrology chart that they brought before the widower-king Gurkar. They said to him, "If you wish to find a magnificent queen, then at dawn tomorrow—Gochö Dikchö[2] Shenpa (Efficacious Evil Butcher), Tobchen Langpo Trobar (Mighty Wrathful Elephant), Shechen Riwo Punglen (Strong Shoulder Mountain), the warrior[3] Padur Chonglha Mukpo (Warrior Divine Maroon Agate), as well as the skilled archer Dakyen Anga Thebdruk (Great Archer)[4]—these five ministers you must send to the far side of Dzari Ngamchen, where there is a man, handsome as a flower born from a poisonous thorn, stuck in the blizzard. The mo divination, prophecy, and astrology chart clearly predict that he has something worth hearing."

King Gurkar was delighted and summoned the five ministers, telling them, "According to the divination and prophecy of our two lamas, it seems there will be a person of use to me over there on the far side of Dzari Ngamchen. Go there now and see what the situation is." The five warriors went quickly and when they arrived, they saw several drong on the mountain peak. Some of them went running after the drong, but Dikchö Shenpa continued on, and at some distance, he saw a man astride his horse. He approached the man and there was Michung seated on his small horse, Marchung Droden,[5] looking this way and that, searching for the path. Dikchö Shenpa said, "Listen, son of such a great father![6] Both of you, man and horse, so ruddy red, you really make a pair! A small man and small horse, a small saddle and small man, fitting so well together! What is your name?" he asked, "And that of your horse?" So saying, Dikchö Shenpa sang these words.

> Sing "Ala thala thala."
> "Thala" begins.
> The song unfolds in three parts.
> Today, I call to the gods.
> Three divine teurangs—Namthel, Barthel, Sathel of the high
>   heavens, the middle skies, and the earth—
> please do not be distracted, today come to assist me.
> If you do not recognize this place,
> it is Dzari Ngamchen, the great rocky crag of Gurnak,
> known as the slopes of the dark forested mountain Sölri
>   Nakpo (Black Coal Mountain).
> Perhaps you do not recognize me,
> but of course you do!
> From the kingdom of Achen Hor,
> at the foothills below Raduk Khar (Poison Horn Castle),
> upon the cliffs of Phulung Dorjé (Indestructible Upper
>   Sloping Valley),
> from my castle Dzomo Rudzong,
> I am known as Dikchö Shenpa,
> the man from whom no one escapes alive.
> I will explain why I am so relentless.
> In the land of Achen Hor
> it is a crime to recite the MAṆI mantra.
> If you recite a single MAṆI OṂ
> the fine is one horse.
> For killing even a single flea,
> the penalty is a dzo.
> Listen, pale, red one,

what is your name?
What is your father's name?
What is your mother's name?[7]
What is your birthplace and heritage?
The style of your armor
is not local.
You are a small man, but perfectly clad, tight and powerful in
    your armor,
and your tiny horse has a healthy gait—
a man and horse that suit each other.
You seem a robust man.
As in the examples of the proverbs:

The deafening sound of water surging through a small valley
comes from the height of the snowy mountains;
the shuddering intensity of an avalanche
comes from the steep grade of the mountain.

What land have you come from?
What country are you going to?
Give me an honest answer.

Thus he sang, and Michung said, "What you have said is true. As for me, I had escorted the lord of Ling, Gesar, as he left for the upper land of the north, and I was on my way back to Ling, but snow has fallen on the road and I have lost my way. I ask you to please be my guide." Saying that, Michung sang this song to Dikchö Shenpa.

Sing "Ala thala thala."
"Thala" begins.
As I sing, I meditate on the awakened state,
my voice intones dharmakāya.
Today, I call the deity.
Divine dharmakāya, saṃbhogakāya, nirmāṇakāya,
three divine ones please grant your blessing and look
    upon me,
gaze upon me and assist my song.
If you do not recognize this place,
it is the Münpa gorge in the north,

305

at the junction of three valleys.
There has been a great snowfall
obscuring the path that brought me here as well as the path
    forward.
What is the best way out?
As for my background,
before I took rebirth
I was the horseman who galloped the rocky crags,
siddha Thangtong Gyalpo.
Now, I have taken rebirth in Gok
as the nephew of Ralo Tönpa.[8]
I am an emanation of Thangtong Gyalpo
with the name Michung Khadé,
butler to King Gesar.
I saw King Gesar off on his journey north
and now, on my return to Ling
I have lost my way.
In this worldly land, I meet a wild butcher—
you, the warrior who takes the lives of humans.
Certainly, a man is fierce who devours human flesh,
but who could act with such evil?
To kill me would accumulate great nonvirtue,
especially today on an auspicious full moon day.
I beseech you not to kill me.
From this day onward,
with palms joined, confess your evil deeds.
Wild butcher, the way you portrayed me,
the analogies and their meaning are fitting.
You said that just as a small river runs with a loud sound
because the snowmelt falls from such a high mountain,
I, this small man, have made quite an impression in my tight
    armor,
dressed in the style of distant peoples
and riding this small steed with its smooth gait
for a comfortable ride on a long journey.
My horse and I have only just arrived
but have lost our way in the snow
and with no choice are trapped here.

Luckily, I have met you, Dikchö Shenpa;
I depend on you to show me the path.
How can I return to Ling?
I have a single red khata
and, today, I offer it to you
in return for honest advice.
If you understand my song, please guide me.
If not, I cannot repeat myself.

Thus he sang, and Dikchö Shenpa thought, "In light of the mo divination and astrology that the teurang lamas gave to King Gurkar, meeting this man from Ling seems more than a coincidence, especially since I had a premonitory dream that Gurkar desires to be with the Ling queen Drukmo. Suppose that happens—surely, there will be war between Hor and Ling and eventually one serious disaster after another, such that the Hor districts will burn to the ground with not even so much as ashes remaining." With all that in mind, he said to Michung, "Take the mountain pass Kyaka Tratsé (Variegated Magpie); it will get you close to eastern Ling. But if you don't go quickly, you will likely encounter several ruffians at the end of the path." Offering thanks for his kindness, Michung took to the road.

Dikchö Shenpa was turning back when he saw a large stag some distance away. He felled it with a single arrow shot and had loaded the kill onto his horse when, along the road, he ran into Langpo Trobar and two of the others [Riwo Punglen and Chonglha Mukpo] who called out, "Shenpa-la! There, over on the other side of the mountain, was that you we heard singing?" Shenpa answered, "From the mountain peak, I could see hundreds of mountains and river valleys and I was inspired to sing. Now, you three and I should share this venison." Langpo Trobar winked at his companions, murmuring that he felt that Shenpa had not told them the truth and that his story was a bit far-fetched. Then, he sang this song.[9]

Sing "Ala thala thala."
"Thala" begins.
The song unfolds in three parts.
Today, I call to the three divine teurang
from the celestial firmament.
Look upon me, highest god, Namthel Karpo,
white teurang riding a white goat.[10]
May King Anam Gurkar be sovereign.
Look upon me, middle god, Barthel Tramo,

multicolored teurang riding a multicolored goat.
May father Anam Gurkar be steadfast.
Look upon me, divine one below, Sathel Nakpo,
black teurang riding a black goat.
May King Anam Gurkar's kingdom be firmly established.
May the forces of Hor be excellent
and may bliss and happiness come to the subjects.
If you do not recognize this place,
it is Dzari Ngamchen of Hor Gurnak,
the protector mountain spirit of King Gurnak.
To the three teurang protectors Namthel, Barthel, and Sathel,
I supplicate.
If you do not recognize me,
from within the castle Dzomo Rudzong,
among the five sons of the scorpion father,[11]
I was the youngest of those great sons
and the smallest among them.
I will tell you why
I became known as Tobchen [Langpo] Trobar.
When I was eighteen,
I walked up to Rakar Crag (White Copper Crag).
I got into it with a herd of many powerful drong.
Seizing several of them by the horns,
I headbutted them
and carried the carcasses on my back.
Still, I was not called Tobchen.
I went to the summit of a high snow mountain
and seized a couple of lions.
Holding their legs, I flung them and took their turquoise
    manes.
Only then was I honored with the name Tobchen.
One day I went to the marshlands
where I threw many stags to the ground
and carried their carcasses on my back.
After that, I was known as Langpo Trobar, the powerful
    warrior with the strength of an elephant.
This is the main point of my story:
On the far side of Sölri Ngamchen,

I heard the warrior Dikchö Shenpa singing.
I wonder if he was singing out of happiness;
I think he may have been singing a secret song.
My friend Chonglha Mukpo, let's go [investigate];
the rest of you stay back and cook the meat.
Chonglha and I
are famous far and wide
and are the eyes of King Gurkar
who has delegated us to act on his behalf.
If we fail to carry out these important undertakings,
we cannot be called brave warriors.
If Shenpa had not been singing,
I would have had no suspicions.
One father or one uncle can have many children,
but some will be weak and others strong.
You can saddle up horses to ride,
but if you can't distinguish the fast from the slow,
you do not understand what makes for a healthy horse.
We two, Langpo and Chonglha—
unless we accomplish true deeds of greatness,
it is senseless to wander these barren mountains.
All you warriors, keep this in mind.
If you have not understood, I cannot repeat myself.

Thus he sang. Langpo and Chonglha then left at once, and when they were halfway back [to where Shenpa had come from], Langpo spotted Michung and spurred his horse. He pulled out his iron-hooked wind-lasso from his belt and flung it once at Michung. Michung and his horse were dragged through the swirling gray snow. Chonglha galloped quickly toward Michung and grabbed him by the right shoulder and demanded to know who he was. Michung, trembling in fear, begged to be let go but Langpo Trobar and Chonglha Mukpo brought him to Shenpa. Shenpa and Riwo Punglen told him there was no need to be afraid. "Now, you are going to meet Gurkar the powerful king. There is no harm that will come to you, only good," they said.

Langpo Trobar continued, "Listen, if you are truthful when the king asks you questions, your life will be spared," And Dikchö Shenpa added, "That's a promise!" and they brought Michung to King Gurkar. Michung offered a white silk khata to the king who said, "Now, Michung, you need not be frightened. You claim to be

Michung Khadé of Ling; if that is so, then from today onward you will stay here in Hor. Here, you will be known as Gama Zigo (Leopard Head),[12] and you will be my butler." Michung took off his own armor and put it aside; he dressed like a Hor warrior and sat with his new sovereign, enjoying tea and chang.

In the meantime, Gesar and Drukmo had continued northward for three days, but Gesar could not rid himself of the embarrassment of being a warrior going to meet the enemy accompanied by a young woman. While he was lying awake, trying to think of a way to get her to turn back, Manéné came flying in with a flock of white vultures, and transformed into a tiny golden bee. Buzzing in Gesar's ear, not too loudly, not too softly, she sang this vajra song of prophecy in the melody of "Great Nectar of the Sound of Bees."

> Sing "Ala thala thala."
> "Thala" begins.
> The song unfolds in three parts.
> From the supreme dwelling place of the exalted heavens
>   above,
> from the pure realm of Supremely Perfected Activity,
> the northern buddhafield Lerab Dzokpa,[13]
> Great Mother Consort Prajñāpāramitā,
> do not be distracted. Please help me.
> From the pure realm of Buddha Amoghasiddhi, Lerab
>   Dzokpa,
> powerful Karma Ḍākinīs,
> today come to assist me.
> From Tārā's buddhafield, the Eastern Paradise Arrayed in
>   Turquoise Petals,
> from the highest celestial palace in Akaniṣṭha,
> Longevity Goddess, Noble Mother Jetsün Drölma,
> Protectress White and Green Tārās,
> today please join with me.
> If you do not recognize this place,
> it is the lowland beneath the Münpa mountains,
> the arid land of the northeast, dry as human skulls.
> If you do not recognize me,
> from the supreme dwelling place of the celestial sky realm,
> I am Ané Göcham[14] Karmo,
> the aunt of Amitābha

and the consort of Padmasambhava.[15]
Today, Precious King Gesar,
pay attention and listen.
You are the incomparable leader of this world,
your enlightened mind holds the five wisdoms,
and your enlightened body is free from obscurations.
There is no need to tell you what you already know,
but I have a few words to remind you.
Although Drukmo has been with you from the outset,
it would be better if she turned back now.
She is the finest woman in the world,
always dressed in silk brocade
and accustomed to a lambskin chuba—
she could never withstand the piercing cold of the north
    winds.
This great vast land of the north
is the homeland of demons and cannibals;
it is no place to take Drukmo.
Whatever it takes, you must find a way for her to turn back.
On the far side of the mountain are three antelope.
As soon as they run down to the arid flatlands,
you must shoot one with an arrow
and send Drukmo to get the meat.
She will hesitate, but you must insist that she go,
and as soon as she has the antelope in hand,
you and your horse must vanish like a rainbow.
Your divine steed Kyang Gö
must then manifest as a nine-headed wolf, black as a charred
    teapot,
with the skill to take Drukmo back to Ling
all the way to the doorstep of the Tea Castle Jakhar.
Joined inseparably, you and your horse
must cross the muddy lake Damtsho of Minub[16] without
    sinking.
Then, when you come to the highlands,
from the snowy peaks
the demoness Acham Karmo
will come with her retinue of many teurang.

Your arrows and swords will be useless.
In the country Minub there resides
Lhamo Rizan (Mountain Eater Goddess),
an emanation of Palden Lhamo[17]
known as the northern family Green Tārā;
you must bind her under oath to be the protectress of the side
    of virtue.
Then, Gesar, farther on
there will be the seven [menmo] sisters of the north;
you must call to them to be your allies.
A bit farther along
will be the iron-hoofed māra sheep,
the guardian of all life in this world
and the life-support talisman of the māra Lutsen;
you must tame that māra sheep.
The Zhugadar minister Ching-ngön
is their shepherd;
he must be turned to the Dharma.
Gesar, keep all of this in mind.
If you did not understand, I cannot repeat my song.

Thus she sang, and Gesar's face darkened with the realization that there was no option other than for Drukmo to return home. He stood up from the lavish meal that had been offered to them by the dralha and protectors,[18] who had also graciously given grain to both of their horses. Gesar and Drukmo mounted their steeds, heading north. A short distance away, Gesar saw three antelope meandering back and forth, and he told Drukmo that he was going to shoot one and that she should go and get it. This reinforced what Drukmo had been thinking—that since Michung had left, Gesar was acting strangely. All this had put her on edge, and she thought to herself, "This is not a good sign: I am afraid he will leave me wandering alone in this desolate wilderness."

With a single shot from Gesar's bow, an antelope fell to the grassy plain. When the noble being said, "Now, please go get that antelope," Drukmo replied, "First listen to my song."

Sing "Ala thala thala."
"Thala" begins.
Today, I call to the deity.

From Tārā's buddhafield, Arrayed in Turquoise Petals,
from the supreme dwelling place of Akaniṣṭha,
Mother Jetsün Drölma White and Green Tārās, look upon
    me.
You who are omniscient, please lead my song.
If you do not recognize this place,
these are five peaks nearby the mountains of the north.
If you do not recognize me,
from the kingdom of Upper Ling in the east,
I am Sengcham Drukmo of the family Kyalo.
If you do not recognize my song,
it is my resonant "Melody in Six Reverberations."
I do not sing this song just anywhere,
but today I have no choice.
Precious Sengchen,
you have changed.
You have always greeted me with a smile
and reassured me with your sweet words,
but today your face has become dark
and your words have hurt my ears.
I don't understand.
A few days ago,
upon seeing the lovely Hor mountains, I yearned to visit.
Then, you said I had bad karma with Hor.
Why did you keep saying that?
There are several things you should explain.
After Michung left,
you nearly dissolved into a rainbow,
but a rainbow will vanish, it cannot be held.
You nearly dissolved into the wind,
but gale wind cannot be contained.
You are like the rays of the sun,
falling just where you land.
Precious Sengchen Gesar,
I implore you to stop acting that way.
Take me with you; do not leave me here.
As in the examples of the proverbs:

Within a great lake that forms from the flow of rivers,
the swan is not truly free,
as it must trust the lake
neither to become a spot of dry land
nor freeze over.

Just so, you could make this either a joyful place
or a place of sorrow.
Precious Sengchen Gesar,
we are destined to be together in this lifetime;
I have come with you.
Please do not abandon me in this uninhabited wilderness.
If I am left in this desolate valley,
how will I survive?
Sengchen, do you care for my happiness?
Watch over me, that I am not sad.
Although the fierce northern winds can pierce like an arrow,
I have a fox-skin hat that is the kindness of my parents.
How could I not have enough fortitude?
Don't you agree?
I rely upon you completely
and trust in you.
Do not see to it that I am sad;
look after my happiness.
You have a mind more gentle than silk;
please look upon me with your tender heart.
I offer you a silk khata
that the kindness of your mind may remain steadfast.
As for me, I will get the antelope meat.
Not to go would be to defy you;
to go is to think of you as a living buddha.
You are no different than a rainbow in the sky,
no one knows what will happen.
Supreme king, hold this in your heart.
If you have not understood, I cannot repeat it.

Thus she sang, and Gesar said, "All that is true. Now, go get the antelope meat."
Drukmo went, unable to go against his wishes. Just then, Göcham Karmo-Manéné,[19]

314

Dungkhyung Karpo, Lutrül Öchung, Thalé Ökar, and the dralha Nyentak Marpo surrounded Gesar and his horse, as well as Drukmo's horse, and the entire entourage vanished into a rainbow, leaving Drukmo behind. With the antelope carcass now slung over her shoulders, Drukmo turned. She was all alone with Gesar and the horses nowhere to be seen. She was wearing a fine red silk brocade sash and blouse Norbu Gakyil (Jeweled Coil of Joy) beneath her apron Riksum Gönpo (Three Protector Families). She took off the apron and beat it into the ground.[20] She flung the loops of her turquoise hair ornament and agate necklace, strewing the beads, and as though she was pulling her own hair, slammed her head on the ground. Then, one after another, her tears fell. Two black nine-headed wolves ran at Drukmo, circling around her three times. One said, "Ya, maiden! We wolves howl when we have eaten, but isn't it said that maidens cry when they are drunk? If you cry, we will cry with you." The mountain valleys filled with the great howling sound of the wolves but Drukmo dried her tears and said, "Well wolves, since you are the carnivores, just eat my meat and drink my blood." And she sang.

> Sing "Ala thala thala."
> "Thala" begins.
> The song unfolds in three parts.
> Just now I call to the deity.
> Dwelling in the supreme divine buddhafield,
> from the palace of Akaniṣṭha,
> Divine Khachöma (Vajrayoginī), please look upon me.
> Also, I call to the deity:
> Mother Lineage Vajrayoginī, know me.
> Surrounded by your retinue of hundreds of millions of
>   ḍākinīs,
> assist me in my plan.
> If you do not recognize this place,
> these are the eight mountains of the kingdom of the upper
>   north,
> a great plain in the north, dry as a human skull.
> If you do not recognize me,
> I am the daughter of Kyalo Tönpa.
> When I was seven years old,
> there was strife in Upper Ling.
> I was promised to Joru—
> until he turned thirteen,

the boy Joru behaved badly
and in front of me
showed his worst—he was ugly, ill-mannered, and mean.
Not only was he scrawny and emaciated,
but even though he was young, his hair was gray.
He was cold and hard-hearted—
this was the man they said was to be mine,
the one said to be my companion in my youth and in my age.
I wondered how this could be possible.
When he turned thirteen, Joru
showed his true nature and good looks.
I could not help but trust in him
and consider my good fortune in this life and the next.
But now this year, he
has turned fifteen
and is intent on going to the north.
He says he cannot rest until he starts out for this faraway
    place
nor slack up on spewing out hurtful words.
The truth of the matter is, it looks like all he is after is another
    girl.[21]
This is the day
I have lost that shameless Joru—
when I look up, the heavens are empty,
when I look down, the ground is empty.
It is over. I am left alone.
I have no father backing me,
and no mother leading me.
You wild wolves, do you know just how wretched I am?
Joru has abandoned me, gone I know not where.
Isn't it like the folk sayings of old?

If one has neither interest, respect, nor trust in another,
they should not pretend otherwise.

If a man desires another maiden,
one minute he looks after you, but the next moment, you are
    invisible.

In the eighteen regions of this valleyed land
are eighteen great queens.
Three are above me:
one, Yangmen (Prosperity Maiden) the Queen of Zima,
two, Tongnyi Garza Chödrön (Emptiness Blacksmith Lady
    Dharma Lamp),
three, Gesar's mother Queen Gokza—
these are the three women famed through the world.
Yangma and Garza
are the foremost women in Jambudvīpa.
It is strange that Joru does not desire them,
but quick as a flash, he is head over heels for the maiden
    Meza.
Joru is as unsettled as the wind,
here one minute and gone the next.
If I think about it, it is Meza he is after.
There is a saying in ancient Tibet that three things make one
    crazy:

Old donkeys go crazy at the arrival of a wild kyang.
Old monks go crazy at the arrival of a beautiful woman.
Old crows go crazy over a cuckoo.

Crazy, but that's the truth,
and today it seems to be Joru who has lost his mind.
Misfortune comes to men who chase after women;
in the end their precious lives are lost.
Misfortune finds women who chase after men;
in the end they fall into a barren wilderness.
Just like that, Joru is nowhere; he is gone,
and I am left behind in this desolate wasteland.
In ancient Tibet, there were said to be three essentials:
No day passes that a wrongdoer, fallen into hell,
does not need the teachings of the excellent guru.
No day passes that a child engaging in the world
does not need the advice of excellent parents.
No day passes that a woman wandering alone in the
    wilderness

does not need the heartfelt words of her life-long companion.

Those are the words, but their meaning is hollow.

In ancient Tibet, there were said to be three things that bring
    ruin:

a leader's embezzling brings ruin[22] to his subjects,

a man's gambling brings ruin to his family,

and a woman's promiscuity brings ruin to her life companion.

These are examples, but true.

Meza Bumdrön Trishok

has both a good and a bad side.

In the morning, with the temperament of the gods,

Meza possesses the divine marks.

In the evening, she has a demon's temperament,

with all the marks of a māra.

Within a single day,

her mind vacillates from one extreme to another.

Joru, my sweet companion[23]—

one day there will be a tale to tell of how Meza's flirting
    ruined him.

You nine-headed black wolves,

karmically destined to be carnivores,

make mine the meat you eat today

and mine the blood you drink.

There is no greater delicacy than my flesh,

nor nectar more nutritious than my blood.

I am the daughter of such excellent parents,

and honey, brown sugar, and molasses, the three sweets,

were my constant enjoyments.

Today, wolves, devour me,

do not hesitate in taking my life.

I received this human body,

and in the end, everything that is born, dies.

All accumulated wealth is fleeting.

Today, Drukmo is the sacrificial offering.

Do not wait, wild wolves; come quickly.

My blood and flesh I present as an offering torma.

I will perform my own phowa

into Tārā's buddhafield,

or perhaps elsewhere.
For Gesar,
as he journeys north to tame the king,
may no obstacles arise
and may any that do fall to me.
In this lifetime, may his good fortune prevail,
and may any misfortune follow me.
May this aspiration prayer be accomplished.
May I forsake my own life.
But if I am not eaten by the wolves,
may I dive into the frothing blue waters,
may I leap from the rugged high cliffs.
If I am unable to do that, I am not Drukmo.
Wild wolves, keep this in mind.

As her song ended, the mountain valleys were filled with the roar of the two wild wolves. They came closer, beating their tails against the ground, and one said, "Maiden, despite your misery, you have made an excellent offering. There is a place for this gift of your flesh and blood. Up in the highlands of this rocky valley is a vixen with nine cubs. Even if they wolfed down both sides of the mountain, they would not be satisfied. Even if they gulped down the entire river, their thirst would not be quenched." And without taking another breath, the wild wolf offered this song to Drukmo.

Sing "Ala thala thala."
"Thala" begins.
The song unfolds in three parts.
Today, I call to the deity.
From the right-hand side of the snowy mountain peak,
youthful lion with turquoise fur,
the dralha Dungseng Karmo,
please be constant in looking upon this wild wolf with
    kindness.
Here in these flat, white, mountain meadows,
may I, this black nine-headed wolf,
be imbued with this dralha's gift of speed.
May the Bengal tiger of the dense jungle,
by many said to be luxuriant with the six smiles,

look upon this wolf.
If you do not recognize this place,
it is the great plain Migo Kampo, dry as human skulls.
If you do not recognize me,
I am the nine-headed black wolf.
Last year, I came from Jeri, the sand dunes,
where the king had many livestock
that I come to devour.
This whole year, I have been in the north,
and here in these eight mountains of the upper land of the north
I am said to be the wild wolf that eats meat and drinks blood.
Yesterday, before noon,
circling the peak of the high crags,
I felled three drongs.
I am stuffed from eating their meat
and satiated from drinking their blood.
Then, today I circled the mountain
and killed three stags.
I am stuffed from eating their meat
and satiated from drinking their blood.
Now, I have met up with you,
a maiden who says her own flesh is delicious
as she is the daughter of excellent parents;
who says there is no flesh tastier than her own,
nothing sweeter than her blood;
who offers her very flesh and blood,
without regret;
and who says she is without attachment to her life.
These are the words you have spoken.
If there is truth in what you say,
in the rocky valley above,
a vixen and her nine cubs
are hungry, with not enough to eat;
neither the front side of the mountain
nor the back side of the mountain could fill their stomachs.
Even the great river
would not quench their thirst.
This select offering of your flesh and blood

is an excellent gift.
However, Drukmo, listen
and don't be sorrowful.
As said in the ancient proverbs of Tibet:

The morning star is luminous over the mountain pass,
but no matter that it sinks below—
in turn the sun and moon will shine forth.

Gesar, the divine lama,
no matter that now he has left to tame the māras,
after he has shot an arrow into Lutsen's skull,
he will return to Ling,
and in his castle Sengdruk Taktsé,
there will be joyful celebration
with song and dance.
Keep that in your heart, Drukmo,
and contrast his actions with what could be.
Take the example of some of the highest kings
who wear their titles like a hat
but abdicate the rule of law to their ministers—
in the end, the enemy takes over
and their kingdoms are lost.
Then, it is too late for regret.
Isn't that so, Drukmo?
If you have understood, keep this in your heart.
If not, I cannot repeat it.

Thus his song ended, and Drukmo said, "Well now, black wolf, you must take me to the wolf cubs." She rode astride the wolf, but through Gesar's power to bring on sleep, she drifted off and instead, surefooted in his step, the wolf took her back to her homeland of eastern Upper Ling. The wolves had collected all the jewelry—turquoise, coral, and so forth—that Drukmo had scattered, and when they arrived, the wolf placed it upon the mounting stone Yungdrung Barwa (Ageless Blaze) at the eastern gate Padma Druzhi of the Maroon Tea Castle. Gesar's horse Kyang Gö[24] had already brought Drukmo's horse Dromuk Dingshé, the one with a single agate horn, back to Ling and had slipped away unnoticed to return to Gesar. As Dromuk Dingshé was led into the crystal stable with its bridle and saddle of rainbow light,

Drukmo woke from sleep. Looking around, only then did Drukmo realize where she was. She was amazed and overwhelmed and thought, "Certainly I am here only through Gesar's magical power." She stood up and shook the dirt from her hair, rubbed her face, and dusted off her clothes. She rewrapped her sash Norbu Gakhyil, tied her apron Riksum Gönpo, and put her jewelry inside her chuba pocket. She entered the castle and came upon Senglön, Gokza Lhamo, and Neuchung who spoke through a smile, saying "Drukmo! It is wonderful that you have returned. You must be very tired! Where was Gesar when you last saw him? Tell us where you have been." Neuchung set out an abundant feast of tea, chang, and so forth, and Drukmo relaxed and sat to talk with the women of Ling.

All the while, Gesar had been tacking his capable steed Kyang Gö. The horse wore the halter Meri Khyilkhyil, and the conch-white stirrups Gyangdrak (Calls from Earshot). Around him was the saddle cinch of brocade Drukri Shenkhor, held in front by the cinch Lhadré Zilnön (Quells the Gods-Demons), and below by the crupper Tashi Yangkhyil (Auspicious Swirling Prosperity).[25] His golden saddle Rinchen Wangyal (Precious King of Power) was adorned in the front with the rising sun, and at its rear with the full moon. The stirrups were imposing when they glinted in the sun, shining like the great constellations, but impressive even when they merely flickered like stars. Gesar wore the helmet Mokchen Gyalwa surrounded by the lords of the three families, with its garuḍa-feathered top ornament Khamsum Zilnön surrounded by 1,022 buddhas. His great armor Zilwa Bumdzom was surrounded by the one hundred peaceful and wrathful deities, and the shield Bakar Lebchen by the dralha protectors of the four continents. Ninety-nine arrows were bundled on his right[26] and Ragö Kyilwa, his curved bow of goat horn, rested in the leopard-skin case on his left. Around the sword Thapa Lenmé was the dralha Sokchö Nyurwa (Quick to Sever Life) and the victory banners of war were around the lance Khamsum Urdül (Effortlessly Taming the Three Worlds). Beautifully adorned with these many weapons of the dralha, he came to the bank of the great mud lake Damtsho in the north. Gesar called upon the lha, lu, and nyen for support and, gesturing to his horse, began a short song.

> Sing "Ala thala thala."
> "Thala" begins.
> As I sing with awakened mind,
> I set the melody[27] with the meditation of the buddhas.
> Today, I call to the deity
> from the pure realms of the three places, body, speech, and
>   mind:

Dharmakāya Samantabhadra, know me.

From the eastern realm of Potala,

Saṃbhogakāya Avalokiteśvara, know me.

From the supreme dwelling place on the western continent of
  Chamara,

Nirmāṇakāya Padmasambhava, know me.

Today, come to assist me.

Don't be stingy; grant your blessings and look upon me with
  compassion.

From your dwelling place in the thirteen levels of the azure
  sky,

Manéné, come to assist me.

Now, I call the deity

from the supreme dwelling place of the highest celestial
  realm,

the divine realm of the thirty-three,[28]

Great Divine Brahmā,

wearing the divine white helmet,

your white turban sways, *shik sé shik,*

tour rainbowlike hair swings, *hem sé hem,*

snow crystals[29] flutter down, *ta la la,*

flowers tumble here and there, *si li li,*

sweet incense smoke scents the air, *hang sé hang,*

and garuḍas spread their feathered wings, *dem sé dem.*

You wear white armor,

a tiger-skin quiver on your right and leopard-skin sheath on
  your left.

You bear the threefold weapon panoply.

Holding a crystal sword in your right hand,

brandishing a bloody lance[30] in your left,

mounted on your divine gray horse

and surrounded by an army of millions,

today come to assist me

to traverse the muddy lake Damtsho of Minub.

Today, I invoke the deity

from the palace of the crystal snow mountain,

atop a blazing jeweled throne,

Nyenchen Kulha Gedzo,

wearing the red tsen helmet,[31]
its red silk waving, *hab sé hab*,
wearing red armor,
holding a thunderbolt sword in your right hand,
and brandishing a bloody lance in your left.
Mounted on a red horse
and seated on a red throne[32] that shimmers, *khuk sé khuk*,
surrounded by your retinue of hundreds of thousands,
now today come to assist this king
to traverse the muddy lake Damtsho of Minub.
From the midst of this great swirling ocean,
in the colorful nāga castle of the sense pleasures,
Nāga king Tsukna Rinchen,
wearing a turquoise helmet,
its blue water-silk waving, *hab sé hab*,
wearing turquoise armor,
a tiger-skin quiver on your right, and a leopard-skin sheath on
    your left,
you possess the threefold weapon panoply.
Your right hand grasps the All-Accomplishing Lasso of
    Amoghasiddhi;
your left holds the Wish-Fulfilling Jewel of Avalokiteśvara.
Mounted on a turquoise horse
and surrounded by one hundred thousand nāgas,
today come to assist me
to traverse the muddy lake Damtsho of Minub.
This very day I expressly supplicate you.
In the eastern land of Ma in Ling,
I was happy within the divine colorful castle,
enjoying delicious tea and chang
and singing and dancing,
when you, the highest gods, sent down the prophecy
that I could not remain in Ling but was to go north.
Without hesitation, I sped to this dreary northern plain
and just today have come to this muddy swamp lake
    Damtsho.
According to the prophecy,
it is the time to ford this lake

and demolish its paired rock overhang.[33]
I had never seen this place
but had only heard far-off stories
that it was easy to cross,
that it could be done in the blink of an eye.
Thinking what was said must be true,
I hastened to its banks,
but its waves heave ominously.
Not knowing how to navigate, I have faltered.
The waters are muddy, deep,
and boundless. Yet crossing,
to hear a cunning person tell it, is easy.
Destroying the double rock overhang, those brass- and
    copper-colored rocks,
to hear a deft person tell it, is simple.
The mud lake Damtsho that I face today
is an ocean beyond my wildest imagination.
Above, in the heavens, masses of dark clouds roil;
below in the swampy lake, dark waves seethe.
Even though their clamor is the same,
the earth is swallowed up in the churning waves.
From the azure sky the dragon's roar resounds, *ur ru ru*;
ur ru ru is the roar of the waves in this northern swamp lake.
The sound may seem the same,
but in one's own ears, the wave's roar is deafening.
So now, how can we make it across?
You, the all-knowing supreme steed Kyang Gö,
you are the divine horse of channels and winds.
It is time for us to soar the skies
and cross the northern mud lake Damtsho.
But when the waves march in file, skyward,
we will realize how difficult it is to cross this boundless lake.
Divine ones dwelling in the pure land,
do not rest and merely send a prophecy;
rather, come with us, man and horse,
that we may cross the swamp lake together.
From the snowy mountain of Mount Kailash,
Demoness Acham Karmo,

now is the time for you to rush to our aid.
If my words ring true, you gods and nāgas must consider
    them.
If you have not understood, I cannot repeat the song.

Thus the song ended, and Kyang Gö neighed three times with an earth-shattering sound. His words came out in a human tongue, and to Gesar he offered the song, "Six Reverberations of Neighing."

Sing "Ala thala thala."
"Thala" begins.
"Ha ha ha la ho ho ho
ha ha ho ho" is the language of horses.
It is the neighing sound of the capable steed Kyang Gö.
"Ha ha," I shout out thrice.
"Ho ho," I shout out thrice.
Those three shouts today call to the gods.
From the supreme dwelling place of the sky gods,
supreme steed Shelgyi Gyalpo (Crystal King), know me.
Look upon me with kindness.
From the peak of Sipa Gangri,
supreme steed Maha Barlha (Blazing Divine), know me.
From the five-peaked mountain Wutaishan of China,
Dharma horse Zhönu Lodrö (Learned Youthful One), know me.
Please assist me, this steed Kyang Gö.
If you do not recognize this place,
it is the left shore of the northern swamp lake Damtsho.
If you do not recognize me,
I am in fact Kyangshé, the all-knowing steed.
From the pure land of the highest gods
atop a golden peacock throne,
most exalted dharmakāya Amitābha,
I am your reincarnation.
I am the divine horse of channels and winds
known as the Capable Steed Kyang Gö.
I am not a white kyang; I am a maroon kyang
with the amazing color of my mother's coat,
lustrous and like a ruby.

My body is radiant with three colors:
the lustrous richness of red, sorrel, and the divine glow.
My body is thrice resolute:
my shoulders are steady as a general's flag,
my hindquarters have the piston-power of the victorious
    ones' enlightened activity,
and my barrel[34] is unwavering in its good fortune.
There are three lights of my body:
the boundless dharmakāya light of protection,
the boundless saṃbhogakāya radiance of compassion,
and the boundless nirmāṇakāya light of compassion.
These three lights are the divine channels and winds.[35]
My shoulders are gifted with wheels of wind
and I am as swift as a bird in the sky.
I am the horse endowed with magic.
I will explain how this is:
As you look at the right side of my body,
there are eighteen white vulture wings
and sixteen wings of the garuḍa, king of birds.
As you look at the left side of my body,
there are the eighteen dark vulture wings
and sixteen wings of the garuḍa, king of birds.
I have attained mastery of the channels and winds
and I am unfettered wherever I go.
My head is the long-life vase of the ḍākinīs,
consecrated by Amitāyus
and empowered with his deathless amṛta.
I am the one horse with super-knowledge.[36]
Within my eyes
is the radiant rainbow path of dharmakāya.
From my nostrils
comes the unceasing voice of the father guru's enlightened
    speech, *ta la la*.
In the elegance[37] of my mane[38]
is the surging fire of a thousand great blacksmiths.
My forty-nine[39] vertebrae
are surrounded by the eighty mahāsiddhas.
The spokes of my right rib cage

are adorned with the nine astrological diagrams.
The spokes of my left rib cage
are surrounded on the eight sides by the eight trigrams.[40]
my tail is like a gentle waterfall,
the stretched silk weaving of one hundred thousand ḍākinīs.[41]
My abdominal cavity is a maṇḍala
with an assembly of 1,022 buddha statues.
Unless you, Gesar, are off the mark,
there is no chance that I, the horse beneath you, will blunder.
As for crossing this muddy lake of the north,
there is no reason to be frightened.
That lake may seem vast,
but, ultimately, it has a limit.
Wide as it is, an ordinary stallion can cross it in eleven days.
Even though its waves surge to the heavens,
they swell methodically,
and we can move through them in a line.
Today, without a doubt, we can cross the northern swamp
  lake Damtsho.
Don't you think so?
You, Gesar, for one,
and I, the capable, great-gaited Kyang Gö, for another,
should not be sitting here relaxing.
One day we will go to the western land of Persia
and must cross its plains of fire.
There are eighteen fire plains of Persia
and the vast expanse of each
is an eighteen-day ride on a stallion.
An inferno spreads over their entirety,
and its blazing flames lick the skies
as though the splendor of fire consumes the sun[42]
and the god of fire drinks up the rivers.
Then, what will we do?
We will come to the country of Mongolia
and must cross its desert sands.
As for the sixty-eight desert hills there,
the upper sands are full of carrion birds.
Vultures lie in wait for meat and bones.

Fresh human flesh is there to be eaten.
Human skin is there to be sewn into aprons.
The middle sands are full of doves
singing a cooing sound *ung ung*.
Twirling right, they dance;
turning left, they twirl their heads.
Each day, the doves sing for their supper.
The lower sands are full of monkeys
cracking open the hills and mountains of sand
to roast grain.[43]
The deserts are overrun with pikas
burrowing and nesting in the sands
and reveling in play.
As we cross each of these desert lands,
the great vultures will knock us down with their beaks,
the doves will whip us with their wings,
the monkeys will charge and claw our flesh and skin,
and the pikas will gnaw at our calves.
When that happens, what can we do?
Keep listening, Sengchen.
Then, we must go to the deserts of Jeri in the north,
where there are thirteen great salt seas
that we must cross.
But today
there is not much more to say, Sengchen.
A soft-minded man is too careful; don't be that man—

everyone knows that the wind cannot carry a rock.[44]

We should both bear in mind what this means.
Let us get ready to cross Lake Damtsho.
Tonight, we should have a good rest
and in the morning cross the churning waters,
heading for the far shore.
Even if doubts arise, we must not look back.
Keep this whole situation in mind.
If there are faults in this song, they are mine.
If my words have caused confusion, I take the blame.

Thus he sang, and Gesar smiled and nodded and then drifted off to sleep. The next morning, by the time the sunlight was touching the mountain peaks, Gesar and his horse had reached the banks of Lake Damtsho. Kyang Gö said, "Now, we must be fearless and cross the waters." Gesar agreed, but as they waded in, the force of the waves lifted them up toward the clouds. As the waves broke, Gesar became frightened, feeling as though he was falling from the sky. Right at the moment that they were pulled underwater and disappeared from sight, the lha, lu, and nyen—and even more importantly, the water gods—arrived, propelling them across the lake and onto the far shore. Gesar was overjoyed and said, "But for the help of the gods, not only would we have failed to cross the lake, we would have drowned." Kyang Gö simply said, "Things went wrong because you were afraid, noble being."

Gesar kept on, "It is fortunate that we made it across; however, the creatures who live in the water and the mud, the tortoises and so forth, so many creatures living in the lake—it was not right that they were crushed under your hooves. It would be best if we found a way to guide them to the higher realms." The horse replied, "There is no need to worry about the living creatures down below. Those I trampled with my front legs I will guide with my rear legs, and those I trampled with my back legs I will guide with my front legs. Those creatures, not even a single insect, will fall to the hells. Gesar, listen to the song I will sing to you."

> Sing "Ala thala thala."
> "Thala" begins.
> The song unfolds in three parts.
> I take refuge in the Buddha, the Dharma, and the Saṅgha;
>   these three,[45]
> please grant your blessings.
> Three sacred gods, know me.
> Today, may your light rays of compassion shine.
> If you do not recognize this place,
> it is the near bank of the mud lake Damtsho of the north.
> If you do not recognize me,
> I am an emanation of Amitābha.
> Now, supreme king Sengchen,
> do not let your mind be petty.
> If you are small-minded, you will lose sight of the goal.
> You are the king of all of Jambudvīpa,
> and I am the capable supreme steed Kyang Gö.

We are the ones entrusted to send the māras to the hell realms
and to lead the six classes of sentient beings to liberation.
If you are petty-minded, you will lose sight of that,
and we will inherit the succession of māra obstacles.
I, the supreme steed Kyang Gö—
those who perished beneath my front legs, I will lead with my
    back legs, and
those who perished beneath my back legs, I will lead with my
    front legs.
You and I,
in the morning, are murderous butchers,
and in the afternoon, guiding gurus.
Don't you remember this?
In the pure land of the highest gods
all the way up to Brahmā
and in the eighteen hells below
all the way down to the lord of death, the Dharma king,
if anyone is to be liberated,
we are the ones to guide them to the pure realm;
if anyone is to be sent downward,
we are the ones to lead those sinners to the hell realms.
Between heaven and earth,
we are the ones to benefit beings.
That is our heavy responsibility.
In this great existence,
there are countless sentient beings of the six classes,
and therefore no end of enlightened activity required for
    their benefit.
In this samsaric world,
although you and I will endure great hardship,
there is no reason for regret.
That is the nature of what we have been asked to do.
Please take this to heart, King Gesar.
If you have not understood, I cannot repeat it.

When the song was over, Gesar and his horse left for higher ground but there, blocking the way, were the paired boulders, Rakchuma and Zangchuma, protruding like lips. As neither the birds of the skies nor the insects of the earth could pass, certainly a man mounted on a horse could not. Gesar stood up in his stirrups, drew out his sword Tabpa Lenmé, and sang.

> Sing "Ala thala thala."
> "Thala" begins.
> The song unfolds in three parts.
> I call to the gods:
> From the upper story of the colorful fortress of the warrior dralha,
> dralha king Sengtak Ökyi, know me.
> From the middle story,
> Dralha Dungseng Patrab, know me.
> From the lower story,
> Dralha Nyentak Marpo, know me.
> There are none higher to call.
> If you do not recognize this place,
> it is a great ocean[46] in Gowa Thangchen (Antelope Plain),
> and to the left of this low-lying plain
> are Rakchuma and Zangchuma.
> Theses two boulders paired into a slit
> are the butchers of unfortunate beings.
> If you do not recognize me,
> I am a man from the east,
> sped here by the wind.
> An icy wind and a wild man such as myself
> are unpredictable.
> My horse and I have come far,
> journeying along the rays of the sun.
> Rakchuma, move up!
> Zangchuma, move down!
> If you persevere and remain clenched together,
> my sword Tabpa Lenmé,
> the blazing sword of wisdom,
> will hammer unrelentingly
> and split you apart.
> Even though you are vajra-like, you will be reduced to dust
> by the thunderbolt that is my sword—
> won't that be a sight to see.
> If you have understood, keep this in mind.

The song ended, and from the crevice between the two rock outcroppings, Rakchuma and Zangchuma, came two *teumo*, both one-legged and with bright white teeth. Instantly a black rock no smaller than a sheep sat within the web of their slingshot. Whirling it overhead three times, they aimed at Gesar. The earth quaked and a roaring sound erupted into the three-thousand-fold world. Gesar swung his sword, Tabpa Lenmé, once and struck the slingshot stone, pulverizing it. A blinding dust cloud thickened over the earth and enveloped both teumo. Gesar again raised his sword and, in a single slashing blow, cut both teumo in half: their upper bodies were left with eyes that darted around, and their lower bodies with their single leg trembling in fear. However, being magical, both teumo reappeared in their original one-legged form, and one of them lunged right up to Gesar and sang this boasting song.

> Sing "Ala thala thala."
> "Thala" begins.
> The song unfolds in three parts.
> Today, I call the gods.
> From the dwelling place of the sky realm,
> yak-headed three-eyed teumo, know me.
> From the ocean of heart blood,
> black serpent with a fresh human head, know me.
> Kindly assist me.
> If you do not recognize this place,
> it is that of Rakchuma and Zangchuma,
> the boulders paired like lips.
> If you do not recognize me,
> I am the lord of life, the one-legged teumo Khenpa Genmo,
> the mother of the evil black serpent,
> the gatekeeper of the māra king Lutsen.
> Such an arrogant man and horse,
> you displaying the threefold panoply of weapons
> and your stallion flaunting his skilled gait,
> have come here to these paired boulders
> to smash Rakchuma and Zangchuma
> and cover the great earth with their dust,
> and not only that, to fill the air with your shouts of "Ki!"
> Thinking you and your horse were so fierce,
> you leapt right in front of me.

This karmic ledger of the teurang lord of death
today includes both your names.
Outwardly, your bony skeleton will be destroyed;
inwardly, the candle of your consciousness will be
    extinguished.
If none of this happens, then I am not a teumo.
If you have understood, may this be music to your ears.

The teumo finished singing and threw the karmic ledger at Joru. Above were the troops of Brahmā, then the army of Nyenchen Kulha Gedzo, and below the troops of the nāga king Tsukna, as well as the dralha, werma, and so forth. With sharp swords they sliced the karmic ledger, while Brahmā and Nyen Kulha threw their spears, simultaneously killing both teumo. The lha, lu, and nyen buried the corpses in an inlet on the ocean shore, and upon the grave they constructed a stupa to suppress the return of the barbarian cannibals. Furthermore, the paired boulders naturally parted, and the road became wide, open, and easy to cross.

CHAPTER FOURTEEN

Acham Karmo turns to the Dharma.
An arrow message is sent to Meza.
Meza stirs up various falsehoods and discords.
After quarreling, Lutsen Gyalpo devours his minister
    Beu Natra.

MOVING IN SINGLE FILE, Gesar and his horse reached the foothills of Sipa Gangri where, like a flash of lightning, the demoness Acham Karmo appeared. Seated upon her white lion with its turquoise mane, she wielded the lasso of the lord of death. Detaining Gesar, she sang this song.

> Sing "Ala thala thala."
> "Thala" begins.
> Today, I call to the deities.
> First, from the supreme dwelling place of the sky gods,
> the teurang Lhamo Ökar (Goddess White Light),
> second, from the black rock inlet of the cannibals,
> the teumo, one-legged mother Khenpa Genmo,
> and third, the 360 teurang—
> today kindly assist me.
> If you do not recognize this place,
> it is the middle of the Antelope Plain, Gowa Thangchen,
> below the foothills of Sipa Gangri,

the home of the white-muzzled kyang
and the sorrel drong,
an unpeopled land.
If you do not recognize me,
from the heights of Sipa Gangri,
I am Acham Karmo, a teumo,
in essence the demoness Acham.
Hey boy, listen—
your body is encircled by the threefold panoply of dralha,
adorned with the exquisite accoutrements of a warrior
and riding the magical horse of channels and winds
that rivals any bird in flight.
You have disturbed the fish and mammals of our blue waters,
for what reason?
I, the keeper of these watery sacred māra lands,
this very day have met you, the stag.
Now, I have not seen it for myself
but only heard that
from the land of Ma in Ling,
that nasty snot-nosed Joru
recklessly
went far into India—
up to India, dressed in the Dharma,
and over to China,
dressed like a ruler,
and in between, to the four regions of Central Tibet,
traveling wherever he wanted,
saying there was no place that he did not go.
But in India he did not ask for Dharma teachings,
in China he did not respect the laws,
and in between in Ling he ran around like a crazed elephant.
That is nothing but the boasting of a brazen man,
and without doubt, that is exactly your style.
Today, we two shall meet
and vie with each other.
Listen. Here is the story.
As in the ancient proverbs of Tibet:

When human life is spent, the aged come to the door of the cannibals
and enter that house.
When life is spent, the insects come to the door of ants
and enter their nest.

These proverbial words are coming true.
You, the Ling child, have come to the north.
Who are you after?
Who here can you trust?
The inner meaning of my words is:

The sun in the azure firmament—
can it escape the great Rāhula's mouth?
The raging tiger with its fur pelt—
can it escape the hunter's trap?

You who bragged of not staying in Ling
came to the kingdom of the unrivaled Lutsen,
that man-eating king of demons.
Are you deaf?
Are you blind?
Look around, Ling child, your life is over.
This lasso I wield
will whip to the heavens above,
barring the path of the sun and moon
and demolishing the stars' array.
It will thrash at the mouth of the rivers below,
reversing the flow of the great rivers
and drying up the oceans.
Today, this butcher comes for you,
outwardly binding you like a ring,
inwardly binding you like string.
If that does not happen, I am misreading the signals.

She sang and flung Yama's lasso at Gesar and his horse, forcing them back the length of an arrow shot. Gesar unsheathed his sword, Tabpa Lenmé, swung it once, and the māra lasso was cut to pieces. Gesar realized that he must find a way to turn the teumo Acham Karmo to the side of virtue. Thus, he sang "Self-Utterance of the Unobstructed Vajra."

Sing "Ala thala thala."
"Thala" begins.
The song unfolds in three parts.
Make the first, second, and third offerings
to the Three Jewels,
next, the fourth to the four orders of the great kings,[1]
the five families of the victorious ones,
the six sages,[2]
and finally, to the seven buddhas of antiquity.[3]
If you do not recognize this place,
it is Gowa Thangchen of the north.
If you do not recognize me,
in the forenoon I am the murderous butcher,
in the afternoon, the guiding lama,
entrusted by one thousand buddhas,
the warrior who subdues the four māras,
the leader who unites the three worlds.
I am Gesar, the king.
But you know all this, Acham.
In the past, in Tramo Ling
I was known as the snot-nosed boy Joru,
but, in fact, I am a divine lama who knows the Dharma path,
a high minister versed in secular law,
and a skillful warrior.
Today, Acham, we met face to face,
and you hurled Yama's lasso at me.
I sliced it with my sword, and it fell into a heap.
Let go of your lasso;
turn your mind to virtue.
First, the teachings of Śākyamuni Buddha,
second, the oral instructions of the sublime master,
and third, the direction of the unrivaled king—
these three, if accepted, bring joy.
Demoness Acham Karmo,
grasp instead the teurang lasso of emptiness
that brings unrivaled delight.
I have cut Yama's lasso,
severing your ties to the māras

and creating the tendrel to accomplish the benevolent
  Dharma.
The māra Lutsen remains;
I have come to help annihilate him
in accord with my destiny.
Acham, you are concealed in the crook of my arm.
If you have understood, keep this in mind.
If not, I cannot repeat my song.

At the song's end, Acham burst out laughing, flashing her teeth, and questioned, "If you are an emanation of the Buddha, then what is all this . . . your helmet, armor, and threefold panoply? It's shameful." She demanded that he listen to her song.

Sing "Ala thala thala."
"Thala" begins.
The song unfolds in three parts.
I call to the divine one.
From the sky, the dwelling place of the gods,
Dharmakāya Supreme Mother Dakmema[4]
if you do not recognize this place,
it is the interior of Gowa Thangchen
at the foothills of Sipa Gangri.
If you do not recognize me,
I am the demoness Acham Karmo.
Listen,
you say that you are from Ling,
a divine lama who knows the Dharma path,
a high minister versed in secular law,
and a skillful warrior.
You say that in the forenoon, you are a murderous butcher,
and in the afternoon, a guiding lama.
You say that you have accomplished the teachings of virtue.
There is much talk that you are some marvelous lama,
but probably you are just a charlatan.
This white helmet that is on your head,
is it really the hat of a great meditator?
The white armor that you wear,

are they your Dharma robes?
The supreme white arrow and bow that are your
    accoutrements,
are they the drum and bell of a lama?
A divine lama then, is that what you are?
Even if you spew Dharma from your mouth,
the wrathful weapon-wheel turns around your body.
Even if you lead the six classes of beings to the higher realms,
they will quickly be ushered into war's slaughterhouse.
Even if you wear Dharma robes,
who is it that will say you are a great meditator?
For the subjects of Jambudvīpa,
a genuine guiding lama is
one with mastery of the Dharma teachings
from the kingdom of dharmic India,
a supreme emanation of Śākyamuni
wearing a meditation hat
and the Dharma robes of emptiness,
a guide who holds sentient beings of the six classes in his
    heart
and proclaims the Dharma, *ur ru ru*.
On the peak of the Glorious Copper-Colored Mountain
dwells the supreme nirmāṇakāya Padmasambhava.
His head is adorned with his secret lotus hat and
he wears the Dharma robes of the three attributes,
holding samsaric beings in his heart
and leading them in a dohā, *sil lé lé*.
His outer mind, inner heart, and his conduct are one and the
    same;
his body, speech, and mind are one and the same.
That is what it means to be a guide,
a great meditator.
In the southern land of Jambudvīpa,
Buddhadharma flourishes,
many temples have been erected,
there are many lamas
and many disciples.
Beings have been led from suffering

and guided to the pure realm.
You, with your armor, helmet, and weapons,
entered the killing field
and from your threefold panoply surrounded by the weapon-
      wheel,
killing weapons rained down.
You should be ashamed to call yourself a compassionate
      meditator.
Who put you into the ranks of divine lamas?
Nevertheless, today is a good day.
Are you not the Ling youth who has come to the north
and now stands facing me?
It is just as the ancient proverbs say:

It cannot be the uppermost mountain peak
if it is not snow covered.
It cannot be the depth of the blue ocean
if it is covered with frothy foam.

Formless beings do not make a shadow.
The law must not punish the innocent.
Water, whether on the rocks, in the meadows, or by the
      riverbanks,
starts from the white snow mountains
and travels on to the turquoise blue ocean.
The three of them, Achung, Chakchung, and Mukchung,
are the heirs of the māra families;
their target is the flesh and blood of humans—
no surprise in that.
That suddenly we two have met today
indicates our karmic connection
and that the fiercest of us will bear the trophy.
From deep within the leopard-skin case on my left,
I will draw the bow Karmo Lebchen (The Great White)
and from deep within the tiger-skin quiver on my right,
the arrow Karpo Shaza (White Flesh-Eater)
and impale you with this single arrow
like a thunderbolt splintering white rock.

If that does not happen, I am not who I said I am.
If you have understood, think it over.
If not, I cannot repeat the song.

When Acham finished her song, Gesar spoke, "Today, the story will unfold: Are you an expert with your bow and arrow?" and with the lasso of emptiness in hand, he sang to her.

Sing "Ala thala thala."
Thala begins.
The song unfolds in three parts.
I call to the deity.
In the celestial dwelling place of the gods,
from on high, Brahmā, know me;
from in between, Nyenchen Kulha, know me;
and from below, nāga king Tsukna, know me.
Warriors, dralha, and werma, kindly assist me.
If you do not recognize this place—
but of course you do—
it is the interior of Gowa Thangchen.
If you do not recognize me,
from the kingdom of Ma in Ling,
I am Gesar who has come,
entrusted by the highest gods.
I am the Ling youth with a white top ornament,
and today my horse and I have arrived in the north.
We have come here to benefit beings
and to deliver an arrow into the demon's skull.
Acham, you said I was a braggart
and that I had come, a Ling youth
surrounded by the threefold panoply,
to enter into a killing field,
such that human blood would rain down.
Acham, what you believe is based on rumors,
nothing more than your opinion.
You perceive the outward appearance but not what is within.
I, Ling Gesar,
in the forenoon, am a murderous butcher

with a threefold panoply of armor,
repeatedly battling the demons.
In the evening, I am a guiding lama
who has accomplished the enlightened activity intent,
guiding sentient beings from suffering.
This, my great helmet
surrounded by one thousand buddhas,
is the meditation hat of a sublime lama.
This, my body armor
surrounded by the protectors of the three families,
is none other than the three Dharma robes.
The threefold panoply of armor encircling my body
and surrounded by the sublime peaceful and wrathful deities
are the weapons of the dralha Dharma protectors.
This lasso that I hold,
suppose I whip it to the highest reaches of space,
the turquoise dragon will seize it.
If I whip it onto the lowest ground
the makara below will snatch it,
and if I toss it into the skies above,
the icy wind will take it away.
Keep those things in mind, Acham.
If you consider me a lama, repent and confess.
If you consider me a buddha, meditate with devotion.
If twenty-one days and nights pass without meditation,
your precious life force will be no more.
If you have not understood, I cannot repeat the song.

When his song was finished, Gesar readied his lasso but Acham shot first, striking Gesar though not wounding him. She drew back, frightened as Gesar leapt at her with his sword unsheathed. He threw his lasso and in turn Acham threw swirling, acrid ashes. Gesar's connate protector brothers, Dungkhyung Karpo and Lutrül Öchung, each grabbed one of Acham's hands and with a single piece of white silk tied them behind her back, fettering her with a loop that they spun around her like ball of yarn. Gesar said, "It is clear that our competition is over. I could easily have turned you peacefully to the benevolent Dharma, but you chose not to listen." Acham addressed him now with respect, saying, "Sengchen Norbu Dradül, I did not understand you to be a buddha. I did not realize the pith of the instructions. Today, I confess to you and repent. I ask to be spared." And she sang this offering song.

Sing "Ala thala thala."
"Thala" begins.
The song unfolds in three parts.
I call to the deity.
Dharmakāya, saṃbhogakāya, nirmāṇakāya,
three divine ones with your blessings, know me.
Hosts of dralha and werma,
today, please assist me.
If you do not recognize this place,
it is Gowa Thangchen
at the foothills of Sipa Gangri.
If you do not recognize me,
from the eight snow mountain ranges of the great northern
    continent,
from the summit of Sipa Gangri,
I am the demoness Acham Karmo,
the guardian protectress of the snow mountains
and gatekeeper for King Lutsen of the north.
Previously, in the distant past,
before I had mistakenly acted so harmfully,
the forebears of the noble saṅgha
had given me the blessings of dharmakāya,
and I was the wisdom ḍākinī Chamseng (Lion Sister).
But I wasted my merit in evil action
and became the north country teurang guardianess.
Nevertheless, today,
the planets, stars, and moon are in good alignment,
and the unrivaled Sengchen has come to the north.
With compassion, he has led me to understanding
and blocked the path of ignorance and delusion.
He turned the wheel of Dharma with his illustrative words,
but I welcomed him with the evil demon lasso.
Until today,
my mind knew only arrogance.
Sengchen Lama,

your body is the Buddha;
that I did not understand until now.
Your speech is the amṛta of oral instructions;
that I did not understand until now.
Your mind is primordially liberated wisdom;
that I did not understand until now.
Today, I have met the Buddha
and heard the oral instructions.
I offer repentance for past deeds.
I confess to the noble being and atone.
I request refuge,
please consider me and bestow *abhiṣeka* and blessings.
I bow my head for abhiṣeka
and with folded hands, offer this shaven head
from my heart.
Sincerely, I ask for your blessings.
You who are the Buddha, please grant your blessings.
From my crown cakra
with one-pointed mind, I request refuge.
I request refuge in you, the Buddha.
Your body is the maṇḍala of the victorious ones.
Within it reside the three channels: *avadhūtī, rasanā,*[5] and
    lalanā.
Out of compassion, do not forsake me,
bestow the transmission of the sacred Dharma.
Whatever teachings of virtue you set out,
I will accomplish.
Listen to me, Sengchen Gesar.
Today, you have come to the upper lands of the north,
and now is the time.
The demon Lutsen
is sixty-nine years old.
The time has come to tame him,
as next year it will be more difficult.
Trishok Meza Bumdrön
will be eighteen years old,
a wise woman with all the excellent qualities.
Although she has great wisdom and omniscience,

if she turns nineteen, she will drift away
and risk being with the demon Lutsen.
Meza and Lutsen—
if they couple, the chance to tame Lutsen will be lost.
Atak Lhamo—that foreigner from the north,
she who is the emanation of the Lion-Faced One,
    Siṃhamukha,
whose father is the empty sky
and whose mother is the vast expanse of earth—
was born among kuśa grass.
Atak Lhamo—the northern outsider,
fifteen, with the gathered six powers of a warrior—
throughout the southern continent
is called a woman, but her strength
is greater than that of one hundred warriors.
This is the time to bring her under your power.
Now is the time to bring her into the Dharma.
The long-horned demon sorrel yaks
are unrivaled in strength.
Their horns reach the sky
and their tails mass like clouds in the heavens;
red lightning flashes from their horn tips,
and their four legs kick up a dust storm.
When these yaks run,
their hooves thunder like the roar of the turquoise dragon,
darkness descends beneath the swirling dust and vapors.
It is not easy to subdue even one demon yak.
Gesar, there is danger that she, Atak Lhamo, will defeat your
    army.
The demon Lutsen's minister, his disciple,
is the wild one Beu Natra,
a rebirth of the rudra king,
and the enemy of the Buddhadharma.
Likewise, he must now be tamed.
All this, Gesar, take to heart.
I take full blame for any mistakes in this song.
If my words have been nonsense, the fault is mine.

Thus she supplicated, and Gesar answered, "You have spoken openly and elegantly. Your words and the divine prophecy are in complete harmony. Acham Karmo, this is the tendrel of your turning to the Dharma, and you will be granted abhiṣeka." Acham vowed henceforth never to harm sentient beings and prostrated to Gesar, bowing deeply. Gesar, taking heed of Acham's prophecy that the demon Lutsen must be tamed without delay, before Meza turns nineteen, said, "Now, I will send Meza a message to relax and that she and I must collaborate." Drawing the divination arrow Ngangpa Dradül (Golden Swan Enemy Tamer) out of the tiger-skin quiver and the bow Ragö Kyilwa from the leopard-skin case, he strung an elephant hide bowstring,[6] and, in a flurry, attached to the arrow a folded yellow parchment on which was written his message in ḍākinī script.

Gesar respectfully composed a letter to Meza, which read:

> I, the incomparable king, Gesar, without faltering, am just now arriving at the foothills of Sipa Gangri. You have never turned away from the divine ones and have skillfully persevered in the foolproof plan to deceive the demon Lutsen, enduring hardship beyond imagination. Now, delight is at hand; it will not be long until you and I are together. As you have before, you must use your wisdom and skillful means to destroy Lutsen's three life-force supports.

Thus it was arranged, and Gesar spoke to his divine arrow, "Ngangpa Dradül, the time has come. Go quickly to Meza so that she can receive your golden arrow message. Remember every word of her reply, keeping it close to your heart. Arrow, go quickly and make an awesome show of your unrivaled force. Send fear into the heart of that shameless demon and overpower him. May he cease to exist." He loosed the arrow and with a whirring sound it went like a flash of lightning. Overnight it reached the skies high above the land of the north. The air trembled as the arrow zigged and zagged across the celestial expanse, and a rumbling sound welled up from the quaking earth. Those who lived there became agitated and fearful, wondering what had happened. The soldiers of the north said that it could have been almost anything.

A great sound arose from the very top of the māra castle Shari Tsegu and red lightning flashed. Lutsen, terrified, ran this way and that, shouting, "What was that? What was that?" Just then, the arrow Ngangpa Dradül whistled past, grazing Lutsen's skull and wounding the tip of his right horn, and he let out a yelp. To his eye, the arrow vanished like a rainbow, but Meza understood that it was Gesar's divine arrow, and she took it in her hands, touching it to the crown of her head as she offered an aspiration prayer. Tied at the midpoint of the arrow was a red silk flag that depicted Gesar on his mount, and she could see the lettering. She glanced at it quickly three times and realized that Gesar was not far away and was on his way to meet her. A joyful smile shyly spread across her face. Bending her head to the divine arrow, she sang this song.

Sing "Ala thala thala."
"Thala" begins.
The song unfolds in three parts.
I call to the divine one.
From the supreme dwelling place, the expanse of space,
Mother lineage Vajravārāhī, know me.
If you do not recognize this place,
these are the eight mountain ranges of the upper north.
Blood rains down from above,
between, consciousnesses swirl like a snowstorm,
and from below wafts the stench of flesh and bones.
The great plain is covered with human corpses—
the world that has come into being from the demon's desire.
If you do not recognize me—
but, surely you know a face like mine.
From the precious sacred land of eastern Ling,
where the utterance of the turquoise dragon
and the perfect timbre of the cuckoo's melody are heard,
there, in the Akyi family home,
my father, mother, and brother
were swallowed up by Lutsen,
and nine years ago, he brought me here.
I have had no means of escape.
Thrice he chewed me with his sharp jagged teeth;
thrice he licked me with his red ironlike tongue.
Desperate, I sat still as an iron boulder,[7]
hidden among his sharp, gapped teeth.
Three times the demon sucked me in but was unable to harm
    me.
He spit me out onto the tip of his finger,
and I transformed myself into a ravishing woman,
a maiden of divine charm and elegance.

The demon's mood changed quickly,
saying I must be his wife.
And though he had previously eaten my father, mother, and
    brother,
he immediately spit them out, saying he would spare them,
spewing them out of his mouth
and into his hands.
He was tossing them from one finger to another
as he asked, "Is this your mother?
Is this your father?
Is this your brother?
If so, I will spare their lives;
if not, they have no future."
The man had vomited them out of his guts,
and, without question, there I saw my father, mother, and
    brother.
As set in motion in a previous life,
my karma was to become the demon's wife.
I thought I would be better off dead
and nearly took my own life.
He, the young minister Joru,
arrived, mounted on his staff, Changkar Berkar,
saying to me that this was the opportune moment,
this was the time
for deceiving the demon,
that the loss of my father, mother, and brother
he would eventually revenge.
Gesar is now fifteen
and I, Meza, am eighteen.
Gesar has said that Lutsen must be annihilated
by an arrow shot into his skull,
saying over and over that today is the day to tame the demon.
You, Sengchen's divine arrow,
have come today. Greatly kind,
divine arrow Ngangpa Dradül,
I am overjoyed simply to have met you;
it is as though I have met Gesar himself.
From today onward,

I will act as the wife of the demon.
Outwardly I will show him a smiling face,
but inwardly my mind will hold to Gesar,
deceiving the demon.
Naturally, I hope Gesar will wait for me,
just as the cuckoo waits and waits for rain.
This year, the stars and planets are favorable.
The supreme king Sengchen has come north
and sent the reassurance of the divine arrow to me
with its dear message displayed.
That message on the parchment encircling the arrow,
vivid, as though meeting Gesar face to face,
brings a smile of delight to my face
and ease to my being.
Just as Sengchen asked,
with the methods of destroying Lutsen's three life forces,
I will greet Gesar's auspicious arrival.
As for this land of humankind,
there are many great deeds.
Three prevail in the heavens:
those of the sun, the moon, and the stars.
Which has the greatest import?
Here in this world, greatest
is the sun's kindness
for the brown earth.
As for India, China, and Ling,
here in this world, the greatest kindness
is probably that of Ling.
There are three beautiful women renowned in all the world—
in India, the maiden Rati,
in China, the maiden Lhadarma,
and in Ling, the maiden Drukmo—
renowned in all the world as the most beautiful.
They could lay their own bodies down,
but what would that accomplish?
Who would say this is such a great turn?
Meza is the maiden
whose sorrow no one knows.

But I have an ally in Gesar,
the one to accomplish great meaning.
Today, divine arrow Dradül,
do not be too weary; come quickly.
Here is my advice to Gesar:
When you arrive at Gowa Thangchen
and meet the seven menmo sisters,
please be careful of them,
especially of Atak Lhamo,
one as savage as any warrior,
the skilled archer
whose dexterity is unrivaled.
If you are not prudent,
you will fall into her clutches,
she who is vital life essence of the demon Lutsen.
But everyone knows the demon is not so brave;
it is I, Meza, who has been the courageous one.
And as Gesar has avowed,
all I have hoped for these many years
is finally at hand.
The joyful sun appears,
clearing away bad karma.
Delicious barley ale boils,
and the patiently awaited guest arrives.
All the auspicious signs and marks have come together.
Divine arrow, take this to heart.

Thus she finished her song, and Meza, cloaking the divine arrow with a single white scarf, offered it to the sky and it flew away like a bird. Right away, Meza boiled tea and cast the mantra spell of the Lion-Faced Ḍākinī, Siṃhamukha and Lhamo Marchungma [the wrathful wisdom Vajrayoginī]. The gleaming splendor of the divine arrow had caused Beu Natra, the foremost of Lutsen's ministers, to faint dead away, and he was just recovering. Moreover, the tip of Lutsen's right horn had been gashed and he was lying senseless, face down in a pool of his own blood. The māra ministers Beu Natra, Chiwa Lakring (Long-Armed Marmot), and Jangma Kangring (Long-Legged Northerner) came to help, and as soon as she saw that Lutsen was able to stagger to his feet, Meza rushed to his side sprinkling ablution water, and he gradually came around.

Meza had seen a red streak of lightning when the arrow struck Lutsen, and she said, "Lutsen, are you ill? What happened to your right horn? Last night, lightning was tossed from the sky. Do you believe this too was an emanation of demons, cannibals, and evil spirits?" While she spoke, Lutsen wrapped a red cloth tightly around his bleeding horn, wiping off the blood. Then, he said, "Today, seeing all that has happened, is it that snot-nosed black-headed worm of the world Joru has arrived? Did you see him?" Meza said, "I have no idea what you are talking about. You, a mantra practitioner sleeping while you pretend to be meditating, explain everything by calling it the work of demons, cannibals, and evil spirits." They were sitting in Lutsen's castle with its endless supply of amṛta to which she had added poison. She lifted a glass up to him, and Lutsen took three gulps and immediately became ill. His minister Beu Natra said, "Sir, I was afraid of this. Today, the strangest things have happened." And he sang this song.

> Sing "Ala thala thala."
> "Thala" begins.
> The song unfolds in three parts.
> I call to the divine one.
> From the pinnacle of Mount Meru,
> little white snow mountain, Sipa Gangri, look upon me.
> Omniscient father mountain, lead me in my song.
> There is no one above you to call.
> If you do not recognize this place,
> these are the eight mountain ranges of the upper north,
> the land that brings happiness to the māra demon,
> the dancing ground of the demons and rākṣasas.
> Human blood rains down from above,
> consciousnesses swirl like a blizzard in between,
> and below, the insects clean flesh from bones.
> It is the land of wine made from human blood
> and of feasts of human flesh.
> Here, Lutsen and his ministers revel.
> If you do not recognize me,
> by way of explanation,
> I am Beu, from the land of strong young bulls.
> Here in the precious jewel of our homeland,
> you are the leader of 1,3000,000 people,
> and I am the māra minister Beu Natra.

This year at Losar,
I will be twenty-seven years old,
with claim over nine hundred households.
To be a man like that in the world is a great responsibility.
Great and powerful King Lutsen,
today listen to my song.
This year in the north,
many strange things will happen.
If we look to the southern continent Jambudvīpa,
the wives there, I can differentiate;
I can glean the good from the bad.
Dwelling in the royal seat of India
with the Dharma king
is a wise woman, chosen to be his wife.
The king can rely on her pure mind,
and she holds him close to her heart.
Repaying the kindness of her parents,
she is a maiden known for her good character.
Dwelling in the royal seat of China
with the secular king of China
is a wise woman, chosen to be his wife.
The king can rely on her sincere good intention.
She honors and serves her aging parents,
caring for them with the love of a good daughter.
Those are the supremely excellent women.
As for the eight mountains of the upper kingdom of the
    north,
to this land that is your home, demon Lutsen,
Ling's Meza Bumdrön
you invited as your wife.
But those smiling white teeth are not for you,
her pure intentioned mind is not entrusted to you
but rather to the legacy of eastern Ling.
Isn't that startling, King Lutsen?
Today, all day,
from the sky above, lightning struck down,
from the gap of the middle sky, sparks swirled,
from the solid earth, dusty vapor thickened,

from atop the many-peaked iron mountains,
a fearsome trembling din arose.
The red inferno of a blazing fire spread[8]
and the sound of the feathered flesh-eating arrow whistled
    past.
Many castle fortresses were destroyed,
and the horns of the king were left unprotected.
This is a truly amazing arrow;
look how it was constructed:
the nock of the arrow is made from white conch
as though the great god Brahmā conceived it,
the shaft of the arrow is made from precious gold
as though Nyenchen Kulha conceived it,
and the arrow point is made from blue turquoise
as though the nāga king Tsukna conceived it.
The arrowhead is made from black iron,
quickly drinking blood and eating flesh.
When that arrow of awesome brilliance flew,
everyone was frightened, running everywhere,
covering their heads and hiding.
Gradually, the sound of the arrow faded away
and everyone stood around talking.
Some said that the arrow was quite amazing,
others said that they were terrified,
talking and talking. Although they said many things,
to me this is what happened:
That particularly marvelous swift arrow
went toward Meza's castle.
I heard Meza sing a song,
and then I saw the arrow fly like a bird from the castle,
no doubt that wondrous arrow, the courier
of Joru's behest.
Moreover, the Antelope Plain, Gowa Thangchen,
is where Joru had been.
Yet, he had not stayed there,
and, just then, the marvelous splendor of the arrow
    manifested,
followed by Meza's happy song.

Don't you think she was looking for a way to freedom?
Meza Bumdrön is difficult to understand . . .
today it is time to make a blood sacrifice.
Furthermore, if Meza stays,
harm will come to you.
Lutsen, please think over this very important matter.
If you have not understood, I cannot repeat my song.

He sang, and Meza confronted him, saying, "Demon minister Natra, the story you just told so melodiously—suppose things are really like that." And Meza turned and sang this song to King Lutsen.

Sing "Ala thala thala."
"Thala" begins.
The song unfolds in three parts.
The song begins with entreating the gods and lamas,
the middle seeks the motherly ḍākinīs,
and the song ends with the gaze of the dharmapālas.
From the land of the māra demon cannibals,
powerful nine-headed cannibals, please lead my song.
If you do not recognize this place,
it is the eight mountains of the upper north,
the lowest plain strewn with rocks,
the land of rocky crags, dark as night.
If you do not recognize me,
in the kingdom of Ling in the east,
I was the daughter of a happy home,
but I was exiled to the north nine years ago
and have endured great hardship and suffering,
put into the hands of the enemy by the boy I love.[9]
As is told in ancient stories:
the demon king Lutsen,
saying I was beautiful, welcomed me with a smile
and said I would be happy as his wife.
I had precious silks to wear
and delicious food to eat.
There, I was in the castle of happiness,
forced to deny my suffering.

Chief minister Beu Natra,
now you turn the wheel of these falsehoods,
saying an arrow was launched from the east
and calling it the divine arrow of Brahmā,
saying it was a divine arrow with the power of awesome
     brilliance,
the necklace arrow of Nyenchen Kulha,
and saying it was the messenger arrow of Joru
coming to Meza.
Although many things were said,
the truth of it,
Lutsen, is up to you to decide.
Beu Natra, you
came to Lutsen with your sweet little story,
but all you wanted was to provoke an argument
between Lutsen and me;[10]
that is all you were doing.
The arrow that you said came from the east,
was it an arrow or just red lightning?
Natra, can you tell the difference?
The arrow that you said brought Joru's message—
when he commissioned it as his courier,
were you nearby, Natra?
You said that I, Meza, could read what was written,
but I came north nine years ago
and, as Lutsen knows, I never learned the script.
Here, out of the 360[11] most important ministers,
each one possessing several arrows,
let us see if there is one who has an arrow that sings.
If there is an arrow that can sing,
your flesh, Natra, will be mine;
if there is no arrow that can sing,
my flesh will be yours.
Last night, the sky swirled with clouds,
the turquoise dragon roared *ur ru ru*,
red tongues of lightning flashed *khyuk sé khyuk*,
like thunderbolts falling from the skies,
a roaring sound filled the valley

and the earth trembled,
castles crumbled,
and Lutsen's right-sided horn
was shattered at its tip.
I was the one who came to Lutsen's side—
not a single one of his ministers showed up.
King Lutsen, as for your injured horn,
unless the six precious medicines are compounded,
how will you rouse yourself?
Today, every piece of this story
the interior minister Natra
has fabricated out of nothing,
making false accusations.
Lutsen, you decide what is true and what is false.
If you cannot, then from now on,
I cannot be happy staying here.
King Lutsen, keep this in mind.

Thus she sang, and Lutsen, thinking that he should see if what Meza had said was true, said, "The 360 māra ministers carry 360 arrows. One after another, we will see if there is or is not one that can sing." And immediately, Lutsen sang to his minister Beu Natra this song of how he saw things.

Sing "Ala thala thala."
"Thala" begins.
The song unfolds in three parts.
I call to the divine ones.
Twenty-nine māra gods, know me.
May my heart be protected by the valued life keeper.[12]
Lord of life[13] over millions, know me.
Today, assist this king.
If you do not recognize this place,
they are the eight mountains of the upper north.
This māra castle is called Shari Tsegu.
If you do not recognize me,
from these eight mountains of the upper north,
I am the māra Lutsen.
There are 360 interior ministers,

twelve māra myriarchies.
The country of Düd flourishes with power and influence.
Why wouldn't we make war?
Today, wherever
there is no quarrel, we will stir one up.
Just as the sky abuts the earth,
to act is unavoidable.
Is it not just like these examples?
When black clouds swirl in the skies,
the turquoise dragon roars in the azure firmament
and lightning flashes down;
even the adamantine rocks cannot endure.
Is that not the way it is, Natra?
As one of my 360 ministers,
Beu Natra, listen.
Between me and Meza,
starting a pointless fight
is not your prerogative.
You said that an arrow appeared out of nowhere,
that clouds swirled in a cloudless sky,
and that there was a man in an uninhabited place.
Can you explain what you mean by all this?
Here in Düd, this land of cannibal demons,
from above, blood rains down,
in between, consciousnesses swirl like a blizzard,
and below, maggots pick bones clean.
The great plain is piled with the bones of humans and horses,
the mountains look like they are made of human and horse
    skulls.
In this very same kingdom,
there are tiers of gatekeepers.
On the highest northern great slate plain, Yama Thangchen,
live the cannibals with their breath-bag.
The teurang Khenpa Genmo
and her 360 teurang children
live by the great muddy lake Damtsho of the north.
There stand the two boulders
clamped like copper and brass lips

and counterbalanced
such that neither one can be easily rolled away.
On the right side of the snowy world
live the demoness Acham Karmo,
the one hundred material and one thousand immaterial
    beings,
and more than one hundred wild men.
In between live the seven menmo sisters
and the mistress Atak Lhamo,
the long-horned māra yak,
the iron-hoofed māra sheep,
and finally, the Zhugadar minister Ching-ngön.
The three gates, outer, middle, and inner—
you might get through one, but not the other two.
Even the icy wind cannot escape.
Meza and Natra, you two,
has this become a quarrel or not?
Is there truth to any of your words?
That is something the māra ministers must know.
It is like the ancient proverbs:

The wind brings on the rain.[14]
Evil spirits bring on epidemics.
Wickedness leads to scheming.

What is most important is the root of a mistake.
Today, Beu Natra,
you accused the innocent
and set in motion your own harsh punishment.
I, King Lutsen,
delight in human flesh
and thirst for human blood.
Natra keep this in mind.
All of this is the way of Lutsen.

King Lutsen finished singing, grabbed Beu Natra around the waist, and, clutching him, flew into the sky. Natra fell, his body twisted into a heap, and he struck his head on the ground, bleeding. To the horror of the other māra ministers, with a chomping sound Lutsen devoured Natra. But Lutsen still could not discern what was true or false by the look on Meza's face. As for Beu Natra being able to clarify anything for Lutsen, it was too late, as Lutsen had eaten him. Furthermore, seeing that no good was going to come of what had just happened, Lutsen was fed up with talking and became furious. His face was a turbulent black cloud, his eyes flashed with red lightning, his mouth was smacking, and he beat his chest as though it were a large drum. The northern minister brothers, Dadri Trikdruk, Rudra Pawo, Mudü Jamnak Damdrub, together with the Zhugadar minister Ching-ngön, were about to sing a fierce song, when Ching-ngön took over and sang this song to Lutsen Gyalpo.

> Sing "Ala thala thala."
> "Thala" begins.
> The song unfolds in three parts.
> I call to the deity.
> From supreme celestial space,
> great divine Brahmā, know me.
> Today, assist this hero warrior.
> From the snowy tsen lower valley,
> local deities numbering 990,000, know me.
> Today, assist in this hero's plan.
> If you do not recognize this place,
> it is the eight mountains of the upper land of the north,
> the māra land of dense darkness
> where evil deeds are readily undertaken.
> No matter where you find yourself,
> human blood rains down from above,
> a blizzard of consciousnesses swirls,
> and the ground is full of insects stripping flesh from bones.
> You cannot tell it apart from the garden of the lord of death.
> If you do not recognize me,
> from the lotus fields of the upper plains of the north,
> I am the shepherd of the white prosperity sheep,
> the Zhugadar minister Ching-ngön.
> The māra sheep with iron hooves—
> I am their shepherd, the one who watches over them.
> If you do not recognize this song,
> it is a short song of mine, this warrior boy.
> Māra king Lutsen, listen.

To all the world
you are the unrivaled demon king.
Throughout all time,
you have been called the devourer of humans.
That is what is said, and it is true.
He will scarf down any foreigner,
but his own people he will gather like gold dust.
The king protects his own domain
and in turn is venerated by those who live there.
Here are some examples from the world itself:
the king of India lives to the west,
the king of China to the east,
and there are four distinct borderlands
within which many people live.
But there is not one who devours human flesh like you,
nor two others who drink human blood like you.
But this year, the māra son,
the one out of your many ministers
who was the apple of your eye, the Minister Natra,
you devoured!
Was it that you were possessed by evil spirits or urged on by
    demons
or so drunk with liquor or crazed by poison
that you could not distinguish truth from falsehood?
Why would you devour your own minister?
According to the ancient proverbs:

Life companions who are cannibals
must promise not to devour each other.
For carnivorous wolves,
there must be a better meal than their mate.

That is what the proverbs say, but you have contradicted them.
If the high king is the protector of the kingdom,
he cannot cast down the ministers who serve him.
If a great man is to achieve great things,
it is said that his mind and actions must be worthy.
If he is worthy, the populace will serve him,

but if not, they will revolt.
Is that it or not?
This is the crux of what I am telling you:
when the rain clouds and rainbows gather in the heavens,
even the sun on high is insignificant.
When waves swell in the great waters,
even the makara is caught in the turbulence.
When the high king fights with his own country,
even he has no path to liberation.
If you have understood, let its meaning sink in.

Thus Ching-ngön offered his song, but Lutsen answered that he had punished the minister Natra for speaking arrogantly. He reassured the other ministers that they had no reason to be frightened, saying that they should not think that he would devour anyone without first distinguishing who was right and who was in the wrong. "Now, these are my thoughts," Lutsen said, and he stood up, pridefully singing this song.

Sing "Ala thala thala."
"Thala" begins.
The song unfolds in three parts.
I call to the divine ones.
Twenty-nine māra gods, know me.
All the māra gods of longevity, know me.
Today, please lead the song of this brave man.
If you do not recognize this place,
these are the eight mountain ranges of the upper land of the
    north.
If you do not recognize me,
from the māra castle Shari Tsegu,
I am the demon king Lutsen,
famed throughout the world
and born to be the warrior who devours humans.
There is no one like me in all of Jambudvīpa.
Listen, Ching-ngön—
what you said is true.
The 360 māra ministers
did not consult a divination, astrology, or trigram,

and just as no grain would ripen unless seeds were sown,
all the blame fell on Natra's head.[15]
You said that I was watching Meza's face
but that still I could not tell who was truthful and who was
    lying.
All these rumors just rumble around, *ur ru ru*;
wheezing and groaning, advice swirls around, *ur ru ru.*
Although all this chaos shows their quarrel coming to a head,
no one understands just how deep the roots lie.
But today we come to it:
Beu Natra and Meza were together
when a red lightning bolt struck us all,
yet when everyone lost consciousness,
Natra alone was uninjured.
Ask all the other ministers if they realize that.
It was Beu Natra
who said a divine arrow came from the east,
an arrow that he said was the messenger arrow of the Ling
    boy Joru
and that Meza sang a song to that arrow.
Natra alone heard this;
none of the other ministers knew.
Natra was said to be my closest minister,
and a close minister is dangerous, don't you think?
Ask the other ministers what they knew.
It is just as the proverbs say:

Unless the heights of the lofty mountains
have snow-covered peaks,
there will be no swirling turquoise lakes below.

All you ministers here, don't you think that is it?
Nothing is built from shapeless shadows.
The innocent are not to be condemned by the law.
Still, there is more. Listen, all you ministers here.
The water, whether from cliffs, meadows, or riverbanks,
flows from the white snow mountains
and runs down to the turquoise lake.

Achung, Chakchung, and Mukchung, those three
are the heirs of the māra lineage.
Their target is the flesh and blood of humans,
no surprise in that.
Listen closely, Meza,
as among these twelve māra myriarchies,
there are many slanderous stories.
I, King Lutsen,
was said to be watching your face.
Between you and Natra
was the original root of the quarrel.
Meza, some people think you are right;
others think you are mistaken.
The old stories remark on this.
It is just as the proverbs say:

A wild mare's gait is not matured;
a young woman's mind is unfettered.
The morning's tales do not hold in the evening,
and what holds in the evening is gone by morning.

No one sticks to what they say.
A woman's mind is like snow or rain,
clear and bright as they fall,
but just as you think them most vibrant, clouds roll in.
From the land of Ma in Ling,
this evil snot-nosed boy Joru
has come, acting as though Meza knows him
and with his face hanging after her.
That beguiling, sweet-talking Meza,
fickle as the spring breeze
that, just as you think it is blowing from the east,
turns and rushes from the west.
Flattery is good and criticism is bad,
but all of this has been gossip; none of it is true.
May your ears burn.
All of you deceitful women, keep this in mind.

His song was over, and Meza Bumdrön, carrying chang in a gilded copper pot, tea in a silver-plated copper pot, and yogurt and milk in a conch-covered copper vessel, gracefully offered them to Lutsen, saying, "Māra king Shenmarpo, you said that my explanations and stories are untrue. But how can you say that? Toward you, my mind is as pure as new-fallen snow and as trustworthy as the sun and the moon." Then, she sang this short song.

> Sing "Ala thala thala."
> "Thala" begins.
> The song unfolds in three parts.
> I call to the divine ones.
> From the celestial pure realm,
> Mother Vajravārāhī, look upon me with compassion.
> From the immeasurable divine palace of dharmadhātu,
> Mother Lineage Vajrayoginī, know me.
> Surrounded by your retinue of one hundred thousand
>   wisdom ḍākinīs,
> today, assist this woman's plans.
> If you do not recognize this place,
> it is the eight mountain ranges of the upper lands of the
>   north,
> the homeland of demons and cannibals,
> the butchering evil spirits.
> If you do not recognize me,
> I am Akyi Meza Bumdrön,
> Meza who is afflicted with suffering.
> As you wished, I came to the north,
> where you are sovereign of these five supreme fortresses.
> Demon Lutsen, listen to me.
> I came to the north nine years ago
> without womanly desire for a man.
> Rumor is that a divination arrow pierced the meadow;
> if it is there today, tell me.
> Just as a foal, nourished with grain,
> can be saddled when it is three years old
> and be the horse beneath a rider
> but, until then,
> can only run and not be ridden,

I am too young to become your wife.
A maiden must be beyond the age of eighteen
before she can lie with a man.
But it seems you have forgotten all of that—
doesn't it seem so, Lutsen?
Yesterday morning,
between Natra and me,
you sorted out truth from falsehood
and punished Natra for his crimes,
devouring him.
Now, today, there is more gossip
revolving around Natra and me,
implying that you said that the truth could not be separated
    from lies,
and now I am being accused.
Aren't you ashamed, Lutsen?
Even though you hold down the golden throne of the north,
are you certain of anything that you have said?
Yesterday, you claimed to separate truth from falsehood,
but did you see if there was an arrow able to sing?
There was not a single one.
You are inattentive and confused by lies,
unjustly blaming me
and reproaching others but never yourself,
acting one way toward others and another way toward
    yourself.
Alas, Lutsen, that is it.
Between Natra and me,
if you had not sorted out the truth from the lies,
the inner minister Beu Natra—
did you really have a reason to accuse him,
let alone hand him a death sentence?
You brought down the force of the law on an innocent man.
Today, is it not you who should be judged?
Just as in the ancient Tibetan proverbs:

Great rivers flow beneath a bridge.
Great people are subject to the law.

That is what is said, and that is the truth.
If the king violates the laws,
then anyone can transgress them.
I, Akyi Meza Bumdrön,
have stern authority to be the judge.
You are the butcher taken to court
to pay back your killings with your own life.
King Lutsen, don't you think that is true?
Regardless of the details of all this big talk,
Lutsen, you and I
were destined to be together from previous lives.
But if we do not believe that, we should go our separate ways.
By the time you meet justice, Lutsen,
it will have been nine years that I have been held here.
On my right, I have a gilded copper vessel of chang.
I will serve it to clear your mind;
confess and repent your past evil deeds.
On my left I have tea in a silvered copper kettle.
I will serve it to change your mind;
confess and atone, promise not to commit further evil deeds.
That is the advice of your good wife.
Lutsen, keep this in mind.

She finished her song, and Lutsen hung his head as he thought to himself, "Meza has spoken the truth; I did falsely accuse and punish Natra. My ministers certainly think that everything that Meza has said is true and that I was completely in the wrong. First, I rendered judgment and accused Natra, and then without even considering what Ching-ngön had to say, I fabricated completely outrageous falsehoods about Meza and piled on the guilt. Ching-ngön has told me to accept the criticism of what I did in acting hastily yesterday in shedding Natra's blood and accusing Meza even though she was innocent. He said that I am wrong from the root, and to prevent disharmony, just as Meza said, I must answer for my crimes, confess and repent my evil deeds. That is what I should say." Accordingly, the demon Lutsen offered confession.

Just then, Gesar had descended the foothills of Sipa Gangri and had arrived on foot at its vast rocky valley. He intuited that the divine arrow was returning to him. There was a boulder, white as a conch shell, beneath a clump of tamarisk bushes, and on the ground in front where he sat to rest, to his right, were many musk deer pellets and to his left, rabbit pellets. He took eight deer pellets and a single rabbit pellet and began a divination with the nine black pellets. Just as he had begun meditating on his lama and yidam, the divine arrow swirled and, with a whistling sound, landed next to Gesar. He smiled upon seeing Meza's message, nodding "Oh yes. Oh yes!" and rested there.

CHAPTER FIFTEEN

Ling Gesar draws in the seven menmo sisters,
Atak Lhamo, and Ching-ngön as allies.
The three life-supports of the demon Lutsen—
the talisman drong, yak, and sheep—are liberated.

AT DAWN THE NEXT DAY, Gesar mounted his horse and took to the road in a swirling cloud of dust. At midday, he arrived alone in the valley of Sölri Nakpo. It was walled in by towering rock mountains and was so deep it seemed a bottomless ravine. A waterfall cascaded down, searching for its depths with a deafening roar. The only path was rugged and precipitously steep, narrow and winding like intestines. Moreover, the mountain walls to either side were so close together that they pressed like drums against Gesar's skull, and he and his horse were wedged there such that not even a gale wind could have freed them. Seeing this, immediately Gesar sang a summoning song to the dralha Nyentak Marpo and his retinue.

> Sing "Ala thala thala."
> "Thala" begins.
> The song unfolds in three parts.
> I call to the divine ones.
> Dharmakāya, saṃbhogakāya, nirmāṇakāya,
> The divine three endowed with blessings, know me.
> With your omniscience, assist me.
> If you do not recognize this place,
> it is the eight mountain ranges in the country of the north,

where the black crags meet your skull;
even if you were a bird, you could not escape.
If you do not recognize me,
from the kingdom of Ling in Lower Ma in the east
within the celestial castle,
I am known as Dradül, the Tamer of Enemies.
If you do not recognize this song,
it is the magical song of channels and winds.
The start is majestic and stately,
mirroring the great Brahmā,
the middle is fast and lively,
reflecting that Nyenchen Kulha fills the space with his every
     movement,
and the end reaches beyond the boundaries
just as Tsukna's realm is distant.
This song is free from center and fringe
and calls out its unceasing melody.
Today, may the hosts of deities accompany me.
These eight mountain ranges in the country of the north
are the homeland of the evil māra clans,
the gathering ground of demons and cannibals.
The demon of the north, Lutsen,
is the enemy of the Buddha's teachings throughout the world
and the one who has come to slaughter humans.
According to the prophecy, I have come north,
but while the time has come to tame the māras,
that path is obstructed by demons, cannibals, and hungry
     ghosts.
Of the seven menmo sisters of the north,
the one who leads these demons, cannibals, and hungry
     ghosts
is the gatekeeper of the middle gate of the northern māras.
The land that funnels to the upward path
is hemmed in by high rock mountains.
To the right runs Sölri Draknak (Black Rocks of Sölri)
and to the left runs Dorjé Draknak (Black Rocks of Dorjé),
day and night, relentlessly knocking your skull,
the incessant strike of a drum.

The knocking mountains,
the drumming crags,
along with the guardian menmo
serve to assure that to travel this path is arduous
and that escape from its lands is difficult.
However, today,
my horse and I must proceed.
The supreme steed, the capable Kyang Gö,
is the divine horse of magical channels and winds.
I, Gesar of Upper Ling,
am only half human, a magical divine child.
Today, I flash like lightning,
a fearsome light
that splits the rocky crags.
As in the folk tales of old:
all deeds, all actions
must be earnest and firm
or they will be senseless and lead only to trouble.
This is a song of magical channels and winds.
May the divine ones and lamas grant their blessings.
May my words invoke the dralha
and may Nyentak Marpo, supreme among them,
arrive with his entire retinue.
It is time to cleave the skull-knocking crags.
May the dralha clear all obstacles.
May the Seven Protectress maidens
be summoned by the dralha as allies
and may they turn Atak Lhamo of the north
to the Dharma.

As the song ended, the dralha Nyentak Marpo came with his entire retinue. As this was the opportune moment to split the crags of Sölri Nakpo, the steed Kyang Gö came right up to Gesar, stomping a hoof on the ground three times as he made a single, staccato neighing sound. Gesar bent his head to the steed, agreeing that they should sunder the mountain pass of Sölri Nakpo. Again, Kyang Gö whinnied with a sound like cracking thunder. The crags struck each other and shattered with a final swish of the divine horse's tail, which inadvertently slightly slit the pennant of Gesar's helmet, but Gesar was protected by the dralha gathering and he thought that this would be an excellent time to get moving. But one after another, the seven menmo slipped from between the rocks, blocking the path of Gesar and his horse. However, just as Gesar was unsheathing his sword, the retinue of dralha came to the mountain path and seized all seven sisters. They bound them and presented them to Gesar. Gesar sheathed his sword and said, "There is no way you seven will be able to escape. Ask me for protection and I will show you the path." And he sang the song "Self-Utterance of the Unobstructed Vajra."

> Sing "Ala thala thala."
> "Thala" begins.
> The song unfolds in three parts.
> I call to the divine ones.
> From the abode of celestial prosperity,
> divine dharmakāya, saṃbhogakāya, nirmāṇakāya,
> the divine three endowed with blessings, know me.
> From above, three excellent buddhas, know me.
> From below, ḍākinīs and dharmapālas,
> with unwavering minds, please assist me.
> If you do not recognize this place,
> it is the great northern plain of the menmo sisters.
> The demons' land is off to the right,
> and the demonesses' land is to the left.
> The songs of the preta-demons whistle through this land.
> If you do not recognize me—
> but of course you do—
> from the pure land of Ling,
> I am the famed steadfast warrior,
> Joru, the Gok nephew of a loathsome mother,
> who opposes the hateful mind of the enemy
> and dwells within the view of the Dharma.
> I am a guide for those who wish refuge.
> If you do not recognize this song,
> it is the long song of the warrior.
> You, the seven menmo sisters of the north—
> before we met, I thought of you with great repute,
> and when first I confronted you, you were wrathful and
>   terrifying.
> But now I see that you are toothless,

pitiful, and bound by this lasso.
You wretched, suffering women
say that you are the gatekeepers of the māra demon,
but once so fearsome, you are now frightened,
tormented, and suffering.
Forget about dwelling in a castle;
you will have to live among the rocks.
Forget about having anything to eat;
black wolves roam these mountain peaks.
Forget about having anything to drink;
black foxes run through these lands.
Forget about hearing the melody of enlightened speech;
black mice will just call to the demons.
Unimaginably wretched, all of you seven maidens,
although you are the fierce māra gatekeepers,
you will not come out of this alive.
You, gatekeepers who protect another's life,
finally find yourselves imprisoned by this rope.
But astonishingly, there is refuge in this wilderness.
Now, to be perfectly clear,
either take refuge or go against me,
but give careful thought to what you decide.
If you say you will go to Joru for refuge,
you must be speaking truly.
As in the ancient sayings:

A story and an arrow must be straight,
and the words and a bow bent to them.

Keep in mind what is being said.
Seven sister maidens, listen.
The māra king, Lutsen,
to begin with, what did he tell you?
Where is his life force sheltered?
How will his life force be supported?
Where is his soul tree?
Do not be secretive; be honest.
The māra minister, Atak Lhamo,

famed throughout the world—
what magical power and illusion does she possess?
What threefold panoply of weapons is hers?
How fast can her horse run?
The māra minister Anu Ching-ngön—
from what country, what place did he come?
Does he possess courage and the six powers?
Is he loyal to Lutsen?
The māra long-horned sorrel yak—
how can he dwell in such brutal terrain?
How can he find grass to eat and water to drink?
How fierce and powerful is he?
The māra iron-hoofed sheep—
what pastures does he usually roam?
Where is his home and grazing land?
Who is the herdsman watching over him?
If you answer honestly, you will rise above all this,
otherwise you will come to harm.
Take these as examples:
Dharma, sūtra, and mantra are to be spoken in the presence
    of the lama.
If you do not ask for refuge in this life and the next,
and instead take pleasure in evil deeds,
when you die and wander the bardo, you will reap the results.
I, the chieftain, bring down the strict justice of the law.
If you do not accept the punishment that is your due
but instead act with deceit and cunning,
you will be locked in prison, reaping your karma.
I, the physician, have compounded the six excellent
    medicines,
if you do not examine the diseases of your mortal body
but instead badmouth treatments as useless,
you will die and fall into the hell realms, reaping the results of
    your actions.
That is what is said and it's the truth.
Request refuge in my horse and me,
without deceit or pretense.
If you explain everything truthfully,

you will be set free today.
Wherever you decide to go,
I will give you a place to live.
You will have the blessings of genuine empowerment
and the blessings of unsullied Dharma.
If you have understood, keep this in mind.
If not, I cannot repeat my song.

Thus the song was finished, and, together, the menmo sisters, palms together in reverence, spoke, "Noble Gesar, we did not understand that you are a buddha. The oral instructions are amṛta; we did not realize their meaning. We did not understand until now that we should request refuge. Today, we seven sister maidens have this to request of you," and one of them sang.

Sing "Ala thala thala."
"Thala" begins.
The song unfolds in three parts.
I call to the divine ones.
Earthly Tsendü Nakpo (Fierce Black Māra), look upon me.
Teurang, white, black, variegated, all three, look upon me.
Look upon and guide the song of these maidens.
If you do not recognize this place,
it is the great plain of the menmo of the north.
On its left are the female warriors,
to the north are the eight mountain ranges,
to the east, is Chöten Karpo (White Stupa),
then, spreading to the west is Minub,
and to the south are the jungles and farmlands.
Within these four borderlands dwell the seven menmo sisters.
If you do not recognize me,[1]
I am King Lutsen's gatekeeper,
one who guards the middle gate.
Now, listen,
when you look up, the sky is empty;
when you look down, the earth is empty.
The three-thousand-fold universe is a hinged amulet box.
When you, the Ling child Gesar, come,
there will be a canopy of rainbow light from above,

the sun of happiness will rise in the east,
flowers will rain down on the earth,
and fragrant incense will permeate the valleys.
To meet a buddha of great kindness,
may its blessings last for all time.
Until now, we had no devotion,
but now our faith in you is unshakable.
We seven sister maidens—
if we do not go to you for refuge, to whom would we go?
Whatever you ask, we will do.
Now, look at what I have to show you.
To your right, there is a spectacle:
The dark mountain of the māras on the shady side
at first glance looks black,
but look again and you will see that it is red,
its very tip, which nearly reaches the sky, is red.
It is the soul mountain of the māra king Lutsen,
known as the māra mountain Sölri Nakpo.
Look to your left, and there is a spectacle:
A boulder that looks like a monstrous snake head.
At first glance, it looks like a golden yak,
but when you look again, it is a black serpent,
a rock that looks like a meteor that has fallen from the sky.
It is King Lutsen's soul rock,
the boulder called Yangchong (Leap at the Precipice).
Look up high and there is a spectacle:
The red cannibal lake of the māras.
At first glance, it is a turquoise lake,
but when you look again, you see red blood
roiling like molten metal.
It is King Lutsen's soul lake,
called Sintsho Marpo (Cannibal Red Lake).[2]
Look down below and there is a spectacle:
a tree with a nine-pronged great trunk.
At first glance, you see worms writhing on it,
but when you look again, all you see are demons and
    cannibals,
spirits of the dead circling that māra tree.

It is King Lutsen's soul tree,
called Düshing Tsegu (Nine-Pronged Māra Tree).
The māra minister Atak Lhamo
was born among kuśa grass.
You will not find anyone wiser.
Her bravery and intelligence are without par;
her strategizing and six powers are limitless,
greater than that of one hundred warriors.
She has a threefold panoply of vajra armor,
and no sword swings as freely as hers.
Her chestnut horse with its gilded bridle
is only half horse, a magical great steed.
The māra minister, Anu Ching-ngön,
is the son of the Trimar Gyalpo of Rong.
Since he was a lad of thirteen, he has been in the Rong Valley
as the shepherd of Lutsen's sheep.
The iron-hoofed māra sheep of unrivaled strength
is the life force of the māra king Lutsen.
His minister Anu Ching-ngön and the sheep are one and the
    same.
None of us know who to trust.
The long-horned māra sorrel yak
is King Lutsen's central life channel.
His grazing pasture is a grassy meadow called Tanak
    Thangchen (Black Horse Great Plain);
his shelter is the gate of Atak Lhamo.
That is what people have explained,
but actually no one knows where he comes and goes.
When the māra yak plunges downhill,
it feels as though all the mountains are crumbling,
and when he runs uphill,
it seems that the skies are filling with dust.
May you keep all this in mind, King Gesar.
If you have not understood, I cannot repeat my song.

Thus the song ended, and the sisters bowed again and again. Gesar and the dralha, Nyentak Marpo and Dungseng Patrab, released the rope binding the seven menmo. King Gesar gave the abhiṣeka of the nine-pronged vajra thunderbolt, turning all seven to the Dharma and exhorting them, "You must never again drink blood and eat flesh, and you must remain in the retinue of the twelve tenma goddesses who guard Tibet."

Gesar departed for that great plain of Tanak, just below the dark rock outcroppings, and by the time he reached the grasslands among those jeweled slate rocks, he saw that Atak Lhamo was there at a shimmering crystal palace. Facing her, Gesar swirled with light, impressively attired in the nine dralha weapons. She thought, "Never have I seen such a man as this and, considering the wondrous arrow that came yesterday to these eight mountain ranges, he must be that snot-nosed Joru from Ma in Ling who is on this mountain pass with his threefold panoply." She mounted her steed Rakar Tsubshé (White Copper Swirling) and, like a golden vulture hovering in the air, she quickly faced and confronted Gesar. She took out her iron bow Riwo Gukchen (Summons the Great Mountains) from the leopard-skin case on her left and from the tiger-skin quiver on her right, her metal arrow Dongdro Zhipa (Fourth Winged Face), and holding the bow aloft, she sang this song.

> Sing "Ala thala thala."
> "Thala" begins.
> I call to the deities.
> Teurang, white, black, blood red, look upon me;
> look upon this maiden with kindness.
> Three hundred sixty demon gods,
> today look upon the situation of this heroine.
> If you do not recognize this place,
> it is the eight mountain ranges of the upper north,
> the great plain Tanak Thangchen.
> If you do not recognize me,
> from the peak of the Glorious Copper-Colored Mountain,
> from the supreme dwelling place of Chamara in Ling,
> I am of the lineage of the Lion-Faced Ḍākinī, Siṃhamukha,
> Atak Lhamo of the kuśa grass,
> the one who guides the single-notched arrow.
> In my wrathful form I am a cannibal demoness,
> and in my peaceful form, a goddess with the major marks.
> I am famed throughout the lands and skies.
> If you do not recognize this song,
> it is my song, the "Six Reverberations of Tsalung."
> I do not sing it just anywhere,

but it is vital that I sing it to you.
Listen and I will tell you several stories.
This year, many strange things have happened.
From the east, a black swirling wind has arisen,
and whether they were high or low, all the mountains are
    enveloped in a driving rainstorm.
The eerie sound of a cursing mantra echoes *tha la la*;
the terrifying energy of suffering fills the northern māra
    lands, *tha la la*.
All of these are the shocking signs of this year.
From the azure firmament above the eight great valleys,
a thunderbolt of red lightning arose;
the sky was full of fire,
the earth trembled,
the mountains quaked,
the nine-storied castle of the māras was reduced to dust,
and the fortress to the west, Drongra Mukdzong, was
    partially destroyed.
The māra commoners fell unconscious.
The māra minister Beu Natra
said that there was a single arrow that shot through the sky,
an arrow with a written message,
and that Meza sang a song.
Thinking about it, it must have been you who did this.
There is no warrior like you.
Wearing the armor and weapons, threefold panoply,
so handsome[3] in your finery:
one, the silk on your helmet hovering like a vulture,
two, your chest armor, weighty as a boulder,
three, your great rainbow boots hunting like a tiger,
fearsome are these three that adorn your subtle body
like a flower's poisonous thorns.
Are you a material being or not?
The horse beneath you has great power;
he had speed unlike any other.
His body is surrounded by rainbow colors,
and on his right are hundreds of warriors,
while on his left are hundreds of thousands of ḍākinīs.

His hooves swing far into the azure firmament
as feathered as the birds.
Is that horse a material being or not?
You and your horse who have come here
must have come from Ling.
Why would you choose to squander your life this way?
The proverbs have examples:

A human whose life force is spent arrives at the doorway of the jackal
and enters the cave completely exhausted.
An insect whose life force is spent arrives at the ants' door
and enters the ants' colony.
A child whose life force is spent roams as a cub in the north
and leaps, exhausted, into the home of the cannibal demons.

You have appeared as the target of my arrow and sword.
I, the heroine of the north, have a black iron arrow in hand;
we are as inseparable as thunder and lightning.
Today, for you, the hero,
you the dark man with dralha weapons
and the face of a conch-white moon,
what an enemy you have for a companion.
What should we talk about first?
I am the gatekeeper of King Lutsen,
the life-ruler of 920,000
and the mistress of both demons and evil spirits.
Among the 360 māra ministers,
there is not one who rivals me.
They say my arrow can reach the azure heavens,
toss the sun and moon to the ground,
and smash the core of Mount Meru to dust.
They say my arrow can be thrown to the water's depths,
dry up even the vastest lake,
and annihilate a makara.
This very day, my arrow comes for you, wandering young boy.
First, it is certain to destroy your bony skeleton,
and then it will surely extinguish the inner butter lamp of
    your consciousness.

If what I have said does not happen, I am not a heroine.
If you have understood, keep this in mind.
If not, I cannot explain it.

Saying that, she loosed a single arrow, striking the right side of Gesar's shield Bakar Lebchen. However, Brahmā's divine army of 1,800,000,000, Nyenchen Kulha's army of 990,000 nyen troops, the oceanic army of the nāga king Tsukna, the dralha Nyentak Marpo and 360 dralha and werma, and so forth—the gods and nāgas together with the local earth deities—took the strength[4] of her arrow, and no harm came to Gesar. Gesar made a big show of falling from his horse Kyang Gö. Atak Lhamo shouted, "Ya! Today, the Ling youth has succumbed to my arrow!" and she sat down in a cross-legged posture, thinking that it would be best to perform phowa for him, but at the moment she started to do so, the hosts of werma seized her. Gesar stood up and said, "Amazing! Though you are the excellent archer, here you sit, trapped right in front of me, this warrior, complete with the six powers. Well now, listen to this song that tells the story of the way things actually are." And he sang this command-song.

Sing "Ala thala thala."
"Thala" begins.
The song unfolds in three parts.
I go for refuge in the Buddha, Dharma, and Saṅgha;
grant your blessings and look upon me with compassion.
May the six classes of beings turn to the Dharma.
If you do not recognize this place,
it is the lowlands of the windy and savage eight mountains of
   the north,
the edge of Tanak Thangchen,
a cavernous corner of dark, black rocks.
If you do not recognize me,
I am the steadfast warrior famed to the heavens,
the one of immutable strength, King Gesar
from the jeweled seat of eastern Ling,
the land turned to the happy cuckoo,
the land famed for the sound of the Dharma, *ur ur*,
the monastic center of the Buddhadharma.
My true name is Norbu Dradül.
Atak Lhamo, daughter of Rizhi of the north,

is known as the skilled archer.
You said your homeland and birthplace were in a divine land
and that you were an emanation of the Lion-Faced One,
who took rebirth in the north
to be the demon Lutsen's gatekeeper.
Not purified of karma, you were born in the māra land,
and not purified of evil deeds, you became a māra minister.
This very day,
when a buddha arrived at your doorway,
it was your evil karma to bring arrows and swords in greeting.
When scriptures spread through the lands,
it was impure to strive for nonvirtue.
Receiving an eminent guest
without offering delicacies and chang,
pridefully singing many songs,
and intimidating me with your arrow,
consider that you will die and go to the hell realms.
Without realization or phowa transmission, you pretend that
    you are a lama
and insist that you can perform healing ceremonies. How
    pitiful!
I, as the celestial child Döndrub of eastern Ling,
was entrusted by one thousand buddhas.
In the morning, I am a murderous butcher
and in the evening, a lama who guides beings,
the guru who steers the six classes of beings.
Atak, do you understand that is how it is?
Here are some examples:

Although the moon lights the way,
when the sun journeys through the heavens,
the moon cannot help but be outshone.

When I, the awakened one, come to the north,
there is no way that the demons can sweet-talk and dance,
nor māras and cannibals gnash their teeth.
Although you have met your arch enemy,
the arrow you loosed was without impact.

If your own strength does not keep you out of the grip of
    your bitter enemy,
shooting more arrows will be futile.
Today, I have an arrow for you;
let us see if you, Atak Lhamo, receive it.
Passing through the heavens above the high snowy peaks,
the sun's rays illuminate the day.
Yet, since those same rays do not melt the snow,
that is all the better for the snow lion.
By accepting the arrow
you will be a genuine heroine,
an authentic emanation of Siṃhamukha, the Lion-Faced
    One.
But if you do not accept the arrow, you will not be
    liberated.
Before you release this composite body,
it would be of benefit to give some explanation.
Being the guardian for Lutsen's inner and outer gates—
how were you entrusted with this situation?
How did Lutsen delegate you as the heroine?
Tell the story without holding anything back.

A story and an arrow must be straight,
and the words and a bow bent to them.

Isn't it the way the proverbs say it is?

A superior woman's story is like a rock at the door:
it is immutable.
A middling woman's story is like a horn:
it twists around forcing you to think about it.
An inferior woman's story is like a blanket:
it is spread on ground already warmed by the sun.

Keep all of this in mind, warrior woman.
If you have understood, its sound is sweet to your ears.

Thus he sang, and Atak Lhamo took refuge in Gesar, saying, "I did not realize that you were the awakened one. I was ignorant of the profound meaning of your oral instructions. My negative karma blocked the path of awakening and I shot the arrow of hatred at you. Ardently, I confess," and she sang "Song of the Heroine."

> Sing "Ala thala thala."
> "Thala" begins.
> Today, I call the divine ones.
> From the dwelling place of the palace of dharmakāya,
> mother lineage Vajrayoginī,
> please look upon me with your eye of wisdom.
> From the pure realm of Buddha Amoghasiddhi,
> wisdom mother divine Crystal White Tārā,
> without wavering, come to assist me, Atak Lhamo.
> From your dwelling place, the palace of Akaniṣṭha,
> mother lineage Khachö Lhamo, please watch over me.
> From the Eastern Pure Land Arrayed in Turquoise Petals,
> five classes of motherly ḍākinīs, please watch over me.
> Today, come to assist me.
> If you do not recognize this place,
> it is the eight mountains of the upper north.
> If you do not recognize me,
> I am Atak Lhamo, the heretic of the north,
> an emanation of the Lion-Faced One, Siṃhamukha.
> It would have been better had I not been born,
> but, as it was, I was born among the kuśa grass.
> My father is the empty sky,
> my mother, the empty earth.
> This hinged amulet box is the three-thousand-fold world.
> I, this woman, Atak Lhamo of the kuśa grass,
> was raised by an old man, Rizhi (Four Mountains) of the
>   north.
> He was killed by a drong,
> and as a young woman, I was seized by King Lutsen
> and became the guardian of his inner gate.
> King Lutsen had
> gatekeepers at the outer, inner, and middle gates.
> I escaped the outer gatekeeper but not the middle gatekeeper.
> I escaped the middle gatekeeper but not the inner gatekeeper.

Then, I was commissioned to be the inner gatekeeper.
The demon Lutsen
said that from Ling
the wretched Joru has come
to rescue Meza.
Lutsen said that Joru aims to cast an arrow to the heavens,
to brandish a knife betwixt,
and to sprout spears from the ground.
Lutsen said that the four borders must be fortified,
making a tight guard at the four entrance points
so that here in these northern regions
no one can travel freely.
Here, vapor fills the skies of the māra land, dark as massing
    clouds,
and arrow tips[5] flash like red lightning.
Overhead, evil cannibal demons roam, looking for lives,
and sword tips fall like a hailstorm.
On the ground, the dark energy of nāgas and tsen pervades,
and spears fall like meteors.
All of humankind is butchered.
Walls are built of dry human skulls,
pillars and beams are made from human bones,
and fresh human skins are stretched as roofs.
The ghosts of men wail a song;
the ghosts of women dance.
There is no place more terrifying.
Just to hear of it makes you shudder[6]
and puts your heart in your mouth.
Just to see it makes you stammer
and your arms and legs cringe in fear.
You, noble being, have come to this wretched land
and, without a thought of your own life, have come to the
    mouth of the māras.
Although you must be weary, you have come to benefit beings.
I come to you for refuge.
Today is an auspicious day.
I have met a buddha face to face,
finally clearing the ignorance and delusion of confused mind.

Body, speech, and mind—these three I offer to you.
I request the amṛta of your oral instructions.
I request by accomplishing whatever you command.
Today, as for the details of the story:
you, noble being, came to these highlands
and asked this queen to be your guide.
When you come to the place where there are both rocks and
    valleys,
where there is a pitched tent of black and white yak hair
and the precious crystal ritual vase,
the five family ḍākinīs will be resting there
with rainbow light rays streaming out in the four directions.
Within is a vast lotus grove,
the aftermath of my birth in the kuśa grass
and the scene of my birth as Siṃhamukha.
Then, Sengchen, as you go higher
among great bright coppery rocks,
there will be the long-horned sorrel māra drong
whose horns seem to reach the sky,
as though it were the sentry of the four directions.
Then, afterward, as you go still higher
in the māra valley among rocks strewn as from an avalanche
is a speckled black spirit drong.
That spirit drong is like a healing agate stone,
and has horns like flames.
Then, if you go even higher,
to the right is a great flat meadow
where the iron-hoofed māra sheep dwell.
Their iron hooves are like red thunderbolts raining down.
One, the māra spirit wild black drong,
two, the long-horned sorrel māra drong,
and three, the iron-hoofed māra sheep—
this will be the time to tame the soul of the māra.
The shepherd Anu Ching-ngön will be there.
Ching-ngön has turned to the Dharma
and he is your ally.
Sengchen, keep this in mind.
Now, gradually, I have told you all that you asked.

Thus, Atak Lhamo offered this song, and Gesar said, "Excellent, may all be auspicious." At Atak Lhamo's prompting, she and Gesar set out on foot, and when they came to a black and white yak-hair tent, she invited him inside. There were many statues of the five classes of ḍākinīs, bowls of offering water, and brilliant butter lamps. To see them was a delight. Outside, the tent was encircled by an immense, broad meadow whose fragrant wildflowers perfumed the air. It was a joyful place. Next to the tent, dewdrops on the kuśa grass shimmered with rainbow light. In its midst was a luminous and colorful area where Atak Lhamo, the emanation of the Lion-Faced One, Siṃhamukha, had been born. Gesar was delighted and said to Atak Lhamo, "We must have a feast for your auspicious good fortune in turning toward the Dharma."

Atak Lhamo took refuge in Gesar, saying, "Today, the tendrel is excellent, although right now, without meat and liquor, it will be difficult to make a feast. Yet, now that you and I have met, I thought it best for me to be peaceful rather than wrathful, don't you think? Today, I will offer to you all the weapons that I possess." But just then the Lion-Faced Ḍākinī appeared to her, saying, "Atak, taking on a peaceful disposition will merely make you Gesar's tea maker, never his ally. Not only that, the name of 'warrior' will not befit you." The ḍākinī accepted an offering of yogurt, milk, and so forth, the white foods[7] and all that could be desired to eat, and then vanished like a rainbow.

Gesar and Atak openly praised the prophecy of the Lion-Faced One, saying in unison, "We must follow the instructions of the ḍākinī." Satisfied with their offering of the white foods, they set out on the road at once, gradually ascending on foot up to the dark, rocky peaks. Atak Lhamo pointed, saying, "Look over there on the other side." Gesar turned and saw a rock mountain that seemed to reach the sky. The foot of the mountain was shrouded in gloom, and there was the fearsome long-horned sorrel māra yak running back and forth and howling "Di ri ri." He shook his horned head with a thundering clack, his tail whipped around like massing southern clouds, and the air was thick with dark vapors. The thunderous sound of dragons was heard as red lightning flashed. The yak, with its four legs whirling like an icy wind, went higher and higher, nearly escaping. Gesar quickly pulled out an arrow, but just as he turned to face the yak, the divine horse Kyang Gö, having emanated into an adult drong, collided with the māra yak, locking horns. As their grappling hooves brought up a swirling cloud of dust, *thul thul*, and their horn tips sparked like flint, *chem chem*, Gesar let loose his arrow Shaza Trakthung (Flesh Eater Blood Drinker). It struck the māra yak's heart, shredding his aorta and continuing out from his back with such force that it struck the backside of the mountain and turned the rocks to dust. Nonetheless, the māra yak was so strong that despite the blood matting his coat, he leapt, confronting Gesar and Atak. Atak at once shot two arrows: the first one struck the dark horn of the māra yak and the second one struck high in his skull, right in the middle of his forehead, and he fell to the ground like a pile of rocks. He bellowed loudly and stood back up. The drong emanation of Kyang Gö struck the māra yak. It ran, swaying, for about three rope lengths and then collapsed, unconscious.

Gesar and Atak Lhamo were together. Atak welcomed Gesar back into the tent and offered excellent tea, saying, "My father Rizhi was killed by a drong, and in revenge I have shot many drong with my arrow. Is this enough retribution?" Gesar considered carefully and explained that, even though she had killed many drong, justice had not yet been served. Raising his eyebrows, he went on to say, "Isn't that māra yak at your doorstep just now the very one that killed your father?" With a look of disbelief Atak said, "That cannot be possible." Gesar went on, "Look, and you will understand," and Atak saw what Gesar meant—there was blood as well as pieces of her father's white chuba on the tips of the drong's horn. Anger blazed up from her heart, and smoke poured from her mouth. With an angry wail, she wielded her nine-pointed red-bannered spear and ran at the māra drong thinking, "Surely this is the day . . . I will be the heroine who avenges the death of my father." All at once, she emanated a small black raven that flew off, and she followed behind on the mountain pass riding her splendid steed Rakar Tsubshé.[8]

Gesar winked once at his own divine horse, and instantly, they both emanated as small white birds of prey and took off in pursuit. Just as they were about to catch up with Atak, they saw the small black raven in pursuit of the māra drong. Gesar loosed an invisible arrow, striking the drong's horn tip, and sparks flew as the drong fell to the ground, dazed. Atak, with her spear in hand, red banner flapping, came at the drong, roaring "Ki!" The māra drong roared and stood up, tail raised, kicked up the dust and ran. Immediately, Atak loosed an arrow, striking the shoulder blade of the drong, which staggered momentarily to the ground, stood back up, and bellowed. As it appeared lame, Atak ran like lightning after the drong, pointing her spear. She was faster, but just as she was about to overtake the drong, the spear slipped from her hand and she was in danger of being impaled on his horn tip. As luck would have it, Gesar was there to draw out his sword. With a single swing he severed all four of the drong's legs, and they fell into a pile. Picking up her spear, Atak stabbed the māra drong in the heart. He lay motionless. Atak butchered the corpse and offered the blood, flesh, and bones to the birds, dogs, and wild animals but took the heart and heart blood and, with Gesar, returned to the tent.

They both enjoyed a good meal and rested. The next day at dawn, Atak set out an excellent meal for King Gesar and said, "Yesterday, you said that we should have a great feast to celebrate my mind turning to the Dharma. Now, I offer the māra drong's heart flesh and blood as the meat and liquor." Gesar replied that that would be excellent, just as Padmasambhava and his consort Mandāravā, the ḍākinī Yeshé Tsogyal, and Siṃhamukha, together with the ḍākinīs, dralha, pawo, and *pamo*, innumerable as snowflakes in a swirling blizzard, came to the gaṇacakra. The ceremony and empowerment were excellently done, and the tent became a measureless palace of goodness. Upon Atak was conferred the abhiṣeka of undefiled samādhi and, with bodhicitta aroused, she understood that, in particular, it would be best to perform the enlightened activity of leading the six classes of beings to the higher realms.

At predawn the next day, according to Gesar's wishes, Atak tacked up the steed Rakar Tsubshé. Flying like a bird, she went on horseback to the spot where Ching-ngön was shepherding the māra sheep. It was nearly noon when she arrived and after Ching-ngön asked Atak why she had come, she said, "Listen, here is my story" and sang this song to Ching-ngön.

> OṂ MAṆI PADME HŪṂ
> Sing "Ala thala thala."
> "Thala" begins.
> The song unfolds in three parts.
> Today, I call to the deities.
> From the celestial divine pure realm,
> dharmakāya, saṃbhogakāya, nirmāṇakāya,
> three divine ones, bless me and know me.
> From the peak of the Glorious Copper-Colored Mountain,
> from the supreme dwelling place of Chamara,
> within the immeasurable palace of Lotus Light,
> Lord Rikdzin Padma Thötreng.[9]
> With your retinue of hundreds of thousands of myriads of
>   ḍākinīs,
> today, please come to assist this maiden.
> If you do not recognize this place,
> it is the land of the evil māras
> called Münpa Chutrik.
> If you do not recognize me,
> I am Atak Lhamo of the northern pika-lands.
> Until several days ago,
> in the lowlands of these dark rock mountains,
> was there ever anything so amazing?

High above, a tent of rainbow light,
overhead, flowers raining down,
and below, the sweet fragrance of sandalwood incense—
delight spread from the lowlands to the heavens.
There is a multitude of male kyangs on the right
and a host of female kyangs on the left,
all surrounded by countless baby kyangs.
At the center is the white-muzzled kyang,
the most celebrated,
the one called the divine horse Kyang Gö
with his precious golden saddle.
In the immeasurable tent of rainbow light,
within that rainbowed dome
is the glorious unrivaled being Gesar,
with his retinue of hundreds of dralha on the right
and one hundred thousand ḍākinīs on the left,
all bounded by the sacred peaceful and wrathful deities.
He is the unsurpassed great being—
a man dark as agate,
his divine eye red as coral,
his teeth white as a conch mala,
handsome as a heruka.
His upper body dazzles as the form of a deity, *khuk sé khuk*,
like the heart-son of divine ancestors.
His torso dazzles as the form of a nyen, *khuk sé khuk*,
like the fierce son of the middle nyen.
His lower body dazzles as the form of a nāga, *khuk sé khuk*,
like the wealth heirs of the nāgas below.
He is the one entrusted by the lha, lu, and nyen,
the lama who guides beings of the six realms,
the butcher of the bitter enemy,
and the king of Tibetans.
Devotion arises from merely seeing his face;
hearing him arouses bodhicitta.
Today, Ching-ngön,
ask Gesar for refuge
and meditate upon him as your root guru.
In the next life, you will achieve a higher path.

You have been born into this human body;
think to practice the sacred Dharma,
think of accomplishing benefit in this life.
What use is there to dismiss these thoughts, Ching-ngön?

Thus she sang, and the Zhugadar minister Ching-ngön asserted, "Indeed, Atak, that sounds just like the powerful king of Ling, Gesar. Where is he right now? Did you see him or not? I heard that an arrow had arrived in the māra country, and I was overjoyed to think that it could be King Gesar, the Ling lord, who sent it. I hope to meet him, but first do you have blessing substances from the noble being for me?" Ching-ngön ate the unsullied dütsi pills that Atak had received from Gesar, and the obscurations of his body were purified, the ignorance of his mind cleared, and his bodhicitta manifested. Ching-ngön thought, "Today, all the obstacles of the māras have been cleared."

Atak said, "Excellent, let's go," and they went slowly uphill. Shortly, they came to a flat grassy plain where there was a large boulder from behind which came a man in white and a white horse with many colors swirling around them. Atak affirmed that it was Gesar, the powerful king, and Ching-ngön went right up to him. He offered prostrations, saying, "Unrivaled king, you are renowned throughout the lands, but owing to my lack of merit, until now I had not heard of you. Today, through great kindness, I have met you." Over and over again, he requested refuge, and Gesar replied, "Excellent, Anu Ching-ngön, listen." And immediately he sang "Self-Utterance of the Unobstructed Vajra."

> OṂ MAṆI PADME HŪṂ
> Sing "Ala thala thala."
> "Thala" begins.
> The song unfolds in three parts.
> Now, today, I call the divine ones.
> Dharmakāya, saṃbhogakāya, nirmāṇakāya,
> three divine ones, bless me and know me.
> If you do not recognize this place,
> it is the eight mountain ranges of the upper north
> and in its midst is Kyangkar Thangchen (White Kyang Great
>   Plain).
> If you do not recognize me,
> I am Gesar, the steadfast warrior of Jambudvīpa.
> If you do not recognize this song,

it is the song of unobstructed channels,
the song of mastery of the channels and winds,
the song that expresses unobstructed self-utterance.
Now, listen. This is the way it is.
In the eight mountain ranges of the upper north,
you are three persons of power and might:
first, Jang Chiwa (Pike North) Atak Lhamo,
second, Ling Akyi Meza Bumdrön,
and, third, you the Zhugadar minister Ching-ngön.
You have might and wealth
and are vigorous warriors with the six powers.
You are broadminded
and leaders of visionary policies.
You three live in the north, even though
the north land is not your birthplace.
Atak Lhamo of the north
is the emanation of Siṃhamukha
and holds nearly half of the northern districts.
Zhugadar Anu Ching-ngön, you
are among the eighty mahāsiddhas
and hold nearly half of the country of the north.
Akyi Meza Bumdrön
is an emanation of Vajravārāhī
and reigns over the estate of the māra king.
You three are allied with me
and I am the messenger of the dharmapālas,
the yoke upon the evil māras.
Now, what I am telling you is that
the demon king Lutsen
is not going to destroy the teachings of virtue.
He is not going to establish the teaching of the dark side.
He is not going to kill humans.
He is not going to make liquor from their blood.
He is not going to make a feast of human flesh.
He is not going to gulp down human bones.
Zhugadar Anu Ching-ngön,
you were reborn in the lowlands of Rong
as the heart-son of Trimar Gyalpo (Red-Throned King)

and wound up being captured by the evil māras
to be the Lutsen's shepherd.
Those iron-hoofed māra sheep
that are the talisman of the demon māra,
you have been their nurturing[10] protector.
Can there be any good karma in that?
Within the iron-hoofed māra sheep,
isn't that where the māra life force abides?
Isn't that where Lutsen's soul rests?
I must shoot an arrow into the forehead of the demon,
but first I must bring down these talismans.
Today, I, the Ling lord king—
wearing dralha armor and weapons
and mounted on the magical steed of channels and winds—
for that purpose, have come to the land of the māras.
It is as the proverbs say:

If the makara in the depths of the ocean is disturbed,
it will create a blizzard that envelops the mountains.
There, it will rip out the snow lion's turquoise mane
and seize Sipa Gangri.
If the red Bengal tiger escapes the forest,
it will roam the highest slate rocks.
There, it will destroy the horns of the golden brown drong
and seize the coppery crags.

The invincible Gesar has come to the north
to put an arrow into the forehead of the demon,
to turn the māra land to the Dharma
and light the lamp of virtue.
From today onward,
the iron-hoofed māra sheep—
how can it be tamed?
It is you, Ching-ngön, who has it in mind;
do not keep it a secret.
You took refuge in me,
and the blessings of a thousand buddhas,
the hairs of one hundred thousand ḍākinīs,

and the longevity nectar of the sole mother Queen of Siddhis,
today, are yours, Ching-ngön.
Your mind inclines to the virtuous Dharma.
Through devotion to the Three Jewels
and to the government of Ling
with its eighty Pathül warriors,
you have become my inner minister.
Zhugadar, keep this in mind.

Thus Gesar sang, and Ching-ngön offered prostrations, saying, "As I have met the face of the Buddha, I will not fall into the lower hell realms. As I have heard the voice of the Buddha, I will be guided to the higher realms. Sengchen Lama, I have met you and clearly heard your words. I ask for your great kindness." Taking out a white khata from the amulet box, Ching-ngön offered it to Gesar and sang this song of aspiration, requesting blessings.

Sing "Ala thala thala."
"Thala" begins.
The song unfolds in three parts.
Today, I call to the deity
from the prosperity enclosure of Rong—
great divine ruler of these lands, know me.
Look upon me and lead my song.
If you do not recognize this place,
it is the great northern plain Kyangkar Thangchen.
If you do not recognize me,
I will explain myself.
I was born into one life but ended up in another:
one lifetime, two destinies.
I adopted the lowlands of Rong as my home,
and I am the heart-son of Trimar Gyalpo.
When I was a youth of eleven,
I fell into the hands of the demon māra
and for nearly seven years, I have lived in this māra country
as Lutsen's shepherd boy.
I have three names:
some called me Minister Ching-ngön,
a few called me Anu Sengtren,

and several knew me as Apho Gadar.
Just call me Anu Sengtren.[11]
If you do not recognize this song,
it is the magical song of channels and winds.
Today and from now on,
Gesar, you, the powerful awakened one,
Precious Supreme Being—
just to see your face purifies one's intention
and clears the obscurations of mind.
Just to hear your voice clarifies one's understanding
and arouses bodhicitta.
Please keep me in your heart.
Whatever you request, I will do.
In the eight mountains of the upper north,
there is no end to the number of white prosperity sheep;
they cover the mountains
and fill the lower plains.
Among their countless flocks
is the iron-hoofed māra sheep.
This iron-hoofed māra sheep
is the talisman of the evil māra,
the channel of Lutsen's vital essence.
Without his māra sheep,
by no means can he attain the kingship.
He cannot just lead the sheep with a flick of his finger
and achieve the iron life force of a teurang.
Only someone who has spent their life shepherding māra
    sheep
could distinguish one sheep from another.
My point is that the iron-hoofed māra sheep
ordinarily is indistinguishable from the other sheep:
its bodily strength is about the same,
it is just as strong and healthy,
its horns are the same length as those of the others,
its four limbs are neither thicker nor thinner,
the color of its wool is not distinctive,
and it is not set apart by how it jumps and runs.
Among this flock of apparently identical sheep,

there is no way to single out this talisman māra sheep.
This iron-hoofed māra sheep,
in the daytime, runs through meadows and along the water
but by night is hunted for meat and blood.
Moreover, for several days
Lutsen has been making a chomping sound as though
    chewing meat,
but it is unclear if it was his spirit sheep being eaten.
If Lutsen and his spirit sheep
had so joined, Lutsen will be most difficult to tame.
Today is the day
you, Gesar, must depart,
leave this side of the grasslands,
and become disguised as a great boulder,
motionless, watching the flock of sheep.
Atak and I, Ching-ngön,
will be among the flock of sheep.
I will have come carrying flesh and blood,
and when I drink the strong-smelling clotted blood,
only one sheep will sniff the air:
it will be the iron-hoofed māra sheep.
Cutting off its head is futile.[12]
That iron-hoofed māra sheep of the north,
low down on its forehead
above its small beady left eye,
within the white wool, a black coil of energy swirls like a
    tornado,
and within that is a black dot, the width of the eye of a
    needle.
If you do not strike right there with a sharp sword,
you are a fool to think that you could win.
You must take the meaning of this very seriously,
precious King Sengchen.
Now, to be clear,
Akyi Meza Bumdrön,
although she lives now in the evil māra land,
she will come to reside in Ling.
That coat of dark black,

although that is what she wears,
hers is a white snow mind
for you, Gesar.
She turns her head to Lutsen with a smile,
all the while waiting for you.
With skillful means, you changed my view,
and I will act according to your words.
Please keep all of this in mind, noble being.
May my song be unerring.

Thus he sang, and Gesar broke out in a smile. Nodding his head, he said, "I will." Atak and Ching-ngön left for the mountain pass, where they came to a flock of māra sheep, but they were thinking that it would be unheard of to see the iron-hoofed māra sheep out in the daytime. Furthermore, though they would soon be in the midst of the flock, they realized that even if the special one *were* there and they were looking right at it, it would look no different from the others. In any case, like a flash of lightning, the sheep vanished.

Atak and Ching-ngön did not realize for quite some time that the sheep were gone and thought that the flock was still coming. In the meantime, Gesar had emanated as a boulder and was waiting an arrow-shot length away. Only then did they realize that the māra sheep were gone, and Atak asked Ching-ngön, "Why can't we see any māra sheep?" to which Ching-ngön replied, "It is strange, we have looked far and near." Wondering what to do, he went quickly to the māra storehouse, returning with human flesh and blood and all the while searching for the māra sheep. By then, it was nearly nighttime, and at the edge of the meadow by the rocky crags, there was the flock. The sheep perked up their ears, looking around as they smelled the scent of human flesh and blood on Ching-ngön's hands, and they ran toward him, like vultures to flesh.

While the māra sheep were eating and drinking the flesh and blood, Gesar saw a māra sheep with a thin black line low down on its forehead, above its left eye, just as Ching-ngön had said. It swirled with dark energy within the white wool, and the māra sheep's wooly body was completely puffed up as though with that same dark energy. At first, Gesar watched without shooting his arrow as he considered what to do. Then, he rubbed his eyes and once again held his breath and cocked an arrow, looking at the forehead of each māra sheep, one at a time. He saw one that was different, one with exactly that continuous coil of black in the white wool above its left eye. As soon as he spotted the black dot the size of a needle's eye, he shot his red-flagged arrow, destroying the iron life-force talisman that was the māra sheep.

It fell to the ground near Ching-ngön in a swirl of acrid dust, and Gesar and Atak came running. Though Gesar said, "This has been of great benefit to the Buddha-dharma, and now we must bury the corpse of the sheep and raise its consciousness to the pure realm," Ching-ngön was troubled. He worried aloud, "What will happen when Lutsen starts looking for his spirit sheep along with his spirit yak and spirit drong?" King Gesar, through aspiration prayer and his dralha, created a spirit sheep identical to the one just killed. The three—Gesar, Atak, and Ching-ngön—left, relaxed and carefree.

The demon Lutsen was ill at ease,
anxious and concerned about his spirit sheep.
Ling Gesar had come to visit Meza
to discuss striking the demon with lightning.

THAT DAY, INSIDE HIS CASTLE SHARI NAMDZONG, King Lutsen was of two minds: furious and frightened. Unable to stay seated on his cushion, he paced and raged at his ministers until dusk. Only as the morning sky brightened was he finally given over to sleep, but even then, he was trapped in the web of an illusory dream, talking nonsensically in his sleep. Concerned, one of his ministers called to Meza, and she came, rousing Lutsen. Drowsily, he asked, "Where is my spirit sheep? Joru and his evil band, where are they? With the sheep?" Meza replied, "What are you saying? That the sheep and Joru are here, inside the palace?" Now, more awake, the demon answered, "Even though I was dreaming, still, I must go find my spirit sheep." Then, he sang this song to Meza Bumdrön.

Sing "Ala thala thala."
"Thala" begins.
The song unfolds in three parts.
Today, I call to the deity.
From the immeasurable palace in the highest heavens,
10,900,000 life-rulers, know me.
Look upon me with kindness and lead my song.

From the far side of the vast ocean,
Cannibal Gombu Nakpo (Black Worm Meditator),
    know me.
Please look upon this demon with compassion.
If you do not recognize this place,
it is the eight mountains of the upper north,
the lowlands below Chakri Tsegu,
and the land of the slate plain, Yama Thangchen.
If you do not recognize me,
I am the māra king Lutsen.
There is no one who can rival me.
The world is my feast;
its humans are merely crunchy popped wheat.
My right horn reaches the sky
and splits the azure firmament.
My left horn pierces the ground,[1]
and the solid earth is mine to shred.
Here in my corner of the earth,
human blood rains down from above;
overhead, consciousnesses swirl like a blizzard;
below, worms get their fill of flesh and bone;
and on the great plains, cannibals erect castles of bone.
There is no place like this in all the world.
This land is the most frightening place of all,
and I, the warrior demon, am the most powerful of all.
What great fortune that these two things have come together.
Such great power and might are respected by everyone.
You, motherless, ruinous maiden,
listen and I will tell you of my dream:
Last night in my dream
many bad omens arose.
When I first went to sleep, I tossed and turned,
I kept on tossing and turning.
Streaming down from the heavens,
I dreamed that thunder and lightning struck,
destroying the rock mountain
and the roof of the fortress below.

From the midst of the great northern plain Drimar (Red Dri
    Plain),
I dreamed that red flames spread,
consuming the great valleys,
and that I was lost in the fire.
On the right side of a great grassy meadow,
I dreamed that there were wolves running after meat,
descending on the flock of sheep
and, in particular, on my spirit sheep.
On the far banks of the northern lake Namtsho Chenmo
    (Great Sky Lake),[2]
I dreamed that wild drongs fought with interlocking horns
and destroyed my three fortresses,
and, not only that, they struck me.
These omens are not good; they are bad.
Bad omens fill my dreams,
calamities and obstacles threaten,
and the spirit sheep is nowhere to be seen.
I am going to see if there is trouble.
You, Meza, came to the north nine years ago,
but we are not yet joined as life companions.
If you are a good wife, your life will be happy,
your days surrounded by kindness.
If you are a bad wife, your life will be unhappy,
your days dark and ugly.
Today, as the sun rose in the east
and its light rays streamed forth over the north,
I dreamed of the sun's warmth.
If you think about it, that is you—
the rising sun is like a welcoming maiden.
But, as for now,
there are obstacles for you to become my wife.
I, Lutsen, cannot stay, but must go to Ling
to see whether that nasty Gokmo's son Joru
and the thirty youths of Ling
have fully matured in their six skills.[3]
Meza keep this in mind.

When the song ended, Meza leapt to her feet. Carrying nine sheep heads and nine sheep carcasses, she dropped them in front of Lutsen and said, "Mighty king, your dreams are not bad; they are good. Don't they signify a good destiny? You yourself spoke the truth: a happy life is surrounded by the sun of kindness, an unhappy life by darkness. I worry about how I can be helpful. Listen to my song about the way things are." And she sang this song.

Sing "Ala thala thala."
"Thala" begins.
The song unfolds in three parts.
Today, I call to the deity.
I call to the distant deities.
From the dharmakāya pure land of the three times,
divine lamp Mother Vajravārāhī,
Red Vajravārāhī, extend your kindness.
With your hundreds of thousands of wisdom ḍākinīs,
today, please come to assist this maiden.
From Tārā's buddhafield, the Eastern Paradise Arrayed in
Turquoise Petals,
from atop a blazing conch seat,
All Mother Jetsün White and Blue Tārās, know me.
Today, please come to assist this maiden.
There are no other gods to call.
If you do not recognize this place,
it is the eight mountains of the upper north,
the lowlands beneath Chakri Tsegu.
If you do not recognize me,
I am the maiden from Ling Akyi
called Meza Bumdrön.
Doubtless, I am to be your wife.
Demon Lutsen,
listen. This is how it goes:
a bird, a crane with broken wings,
has no choice but to fall to the forest floor,
and I, far from the kindness of my parents,
have no choice but to trust in you.
Although you desire a maiden,
you have no choice but to wait,

as I am only eighteen years old.
I have had only raptor birds above me
and pure water beneath me.[4]
When I turn twenty-one
I will be a grown woman,
yearning for intimacy.
A maiden's lotus—
consummated,
inexhaustible.
A young man's vajra—
consummated,
lasting.[5]
There comes a time to make love,
but to desire a woman who is too young
makes you the very lowest of men.

In fields flush with early green,
a farmer who rushes to harvest,
in the end, reaps nothing.
A herd of white prosperity sheep,
their delicious meat laden with fat,
is mouthwatering before but worthless after it is eaten.

Whatever you do is up to you.
Isn't that right, Lutsen?
Demon king, your mind is good.
Just as the clear blue, luminous sky
has no reason to send down lightning,
I—who love you, Lutsen—
have no reason for bloodshot eyes.
If you understand, you are my life companion.
You and I,
if we tenderly mix our bodies,
you will lose your strength,
and China, India, and Nepal
will not fall under your influence.
Human, horse, and dog meat
I neither desire nor would I find easy to swallow.

Keep all of that in mind, Lutsen.
Today, demon king,
you said you had restless dreams.
If I, Meza, examine that dream,
the omens are not bad; they are good.
If I explain what is good:
In the eight mountains of the upper north,
striking from above,
the lightning destroying the crag mountain
symbolizes the māra prophecy
that your tyranny is feared more than lightning.
From the midst of Drimar Plain,
spreading red flames
symbolize the raging good fortune
that your power is supreme.
On the flat, grassy meadow,
the wolf running after flesh
is a sign that you are destined to be a meat-eater and blood-
    drinker,
a fully satiated carnivore.
On the far bank of Namtsho Chenmo,[6]
the fighting wild drongs
signify the great strength of the māra troops
and your flourishing bravery.
That three castles were demolished by the drongs
is a sign that döns, obstacles, and illnesses are overcome.
These are the auspicious signs that your dream is good.
Think deeply, there are no evil signs.
That nasty nephew of Gok, Ling Joru,
holds his homeland and will stay there.
Why heap contempt upon him?
Despising another is pointless.
As is said, evil omens will naturally ripen.
Isn't that right, King Lutsen?
I love you dearly.
Today, there is no need for harsh words,
yet you say you must devour me.
Why would you do that? Do not think that way.

I trust in you.
You say you will eat me—your life companion!
According to the ancient proverbs:

A young steed is saddled and bridled so it can be ridden,
but in the many villages of China and India,
when a horse is old, it is put out to pasture
and abandoned to the midst of a swampy plain.
Even while it still breathes, its eyes are pecked out by ravens.
The sorrel yak is herded through all the mountain valleys
and given grain from the storehouse,
but when the horned yak grows old, it is taken to the slaughterhouse.
If it has thick meat, a small knife is indicated,
but if it has scrawny flesh, it is fed to the dogs.
Many dri roam the vast plains,
prized for their milk.
But when its white milk is exhausted, it is shown the door,
and if it doesn't have tasty meat, it is fed to the dogs.

I, Ling Akyi Meza Bumdrön,
since I was a young girl, I have been guided by you, Lutsen,
and now that I am a beautiful young woman, you desire me,
saying you will be my life companion,
my jewel.
Have you no self-respect, Lutsen?
I am a motherless egg, tossed to the ground,
an empty, dry, withered egg carried by the wind.
If I look up, the great sky above is empty.
If I look down, the solid earth below is empty.
Inside this hinged amulet box is the trichiliocosm.
What will happen is in your hands.
Far to the east, the sun rises—
I thought the darkness of the māra land would be illuminated,
as the bright sun spreads its rays here
because of your sovereignty.
Whether you want to be exalted is up to you.
You must act well—can you do that?
Māra king, keep this in mind.

Thus she sang, and Lutsen, his face twisted with rage, spoke through clenched teeth, "I eat cannibal flesh, not that of my wife. It is the carnivorous wolf that does not distinguish between a lamb and a person." He turned to leave, muttering about the dream he had had regarding his spirit animals [the iron-hoofed spirit sheep, the long-horned sorrel māra yak, and the spirit drong] and, thinking he should check on them, mounted his horse Sinta Phurshé (Cannibal Horse Flyer). He disappeared like a flash of lightning into the mountain valley and before long came to where Ching-ngön was, demanding, "Are the sheep well or not? And where is my iron-hoofed spirit sheep?" Ching-ngön answered, "He is fine, and he is right here. All of the sheep are quite well." But a large white boulder at the water's edge below the foot of the mountain caught Lutsen's eye, and he said, "What is that? I've never seen anything like that before." Ching-ngön said, "Perhaps you just now noticed it, but it has been there all along." Without listening, Lutsen started singing.

> Sing "Ala thala thala."
> "Thala" begins.
> The song unfolds in three parts.
> Today, I call to the deity.
> From the supreme celestial divine castle,
> Trarab, king of māras, know me.
> Guide my song.
> If you do not recognize this place,
> it is the upper boundary of Dzari Mukpo.
> If you do not recognize me,
> I am the king of māras.
> I took rebirth from the māra king Trarab Nakpo.
> I am the lineage son of the nine-headed cannibal.
> Ching-ngön, listen to my song;
> listen, and I will tell you how it is.
> On the far shore beyond the shady side of Sölri Mountain,
> across the great, flat, grassy meadow
> is an incredible boulder
> with a peculiar shape.
> It resembles a great steed reclining on the plain
> with its head turned to gaze over here.
> It is a unique rock
> that I do not remember seeing before.
> Is it strange, or not?

Is it different from the other rocks or not?
In the eight mountain ranges of the upper north,
the earth lord, water lord, and mountain lord, all three
are known to me.
In India hats are worn,
in China small shoes are worn,
and in Ütsang sashes are tied at the waist.
I am familiar with the topography of my land.
Zhugadar Ching-ngön,
of the iron-hoofed māra sheep,
thirty-nine have copper in their hooves.
That is all of them, right?
They have pointed iron-tipped hairs,
a ring of iron at their waist,
and iron hide and fleece.
There is one that has attained the iron life force,
the māra life force;
that iron-hoofed māra sheep
is my aorta.
That long-horned sorrel māra yak
is my heart flesh.
That reddish-black spirit drong
is my heart blood.
Where are they now?
I must see if they are well.
In these eight mountains of the upper north,
there are gatekeepers at the outer, inner, and middle gates.
At the outer gate are Khenpa Genmo
and Acham Karmo,
the protectresses who possess magical illusion.
All three gates, outer, inner, and middle,
are locked with keys—
even a bird, no matter how small, could not get in.
At the middle gate, the seven sister maidens
and, in particular, Mendruk Lhamo (Dragon Queen)
are the protectresses who possess cunning methods.
The elemental gates of earth, water, and wind
are guarded by elemental spirits

such that even the wind cannot enter.
Then, at the inner gate, first is Atak Lhamo
and second, Zhugadar Ching-ngön.
They too are guardians skilled in cunning methods.
The form gate, the soul gate, and the longevity gate
are protected by life-force guardians—
even light rays cannot enter.
These guardians of the outer, inner, and middle gates
protect all that is between sky and earth
such that even our mortal enemy cannot pass,
and they discern which stars form the constellations.

Without the three months of spring in which to plant seeds,
the earth could not distinguish hardy from weak plants.
Without the three months of summer for the lotus to blossom,
there would be no way to distinguish this marvelous flower from the
*   others.*
Without the three months of autumn to harvest ripened grain,
there would be no way to know what is edible.
Without the three months of winter,
there would be no way to tell what would freeze.

The keepers of the three gates
distinguish those who are good from those who are bad
and keep a record of those who are not allowed to pass.
Although this is the way it works,
who can really tell where the enemy is?
My spirit sheep, yak, and drong, all three—
always attend to them.
I will state clearly why this is necessary.
For several days
my dreams have been filled with bad omens,
frightening dreams that have given me a heavy heart.
My body shuddered and shook, *sik sik,*
and pain shot through my back.
My chest burned, *shuk shuk,*
and there was a stabbing pain in my forehead.
My toenails pulsated with heat, *lhang lhang.*

What could all this mean?
To look at this strange boulder
makes one's mind anxious and agitated.
Have you understood, Ching-ngön?
If not, I cannot repeat my song.

The song ended, and Lutsen was heading toward the boulder when Ching-ngön blocked his way, saying, "What good could come of grabbing that boulder? It could be a horse or mule head. But powerful King Lutsen, listen. I have several important things to say," and he sang this deceptive song.

Sing "Ala thala thala."
"Thala" begins.
The song unfolds in three parts.
Now, today, I call the deities.
Dharmakāya, saṃbhogakāya, nirmāṇakāya,
three divine ones grant your blessings, know me.
Today, please assist me in this song.
If you do not recognize this place,
it is Changthang Ngönmo (Blue Wolf Meadow), below the
    crags.
If you do not recognize me,
I am the māra minister Anu Ching-ngön.
This year at Losar,
I turned nineteen years old,
endowed with the six powers of a warrior.
News of this spread throughout the world.
If you do not recognize this song,
it is Ching-ngön's very short warrior song.
I do not sing it just anywhere,
but today I have no choice.
Listen to its essential meaning, King Lutsen.
Listen, it goes like this:
You the māra king,
life-ruler of the world,
rival of Shinjé lord of death,
fearless one of this land,
have no reason to dread that agitated dream.

It is a magical wheel of illusion;
there is no need to give it any weight.
Now, clearly, it is like this:
At the edge of this broad, flat, marshy meadow
is the iron sheep, so robust and thick-wooled.
That iron-hoofed sheep has made its home here
and has attained mastery of the iron life force.
These are the three aspects of this iron sheep
that loves to roam these verdant marshy meadows
and takes pleasure in playing in the grass and water
at the border of the slate meadow and the rocks.
Furthermore, the long-horned sorrel spirit yak
and the wild black spirit drong
love to roam the grassy alpine peaks,
the clear rivers, and the mountain valleys.
That sorrel yak and black drong
are healthy and run with vigor,
have hefty strong limbs,
a tail tip and fur of a wondrous hue,
and a great bellow and powerful horns.
The yak and the drong while they run
are savage creatures and, afterward, are companions,
the life-force talisman of the king who dwells blissfully,
wishing to live happily in the castle.
Now, this is the point of my story:
In this harsh northern land,
a young man is not free to rove.
Likewise, the hundreds of birds in the skies
are not free to fly
if they fly against the laws of the birds.
There are binding laws in these northern lands.
An outsider has no easy entry here,
and those who do come are subject to our harsh laws.
From this dark māra valley so thick with gloom,
only Yama escapes
and only thunderbolts enter.
What I mean is this:
On the very summit of Mount Meru,

the turquoise-maned snow lion rules.
It is said to be unrivaled,
but, Lutsen, when you circumambulate that mountain,
it is said that that lion bows its turquoise mane.
Among the rocky crags and the slate meadow,
the wild, horned drong is fearsome.
It is said to be unrivaled,
but, Lutsen, when you circumambulate that rocky meadow,
it is said that that drong bends it horns to the ground.
In the midst of the mountainous sandalwood forest,
the six-smiled tiger is awesome.
It is said to have no opponent,
but, Lutsen, when you walk that forest,
it is said that the tiger is struck with fear.
These might be just stories, but the meaning is clear.
In all of Jambudvīpa,
Lutsen, you are without rival.
There is no reason for you to be fearful.
Here in this worldly existence, on these ancient massive
    mountains,
there are countless boulders, naturally here.
No one placed them as landmarks.
Why do you think they have some strange significance,
    Lutsen?
You cannot possibly believe that.
Whatever harm has come to you, Lutsen, has not been
    from me,
the Zhugadar minister, Ching-ngön.

Even if a jewel were placed in my hand, I would not steal it.
Even if a lie were put on my tongue, I would not speak it.

But now, today,
it is as you consider me a thief
and have branded me a liar.
Why would you think I would act like that?
The other gatekeepers
yesterday were fine; everything was peaceful,

but I do not know about today.
Try not to worry, Lutsen.
In the ancient proverbs of Tibet,
there are examples of how it is:

A mind free of anger and hatred
does not have to battle to be calm.
A heart that does not take every danger as the end
does not have to battle to be serene.

Worrying will not get you what you want.
There are no actual enemy demons inside of you;
the only enemies and ghosts there are, are those you have
  invited.
You see enemies wherever you go,
but these crags are naturally strewn with boulders.
You are all fired up, worrying about revenge.
Don't you see that you are miserable, King Lutsen?
Ridiculed in the marketplace,
senselessly grasping at that boulder—
why are you doing that? Look at yourself!
Basically, to explain it:

When the rain falls in the three months of summer,
the shepherd wanders, shivering with cold.
But there is shelter in the boulders—
in the three months of summer, a refuge from the rain
and in the three months of winter, a refuge from the chill wind.

Keep all this in mind, Lutsen.
If you have not understood, I cannot repeat my song.

Thus he sang. Lutsen pushed the boulder aside intending to smash it down the rocky incline, but he considered the truth of Ching-ngön's words. He had dismounted his horse Sinta Phurshé and now strode into the flock of sheep, and right there was what appeared to be the very same boulder. Under his breath, he muttered, "I don't remember that such a boulder was ever here, but this year my mind has certainly been very uneasy." He stroked the iron-hoofed spirit sheep three times, and the sheep licked him, rubbing up against Lutsen. The sheep stuck its tongue out and Lutsen patted the sheep's head and scratched its body. Pacing back and forth, Lutsen thought, "There is no doubt that this spirit sheep is fine." He called to his mount Sinta Phurshé and galloped across the great Taknak Plain to find Atak Lhamo.

As soon as Atak saw Lutsen coming, she enveloped him in swirling dark vapor and approached him on her steed Rakar Tsubshé. Lutsen shouted out, "Atak! Are the long-horned sorrel māra spirit yak and the spirit drong both well?" and she replied, "Your spirit yak is up on the peak of Dzari Tongsum Barwa (Blazing Three-Thousand-Fold Rock Mountain) and your drong is in my doorway, asleep." Thirteen full-grown drongs of Ling had emanated to impersonate the māra spirit drong that was resting in Atak's doorway. At the sight of Lutsen, the drong's horn tips blazed, his tailed swirled up into the southern clouds, and his hooves kicked up a thick cloud of dust. A fierce roar came from the turquoise dragon, *drak drak,* and the mountains and valleys quaked, *shik shik.* Overjoyed, Lutsen thought, "There is no doubt that that is my spirit drong." He looked up to be sure his spirit long-horned sorrel māra yak was on the mountain peak, and saw it there, grazing the plentiful grass. Satisfied, Lu-tsen decided to return to Meza and mounted on Sinpa Phurshé, who galloped like the wind for the fortress Drongra Mukdzong, where Meza was sitting on the chair Khuktshur Nakpo (Black Corner Over Here) made from cannibal rock. Wrapped in a cloth behind her were five human and horse corpses that she was planning as a meal for Lutsen. He thought he should see what she was up to, and with swirling bloodshot eyes, he spoke through his yellowed, craggy teeth, "What are you doing?" to which Meza replied, "It was very kind of you to come. Now, what can I get you to eat and drink?" She went on to prepare an elaborate meal, which Lutsen devoured, saying, "Right now, I have had plenty to eat and drink. But tomorrow before the sun comes up, I am going to walk these lands, starting from below the eight high snow mountain peaks and up to India, the door of the Dharma, where there are several yellow-hatted lamas I can eat."

The next day at dawn, mounted on the māra horse Rakgyal Khampa (Reddish Copper Royal), he went as fast as lightning toward India. Meza was left, straddling her loom, weaving a cloth of white and black thread, with the upper thread in her right hand and the lower thread in her left hand. She had smeared the right side of her face white, and the left side black. As she was weaving, Gesar came in, impersonating a proper young man. He had an elephant tusk thumb ring in his hair and carried a blue silk cloth with pearls wrapped in it and bowed his head to the weaving Meza. Meza thought first of her previous night's dream and then of the tendrel that had arisen this morning and was sure that this man must be Gesar, the powerful leader of Ling. Smiling, she asked where he had come from, and he replied, "I am the chief mule-herder in the farmlands of Rong. Some thirteen of my mules were driven away by bandits, and I have come to look for them." Meza said, "It is strange that a young man like you has come to this māra valley, guarded as it is by demon and cannibal gatekeepers. How is it possible that you got through?" Yet, she sat weaving as before, as the young man offered a song.

Sing "Ala thala thala."
"Thala" begins.
The song unfolds in three parts.
Now, today, I call the gods.
Dharmakāya, saṃbhogakāya, nirmāṇakāya,
three divine ones, bless me and know me.
Today, please assist me in my song.
If you do not recognize this place,
it is the eight mountains of the upper north,
the maiden's weaving seat.
If you do not recognize me,
I am of the lineage of the lower farmlands,
and in the marshlands of the white salt flats,
I herd salt-laden mules.
But this year, as I journeyed to the upper north,
some of my mules and horses were thieved by bandits
and, today, I have come to rescue them.
Among those farmlands,
I am known as its only child-warrior.
If you do not recognize this song,
it is the long song of the salty fields.
It is not sung freely,
yet, today, I have no choice but to give it voice.
The start of the song is from a crouching pose, *gying zhing*
    gying,
its middle sways, *tshub ching tshub*,
and it comes to an end, *tha zhing tha*.
I sing a song without center or fringe,
invoking a ceaseless voice.
Today, the story goes like this:
beautiful weaver,
today interlacing black and white—

a woman in white with her right hand weaving white,
a woman in black with her left hand weaving black,
the struggle of warp and woof, white and black.
What does this mean?
Thirteen rollers spin on the loom—
let me explain.
Two of the weaving teeth are very small
so that the woman does not mix up the black and white threads.
How is this like the story?
A woman's hair is braided to the right,
as is the custom.
The right side of her face is smeared with white,
pushing her toward a virtuous mind;
the left side of her face is smeared black,
turning her mind away from hatred.
A woven apron tied in front,
small, colorful boots on her feet,
red-soled boots patterned with a rainbow—
that is how you are dressed.
I am a man from the eastern farmlands.
Today, I came after my mules and horses,
but unfamiliar with the land, I went astray and now wander,
  lost.
If you know, tell me the way.
I am lost—please guide my path.
In this māra land shrouded in darkness,
how can one find their way?
Keep this in mind, maiden.
If you have not understood, I cannot repeat it.

Thus he sang, and Meza thought, "This guest who has come here out of the blue seems like the Ling lord Gesar." Joyfully, a smile spread across her face as she rose from her weaving stool and said, "Handsome young man, I do not know if you are who you claim to be. Listen to this maiden's song."

Sing "Ala thala thala."
"Thala" gives the melody.
Dharmakāya, saṃbhogakāya, nirmāṇakāya,

three divine ones, bless me and know me.
Look upon me and befriend me.
From Tārā's buddhafield, the Eastern Paradise Arrayed in
    Turquoise Petals,
from the palace of Akaniṣṭha,
high atop a golden-petalled throne,
Mother Jetsün White and Blue Tārās, know me.
Look upon me with your light rays of compassion.
From the dharmakāya realm,
mother lineage Vajravārāhī, look upon me.
Lead the song of this naive maiden.
If you do not recognize this place,
it is the land of the evil death māra.
Through your karmic destiny,
you wander the mountain valleys of the north
saying you have come in pursuit and chasing everywhere
in these carnivorous māra lands,
wherever the path takes you.
If you do not recognize me,
in a previous life,
in the jeweled prosperity enclosure of eastern Ling
in the castle Kyilhang Lhanglha (Happy Vivid Divine),
the land of the resounding clear voice of the cuckoo,
I was a maiden in the house of Ling Akyi.
When I was a young girl of nine,
I was trapped by the demon māra,
and, at knifepoint, required to offer respect.
In the end, I will become his wife.
Now that I am eighteen years old,
I am waiting for an important guest.
If you do not recognize this song,
it is mine, Meza's song, "Magpie in Six Reverberations."
It is not a song I sing just anywhere.
My right hand weaves the white thread,
woven as the rainbow path of dharmakāya,
perhaps to become buddha robes.
The warp and woof, white and black, struggle.
The white establishes the dharmic path

and is the banner of the Buddhadharma.
My left hand weaves the black thread,
woven as the death of the rākṣasa cannibals,
perhaps as shrouds for māra corpses.
The warp and woof, white and black, struggle.
The black thread brings down the victory flag of the
    māras
and marks the waning of their teachings.
My hair braided to the right
signifies nurturing the tenets of Buddha.
My hair left loose on the left
signifies my torment by the māras.
That the right side of my face is white
is a sign of the virtue of the divine Lord Sengchen.
That the left side of my face is black
is a sign of the pain of not meeting Lord Gesar.
As for me,
meditating on buddha mind,
my corporeal body has reached the state of loving affection,
my courageous mind is fluid as red blood,
and my white snow mind is empty as the sky.
This woven apron tied across my front
will cover the head of the evil demon.
My red-soled boots adorned with a rainbow pattern
signify the wish to arrive in the happy land of Ling.
This story tells it like it is.
Good man, keep this in mind.
Relax a bit, and ask if you have questions.

Meza placed pale, amber, and dark honey, and white, red, and variegated grapes along with sweet, delicious rice wine and abundant food in front of the boy, saying over and over that this was offered in friendship. Joyful, he stood up and met Meza with a smile. Realizing that he was the Ling lord Gesar, she was overtaken by the poignancy of the moment. Wordlessly, she embraced him, suddenly fainting. Gesar gave her the White Tārā Long-Life Empowerment and authentic blessings, and afterward, she awoke, saying, "Although we have been apart for many years, through your great kindness we have met again. I will tell you the story of my long stay here in the māra land." Meza offered this song.

Sing "Ala thala thala."
Thala begins.
The song unfolds in three parts.
Today, I call the divine ones.
From your dwelling place, the palace of Akaniṣṭha,
mother lineage Khachö Lhamo, please watch over me.
If you do not recognize this place,
it is the eight mountains of the upper north.
If you do not recognize me,
previous to this lifetime,
from Vajravārāhī, surrounded by her retinue,
I was the emanation Red Vajrayoginī.
I took rebirth
as a maiden in the home of Ling Akyi.
From the sheep meadows there,
I had the ill fortune that Lutsen, a wolf-emanation,
carried me off to the māra land.
Now, you are fifteen years old
and have come to my aid
as we previously pledged.
Today, you have come to the north.
How long was your journey?
You seem so tired and weary.
Lost in this north land,
I have been waiting like a cuckoo waits for rain,
waiting so long.
Night brought no sleep, only the torture of time.
Unable to eat, hunger filled my days,
hoping for the time that I would look out and see
    your divine arrow with the message that we would meet face
        to face—
and now, Sengchen, that has come to pass.
Please bless the crown of my head.
I pray that it will not be long until we meet again.
Today, the sky is bright and clear;
the sun shines in the azure firmament,
and the stars and planets are in good alignment.
Today, the earth is warm,

humans are happy,
and the earth and planets are in auspicious alignment.
All the signs and omens are favorable.
I have met your great kindness;
may it not be long until we meet again.
May we dwell inseparably together
in this very lifetime.
The wild golden drong is fearsome in the rivered rocks,
   nam nam,
the great stag roams the marshy meadows, *drim drim,*
swans circle in the lakes, *khor khor.*
You, the accomplished siddha, the awakened one,
will strike the arrow into the demon's forehead,
and the north māra lands will turn to the Dharma.
Do not be secretive; speak to me.
If you keep a secret from your father, who can you tell?
If you hide food from your mother, to whom can you give it?
If I cannot trust your word, who can I trust?
Keep this in mind, noble being.
If you have not understood, I cannot repeat my song.

Thus she sang, and Gesar said, "Oh, excellent! Meza, you are my ally; why would I keep any secrets from you? But before I shoot the arrow at Lutsen, since the location of his small black life-stone is not known, you should be clever and find this out. As tomorrow and the next day are auspicious days, make a skillful plan to send Lutsen to go look for his sheep on the high north plain. Then, we can send down nine thunderbolts from the summit of the nine-peaked rock mountain above the path he must take. These thunderbolts will cause nine birds to hover, a golden rabbit to run down the mountain, and a turquoise rabbit to run across the plain. Like a lamb startled by a hawk, the māra horse Sinta Phurshé[7] will be startled and, without looking, will leap right over the edge. Lutsen will be dragged by the stirrups and injured, suffering great pain in the fall with his horse. Afterward, you will go to Mount Kailash to obtain the mo divination text belonging to Lutsen's maternal uncle Thiklé Ökar (Bindu White Luminosity). Then, we will see that events are unfolding as we had hoped and possible in accord with the prophecy of the highest gods." Gesar finished speaking and returned to Ching-ngön and Atak. Staying behind, Meza made aspiration prayers and performed a white smoke offering lhasang to the gods and, heeding Gesar's instructions, understood through her prajñā mind exactly where Lutsen's life-stone was kept. Skillfully, she was able to have Lutsen lead her there. King Gesar had emanated his horse Kyang Gö as a large, plain boulder and placed it in that very same spot to confuse Lutsen. The Zhugadar minister Ching-ngön and Atak Lhamo welcomed Gesar back, and he sang this vital song.

OM MAṆI PADME HŪM
Sing "Ala thala thala."
"Thala" begins.
The song unfolds in three parts.
Now, today, I call the divine ones.
From above, three excellent awakened ones, know me.
From overhead, all divine yidams, know me.
From below, ḍākinīs and dharmapālas, know me.
Do not be distracted, please come to assist me.
If you do not recognize this place,
it is Taknak Dribkhuk Nakpo (Black Tiger Shady Dark
    Inlet).
If you do not recognize me,
within this world realm,
I am called Prince Norbu Dradül.
If you do not recognize this song,
it is "The Three Word Warrior Song" of the highest gods.
The warrior song is not sung casually,
but I have no choice.
Zhugadar minister Ching-ngön
and the foreigner from the north lands, Atak Lhamo,
listen to what I have to say.
Tomorrow and the next day and the next,
high above in the divine buddhafield,
within the beautiful array of stars,
the sun and the moon will make their paths,
but it is the sun that is all-pervading.
When Lutsen traverses this valley,
Rāhula will throw thunderbolts from the sky,
the māra horse will startle and leap,
and Lutsen will be thrown from his horse.
His skeleton will collapse inward,

and his innards will extravasate.
His great strong body will be given over to disease.
A great pain will fill his upper body,
and a lesser pain, his lower body.
He will be bedridden with suffering.
You both, go quickly, do not stay here.
In the middle lake of three lakes in the upper lands,
there are three menacing antelope.
They are the support of the māra demon.
Atak, you must tame them.
In the great marshy swamp of the north,
there are three three-headed fish.
They are Lutsen's spirit fish.
Ching-ngön, you must catch them.
The iron hook of compassion I give to you
is the auspicious connection of taming Lutsen.
Through astrology and mo divination,
decant milky tea in a white copper vessel
and the prophecy of the highest gods
will gradually become clear.
Both of you, keep this in mind.
If you have understood, keep what you have heard in mind.
If you have not understood, there is no reason to repeat it.

Thus he sang, and Atak and Ching-ngön openly praised Gesar's words. Atak went to kill the three antelope and Ching-ngön, carrying the iron hook of compassion, went to catch the spirit fish from the inlet of the great swamp lake Damtsho Chenpo. As for Gesar and his horse, they were in the rocky valley of Meö Barwa, coming to the divine palace Dralha Mepung Barwa (Dralha Blazing Mass of Fire) and resting there in samādhi.

CHAPTER SEVENTEEN

The Ling lord Gesar, just as in Manéné's prophecy,
strikes the demon with lightning.
Meza returns with the borrowed divination text
and queries the demon as to where he has hidden his
    talisman.

THAT DAY, FROM THE ROCK CAVE ASURA DRAKPHUK,[1] Manéné Namné
Karmo came bareback on a lioness, accompanied by a white buffalo on a leash and
a turquoise dragoness following behind. In her right hand she held a longevity vase
filled with nectar, *kyil lé lé*, while with her left hand she scattered consecrated rice,
tha ra ra. A perfect dohā spilled from her lips, *sil lé lé*. She was unmistakable with the
small white fan in her hair and silken ribbons trailing down, and through a stream
of rainbow light of three colors, white, red, and blue, she said, "Divine prince, great
noble being, do not sleep but awake and listen! Listen, for I have several matters."
And she offered this long, auspicious vajra dohā.

> OM MAṆI PADME HŪṂ
> Sing "Ala thala thala."
> "Thala" begins.
> The song unfolds in three parts.
> Now, today I call the deity.
> From the completely perfect celestial pure realm,
> victorious ones of the five families
> and divine yidams with your retinues,

today, please come to assist me.
From the western dharmakāya pure realm of Sukhāvatī,
atop a golden peacock throne,
Dharma protector and guide, Amitābha,
today come to assist me.
From Khechara, the pure realm of accomplished space-
    activity,
Vajravārāhī, look upon me with compassion.
From Tārā's buddhafield, the Paradise Arrayed in Turquoise
    Petals,
atop a blazing conch seat,
five ḍākinīs of the mother lineage, look upon me,
watch over me with your light rays of compassion.
There is no deity higher than you to call.
If you do not recognize this place,
it is the eight mountains of the upper north.
If you do not recognize me,
I am Tārā the long-life wisdom ḍākinī,
I am Ama Namné Karmo.
Today, precious noble being,
do not sleep but awake and listen!
Listen, there are several matters:

A motionless stone will get stuck in the ice.
If sandalwood stagnates, its roots decay.
A lazy monk will not progress in Dharma practice.
If a leader is lazy, the law will weaken.
A slothful father or uncle is a poor example for the generations that
    follow.
If young warriors are lazy, the enemy will rest.
A slothful matron makes inferior chang.
If a maiden is lazy, the household will languish.
If children are listless, the playgrounds will be deserted.

There is no good to too much sleep,
and the least happiness comes from sleeping all morning.
If you are poor, sleeping late is not a choice.
Tonight, in particular,

you had a good reason for appealing to me,
and therefore I have come, noble being—
I, your aunt.
Do you recognize me?
If you do not recognize this song,
it is the Dharma song of your aunt Manéné.
Now, precious noble being,
this year you have come to the north māra lands.
Here are some examples from the proverbs:

The young jungle tiger,
as soon as he is adorned with the six smiles,
shows off the pattern of his stripes.
The golden brown mountain drong,
as soon as he is adorned with horn tips,
shows off the curve of his horn.

Gesar of Upper Ling,
this year you have come for the great enemy Lutsen.
It is time to shoot the skull arrow.
You of the kingdom of Tramo Ling,
matchless King Sengchen,
and the king of the eight mountain ranges of the upper north,
Māra Lutsen,
will be judged against each other in bravery.
The material being of Lutsen
and the intangible one of King Sengchen
will be judged against each other,
and we will see if the arrow strikes the skull.
Tomorrow and the next day and the day after that—
that third day is the auspicious day.
The great king Rāhula will bring down thunderbolts,
the thunderbolts will startle the māra horse,
and the māra horse will throw the demon Lutsen
whose skeleton will collapse inward
and whose innards—blood, flesh, and bones—will be
    crushed.
Hence, his body will be trapped in lingering illness.

He will be bedridden, motionless.
In the lowlands of snowy Mount Kailash
lives Lutsen's maternal uncle
Thiklé Ökar.
He has three texts: the extensive, intermediate, and concise
    divination texts.
The demon king Lutsen
will have no choice but to send Meza for the divination text.
She should arrive from one side of the great valley,
and you, noble being, from the other
to greet her with a loving smile,
staying three days among the rock-strewn meadows
joined in bliss and happiness.
After three days, without delay,
Meza should retrieve the divination text,
and you must take the life of Uncle Thiklé.
On the way back,
before giving the text to Lutsen,
you must defile it with various unclean substances:
one, hair collected from one hundred widows,
two, pieces of worn-out shoes from one hundred lepers,
three, cloth from the skirts of one hundred prostitutes,
four, dirt from one hundred charnel grounds,
and five, rotten blood from the filthy lair of a female dog.
Then, smear the divination text with all of this,
put the text under a doorstep,
and have Meza get it and bring it to Lutsen.
He, the māra king,
will say the extensive divination is long-winded,
the concise divination too terse,
but the medium length divination perfectly cast.
While the demon is using the text to make a mo divination,
precious noble being Gesar,
between the rocky edge of the low-lying river valley
and the golden grassy alpine meadows above,
you must create nine ridges and valleys all from sand[2]
and build nine bridges over nine rivers.
Fashion a mountain to the right;

elder Brother Dungkhyung Karpo should be this
    mountain.
Fashion a mountain to the left;
younger Brother Ötro Lutrül should be this mountain.
Fashion a mountain in the center;
sister Thalé Ökar[3] should be this mountain.
These three dralha siblings will remain there as the three
    mountains.
Inside an invisible vast copper pot,
put water from a hundred different sources,
place various trees upon the water
and in the treetops,
scatter the feathers of many species of birds.
At the foot of the three emanated mountains,
scatter white rice and wheat.
Put a little *tsampa* on your face
and wear a sorrowful expression,
letting tears fall from your eyes
while bees fill your right nostril
and coral fills your left.
Rest there in your armor
with your helmeted head twisted on the ground,
your tiger-skin quiver pinning you down
and the leopard-skin sheath out of reach.
Your poor, miserable face
will appear in Lutsen's mo divination,
and that old māra will relax when he sees it.
When the time is right,
Meza will ask the location
of the māra life-force black stone.[4]
That life-force stone
is sometimes in Lutsen's eye,
circling around.
Sometimes it is in the sole of his foot,
walking around.
Sometimes it is in the cavity of his heart,
circling the point where the blood exits the aorta.
Sometimes it is right between his eyebrows,

spinning around in his forehead.
Today is that day, the day it circles in his forehead.
On the evening of this, the twenty-ninth day,
may you strike his skull with your arrow.
This is your chance to subdue the demon.
Please bow down and I will confer empowerment.
Look up into my face and receive amṛta.
May your life span be longer than a river,
and may that river be without end.
May your life force be stronger than a rock,
and may that rock be indestructible.
May your merit be loftier than a mountain,
and may that mountain be as stable as Mount Meru.
May your higher perceptions be as illuminated as the sun and
    moon,
and may that light never dim.
Noble being, keep this in mind.
If you have not understood my song, I cannot repeat it.

Her song was over, and Manéné vanished like a rainbow into the distant heavens. Gesar took her prophecy to heart. And from the expanse of the sky, he and his horse watched the mountain range where on either side of the path that the demon Lutsen would take were the nine mountain peaks from which the nine thunderbolts would strike. The steed Kyang Gö emanated as nine birds and remained there while, at the same moment, Gesar transformed into a spotted leopard to watch the events unfold. Meza went to find Lutsen, and when he saw her coming, he said, "I'm starting to think that it is wicked to eat human flesh and nauseating to drink human blood. What would be better?" Meza said, "Well now, King Lutsen, as far as I can see, there is nothing else to eat but lamb. Even though it is difficult, go check on the sheep high up in the northern steppes and bring back a few." Lutsen replied with a song.

Sing "Ala thala thala."
"Thala" begins.
Today, I call the divine ones.
Māra Trarab Wangchuk, please watch over me.
Matram Rudra, assist me
and look upon me with your eye of compassion.

428

If you do not recognize this place,
it is the eight mountains of the upper north.
This is the māra castle Shari Namdzong.
If you do not recognize me,
I am known as a red butcher māra.
When I was a child of three,
I threw a wild golden drong to the ground.
Then, when I was six,
I caught a lion and a tiger by their legs,
and by the time that I was nine,
the southern continent was under my power—
the lands of Mön and Kashmir,
Mukgu and Sumpa,⁵
the snow mountains and the country of Minub.
There is not a single land that I have not visited
nor a place I have not been.
I am famed throughout the world.
But when I think about the past,
there is one thing that I do regret.
Long ago,
at Yulung Sumdo in Lower Ma,
one, the ancestral protector Lawa Lakyé (Musk Deer),
two, the māra child Chakdrub Tobden (Iron Accomplished
    One),
third, the six-smiled spirit tiger and its retinue,
and fourth, the seven iron-bird siblings—
those kindred of mine and their retinue of spirits were slain
    by Joru.
Yet, I have not retaliated.
I wanted to avenge their deaths,
but here I am, held back by your words.
As is said in the ancient tales:

A brave warrior must focus on subjugating the main enemy
and not just shoot an arrow into the wind.
A maiden is either brazen or not;
if modest, she must gather up her modesty,
for without it, she is like a mountain flag in the wind.

Who wants that to be their fate?
The makara in the middle of the ocean
does not usually open his huge jaws,
but once a year when he does,
a bloody rainbow rises from the depths.
There is no difference between the makara and me.
The kyang, both male and female, graze the meadows
joined by their frolicking young,
and the low-lying meadows are filled with bliss and
    happiness.
Likewise, Meza, you and I
are here in my homeland, the māra country,
and I wish for us a time of happiness and bliss.
A delicious little white lamb to eat—
today, I will go get one.
Plus, delicious grape wine to drink—
Meza, you stay and prepare it.
Then, we will have meat and wine to enjoy,
and we can frolic and have fun.
Tomorrow morning early, at sunrise,
I will be on my way
to get a sheep from Upper Bera
and one from Lower Amdo.
The lamb from Amdo[6] is superb
and from the best sheep ranch there
I will get an exceptional lamb.
All of these I will present to you, Meza.
We will enjoy abundant meat and wine
and each other's company.
Meza keep this in mind.
If you have not understood, I cannot repeat my song.

Thus he sang, and Meza said,[7] "Wonderful! But now, have a little bit to eat and drink and relax. Have you decided which horse you are going to ride tomorrow, and who is going with you?" Lutsen said, "What would you think if I rode your horse Rakgyal Khampa?" and Meza replied, "Your journey will take you all the way from below Gango (Snow Gate) of Upper Beri up to Lukdzong (The Sheep Fortress) of Lower Amdo—don't you think you need a faster horse?" In Lutsen's mind, it was not important if it took an extra day to get back, but not wanting to disagree, he said, "Well, I will go alone on my own horse Naktra Phurshé."

The next day at daybreak, mounted on his steed, he departed like a whirling windstorm. Coming to the shady side of the mountains, he saw five black and white sand dunes. A spotted golden rabbit was running back and forth, and just ahead on the path, a turquoise rabbit was leaping about. His horse startled and reared up, but Lutsen spurred him on and was not injured. But then, suddenly, from high up in mountains, blinding lightning struck nine times, and nine birds circled. At that moment, Lutsen realized that the lha, lu, and nyen, together with the dralha and werma, were running straight at him. His horse reared and Lutsen fell. His skeleton caved in, eighteen of his ribs were broken, his entire body was crushed, and his innards, his heart, and lungs were expelled. His breath heaved with great pain and, gasping, he returned to Meza, calling out in unbearable anguish, "Meza, come here! I am suffering, don't you see?" he said. Meza said, "So unfortunate!" and she bent her head down to him as though she were crying and offered this song of encouragement.

> Sing "Ala thala thala."
> "Thala" begins.
> The song unfolds in three parts.
> Today, I call the deity.
> From the Glorious Copper-Colored celestial palace,
> within the measureless palace of Lotus Light,
> Master Padmasambhava, watch over me.
> With your retinue of one hundred ḍākas on the right
> and one hundred thousand ḍākinīs on the left,
> today, assist the song of this maiden.
> If you do not recognize this place,
> it is the māra homeland.
> The sky swirls with the fog of nonvirtue.[8]
> Even though there is a sun and moon, they do not shine
>   brightly,
> and though there are stars, they cannot be seen.
> The māra valley is encased in pitch darkness.
> If you do not recognize me,
> I am Trishok Meza Bumdrön.
> I am famous throughout the southern continent
> and in both China and India.

Famed in the azure firmament
are the sun, moon, and stars,
famed in the intermediate realms
is the southern turquoise dragon,
but the one famed in the upper north kingdom
is the maiden Meza Bumdrön.
Do not sleep, but awake and listen,
as I have a few things to say:
You, the māra king Lutsen,
are famed throughout the world,
and I, Meza Bumdrön of Akyi,
am famed throughout the world.
We, the renowned maiden and the famous king—
I thought it auspicious that we were together,
that you, Lutsen, would partake of lamb,
that I, Meza, would make delicious wine,
that we would have whatever meat and liquor we wished,
and I would drink the honey nectar of your lips.
I thought there would be happiness and joy.
But today those are distant wishes.
Unexpectedly, your horse threw you—
what demonic force could have gotten into that horse?
Your body is now racked with pain,
and I am thrown into despair.
We are both miserable.
We cannot go on like this.
In my right hand there is a gilded copper vessel full of chang,
the chang that contains the six excellent medicines,
which this very day I offer to you.
May it have the potency to cure your illness.
With my left hand I offer you tea from the silver-plated
    copper vessel,
the tea that contains the relic blessing pills from the
    lamas,
which this very day I offer to you.
I pray that you will be cured.
Lutsen, keep this in mind.

After she sang, she offered the first select portion of the tea and the first select portion of the liquor to Lutsen. He gulped them down and said, "Meza, the day after tomorrow at dawn, can you go to Uncle Thiklé Ökar up in the white snow mountains and borrow the divination text?" Meza answered, "Of course!" Lutsen, miserable with his injuries, went on to say, "Besides that, Meza, over there on the far side of that rock that resembles a cannibal is the healing lama Menpa Lhakyé (Divine at Birth Doctor), a nonhuman emanation living among the thirteen māra myriarchies. Can you invite him also?" Meza said, "It is too far for him; he will never come. Rather than that, it would be best simply to make a mo divination and use astrology." Lutsen listened and nodded in agreement.

Meza packed up a delicious feast and some wine and, riding the fast horse Kyaka Dingshé (Skilled Flying Magpie), she went up into the dappled rocky crags high above the lowlands and waited there at the banks of a colorful lake. After awhile, Gesar arrived there on horseback, shimmering in swirls of light, and Meza immediately took his horse by the reins. She asked him to be seated on a carpet patterned with the auspicious symbols and offered him liquor from the gilded copper vessel in her right hand, tea from the silver-plated copper vessel in her left hand, milk from the conch-coated copper vessel, and served a bountiful feast with this song.

> OṂ MAṆI PADME HŪṂ
> Sing "Ala thala thala."
> "Thala" begins.
> The song unfolds in three parts.
> Today, I call upon the deities.
> Dharmakāya, saṃbhogakāya, nirmāṇakāya,
> divine ones, source of blessings watch over me.
> Omniscient ones, lead my song.
> From Tārā's buddhafield, the Eastern Paradise Arrayed in
>   Turquoise Petals,
> atop a blazing conch seat
> on a throne piled high with golden petals,
> Mother Jetsünmas, White and Blue Tārās—
> today, please assist me.
> If you do not recognize this place,
> it is a multicolored lake within the northern marshland,
> the spirit lake of King Lutsen.
> If you do not recognize me,

I am Trishok Meza Bumdrön of the north.
This year at Losar,
I was eighteen years old
and stood up to challenge the demon.
Up until now,
I have known only suffering, as was my fate.

A blue wolf roams these mountains
knowing only hardship; nevertheless, that is its fate.
A vulture eats the flesh of humans
knowing it is unclean; nevertheless, that is its fate.

Ceaselessly thinking of you, Sengchen Lama,
waiting like a cuckoo waits and waits for rain,
I prayed for the day that we would meet.
Now, the one I have longed for has come;
the childhood friend I called out for has arrived.
Today, I surely see your golden face.
I am powerless to contain my thoughts.
Many years have passed while I waited;
now, please give me the bliss and happiness I desire.
Listen, precious Sengchen,
is my body not spread out like a cushion?
Today, in this garden of desire,
are we not to enjoy bliss and happiness?
From the highest heavens,
the turquoise dragon has come.
Is it not to lead the rain?
Is it not to arrange the ripening of the six grains?
From the peak of snowy Mount Kailash,
the white snow lioness has come.
Is it not to see that her turquoise mane is luxuriant?
Is it not to offer her nutritious milk?
From the pinnacle of Mount Meru,
the great garuḍa king of birds has come.
Is it not to assure that his six wings are strengthened?
Is it not to be sure that he is able to soar through the skies?
Sengchen Divine Jewel,

you have come to me.
We two, united as a man and woman—
is it not to bring joy and happiness to each other?
How can we induce the intoxicating nectar of our love?[9]
All my life I have thought of you, Gesar.
If we are not joyful now, when will we be joyful?
If today we are unhappy, when will we be happy?
We must celebrate the union of happiness and joy.
You are the parasol of the sun—
before the sun sinks behind the mountain pass,
may its light rays shine on me.
Your eyes, noble being, are the bright stars themselves—
before those bright stars vanish below the mountain,
may they look down upon me.
Great compassionate lama,
may we be bound as one by the iron hook of wisdom.
This very day,
I am joyful and happy.
Anything can happen in the span of a human lifetime.
Happiness and suffering are interwoven.
If you pull away from sadness,
you will never connect with happiness.

Every mountain climb is followed by a descent,
but unless you ascend the steep mountains,
you will never reach the comfort of the lower lands.

In another proverb, it is said:

Unless your work exhausts you,
nothing worthwhile will be yours.

Precious noble King Sengchen,
I, Akyi Meza Bumdrön,
my body, head to toe,
is purer even than the sacred Dharma.
Only the white vulture has soared above me;
only the clean river has been beneath me.
Never for anyone has my body been a cushion.

Here in this pristine marshland,
quickly shoot the arrow of desire.
Upon this fine brocade blanket,
dearest one, stay and relax.
Sengchen, please keep this in your heart.

With her invitation hanging in the air, Meza gave their two horses feed cakes[10] and led them to the pasture to graze. Sengchen and Meza sat together on the brocade mat Tashi Yangra (Auspicious Prosperity Horn), and propelled by their youth and the intensity of their passion for each other, they made love. Meza was so blissful that time itself seemed to stop. After awhile, as Meza found herself thinking that Gesar would be able to destroy the teachings of the evil māras and establish the teachings of Śākyamuni, her own good merit became obvious to Manéné, Brahmā, Nyen Khulha, the nāga Tsukna, and the lha, lu, and nyen. The next day at dawn, Gesar and Meza set out on the road together. It was noontime when they reached the home of Lutsen's uncle, Thiklé Ökar, where they were confronted by his gatekeeper demoness who appeared as a black wolf. Gesar captured and tamed her with the lasso of emptiness. Quickly Meza slipped inside the castle and presented Thiklé Ökar with the fine silk, brocade, and cotton cloths that Lutsen had sent, along with his message. Meza left nothing out as she offered this song.

Sing "Ala thala thala."
"Thala" begins.
The song unfolds in three parts.
Protector, guru, yidam, and the Three Jewels—
from above, buddhas of the three times, watch over me,
from overhead, divine hosts of yidams, watch over me,
from below, ḍākinīs and dharmapālas, watch over me.
Do not waver, kindly assist me.
If you do not recognize this place,
from above the colorful lake high in the north,
it is your castle, Shelgyi Drubkhang (Crystal Meditation
    House)
If you do not recognize me,
I have come from Chakri Tsegu
and am Trishok Meza Bumdrön of the north,
the intended wife of Lutsen,
and you, Uncle Thiklé Ökar,

are his maternal uncle.

Now, listen, here is what I have to tell you.

From the depths of the great ocean,

a great wave surged up to the sky,

and now the makara is disturbed.

This signifies that the patterns on his head will break up.[11]

From the high cliffs of Mount Meru,

a landslide plunged to the red crags of the wild tsen below,

and now they are disturbed.

This is an omen that the tsen will lose their castle.

From great white snowy Mount Kailash,

the snow has fallen in an avalanche,

and now the white lioness is disturbed.

This portends that her turquoise mane will wither.

There, in the eight mountains of the upper north,

Lutsen, unable to settle down, was wandering

when his steed was frightened by a sudden thunderbolt.

Unfortunately, Lutsen was dragged in the stirrups

and now is suffering from his injuries.

When the six excellent medicines were of no benefit,

Lutsen sent me to you, Uncle,

to borrow the divination text.

Within the eighteen divinations,

it is said that there are extensive, medium, and concise texts.

Lutsen said we do not need the extensive one, as the process
is too long,

nor the condensed one, as it would be unable to reveal the
truth.

The intermediate one with thirteen nine-square divination
charts

is the one he said I was to borrow and bring quickly to him.

That is what Lutsen asked,

and these three beautiful silk, brocade, and cotton cloths

he sent as an offering.

He also wanted to know if you thought he would ever be well
again.

Tell me, lama, and I will convey your words of wisdom to him.

Lama, please keep this in your heart.

When she had finished, Uncle Thiklé said, "Oh how awful, how terrible that he was thrown from his horse! Especially that nine thunderbolts struck from the nine-peaked mountain and that nine birds hovered—that is without a doubt a bad omen. These thirteen nine-square divination charts are drawn accurately and are excellent. Be sure not to defile them and get them quickly into Lutsen's hands. When he does the divination, he will know how to meditate on the refuge lama." He then gave Meza some delicious food to eat, and she left on horseback, carrying the intermediate divination text. As she headed down, Padmasambhava sent three nine-pointed vajra thunderbolts from the nine-peaked Glorious Copper-Colored Mountain, and Lutsen's Uncle Thiklé was reduced to dust. For thirteen generations, the [māra] uncles had amassed great treasures that now numbered some 108 and were kept in a large storehouse within the castle Shelgyi Drubkhang. Gesar and Padmasambhava now revealed these treasures and then went to Münpa Chutrik in the upper sloping valley of the māras where they tamed the thirteen myriarchies of immaterial māra beings. Then, they met up with Meza to talk over the details of what to do next.

Gesar said, "Now is the time to defile the divination text. Meza, take the worn-out shoes of a hundred lepers, the cut hairs of a hundred widows, pieces of the skirts of a hundred prostitutes, dirt from a hundred graveyards,[12] and rotten blood from the lair[13] of a female dog. Pile these unclean substances on top of the divination text, leaving it beneath the doorstep of the main gate." When Gesar went back to the tree line, he manifested nine paths to the sand hill with nine valleys, nine rivers, and finally, nine bridges. There were his three dralha siblings—Dungkhyung Karpo, Lutrül Öchung, and Thalé Ökar—appearing as three mountains that surrounded a huge copper vessel brimming with water. On top of that, in the leaves of various trees were strewn feathers of many birds. Gesar put his great victory helmet down by his feet. Bees filled his right nostril and coral, his left nostril. A little tsampa dusted his face and both his eyes were crusted with what looked like maggot excrement, and quite a bit of wheat and rice was scattered around him. He wore the threefold panoply of dralha. He was pinned down[14] by the tiger-skin quiver on his right, and the leopard-skin case was to his left. With Gesar lying face up on the ground, Meza contaminated the divination text, wrapped it in golden silk, and brought it to Lutsen. He was very pleased and said, "It is good that you came back. What did my uncle, the lama, say?" Meza responded with a song repeating Uncle Thiklé's words but giving a version of how she retrieved the divination text especially made for Lutsen's ears.

> Sing "Ala thala thala."
> "Thala" begins.
> The song unfolds in three parts.

Today, I call to the deities.
Dralha and werma, kindly assist me.
Mother Vajrayoginī, lead my song.
If you do not recognize this place,
it is the māra castle Shari Namdzong.
If you do not recognize me,
King Lutsen, I am your tea maker.
Now, listen.
By the snowy range of Mount Kailash,
there is a blood lake in the marshlands to the north,
and with its fury and splendor,
it is like the spirit lake of the nāga Dölwa Nakpo.
Sometimes it is red as blood,
sometimes white as conch,
black as charcoal,
or blue as turquoise—
resplendent with its many colors.
In that snowy mountain
is Uncle Thiklé's crystal white meditation cave Shelgyi
    Drubkhang[15]
guarded by a wolflike female demoness.
I knocked, and the lama came to the door,
inviting me inside,
and I was led into his meditation cave.
He asked after you, how you were, and then
the lama said
that for you, King Lutsen—
this will be a year of many obstacles.
In its current configuration, your nine squares are ominous,[16]
your dreams will be disturbing,
and the signs show that there will be hardship on your
    journey.
But he said nothing too dire will occur.
He had three divination texts: extensive, medium, and
    concise.
The extensive text had eighteen royal chronicles,
the abbreviated text, the histories of the thirteen ministers,
and the intermediate text, the thirteen nine-squared charts.

The latter was the one the lama said I should bring to you.
He said that to cast this divination, you should set out
    extensive offerings—
prepare as many offering bowls of human blood as possible,
set out burnt offerings of human heart flesh,
offering this burnt flesh and human blood to the deities
and praising Garab the supreme māra.
There is still more that the lama said.
You should understand your main motives in borrowing[17] the
    text.
What is your intention?
What kind of person are you after?
Unless you hold the divination thread straight,
he said that the divination would be unclear and empty.
King Lutsen,
why is it that you are borrowing the text?
Who is it that you are worried about?
Tell me honestly; do not hide anything.
My mind is as white as a snow mountain;
why turn it into a dark slate rock?
The swans circling in the lake
trust its blue waters,
and I, Meza, trust you.
But there are some things you have not told me.
Why do you keep secrets?

A young man's heart is as vast as the heavenly sphere.
Both are open and accommodating.
A superior man has the best inner qualities,
spacious enough for a white eagle to circle and soar, ta la la.
A mediocre man has middling inner qualities,
boastfully displaying his sword, arrow, and knife, the threefold
    panoply, khyil lé lé.
The inferior man has poor inner qualities,
at a mere utterance, his knife handle will fly.

    That is what is said in the ancient proverbs.
    Do not leave before you have heard me out

nor cloud your face in a scowl.

Those are my thoughts.

If you have understood, keep them in mind.

She finished singing, and Lutsen said, "Meza, relax while I cast the divination. Then, we will have a frank and honest discussion." Setting out offering bowls of human blood and an offering of burnt flesh, he threw the divination three times, and each time the same identical divination came down. Delighted with the outcome, Lutsen smiled and said, "Now, Meza, here is my honest tale and an explanation of the divination." He sang this song to her.

> Sing "Ala thala thala."
>
> "Thala" gives the melody.
>
> Without singing "ala," there is no way to sing;
>
> without the melody "thala" there is no way to harmonize.
>
> Today, I call to the deities.
>
> Māra Garab Wangchuk, watch over me.
>
> Trarab Nakpo, kindly assist me.
>
> Matram Rudra, be my ally.
>
> There are no gods higher than you to call.
>
> If you do not recognize this place,
>
> the inner castle is constructed
>
> of nine different metals
>
> and is called Chakdzong Khordeb (Fenced Iron Fortress).
>
> The middle castle was built
>
> of bronze
>
> and is known as Tridzong Barwa (Blazing Throne Fortress).
>
> The outer castle was built
>
> of nine different types of horn
>
> and is called Sharu Namdzong.
>
> There will never be another fortress as mighty,
>
> nor one as exalted.
>
> If you do not recognize me,
>
> I am the demon king of the māras.
>
> Trishok Meza Bundrön of the north,
>
> if you think it over, here is the story.
>
> The white vulture circles just above,
>
> but if its wings cannot bring it to altitude,

its flight is useless.
A horse may have wings of wind,
but if it cannot journey to India and China and back,
it is useless to raise this great breed.
I am the demon king of māras,
but if I do not rule over all the world
and destroy the teachings of the Buddhadharma,[18]
it is useless to be this māra titan.
I am the adversary of the divine Śākyamuni,
and Gesar is my rival.
I must overturn Śākyamuni,
or I am not the demon.
I have borrowed the famed divination text of my maternal
     uncle
and used it for a divination concerning Joru.
Within this mo divination, there is a scene:
Nine paths, nine valleys, nine rivers—
those three nines are in the midst of a swirling ocean.
There is a great mountain, a small mountain, and a middling
     one,
with collections of various trees,
birch, cork, and juniper,
with flocks of numerous birds.
The enemy Joru, nephew of Gok,
is sinking in the lake,
having died at the foot of the mountain.
His great helmet floats on the surface of the water,
his great armor drapes over the treetops,
and his great weapons are strewn everywhere.
The hair on his head fans out,
his face is slack,
with his mouth and eyes covered with worm dung,
and his nose seeps blood and pus.[19]
Vultures circle his corpse,
his rotting body, already cooked, crawls with maggots,
and coyotes run for his flesh.
I am so happy with my enemy gone—
no one could be happier!

You, Meza, and I, Lutsen, are together
and from today onward are life companions.
Just as the sun's warmth offsets the cold, happiness offsets
    sadness,
I will not bring you sorrow, Meza,
and will trust you with pure heart.
My thirty white teeth smile at you,
and I express my love.
Keep this in your heart, Meza.

Lutsen finished his song, and Meza swayed with seeming delight and affection. With a face full of false smiles, she put on warm, soft clothing bound with an ornamental silver belt. Tying up her black woven cloth apron and putting on her rainbow boots, she carried chang from the gilded copper vessel in her right hand, tea from the silver-plated copper vessel in her left, together with yogurt and milk from the conch-coated copper vessel and offered them to Lutsen who said, "Come here and sit next to me. I must send a letter to my two ministers." His message was conferred by the wind, and at daybreak the next day, Atak Lhamo and Ching-ngön arrived just as Meza was saying, "Lutsen, if you are worried about your health, I can watch over you for the next three days and nights. Would you like that?" Saying, "Here is our baby," she thrust an infant into Lutsen's arms. The baby scratched and bit, and Lutsen, taken by surprise, exclaimed, "Meza, what are you saying?" But then, staring at the baby, he went on, "This baby is just like me, and I have many life forces, both visible and invisible, material and nonmaterial, so it is quite possible that a baby like this could exist and suddenly appear. Keep him pure; feed him nothing but human heart blood and flesh." He returned the baby to Meza, and she swaddled it in layers of silk cloth. Lutsen turned to Atak and Ching-ngön, saying, "You must be authentic guardians of each and every life-force support of mine. According to the recent mo divination and astrology, I will be cured of my disease in thirteen days." He spoke with great confidence.

Later on, Lutsen had gone outside the castle and was sitting high atop a black rock that had been used in weightlifting contests, eating about a hundred men, a hundred women, and fifty children and drinking human blood. Meza came, carrying a hundred yak-loads of barrels filled with chang, nine huge slabs of butter,[20] and nine yak-loads of tsampa bags to offer to the demon king. Lutsen said, "Don't come. I have human flesh and blood to eat and drink, and you will get filthy." Meza said, "No, you come here. You have had enough flesh. I can give you some delicious food." She had seven cast-iron caldrons full of water that she used to wash Lutsen's head and hands clean of matted blood. She led him to a cozy room called Dekyi Barma (Between Bliss and Happiness) inside the castle. There, into a kettle she had put the meat of seven small white lambs, and the meat of seven drongs as well as the nine yak-loads of butter and bags of tsampa, and she offered it all to Lutsen. Pouring chang into a great copper vessel, she said, "Please drink this excellent chang, and I will sing a beautiful song." Lutsen was thinking that Meza seemed different some-how: "I wonder why she is being so sweet? Of course, if I consume only human flesh, in the end I will starve when the māra districts and twelve myriarchies are exhausted. Meza has a good idea in offering me something else, this feast of the seven carcasses and nine yak-loads of tsampa with nine slabs of butter." He ate it, and Meza opened one hundred barrels of strong liquor and one hundred khal[21] of chang. She poured two bottles for Atak and Ching-ngön and the rest for Lutsen. Lutsen as usual got drunk. He vomited, his head was spinning, and he turned over onto his back like a scorpion and stayed there unmoving. Meza said, "I will watch over you tonight, as there is no one else you can trust and you are in danger of losing your black life-stone." Meza sang this song of caring.

> Sing "Ala thala thala."
> "Thala" begins.
> The song unfolds in three parts.
> Now, today, I call to the deities.
> Dharmakāya, saṃbhogakāya, nirmāṇakāya,
> three divine sources of blessings, watch over me.
> Today, please assist me in my song.
> If you do not recognize this place,
> it is the eight mountains of the upper north,
> the māra castle called Sharu Namdzong.
> If you do not recognize me,
> am I not the one told of in a story?
> The one with dark, willowy hair,
> as though led by the five colors.
> Each hair, a ḍākinī;
> each ḍākinī, a vermillion red.
> Here is the wondrous garland of descriptors:
> My body is a white bamboo shoot
> straight as a beam of sunlight,
> my face is a white conch moon
> bright as snow struck by the rising sun,

my thirty[22] white teeth
are like a garland of pearly conch shells,
and my two eyes
are like a pair of morning stars.
I am emptiness itself, like no other—
beautiful, with a dancer's sway, *shik sé*,
aware of the sound of a single footstep, *nyil lé*,
melodious, the sound of my voice, *shik sé*,
a beautiful, confident maiden, *yer sé*.
From today on, demon king,
you will be my husband.
A man's mind in harmony with a woman's,
her mind is in harmony with his,
and food and drink in harmony with it all—
these three are our auspicious connection.
As for you, King Lutsen,
I, the famed Meza, am your companion.
Who could be happier than you?
Here are the key points of my song:
An excellent prophecy has come down
to you, the unrivaled lord.
But even though you are happy,
you are still ailing.
If it happens that you die,
what should I do?
Just as in the examples:

If the constellations in the far reaches of space
were bathed in sunlight,
how could the light of their stars shine out?
If the oceans were offered up to the heavens,
how could the fish and water mammals find comfort?

Don't you think it must be like that, Lutsen?
That you have no obstacles
and I, no suffering—
may there be these two excellent benefits.
Your life-ruler

and your life-force talisman—
tell me where they are. Do not keep it secret.
Your black life-force stone
and your golden spirit-protector fish—
where are they kept? Where have you put them?
How can they protect you if they are stored away?
Do not be reluctant; tell me.

The speech of a superior man is like the sun,
not stained by the impurities of the world it illuminates.
The words of a middling man are like the winds,
no one knows which way they will blow.
The chatter of an inferior man is dishonest,
a mere three words can deceive.

That kind of talk is unwarranted;
I will not listen.
If you have understood, Lutsen, keep this in mind.

Meza sang, but Lutsen was too drunk to understand what she had said and so intoxicated with her voice that he insulted her by brazenly propositioning her. Meza rebuked him, so he went on, "Well, maybe tomorrow or the day after will give us cause for happiness. However, I have never found a single person worthy of knowing the location of my life force. If I did and word got out, my elemental forces would decline and I would be beset with the greatest of obstacles. Yet, today, Meza, I cannot deprive you of an answer." Lutsen's lips warbled as he sang.

Sing "Ala thala thala."
"Thala" begins.
The song unfolds in three parts.
Today, I call to the deity.
From the supreme dwelling place of the celestial divine castle,
Trarab Wangchuk, king of māras, watch over me
and guide the song of this warrior.
If you do not recognize this place,
it is the eight mountain ranges of the upper north,
and this is the cozy chamber Dekyi Barma.
As for explaining my background,

I am the demon māra butcher,
indistinguishable from the lord of death.
Meza, my closest relatives
are in the upper valley of Draksum, the three crags—
my two brothers Chakchung and Mukchung[23]—
regretfully, it had been a long time since I have seen them.
As for explaining the location of my life-force talisman,
high on my forehead,
within a blazing gem of merit
is a golden mirror that swirls with light.
When I first lie down to sleep,
I make a snoring sound *haré huré*,
grind my teeth with the sound of popping wheat *cha cha*,
and snort loudly like a wild yak *ngar ngar*.
But I am not really asleep—
the life-taking breath-thieves are all around me,
920,000 lords of life,
the outer, inner, and middle life-takers
maneuvering for food and drink.
From within the mirror in the center of my forehead,
the white light of merit shines forth.
The many white and black poisonous snakes on my head,
one after another, uncoil,
coming, hungry for food and thirsting for water.
They drink the leftover human blood in my mouth,
every last drop.
They eat the human flesh left in my mouth, even that between
    my teeth,
every last morsel.
The black life-force stone—
although I have never before thought to tell anyone,
today I have no choice but to tell you.
For one, you have been insistent in asking me,
second, your intentions are good,
third, your great smile,
and fourth, your white snow mind, attracted to me—
these four are our excellent connection.
My wife Meza,

here within this maṇḍala of our existence
have come the lord of death Shinjé Marpo,
filling all of space and stirring up the earth,
and the Lord of Life Pehar[24]
as an emanation of the black and white teurang.
Neither the Lord of Life Pehar
nor the *jungpo* demon lord, that ill-willed Joru,
can learn these secrets.
That black life-force stone
is hidden beneath my toenails.
Were a great evil enemy to come,
this stone would travel speedily through my channels and
     winds
and swim like a fish through my bloodstream, *khyuk khyuk*.
When it reaches the top of my forehead,
it appears as a coal-black, flat-headed tadpole
with the fixed eyeballs of a golden-eyed fish.
It stares out from its inky-black head, *hrik hrik*,
and I finally fall asleep.
If I do not lose this black life force,
no one will ever be able to defeat me.
I will obtain the iron life force
and you will accomplish your goals.
When those two things come to be and come together,
that will create happiness in our lifetimes
and prosperity for your homeland, Ling Akyi Darthang
     Tramo.
I will provide every need—
gold, silver, turquoise,
gems of the five kinds of coral—
whatever is needed, I will give.
Won't that be good, dear Meza?
Queen, keep this in mind.

Thus Lutsen sang, and a smile spread across Meza's face, as she now understood clearly how the life-stone worked and where it was kept. While she was devising a plan to tell Gesar early the next morning, she realized that their task was nearly done, that the teachings of the divine Śākyamuni and the benefit of all beings were at hand. The wisdom minds of the lha, lu, and nyen were in accord, and she understood them to say, "Lutsen came to slaughter humans—an ocean of blood has accumulated and consciousnesses swirl like a blizzard, but the māra country is now about to experience this excellent tendrel." In the meantime, Meza had been thinking that she must trick Lutsen, and said, "Demon, king of māras, what is on your mind? Although today the mo divination was excellent, perhaps things would be even better if we knew that the spirit sheep was well. You should go look for it." Lutsen agreed that was a good idea and set off to look for it. As soon as he was gone, Meza went to find Gesar. "Gesar, come quickly, do not tarry. Just now, the demon has gone to get the five meats, fresh meats.[25] We must find a way to destroy him." And Meza sang this song to Gesar.

> OM MAṆI PADME HŪṂ
> Sing "Ala thala thala."
> "Thala" begins.
> Dharmakāya, saṃbhogakāya, nirmāṇakāya,
> three divine ones bless me and watch over me.
> If you do not recognize this place,
> it is Takmo Lebchen (Great Flat Tigress Plain) of the north.
> If you do not recognize me,
> I am your wife,
> sent here to the upper north.
> I was sent here for a purpose,
> not for my years here to have been meaningless.
> An arrow that does not tame the enemy,
> an arrow that misses its mark, is of no use.
> It is just like these examples:
> Famed in the azure firmament
> are the sun, moon, and stars.
> Famed on the solid earth
> is Mount Kailash.
> Famed in the upper north lands
> it is I,
> the ḍākinī who protects the ethos of Tibet,
> a wife of yours, Gesar.
> Does this not make you happy?
> The māra king Lutsen
> I engaged with a deceitful smile

and confused with my clever strategy,
wheedling out the hidden whereabouts of his life-support
    talisman.
I questioned him precisely, and here is his answer:
When he first lies down in bed,
he snores, *haré huré,*
and grinds his teeth with a cracking sound, *cha cha,*
not yet fully asleep.
Then, while he falls peacefully to sleep,
the poisonous snakes on his head
writhe and uncoil, one by one—
poisonous snakes, black and white, all slithering.
The blood in his mouth and the flesh stuck between his
    teeth—
those poisonous snakes devour it all.
When he is first asleep,
the black māra life-force stone
is underneath his toenails, he said.
But the stone does not stay put;
rather, like blood circulating through his veins,
it travels throughout his body.
Sometimes it is in his fingertips,
sometimes in the middle of his tongue,
and at other times it swirls in the chambers of his heart
or on top of his head.
Its location was never certain, a mere probability.
Next, when he is sound asleep,
it rests within the spot of merit high in his forehead,
a spot that is in the form of a precious golden mirror,
appearing like an inky-black, flat-headed tadpole
and staring out like a golden-eyed fish,
a single form, clear in the mirror.
He said that the pitch-black color is his soul
and the yellow of the piercing eyes is his life force.
The time to shoot the arrow at his skull is
in the Tiger year[26]
on the twenty-ninth day of the middle month
when astrologically the chart of nines comes together.

It is time to tame the enemy.
Tonight as the sun is setting,
inside the great castle Chakri Tsegu
you must ready your arrow.
Then, there within its walls,
where the sun's last rays are streaming in
is where you should sit
and aim the arrow
with Lutsen's forehead the target.
There will be two[27] copper pots brimming with milk.
I will dig a pit beneath them
and mound up some one hundred cinnamon trees on the
      right
and one hundred animal carcasses on the left.
Within that iron castle,
I will strew many dried peas.
Sengchen Gesar Rinpoche,
tonight, be attentive, do not get sidetracked
for, if you miss, it will be a mistake for all time.
Tonight, if you lose, all will be lost.
Still, consider what you are doing.
These are merely my ideas.
What do you think, noble being?
If you have any instructions, let me know.

Thus Meza sang, and Gesar said, "Your plan is good. You have been here in the māra country for the past nine years for the benefit of sentient beings oppressed by suffering, and you must be quite tired. We must quickly prepare an exorcism ritual to tame the northern māra and invite the lha, lu, and nyen to help. Go now to the invisible domed tent that I pitched around Sharu Namdzong. My dralha siblings Dungkhyung Karpo,[28] Lutrül Öchung, and Thalé Ökar are already there, and I will be sitting at the spot where the sun strikes."

Meza retrieved two large copper kettles from inside the reception hall of a thousand pillars, Kawa Tongden; she filled them with chang and milk. She stealthily dug a hole beneath the pots, on the right she piled a hundred cinnamon trees, on the left a hundred slabs of butter, behind she arranged a hundred slaughtered sheep carcasses, and in front she placed the life-force copper cup filled with liquor. She draped fresh human skin over the back of the throne made of human bone and set out a cushion of exotic animal furs edged in the best black felt. The deity table in front was adorned with fresh blood, so red that it seemed to be bleeding out, and a garland of dried human heads. The skull cups were filled, one with brains and the other with heart blood, and were elegantly arranged on the deity table. She was just finished when Lutsen returned, stomping and crashing such that the whole earth shuddered, *sik sik*, the mountains trembled, *shik shik*, and the valleys echoed with a thundering sound, *ri ri*. Standing in the doorway, he shouted, "Meza, I have returned. You sent me out while you stayed happily inside. I have never been this hungry, thirsty, and tired before. You must quickly run and bring me something to eat and drink!"

Meza rushed over to the demon and said, "King, here you are! I am sorry you are so hungry and thirsty, and you must be very tired, but I am glad the spirit sheep is well." She invited him to sit down and then, with her body lithe and her face with a smile like a flash of lightning, she brought excellent food and drink. The demon was thinking, "Meza seems different. Here I am in the midst of this trouble, and she is just smiling happily. That seems very strange. Maybe she has another man. After all, just as when a spring makes a loud roaring noise, there must be a mighty glacier above it; when a young girl acts so self-confident, there must be something behind it." He turned and sang this song of suspicion to Meza.

> Sing "Ala thala thala."
> "Thala" begins.
> Today, I call to the deity.
> From the supreme celestial dwelling place,
> from the pure land of the nāga serpent demon,
> Wangchuk Chenpo, watch over me.
> Guardian of the teachings of Trarab Nakpo,
> today, kindly assist me.
> If you do not recognize this place,
> it is the imperial Sharu Namdzong;
> actually, it is Chakri Tsegu.
> If you do not recognize me,
> I am the demon king Lutsen.
> My father, the nine-headed cannibal, had three offspring:
> The eldest Chakchung Gyalpo,
> the youngest Mukchung Guru,
> and myself, the middle one Achung.
> The eldest was given the three regions called Lho, Do, Po,

and is the son with power.
The youngest was given three regions, Dang, Khong, Nyön,
and remains as the leader of those three villages.
I, the middle son Achung,
hold these eight mountain ranges of the upper north
and am famed for my power and influence.
The southern continent is mine to gobble up.
Throughout the trichiliocosm
I chew up living beings, *cha cha.*
Even the lord of death Shinjé would retreat if he saw me.
I captured you, Meza,
but since you were so young, you became my tea maker.
I gave you whatever you wanted, as though you were my
     child.
I gave you clothes of precious silk
and tasty and nutritious food.
I clothed you in white silks
and cherished you like a precious jewel.
You, Meza, the one I treasure above all others, will perhaps be
     my ruin.
You don't know good from bad, friend from foe—
ruinous Meza, hiding another man.
Me, this countryman who loves you—you try to gouge out
     my eyeballs,
while, with fluttering eyelids, you welcome in that deceitful
     foreigner.
You talk in riddles,
two-faced as a ḍamaru,
your tongue forked like that of a poisonous snake.
Listen! Isn't this the way it is?

When dark clouds envelop the western skies
while the eastern skies are bathed in light
and black rain falls to the earth—
just so, your good and bad sides rival each other.

You deceive by turning everything inside out,
a crafty woman full of lies and duplicity—

all the signs suggest you have created a great charade.
Nothing about you is the same—
the way you look at me,
the way you flash your smile,
the expression on your face,
the way you color your face,
the way you carry your beautiful body—
well versed in all five.
Who is your important guest?
Do not hide the truth; tell me honestly.
Meza, keep this in mind.
If you have not understood, I cannot repeat my song.

Thus Lutsen sang, and Meza retorted, "There is no reason for you to talk like that nor for me to listen when you do. One must trust the one to whom they are attached, and since I am your wife, you should trust what I say. A married couple is joined; they have a natural bond, believing and trusting in each other." She sweetened her tone and continued, "After all, I welcomed you with my smile and held you in my arms when you returned. When you finish your food and drink, we can have all the delights that you desire." Pleased, Lutsen gave Meza a sweet kiss, and hand in hand they went into the courtyard of Kawa Tongden and curled up on a fine silk-cushioned seat. Meza had prepared an abundant feast of tea, chang, meat, cheese, and fruit and had brought year-old aged brown chang. The demon was already a bit drunk, and there on the deity table was the skull filled with human blood, brains, and strong liquor. He gulped it all down noisily. Now completely drunk, without even a shudder he fell soundly asleep as the deity Brahmā, the Nyenchen Khula, and the nāga Tsungna repeatedly bestowed upon him the empowerment of nine delusional obscurations, and he fell even more deeply into oblivion. In three hours' time, he woke to see Meza sitting there with a ball of fine, red silk thread and some black yarn and heard her saying, "Relax, go back to sleep. I am watching over you." As darkness fell, Lutsen was struck with severe pains in his chest and lesser pains in his head, and then a knifelike pain that shot up from the base of his toenails. He tried to stand, but he was stuporous and in so much pain that he collapsed, trembling and jerking.

CHAPTER EIGHTEEN

Gesar finally tames the demon
and the māra subjects take refuge in him.
But spurred by her doubts, Meza brings Gesar the water
    of forgetfulness
and, clouded by delusion, he remains in the māra land.

THAT EVENING, LIKE A BOLT OF LIGHTNING, Manéné had arrived at the māra castle Shari Namdzong from her realm in the upper heavens. She said, "Gesar, noble being, listen attentively. The time has come to tame the demon. Quickly shoot the arrow; do not miss striking Lutsen's forehead." As Gesar pulled out the best of his ninety-nine arrows, Shaza Trakthung, from his quiver, he made a soft rustling sound with its feathers, and Lutsen startled awake.[1] Thinking that Meza was hiding someone, he shouted, "What was that? I heard the sound of arrow feathers." Meza answered, "Lutsen, are you frightened? There are no arrows; it was only the sound of my ball of black woolen thread." He said, "That is strange, it sounded just like it came from arrow feathers," and he fell back into a drunken sleep.

Gesar had pulled out a second arrow, Angki Lingmar (Red-Flagged), but just as he was nocking it into the bowstring, it struck his armor, making a twanging sound, and again Lutsen awoke. "Now, I heard the sound of a bowstring being pulled taut—what enemy is here?" he said, as once more he tried to stand. Meza said, "I don't know what bowstring you mean; I was thirsty and wanted some chang, and as I ladled it into a copper cup, I touched it slightly to the copper and it reverberated making a sound just like the twang of a bowstring." Lutsen thought this seemed like a made-up story, but as he saw no enemy, he fell back asleep. Now, two poisonous snakes, black and white, encircled Lutsen's head, writhing and twisting, and thirstily sucking the blood filling his mouth and devouring the morsels of dead meat from between his teeth. In the center of his forehead was a golden mirror swirling with light. On its surface, a black tadpole and a golden fish playfully frolicked. Frenzied, Meza silently raised her eyebrows at Gesar as if to say, "If you do not hurry and shoot that arrow, there is a danger that the black life-force stone will be lost." And when Gesar did not immediately loose an arrow, she mimed readying an arrow of her own. But Gesar was busy, with his mouth inside his collar silently praying that his arrow would reach its target.

> First, I offer in order to summon the deities,
> second, I offer for the vanquishing of the northern māra,
> and third, I offer for the accomplishment of the virtuous
>   Dharma.
> These three offerings are my verses of homage.
> Now, I offer to Śākyamuni Buddha.
> I offer to the victorious ones with their consorts. May they
>   watch over me.
> I offer to the excellent buddhas of the three times. May they
>   watch over me.
> I offer to the four orders of the great gatekeeper kings of the
>   four directions. May they watch over me.
> I offer to the five families of the victorious ones. May they
>   watch over me.
> I offer to the six families of protectors. May they watch over
>   me.
> I offer to the seven supreme buddhas. May they watch over
>   me.
> I offer to the eight-petaled lotus. Please watch over me.
> I offer to the nine-spoked wheel. Please watch over me.
> As I make these offerings, may the deities assist me.
> May they lead the arrow point of this noble being
> that it may pierce the demon's skull.
> May this māra land turn to the Dharma.
> This is my heartfelt, auspicious aspiration prayer.

Thus he spoke, and the lord of Ling, Gesar, shot his arrow Shaza Trakthung, and thunderously, it struck the very center of the demon's forehead. The tadpole and the golden fish, that life-force black stone of the māra Lutsen, along with his brains and blood, spattered everywhere. He fell to the ground, unconscious.

After a while, Lutsen had recovered somewhat and was groping around, reaching for Meza. He reached out his right hand but picked up only a mass of thorny trees that he thought must be that nasty Joru, the one who had shot the arrow. He shoved the mass in his mouth, smacking his lips as he consumed it. He extended his left hand and picked up slabs of butter. He imagined this was Meza and bolted up but slipped on the dried peas and lost his footing. Again, he tried to stand, but now he slipped on the butter and was unable to get up. At that very moment, Gesar shot the red-bannered arrow Angki Lingmar. It struck Lutsen's skull, and he collapsed on the ground but somehow survived and gradually regained consciousness. He still had the butter in his left hand that he thought was Meza, and as he put it in his mouth he was suddenly struck with the depth of his isolation and lack of support. He had no one there he could rely on, nor did he know the enemy's whereabouts. It seemed best that he leave at once for the valley of his brothers. Thus, he strode through wide valleys and dashed across narrow valleys, making his way through the Phenpo Valley toward Kongpo Draksum.

However, Gesar had seen precisely where the demon had fallen and knew that the life-force stone would be right there, and he carefully picked it up. He jumped on his steed Kyang Gö and, like a bird in flight, started out after Lutsen. With provisions for the journey, Meza mounted her horse Kyaka Dingshé[2] and followed Gesar. In the meantime, Lutsen had arrived at the upper slope of Phenpo, tired and hungry. As he was looking around for Gowa Kyareng (Antelope Dawn), a secluded spot where he could rest, he saw Gesar approaching rapidly, and he ran on without looking back.

Seeing that the demon was about to escape, Gesar shot his slingshot, pulverizing a large rocky crag. When the thick cloud of dust had cleared away, Lutsen had disappeared without a trace and by noon the following day he had arrived, exhausted, high in the valley of Kongpo Draksum. The two ruddy rākṣasī gatekeepers who guarded the iron gate and the copper gate invited Lutsen in and offered tea and food and he was able to relax a bit, but knowing that Gesar could not be far behind, he thought that nothing good could come of staying there for long. Lutsen dammed one of the lakes of Kongpo Draksum, flooding the valley, and he ascended to the base of the mountain Dongtsen Tsengö Barwa (Blazing Fierce-Faced Tsen). There, he hid in a rock crevice. By that time, Gesar and his horse had arrived at the gates, but the two rākṣasī gatekeepers were blocking his path. Enraged, Gesar swung his sword once, killing them both. Climbing higher, he saw the deluge below and through his magical powers, emptied the floodwaters. On the opposite shore of the lake he saw Manéné, who was sitting under a sandalwood tree boiling tea. When he reached the other side of the lake, Manéné greeted him and said, "You and your horse must both be very tired! Sit and rest, and I will bring some amṛta." And she offered instruction as well as tea.

With Manéné's words fresh in his mind, Gesar placed a single divine stone inside his slingshot Urtra Ringma (Long Striped) and spun it three times around his head, releasing the stone with a reverberation loud enough to fill all of space. A pile of dust was all that remained of the mountain Tsengö Barwa. Lutsen, frightened and confused, had jumped into the lake. Gesar was delighted with this turn of events, thinking that he could capture Lutsen as easily as a fisherman hooks a fish. He spun around on his steed Kyang Gö and came to a halt at the edge of the lake. There, the demoness guardians Traktshoma (Blood Lake Mother) and Otshoma (Milk Lake Mother) blocked his path and said, "You, man and horse—so much arrogant commotion, such a terrifying, wrathful face, grimacing, glaring—what is so important? Why have you come to this place?" Gesar unsheathed his sword, demanding, "This is a road for travelers, there is no reason to block the path. Are you bandits or kidnappers? What so-called brave men are you protecting? Listen, let's not be so hostile. This place is said to be Lutsen's home, the fatherland of that cannibal demon, where no one is free to travel—that is what I had always heard— but as soon as I arrived, that renowned demon Lutsen fled. Did you know that? Those who block the path in daylight wish their lives to be dispatched by a sword blade. Isn't that right?" At Gesar's words, the guardians Traktshoma and Otshoma disingenuously knelt down on that flat roasting pan of land and held their thumbs up begging, bowing their heads in fright. They protested, "We did not realize it was you, Gesar. Please forgive us, and please spare our lives." With that, they offered a song in unison.

> Sing "Ala thala thala."
> "Thala" begins.
> The song unfolds in three parts.
> Today, we call to the deity.
> From the immeasurable celestial heavens,
>   divine Garab Khulha Wangchuk, watch over us.
> Do not waver, please join with us.
> If you do not recognize us,
>   we are Traktshoma and Otshoma,
>   nieces of Garab Wangchuk
>   and sisters of the māra Lutsen.

If you do not recognize this place,
it is the foothills below Draksum.
This is the land of Chakchung and Mukchung,
the fatherland of the cannibal demons,
and the homeland of Lutsen Gyalpo.
It was not a good idea to have come here.
The lake here is
Cannibal Red Lake of Draksum.
The one in control of this lake is the evil nāga demon.
Foreigners are not welcome to circumambulate the lake;
disturbing this lake is not permitted.
We two sisters
entrusted to be guardians of the lake
have no authority to let foreigners pass.
We had no choice but to block your path.
Today, we have unwittingly accumulated negative karma.
King Sengchen, please forgive us,
as today we request refuge.
Please spare our lives.
Warriors of great courage
do not kill helpless women;
if they did, that would be truly evil.
According to the traditional stories of old,
if you kill the northern black crow,
it is said that you will accumulate negative karma,
as neither its flesh nor feathers are of any use.
If you kill these maidens, where is the good in that?
It is no different than killing the crow.
If you kill the yellow-eyed owl in its rocky crevice,
you will accumulate negative karma
as neither its flesh nor feathers are of any use.
There is no reason to kill these maidens;
it is no different than killing the owl.
Don't you think so?
What we are asking of you
is to spare our lives,
and we will do whatever you command.
Precious Sengchen,

it is good that you have come
and that we have had the chance to meet you.
But in this māra land of darkness,
to come alone is fraught with difficulty.
Just as, at dusk, when darkness gathers over the land,
there is no path for the sun to rise.
Take this to heart, noble being.

Thus they sang, and Gesar replied, "I heard your pleasant words and your request is admirable, but your trust remains with the evil outlook of the māras. You have spoken sweet words of falsehood and deception, but you have no talent for lying and your words are unconvincing. Professing to take me as an object of refuge, the hypocrisy of your words is clear: "In the morning I am a butcher who does not spare the life of the hateful enemy, and in the evening I am a guiding lama. Only those whose request for refuge is more than mere lip service have true merit. I am the yoke upon the māra demon, the universal warrior of Jambudvīpa." With that, he threw the lasso of emptiness and bound both demonesses. He tied them to a tree like guard dogs, offering the flesh and blood of the two lake-guardian women to the vultures and leading their consciousnesses to the pure land. Now free to pass, Gesar rode to the edge of the lake and, looking around, saw that Lutsen had transformed himself into a golden-eyed fish. Quickly following suit, Gesar became a golden fish and swam after him. Just as Lutsen was backed against the shore, he transformed into a pigeon and flew off. Gesar turned into a falcon and went after him and nearly had him in his talons when a windstorm arose and the pigeon vanished from sight.

Gesar had no idea where Lutsen had gone and was heading back on his steed toward the lake when he came across a shepherd. When Gesar inquired whether he had seen anything, the shepherd answered, "All I saw was a strange-looking man ride by on a hornless dzo." Gesar thanked him and headed in the direction that the shepherd had indicated. There in the far distance beyond the lake, he saw Lutsen nearing the summit of a mountain pass. Quickly, Gesar cocked and shot his arrow and destroyed half of the mountain. Ashes rained down, only to be blown away by the wind and when the dust settled, again Lutsen was nowhere to be seen. His ideas spent, Gesar sat down on a large boulder to rest and, exhausted and hungry, promptly fell asleep. Padmasambhava intuited all this and immediately came to Gesar, saying, "Noble being, this is no time for sleep. If you rest now, how will anything good result? Lutsen may have a bit of a flesh wound, but his life force is unharmed and at this very moment he is running toward the Lotus Gate." Gesar leapt on his horse and flew off in pursuit.

Looking down from the Lotus Gate, Lutsen saw Gesar closing in, and seeing no escape, he jumped into Lotus Lake. Gesar and his horse transformed into otters and went in after him. Finally, they caught Lutsen by the heels and threw him like a fish onto dry land. Gesar visualized himself as dense as Mount Meru and knelt down as though he were meditating, crushing the demon's chest. The old māra Lutsen let out a cry of anguish, begging for his life. "I did not realize you were a genuine buddha. I did not realize the meaning of your words as precious nectar. I will go for refuge and confess to you. But if you are going to kill me, first hear my song." Those were Lutsen's words, but he was silently reciting the māra iron mantra as he sang this song of petition.

> Sing "Ala thala thala."
> "Thala" begins.
> From the immeasurable divine celestial palace,
> māra Garab Wangchuk, watch over me.
> Do not waver, please listen to my song.
> If you do not recognize this place,
> it is Cannibal Red Lake of Draksum.
> If you do not recognize me,
> in my previous life
> I was born as Trarab Nakpo,
> the one who turned the toothed weapon-wheel.
> The evil weapons of assassination
> were mine alone.
> I am the son of Matram Rudra
> and the enemy of Padmasambhava.
> Eventually, I was born in the northern plains
> on the outskirts of the Dri Valley
> as one of three evil scorpion brothers.
> We three karmically saddled brothers
> were stuck in the farmlands of the Dri Chu (Yangtse River)
>   valley for nine years.
> One day, after those many years had passed,
> Vajrapāṇi gave me transference,
> and before three years had passed in the god realm,
> I was again sent to the human realm,
> where, here in the eight mountain ranges of the upper north,
> I took rebirth in the form of a nine-headed marmot.

I am the nephew of the serpent-demon cannibal,
the destined son of Trarab Nakpo
known as the māra king Lutsen.
I am the enemy of the teachings of Śākyamuni,
the personal enemy of the Buddhadharma,
the general enemy of Jambudvīpa,
and the leader of the evil māras.
I am the one who propagates the evil doctrine,
the one who turns the toothed weapon-wheel
and has descended to slaughter humans.
In this kingdom of Southern Ling,
I was unrivaled.
Unfortunately, today I have been defeated
and have no choice but to request refuge in you.
Noble being Gesar,
in the forenoon you are known as a butcher,
and in the evening, as a lama.
Listen, I have a few things to tell you.
Kongpo, Nyangpo, and Dakpo, the three regions,
are half of Jambudvīpa;
today I offer them to you
in exchange for sparing my life.
The thirteen myriarchies of the north,
from down in Drimo Rochen
up to the snow gate of Ladakh
and over to the kingdom of Lhündrub Gyalkhak,
along with countless horses, yak, sheep, cows, and goats—
I offer all these to you, Sengchen,
in exchange for your protection.
The māra districts of Angön
with its farms and forests,
the māra districts of the divine mountain Artsa,
all the inhabitants of the māra district of Kardrub,
and the māra districts of Draksum Valley—
I offer to you, noble being,
in exchange for your protection.
A hundred sheep of the slate plain Yama Thang,

a hundred goats of the longevity plain Tsema Thang,
a hundred dri of the dri plain Drima Thang,
a hundred dzo of the lotus plain Pema Thang,
and a hundred horses of the cave plain Phukmo Thang—
these five types of herd animals I offer
in exchange for your protection.
Inside the māra castle Shomo Gutsek
is precious gold, the paternal treasure,
exquisite silver, the maternal treasure,
the Mukpo clan's gardens of red coral,
necklaces of blue turquoise,
and lattices of variegated agate—
these jewels I offer
in exchange for your protection.
Inside Meza's castle
there are highly regarded riches.
Cat's-eye jewels,
deep blue sapphire,
adamantine diamonds,
indigo lapis,
variously hued agates,
the jeweled lasso of Avalokiteśvara,
and the jewel that fulfills all wishes—
the treasure of these precious jewels
I offer to you, noble being,
in exchange for your protection.
I, this māra demon Lutsen,
have been happy to be a butcher in this lifetime
and eager to accumulate negative karma.
I did not meditate on the guru
nor accumulate even a single OṂ MAṆI mantra.
Today, I confess this to you, Gesar,
and devote myself to you.
This I promise, like words carved in stone,
like a tightly knotted scarf.
Please protect me with your compassion.
Please keep this in your heart.

All the while reciting black magic under his breath, Lutsen finished his song just as Manéné came from the immeasurable palace of the sky, bareback on a lion. A turquoise dragon followed behind her. In her right hand was a longevity vase and with her left she scattered consecrated substances, *tha ra ra*. She sang a dohā, *si lé lé*, as she came up to Gesar and said, "Divine Prince, do not be the fool. The māra demon has a sweet mouth, but all this time he has been accumulating the māra iron life-force mantra. Ignore what he says: the mouth you see speaks lovely platitudes with seeming sincerity, while inwardly he has eight mouths that gather power from his evil mantra. Do not hesitate to pierce him with your sword." Taking her words to heart, Gesar stabbed Lutsen in the armpit and groin. The dralha Nyentak Marpo forcefully thrust his lance, Khamsum Zilnön, into the heart of the demon, yet even then the old māra did not die. In fact, he was about to stand back up when Gesar threatened Lutsen's forehead with his arrow and said, "Recall that in the morning I am a butcher and in the evening the lama who guides one's consciousness. If you want to request refuge, now is the time. You must be sincere, for now you are at a threshold; it is up to you whether your life force continues or you are cast down to the depths of the eighteen hell realms. Until now, you, old man, have stood on the side of the nonhuman demonic forces, slaughtering humans and cherishing your own precious life as though it were a silk-wrapped jewel, while all the while scattering human lives like ashes. You have guarded your own country like gold dust while you scarfed up the human world, serving only to accumulate negative karma."

Lutsen lamented, "Ling lord, you are a genuine buddha—only just today did I realize that—and you recognized that I was reciting black magic while only pretending to request refuge. Until today, I did not know that in the morning you are a butcher who kills and in the afternoon a lama who leads consciousness. I had heard of neither the pure realms nor the eighteen hell realms. If today is the day I am to die, I have one request: although in this lifetime I was born a man, I have never known a woman's body. I ask therefore that you transfer my consciousness to a place where I can look upon a female form with conch-white bracelets tinkling, *lhem lhem*." Gesar, wearing a dharmakāya meditation belt, performed phowa, saying, "I am Norbu Dradül, the one who kills enemies and demons and the jewel who guides humans. You with your evil deeds are the worst of the worst, an assassin surrounded by a wheel of blood. For the welfare of the world, my sword comes down upon you. Today, in accord with your request, I will place your body deep in the azure firmament, at the edge of three sparkling[3] constellations, *go*, *lak*, and *gyal*.[4] I will raise your consciousness there, where you will be surrounded by the sound of women's bracelets and be aware of them uninterruptedly, day and night. But for you, a sinful human flesh-eater, there is no chance of going to the pure realm." Then, at that moment, a tent of rainbow light and a retinue of one hundred thousand ḍākinīs appeared surrounding Manéné as she advised Gesar how to sever the body of the demon and bury the pieces in a deep pit.

Sing "Ala thala thala."
"Thala" begins.
The song unfolds in three parts.
Today, I call to the divine ones.
I take refuge in the Buddha, the Dharma, and the Saṅgha.
Grant you blessings and look upon me with compassion.
From the pure realm of Buddha Amoghasiddhi,
great divine Mother Prajñāpāramitā,
through the rainbow path of radiant dharmakāya,
today please assist me.
If you do not recognize this place,
it is the edge of the spirit Red Cannibal Lake, Sintsho Marpo.
If you do not recognize me,
I am Manéné Namné Karmo,
your auntie,
the one who advises you when you are confused,
the one who calls to you when you do not understand.
If you do not recognize this song,
it is Manéné's pure dohā.
This year you have come to the māra valley in the north
to shoot an arrow into Lutsen's forehead
and transfer his consciousness to go, lak, and gyal.
Your actions are praised by all.
Today, my sweet little one,
you are sent to cut his corpse into pieces.
His head, arms, and legs
drop into the swampy depths of the blood lake Traktsho.
Fly banners on the various trees.
Erect a meditation cave dedicated to Tārā practice.
Bury Lutsen's empty torso beneath the iconic nāga castle.
His lungs, liver, and guts,
along with the impure substances, bury at the intersection of
    three roads
    beneath the great cannibal rock

in a sack cinched tight with a poisonous black snake[5]
and a golden seal yoked around the bag.
As for the darkest heart of this evil māra—
at the edge of Mipak Thangchen (Great Plain of Human
    Skin) in the north,
dig a pit nine handspans deep
and place the māra heart in the pit,
sealing the opening with a boulder
and building a nine-storied stupa to rise above it.
Proclaim this strong samaya command:
"For as long as this world remains, this māra king
cannot arise!" Swear this, Gesar.
To tame the māras is the excellent tendrel.
I am satisfied
that this will bring an excellent future to Tibet
by establishing the teachings of Śākyamuni.
As the teachings of the māras subside
and the māra lands turn to the Dharma,
you will fulfill your purpose.
Listen, precious Gesar,
do not stay here; return quickly to Ling
and the benefit of beings and auspicious circumstances will
    flourish.[6]
But if you tarry, there will be obstacles.
Three years will pass until we meet again; be well until then.
If you have understood, keep this in mind, noble being.
If not, there is no point to repeating my song.

The last notes of her song faded, and Manéné vanished like a rainbow. Gesar set out to follow her instructions, and, accordingly, he separated the demon's head, arms, and legs from his lungs, liver, and guts, and from his māra heart. He dug a pit nine handspans deep and buried the heart in it. On top of that he built a stupa and sealed it with a precious golden seal, saying, "It is decreed that you remain in this pit until the grains of sand on the riverbanks become grain and the boulders of this marshy meadow become yaks."

In the meantime, Meza had collected spring water from Dara Khagu (Nine Water Silks) and cleansed her body with that as well as with divine ablution water. She met up with Gesar by the time she reached the dri plain Drima Thang, and

together they headed toward Mipak Thangchen (Plain of Human Skin) where she
sang this song.

> Sing "Ala thala thala."
> "Thala" begins.
> The song unfolds in three parts.
> May the three divine ones look upon me and grant their
>   blessings.
> From the Pure Land Arrayed in Turquoise Petals,
> White Tārā Goddess of Life,
> who protects from danger,
> may you shelter me from all fears.
> Please pacify all obstacles to longevity
> and bestow the inner siddhis.
> In particular, kindly assist me,
> do not be meager in your blessings.
> If you do not recognize this place,
> it is Mipak Thangchen.
> If you do not recognize me,
> I am Trishok Meza Bumdrön of the north,
> the one with the wisdom and means to naturally remove all
>   darkness,
> with intelligence as open as a sky-door.
> Gesar, please watch over me.
> I venerate you as a divine one upon the crown of my head.
> I meditate upon you as a divine one in the center of my
>   virtuous heart.
> Day and night, I supplicate your blessings.
> I have prayed to meet you again
> and hoped for the liberation of the māra Lutsen.
> Just as in the stories of old:
> The golden-brown drong roams the alpine meadows
> cutting a path through crags and slate and grassy hills,
> developing its muscled body
> and fearsome horns.
> The cuckoo bird of Mön
> sings with six melodies famed throughout Jambudvīpa,
> and this year the melodious tones reverberate in the north

to the delight of those who live here.
Here in these dark māra lands,
the sun is radiant.
My experience of these past nine years
has culminated today—
the planets and stars are aligned,
the tendrel to bring down Lutsen is excellent,
the māra districts will turn to the Dharma,
and the citizens will benefit.
Face to face, we have met,
and now I know happiness.
Sengchen Lama from the east, remain here;
the important matters of Jambudvīpa, you can keep in your
    heart,
cast down the enemies and demons
so that the six classes of beings may experience happiness.
In the chamber Dekyi Barma
we will celebrate our happy reunion,
singing and dancing,
and dwelling in the mind of bliss and happiness.
After the māra districts embrace the Dharma,
will you stay here with us?
If not,
then how could I remain here?
Sengchen, what do you think?
Please, speak openly.
If there is a fault in this song, the blame is mine.
If there is any confusion in my words, the fault is mine.

Thus she sang, and for the moment Gesar said nothing and, while he was wondering how to answer her, the māra minister Ruhri Pawo (Solid Boned Warrior) and the malicious Jana Samdrub (Rainbow Wish Accomplisher), the principal māra minister, came to surrender to Gesar, offering up their incalculable personal wealth. They set off with the ministers, and just as Meza had hoped, they headed for Chakri Tsegu.

The next day, after Gesar and Meza had arrived at Chakri Tsegu, Meza offered tea, liquor, and milk and prepared an elegant and tasty feast of meat, butter, and sweet cheese, and everyone relaxed. Atak Lhamo and the minister Ching-ngön, along with the great northern warrior Jangtri Drukdrak (Dragon Roar), came to request an audience and pay respects to Gesar. Drukdrak made a special offering of a golden tray piled with a hundred gold coins and five precious gems wrapped in a white khata and sang this song requesting refuge.

> Sing "Ala thala thala."
> "Thala" begins.
> The song unfolds in three parts.
> Today, I call to the deities.
> From the divine celestial realm,
> Sublime Brahmā, care for me.
> Sublime Nyenchen Khulha, look upon me.
> Sublime nāga king Tsukna, watch over me.
> Warrior dralha and werma, kindly assist me.
> If you do not recognize this place,
> it is the eight mountain ranges of the upper north lands.
> This is the māra castle Chakri Tsegu
> and its chamber Dekyi Barma.
> If you do not recognize me,
> I am Jangtri the leader of a hundred of the north.
> I heard long ago tales told of Gesar of Ling,
> who in the morning is a butcher who kills
> and in the evening a lama who guides consciousness.
> Finally, today I hear your voice.
> There is no single all-pervading light
> except the light that illuminates the world,
> the sun in the sky.
> No single mind understands the kingdom
> except one mind that fathoms its full extent,
> the mind of King Gesar.
> Sengchen of Jambudvīpa,
> you have come to our country without shying away from
>   difficulty.
> At the age of fifteen,
> you shot an arrow at Lutsen,
>   intending only that the māra country would turn to the
>   Dharma.
> There is no more enlightened activity than that—

your wish to bring happiness to the māra people.
Within the eighteen northern myriarchies
there are innumerable warlords and armies,
and today I offer them all to you.
Without this khata I could not request
to take refuge in you for this lifetime.
I offer first, one hundred golden coins,
second, a cat's-eye jewel,
and third, a vajra diamond, as well as
a rightward-turning coil of joy
and various jewels.
Today, I offer these to you.
Bless and look upon me with compassion.
I entreat you to guide me.

Thus he sang and from the head of the right-hand row, Meza bolted up, smiling shyly and, with a glint in her eye and a dancing gait, said, "Gesar has put an arrow into Lutsen's forehead—an excellent reason to celebrate for thirteen days." At her words, everyone gathered, sang melodious songs, danced gracefully, and feasted. When the earth was covered with the dark robes of night on the final eve and everyone had left to make their way home, Meza realized that Gesar was planning to leave as well. She thought that she must devise a way for him to forget all about Ling and Sengcham Drukmo, and she swiftly went for advice to the demoness Dümo Naché (Various Attributes), who gave her a bag of amnesia-inducing pills. Meza returned and surreptitiously took Gesar's cup, filling it to the brim with amṛta liquor mixed with the amnesia pills. With a radiant smile and coyly darting eyes, she entered the bedchamber and with the cup raised, offered Gesar a bedtime drink with a song.

Sing "Ala thala thala."
"Thala" begins.
The song unfolds in three parts.
Today, I call to the deities.
May this song be supported by the motherly ḍākinīs.
Omniscient One, please look upon this maiden with
    kindness.
If you do not recognize this place,
it is the castle Chakri Tsegu.
Here, lying in the bed Rinchen Barwé (Precious Blazing),

Gesar, watch over me.
From the highest peak of existence above
down to the lowest of the eighteen hell realms,
you are the greatly famed Tamer of Enemies.
You have reached the age of fifteen—
a boy old enough
to know the happiness and suffering of this land
and to strive for the benefit of beings.
Girls of fifteen
can boil milk and not get it too hot
and are expert at churning milk to reveal white butter.
Here is exactly who I am—
Trishok Meza Bumdrön,
who has wandered these upper north lands
and now is a woman of eighteen,
and your wife.
Listen as I have several things to say.
Sengchen Norbu Dradül, you
must be very weary, but still you have come to the north.
The 360 teurang of the north,
the three gatekeepers of the castle,
the deceitful demoness sisters—
you have conquered them all and bound them by oath.
The famed demon Lutsen—
you have shot an arrow into his forehead and transferred his
    consciousness.
Your deeds are like one hundred suns shining
and are obvious to everyone.
Noble being, your kindness is great;
humans will praise you.
However, today I have this to say:
If you are going and not staying,
who will turn the māra people to the Dharma?
Who will bring happiness to the māras and humans?
Although you shot the arrow into Lutsen's forehead,
how will this accomplish benefit for all beings?
As in the ancient proverbs:

The start of a deed may be excellent,
but if the end brings no result, it has no meaning.
The year starts out with sowing excellent seeds,
but if the soil is barren, there will be no hay.

That is the way it is—don't you think so Gesar?
Consider this carefully.
The essence of this nectar, like wine—
sip it three times and you will have a good night's rest
and tomorrow will be refreshed.
Emptiness is the innate nature of the saṃsāric world.

Thus Meza sang, and she casually offered the liquor to Gesar. He declined, but she cajoled him and finally he gave in, saying, "I will drink this, but no more." Gesar was soon somewhere between sick and drunk, unable to speak, and stumbling around as though he were floating. The next day at dawn everyone returned for a final celebration but found that overnight Gesar had become dull and slack-jawed. When he greeted people, he opened his mouth but no words came out; he merely gestured. Furthermore, he had completely forgotten any plans for the benefit of Ling and its citizenry, and, beyond that, he had no memory of his own parents or of Drukmo. Caught in this state of oblivion, he remained at the māra castle for many years. May there be virtue!

For as long as space endures
and for as long as living beings remain,
until then may I too abide
to dispel the misery of the world.[7]

GENEALOGY

This chart delineates the paternal and maternal (in bold) blood lines relevant to this text.[1]

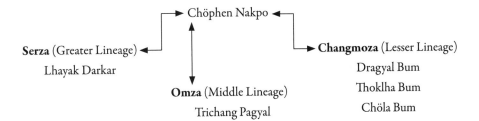

Serza (Greater Lineage)
Lhayak Darkar

Chöphen Nakpo

Omza (Middle Lineage)
Trichang Pagyal

Changmoza (Lesser Lineage)
Dragyal Bum
Thoklha Bum
Chöla Bum

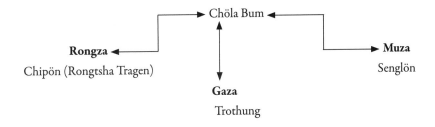

Rongza
Chipön (Rongtsha Tragen)

Chöla Bum

Gaza
Trothung

Muza
Senglön

WARRIOR CHART

Name (Alternate Name)	Lineage/Affiliation	Role
Gyatsha Zhalkar	Lesser Lineage Bumpa clan and son of Senglön and Gyaza Lhakar Drönma	One of the Seven Super Warriors who vies with Shelé Lakring
Nyibum Daryak (Nyima Bumthub)	Greater Lineage Serpa clan	Falcon, one of the Three Ultimate Warriors
Anu Paseng	Middle Lineage Ombu clan	Eagle, one of the Three Ultimate Warriors
Sengtak Adom (Michang Karpo)	Middle Lineage	One of the Seven Super Warriors who vies with Migö Yamé
Denma (Tshazhang Denma Jangtra)	Den clan	A famed archer, one of the Seven Super Warriors who vies with Lugön Tongthub Yamé
Zikphen	Lesser Lineage and son of Trothung	One of the Seven Super Warriors who vies with Tsenkya Bumthub
Gadé (Gadé Chökyong Bernak)	Middle Lineage	One of the Seven Super Warriors who vies with Tongdü Lenmé
Darphen	Lesser Lineage	
Nyatsha Aten	Son of Trothung	One of the Seven Super Warriors
Rinchen Darlu	Lesser Lineage	Wolf, one of the Three Ultimate Warriors
Rongtsha (Rongtsha Marleb; Rongtsha Lhadar)	Lesser Lineage and son of Senglön and Rongza	
Nang-ngu Yutak (Yutak Buyi Metok)	Greater Lineage and son of Chipön and Metok Tashi Tsho	The youngest of the Seven Super Warriors who vies with Shechen Yamé
Dongtsen (Dongtsen Apel)	Lesser Lineage and son of Trothung	
Takphen	Lesser Lineage and son of Trothung	

NOTES

DUDJOM RINPOCHE FOREWORD

1. The four endowments are: Dharma, wealth, desirable objects, and the opportunity for liberation.

TRANSLATORS' INTRODUCTION

1. See Karmay, "The Theoretical Basis of the Tibetan Epic."
2. See Samuel, *Civilized Shamans*, 68.
3. Ju Mipham Rinpoche or Mipham Jampal Gyepé Dorjé (1846–1912) was a nineteenth-century rimé master with a lifelong interest in Gesar. His students compiled the first three volumes of the Gesar epic, which were carved into woodblocks that were printed and translated later on into French by Rolf Stein and more recently into English by Robin Kornman, Sangye Khandro, and Lama Chönam. In addition, Ju Mipham Rinpoche received as mind terma the Gesar supplication, *The Swift Accomplishment of Enlightened Activity through Invocation and Offering* (*Gsol mchod phrin las myur 'grub*).
4. *Bdud gling gyul 'gyed* (Beijing: National Language Press, 2000).
5. Byang bdud klu btsan rgyal po 'dul ba.
6. *Gdug pa spun bdun* (Lhasa: People's Publishing House of Central Tibet, 1993).
7. *Bdud 'dul* (Kansu: People's Publishing House, 1981).
8. *Bdud le'u* (Lhasa: People's Publishing House of Central Tibet, 1991).
9. The term *gods-demons* (*lha 'dre*) does not imply duality but rather the dynamic quality of going back and forth. In wisdom deity practice, one must understand the nature of the wisdom deity, otherwise the deity becomes worldly and thus kingly, demonic, and evil. This is difficult to render in English, because it is a term that implies something inseparable, as in "two sides of a coin." Except for an occasional exception for context, we decided against "gods and demons," "godly demons," "demon-gods," or other terms used in the past and have chosen the more literal, if somewhat awkward, "gods-demons."

CHAPTER ONE

1. We have taken "upper" to refer to the area upriver at the headwaters of the Ma River. In the epic, this is also called "Upper Ling" or "Upper Ma." The Ma River—when it flows from Tibet into China—is then called the Yellow River.

---

2. Throughout the text, the Tibetan often gives directions as "right" and "left," which may correspond to "west" and "east," respectively, but this often depends simply on the position of the viewer with respect to a particular geographical landmark.

3. Takrong (Stag rong) is an area between the Ma (or Yellow) River and the Kho (Nyakchu or Yalong) River, which is a tributary of the Dri (or Yangtze) River.

4. The term *greater* is given to the lineage descended from Serza, the first wife of the ancestral leader of the Mukpo Clan, Chöphen Nakpo; *middle* to the lineage descended from his second wife, Omza; and *lesser* to that from his third wife, Changmoza; but this does not imply that one is better than another. See Kornman et al., *The Epic of Gesar of Ling*, 157.

5. An error in the original text gives the Tibetan *'dzom*, "gather"; it should be *'dzum*, "smiles."

6. The phrase "six smiles of a tiger" refers to the stripes on the sides of a mature tiger. "A tiger in its prime" is a metaphor for a mature and skilled warrior.

7. An error in the original text gives the Tibetan *dzar*, which has no meaning and should be *'dzar*, "tassle" or "tuft."

8. Sengdruk Taktsé (Seng 'brug stag rtse) or Lion Dragon Tiger Peak is Gesar's castle, which is at other times called Sengtruk Taktsé (Seng 'phrug stag rtse) or Lion Cub Tiger Peak.

9. This refers to Tönpa Gyaltsen of Kyalo (Skya lo Ston pa rgyal mtshan), who is a wealthy leader in Ling and the father of Drukmo, Gesar's bride.

10. *Har min hur* translates as "sudden" or "abrupt" and is the name of the tune in which Trothung sings all his songs. Each character in the epic has a signature tune.

11. Traditionally, every song is introduced with these three lines or ones very similar to them, perhaps as in the West we might tap a baton as musicians get ready to play.

12. "Encircling" (*a long*), literally "ring" or "circle," refers here to the idea that the abode of the yidam Hayagrīva is a perfect continuum. This term is sometimes given to a story that is well told, with a beginning and end that come full circle, and also contains the idea of the "circle of life."

13. This a reference to the false prophecy planted by Joru (Gesar's boyhood name) in Trothung's mind, which prompted Trothung to arrange a horse race to compete for the throne of Ling and the hand of the coveted princess Drukmo. Though Trothung imagined himself the winner, Joru won the race, riding his magical horse, and became King Gesar. See Kornman et al., *The Epic of Gesar of Ling*, 317.

14. A reminder to the reader: this is a reference to the meaning of the names Takphen and Zikphen, with *tak* (*stag*) meaning "tiger" and *zik* (*gzig*) meaning "leopard."

15. This refers back to events prior to this volume of the epic. Ralo Tönpa is the leader of the Gok tribe and the one entrusted by Padmasambhava to be the earthly father of the nāga princess Yelga Dzeden, also called Gokza, who would become Gesar's mother. See Kornman et al., *The Epic of Gesar of Ling*, xlvi.

16. The Tibetan term translated here as "life force" (*srog*) is one of three terms referring to life. We have chosen to translate it as "life force," similar to the Western idea of "will to live," while translating *la* (*bla*) as "soul" or "spirit" and *tshe* as "life span" or "longevity."

17. This name is also rendered as Yathö (Ya thod), but, because it more commonly appears as Akhö (A khod), we have left this as the spelling of his name.

18. The Glorious Copper-Colored Mountain (Zangs mdog dpal ri) is the earthly abode of Padmasambhava, Guru Rinpoche, where he resides in his palace, Lotus Light. It is located on the island of Chamara. See glossary of names: "Glorious Copper-Colored Mountain" and "Padmasambhava."

19. The Three Roots are the guru, yidam, and ḍākinī.
20. A tsen (*btsan*) is an evil and powerful nonhuman spirit.
21. The Masang (Ma sang) is an ancestral tribe of Ling, the paternal lineage of Gesar. Masang can also refer to the nine brother nonhuman spirits who were said to inhabit Tibet in times of prehistory.
22. The name given here in the original text as Lion Dragon Tea Palace (Seng 'brug ja mkhar) is more commonly known as Lion Dragon Tiger Peak or Sengdruk Taktsé (Seng 'brug stag rtse). We have chosen to use Sengdruk Taktsé throughout the text.
23. This phrase is literally "cured of the disease of the foot" (*rkang 'bam nad gzhi rtsa nas sangs*), meaning gout, or lymphatic obstruction, i.e., elephantiasis. However, here it is taken as an analogy that he was completely cleansed or pure.
24. Here, "prosperity" (*g.yang*) refers to the idea that something is so respected that it has intrinsic value itself. In the case of a prosperity horse, the horse may not be ridden but just kept and cared for.
25. There is a variation in the original text here: *sa tham* is another spelling of *sa dam*, meaning Sadam, the Jang king.
26. An error in the original text gives the Tibetan *nga*, "I"; it should be *da*, "now."
27. This refers back to skirmishes between Ling and the Gok people. In one of these battles, Chipön's youngest son, Lenpa Chögyal, was killed. Ling warriors went to Gok for revenge but found only an abandoned Gok homeland, save for chancing upon Gokza, the woman destined to become Gesar's mother.
28. An error in the original text gives the Tibetan *rma*, "the land of Ma"; it should be *dma'*, "lower."
29. This name is also rendered as Kyangbu (Kyang bu) but the usual name Kyang Gö (Kyang rgod) is used here.
30. This line in the Tibetan text actually appears six lines up, following "Thala begins." This seems to be the error of the bard or the scribe, and we have moved it down to its usual and more logical place in the song.
31. This name is rendered variously as Sibpa Khölmo Dzong (Srib pa khol mo rdzong), Sipa Khölmo Dzong (Srid pa khol mo rdzong) and, in Kornman et al., as Sipa Khölmo Rokdzong (Srid pa khol mo rog rdzong). Earlier in this text, this same fortress is referred to as Porok Nying Dzong (Pho rog snying rdzong) or Raven Heart Fortress, and, for consistency, we have substituted this more familiar name.
32. This refers poetically to his name, *zik* (*gzig*) or "leopard," and to the rosette pattern of leopard skin.
33. An error in the original text gives the Tibetan *sngag*, "sad"; it should be *stag*, making *stag rong*, "Takrong."
34. The term for liberated (*thar pa*) literally means "free from saṃsāra" but here there is the obvious implication that Nyatsha is threatening Trothung's life.
35. Shenpa (the Hor king Gurkar) and Gyatsha, as well as Chingön and Atak Lhamo, were previously connected in the god realm but have taken rebirth in different ways.
36. This refers to one of the twelve two-hour periods that make up a twenty-four-hour day and is the pig-time (*srod 'khor phag gi dus*), representing approximately 9:00 p.m. to 11:00 p.m., the hours when pigs are fast asleep. See glossary of terms: "time periods."
37. Akhu (A khu) is usually translated as "uncle," but it is also a term of respect used to address a lama or someone who, though not trained as a full lama, can perform pujas, offer prayers, and so forth.

38. An error in the original text gives the Tibetan *byi nag*, "black bird" of Janak; it should be *bya lag* as before, or perhaps it reflects her transformation into a black raven. For consistency, we have kept it as Jalak.

39. The thirteen great mountains are not to be confused with the thirteen hills of Ma. They are thirteen mountains east and south of Ma that protect Yutsé's land and may correspond to the present-day Hengduan Mountains. The thirteen hills of Ma are north and west of these mountains and are in Ma itself.

40. The eight classes (*sde brgyad*) of gods and spirits are often given as: māras, mamos, nāgas, gings, rāhula, tsen, rākṣasas, yakṣas.

41. Samyé Monastery is the first Buddhist monastery built in Tibet, southwest of Lhasa. It was constructed with the inspiration of the Indian master Padmasambhava in the late 770s C.E. during the reign of Trisong Detsen, the second of the three Dharma kings.

42. A damsi (*dam sri*) is a demon obstacle-creator, particularly one that destroys the continuity of samaya vows and morality.

43. Gyalpo (*rgyal po*) are "king spirits" that travel the skies and manifest as anger.

44. The Tibetan for this name varies. Here, it is given as Shelgi Lakring (Shel gyi lag ring) but more often, later in the text, as Shelé Lakring (She le lag ring). We have chosen to use the latter.

45. Rather than Trakrelma (Khrag ral ma), we have chosen to use the English, Bloody Tress, throughout the story, as it is a more powerful image. In Kornman et al., *The Epic of Gesar of Ling*, she is referred to as "Düdmo Trag-gi Relpa [Bloody Single-Tress Demon Woman]."

46. It is odd that Tsenkya Bumthub is singing in this melody, as it is Trothung's signature melody. Perhaps it is the bard's error.

47. Dongrata Genpo (Ldong ra khra ta rgan po) is the most important ancestor of Ling. He is the source of knowledge brought down to the present. The ketaka gem was given to him by the gods-demons and was part of his throne. It had passed down the line of leaders as a national treasure and was then in Trothung's keeping.

48. An error in the original text gives the Tibetan *bsdes*, which has no meaning and should be *bsdebs*, "together."

49. This is a hard and dense cake (*thud*) made from roasted ground dried sweet yams, mixed with dried hard cheese and ghee, often served at fancy occasions such as weddings.

50. Garab Wangchuk (Dga' rab dbang phyug) is the chief māra deity.

51. An error in the original text gives the Tibetan *za mi*, which should be *zi ma*.

52. Mazhi (Ma bzhi) refers to one of the four original clans of Tibet but has also been taken to mean "four-mothered," implying that Trothung had four nursemaids.

53. This refers to Gesar's request to Padmasambhava while he was still in the god realm that he have a human foil, or enemy, when he emanated in the human realm.

CHAPTER TWO

1. The term *am am* (*'am 'am*) has no specific meaning in Tibetan but is meant to convey the quality of the song's disquieting mood.

2. Here the Tibetan text has a second name Jathel Gyüchik (Bya thal rgyud gcig) or Bird Dung Lineage, but, for clarity, we use the name as previously given, Jathül Nakpo (Bya thul nag po) Nakpo.

3. Here, the demoness implies that Gesar is so powerful that he has been able to act without being seen.

4. *bde mchog lha yi pho brang.* This term is used repeatedly, particularly in the volume that tells the saga of the conflict between Hor and Ling. Here, it refers to Gesar's palace, but its inner meaning is that of the sacred land of Cakrasaṃvara or Vajrakīlaya, the sacred space of those who have realization.

5. These are: the Düd king Lutsen, the Hor king Gurkar, the Jang king Sadam, and the Mön king Shingtri. Each of these kings rules a kingdom that Gesar will overcome in this and further volumes of the epic.

6. An error in the original text gives the Tibetan *gtor yang*, "if scattered"; it should be *gter gyang*, "prosperity treasure."

7. See glossary of terms: "vajra tent."

8. An error in the original text gives the Tibetan *ga'u kha sbyor*, which has no clear meaning and should be *ga'u kha sbyar*, "closed spheres" or "closed amulet box."

9. The original text gives the Tibetan for Gyatsha's wife as *ra bza'*, but later (in chapter 8) it is given as *rag bza'*. We the translators take this as indicative of the fact that, as discussed in the introduction, this text was compiled by committee from multiple stories that were not synchronized into a single narrative. This is further evidenced by the inclusion of two dissimilar versions (one here in chapter 2, and the other in chapter 8) of the birth of a son to Gyatsha and his wife. Simply for the flow of the story we have decided to use only the name *rag bza'* Rakza.

10. A kulha (*sku lha*) is a body protector deity.

11. An error in the original text gives the Tibetan *del*, which has no meaning and should be *dil*, "hill."

12. An error in the original text gives the Tibetan *thad*, "about"; it should be *theg*, "carrion," "corpse."

13. An error in the original text gives the Tibetan *byings*, "concealed"; it should be *dbyings*, "state of," "realm."

14. An error in the original text gives the Tibetan *lag*, "hand"; it should be *legs*, "good," "proper."

15. The reader may recall that Lady Margyenma was one of King Trisong Detsen's wives and had played a role in corrupting the kingdom. See glossary of names: "Margyenma."

16. This ablution water (*khrus*) is water with a small amount of milk with which he anointed her head.

17. As a reminder, Gyaza Lhakar is Senglön's wife who had been taken by the demoness and is infected with an evil spirit. As she had lost her spirit, or life force, it had to be reclaimed. For example, when someone is released from prison in Tibet, others shout out his or her name as loudly as they can in order to reawaken the life force.

18. An error in the original text gives the Tibetan *ci skya ze*, which has no meaning and should be *ci byed*, "what's the use?"

19. An error in the original text gives the Tibetan *sna mo*, which has no meaning and should be *sna bo*, "leader."

20. An error in the original text gives the Tibetan *mi stag*, "humans and tigers"; it should be *me stag*, "sparks," and *ze*, "crest," "mane," should be *tshe*, "life."

21. An error in the original text gives the Tibetan *rim gyi*, which has no meaning and should be *rim gyis*, "gradually."

22. The text refers to the Seven Wayward Siblings, each singing a song, but, in fact, Bloody Tress is not there, meaning that only the six male wayward siblings could have sung.

23. An error in the original text gives the Tibetan *ha ri*, "pattern"; it should be *shar ri*, "eastern mountain."

24. An error in the original text gives the Tibetan *sgra lha*, "dralha"; it should be *sgra lhas* giving the instrumental "by the dralhas."

25. Here, he is not referring to a Buddhist lama but to the Düd lama, his guru, Garab Wangchuk.

26. Milk is poisonous to the nāgas.

27. An error in the original text gives the Tibetan *spar*, "claw"; it should be *sgam*, "box."

28. The term for "silk runner" is *do li*, literally, "a palanquin."

29. An error in the original text gives the Tibetan *rang chung*, which has no meaning and should be *rang cha*, "individual or own fortune," "lot."

30. An error in the original text gives the Tibetan *sno mar*, which has no meaning and should be *sngo dmar*, "purple," the color that represents illness.

31. The term *sindri* (*srin gri*) literally means "cannibal knife" but refers to a blade that is not an ordinary sharp knife.

32. The term *nampa dzepa* (*mnan pa mdzas pa*) refers to something like black magic where something or someone is destroyed such that it can never come back to life again, e.g., it is buried with a dog's head, or put into a triangular box under a stupa or temple.

33. An error in the original text gives the Tibetan *bang*, "messenger"; it should be *dbang*, "power."

CHAPTER THREE

1. This refers to the lords of the three families in kriya yoga tantra: Mañjuśrī, Vajrapāṇi, and Vajrasattva.

2. An error in the original text gives the Tibetan *gzhung zhing*; it should be *gzhung shing*, "life pillar."

3. An error in the original text gives the Tibetan *rgyal por*, "to the king"; it should be *rgyal pos*, "by the king."

4. This is another of Gesar's fortresses, presumably not too far from his main fortress Sengdruk Taktsé.

5. The Tibetan gives this as Akhu Gané Gompa (A khu Ga ne gom pa) a nickname for Chipön, meaning something like "the old familiar one."

6. Dritsen (*gri btsan*) are deer-headed demons in the line of samaya-violating gongpo, shapeshifting sorcerers that cause mishap. For example, a beggar may be lucky and get a bowl full of food, and the spirit will cause him to spill it all.

7. An error in the original text gives the Tibetan *mi sngon*, "man of blue"; it should be *mi nag*, "man of black."

8. The twenty-ninth day is the lunar calendar day when offerings are made to demons.

9. This reference is to seven candles made from the oily blood of the samaya corruptors, the nature of which is destroyed by the demoness's heart blood substance.

10. The term *dechok norbu* (*bde mchog nor bu*) literally means "supreme bliss jewel." Here, this refers to Ling, its land, and its governance. This will become clear in the song that follows.

11. This refers to Senglön, Gesar's human father, whose name means "Lion Minister," and to Gesar's mother, Gokza, or Metok Lhadzé, as she is the daughter of the nāga king Tsukna Rinchen.

12. An error in the original text gives the Tibetan *gdangs*, "tune"; it should be *gangs*, "snow."

13. An error in the original text gives the Tibetan *chas*, "thing," "garment"; it should be *ches*, "forces."

14. An error in the original text gives the Tibetan *nyam med*, which has no meaning and should be *nyams med*, "unwaning."

15. The term *chankheb* (*mchan khebs*) literally means "concealed in the crook of his arm" and refers to the Tibetan understanding that all individuals are born with dralha protectors held in the crook of the arm, who accompany them through their lifetimes.

16. An error in the original text gives the Tibetan *lhangs*, which has no meaning and should be *lhang*, "brilliant," "resplendent."

17. The names Zichim and Limibal (Zi mchims and Li mi bal) have been transliterated as regions, but we were not able to identify them historically.

18. Yengmé Rangdröl Chenpo (Great Assiduous Self-Liberated One) and Drubchen Chökyi Guru (Greatly Accomplished Guru of the Dharma) were also listed by name.

19. The reader may recall that Manéné posing as the demoness Wangjema had poisoned the lake with milk, ridding it of the nāga demons.

20. We were unable to identify this as a specific location. Perhaps it could be a mountain if there were an error in the text and the Tibetan *bu rar* should be *bu rir*.

21. An error in the original text gives the Tibetan *ri*, "mountain"; it should be *re*, "each."

22. An error in the original text gives the Tibetan *chos*, "dharma"; it should be *jus*, "affair," "situation," and *gos*, "clothing" should be *dgos*, "must," "should."

23. An error in the original text gives the Tibetan *zil*, "splendor"; it should be *zi la*, "Zi mountain pass."

24. Though Nyibum is listed here as one of the Seven Super Warriors, he is actually one of the Three Ultimate Warriors, and Sengtak Adom would be the other of the Seven Super Warriors. However, as the bard repeatedly refers to Nyibum in this list of seven, we have left it as it appears in the text with the understanding that who is included in these categories is somewhat fluid.

25. An error in the original text gives the Tibetan *'dre*, "demons"; it should be *dre*, "mules."

26. An error in the original text gives the Tibetan *shang*, "tambourine"; it should be *shing*, "trees," "wood."

27. An error in the original text gives the Tibetan *yos*, "rabbit"; it should be *yol*, "afternoon."

28. An error in the original text gives the Tibetan *glu rta*, "singing horse"; it should be *klu rta*, "nāga horse," giving *klu rta lding shes*, Luta Dingshé (Naga Horse Knows How to Fly).

29. An error in the original text gives the Tibetan *phyag*, "bow down"; it should be *phyar*, "held aloft," "hoisted."

30. This specifically refers to the knife used to cut up corpses for sky burial (*las gri*; Skt. *kartika*).

31. This line was two lines in the Tibetan text, a descriptive line and then a line with the warrior's name. We combined them into a single line, feeling that the flow improved. The same is true of the next five lines.

32. The Tibetan has Pönpo Nyala (Dpon po nya la), but we have used his more familiar name, Nyatsha Aten.

33. Each warrior has a large, mirrored shield that protects his heart.
34. This is Denma's song, but there are other songs of six modulations: "Joru's Six Modulations of the Māras," "Gyatsha's White Melody in Six Modulations," and "Drukmo's Six Modulations in Nine Pitches."
35. An error in the original text gives the Tibetan *cum*, which has no meaning and should be *chum*, "crouch in fear."
36. An error in the original text gives the Tibetan *ye shes*, "wisdom"; it should be *e shes*, "Do you know?"
37. This line is missing from the Tibetan text; we assume this is in error, as it is a standard part of the beginning triplet to a song, so we have added it.
38. An error in the original text gives the Tibetan *dgra lha zan*, which has no meaning and should be *sna zin*, which refers to friends or loved ones.

CHAPTER FOUR

1. The Tibetan here has Gulang Wangchuk (Gu lang dbang phyug), but for consistency we have translated this as Garab Wangchuk, as both are names for the main māra deity.
2. An error in the original text gives the Tibetan *zhe spro*, "joyful"; it should be *zhe khro*, "angry."
3. An error in the original text gives the Tibetan *thog mar*, "first"; it should be *thog dmar*, "red lightning."
4. An error in the original text gives the Tibetan *yod nas*, which has no meaning and should be *yod na*, "if it exists," "if there is."
5. An error in the original text gives the Tibetan *'gyod*, "regret," which appears twice in the line and should be *gyod*, "troubles."
6. An error in the original text gives the Tibetan *nag*, "dark," "black"; it should be *nags*, "forest."
7. Nakshö (Nags shod) is the term for forested valley but is also the proper name for the area of Amnyé's sovereignty.
8. An error in the original text gives the Tibetan *gyas*, "right"; it should be *gyag*, "yak."
9. This warrior, though unfamiliar to us in the volumes to date, has a more significant role in later volumes, specifically in Ling's battles with Hor. His name (Ban de dmar lu), almost more of a nickname, connotes an image of a slender and somewhat slight man, dressed in the red robes of a monk, or perhaps one with a ruddy complexion.
10. An error in the original text gives the Tibetan *klu klo*, "naga savages"; it should be *kla klo*, "barbarians."
11. This is the term for skull cup (*ka li*) and refers here to the severed top of his skull, the calvarium anatomically.
12. The name Bethül Chidak Nakpo (Be thul 'chi bdag nag po) begins with the appellation "Bethül," which may be Mongolian in origin and refers to a title of a powerful warrior, similar to the Tibetan designations Pathül (Dpa' thul), indicating a notably powerful warrior; Yangthul (Yang thul), a super warrior; and Zhethul (Zhe thul), an ultimate warrior.
13. An error in the original text gives the Tibetan *hang pa*, which has no meaning and should be *hang ba*, "pant," "gasp."
14. Just as we would say "dharmakāya," this is the field of existence of the māras. He is calling to the māra gods who dwell there.

15. There is a variation in the text here. Thinking that the bard accidentally omitted this usual line, we have added it here.

16. An error in the original text gives the Tibetan *gzhi*, "foundation"; it should be *bzhi*, "four."

17. Rāhula's is the power of lightning—striking quickly and without hesitation.

18. The Tibetan *ruting* (*ru rting*) is an epic word referring to the warrior who is at the end of the line guarding the rear. Here, Yutsé is saying that it is his guess that it must be Joru's horse and therefore Joru whom he sees.

19. It is said that the only creature feared by the mythic makara is the conch.

20. An error in the original text gives the Tibetan *ril ba*, "round"; it should be *ring ba*, "tall," "height."

21. An error in the original text gives the Tibetan *bang ba*, "storeroom"; it should be *bong ba*, "donkey."

CHAPTER FIVE

1. An error in the original text gives the Tibetan *sum cu so drug*; it should be *sum cu rtso drug*, the correct spelling of thirty-six.

2. The Tibetan does not name the judge, but we are quite sure this is Werma Lhadar, the most famed judge.

3. According to the cosmology of the Abhidharma, seven circles of golden mountains (*gser ri bdun*) surround Mount Sumeru in the center of our universe.

4. An error in the original text gives the Tibetan *bde*, "bliss" or "well-being"; it should be *sde*, "district," giving "of the Takrong district" or the domain of Takrong.

5. This refers to an ancient proverb that tells the tale of two well-to-do men wearing golden armor and disputing over a small sum. A pauper in goatskin rags comes upon them and bargains with them that he will resolve their dispute. They agree, and the wealthy men are then bound to abide by the poor man's verdict. What he means here, he goes on to say in the next line, is that this was a matter that should have been handled internally by Trothung's clan. But just as the two golden-armored men should have solved their own dispute but now are stuck with the goatskin-clad pauper's decision, Trothung is now stuck with the judge's verdict and punishment.

6. The Tibetan term *tendrel* (*rten 'brel*) refers canonically to interdependent connection or causal linkage, while in colloquial usage it describes favorable happenstance and is commonly translated as "auspicious coincidence."

7. The term *khyerso sum* (*khyer so gsum*) refers to the three awarenesses of body, speech, and mind, wherein are the three basic principles: regarding whatever you see as the guru, whatever you hear as mantra, and all thoughts as those of the guru's enlightened mind.

8. *Kalpa* is a Sanskrit word meaning an eon or a relatively long period of time (by human calculation) in Hindu and Buddhist cosmology. The concept is first mentioned in the *Mahābhārata*. The definition of a kalpa equaling 4.32 billion years is found in the Purāṇas (specifically *Viṣṇu Purāṇa* and *Bhagavata Purāṇa*).

9. An error in the original text gives the Tibetan *ger mdzo*; it should be *ge dzo*, "Gedzo."

10. Lama Chönam describes the seven stages of sealing as: (1) a *tsek* (*tsheg*), or dot, between words; (2) a *she* (*shad*), or single line stroke, between sentences; (3) chapters; (4) volumes; (5) sets of volumes, or *bumpos* (*bum po*); (6) borders and edging that contain the text; and

(7) the title, which encompasses the meaning. In this same way, samādhi is protected by the vajra tent, fire, sword, and so on.

11. An error in the original text gives the Tibetan *rkan sga*; it should be *rkan sgra*, referring to the palatal sound that comes from smacking the tongue on the roof of the mouth, which in Tibet is a hostile, provoking sound.

12. The term *phamabu* (*pha ma bu*) refers to the principal energy as the "father, mother, child," indicating its magnitude, much as we might say "that was the mother of all storms."

13. Vikramaśila (Rnam par gnon pa) is one of the thirty-five buddhas of confession also known as Ratnapadmavikrami.

14. Se (*bse*) trees are trees growing in thick forests in southern areas of Tibet, members of the sumac family, and like poison oak, they cause contact dermatitis.

15. An error in the original text gives the Tibetan *'od*, "light"; it should be *mdo* as in *mdo ba*, "great steed."

CHAPTER SIX

1. An error in the original text gives the Tibetan *kam kam*, which has no meaning and should be *kam kem*, short for *kam me kem me*, which is a descriptive term for looking distraught (opening one's eyes wide and then closing them with a sigh) and describes how someone might look who is very down, depressed, and worried.

2. Here, he is referring to Gesar and the Ling warriors as fearless in the face of the lord of death.

3. Here, he is spinning a tale that Bloody Tress was not defeated but rather that it was only through the aid of the māra gods that she did survive.

4. This is a goblet filled with an offering drink (*khyems phul*) and is a golden drink (*ser khyems*), likely tea made golden by the addition of a few filings of gold dust shaved from a golden chopstick. This could also be made with turquoise or other precious substances.

5. These would be wrathful tormas, perhaps depicting the sense organs or the heart, or liquor, black tea, and so forth.

6. This means "Timeless Soya!" (*Bso ya ye 'gyur*). This is a Bön invoking expression, much like the Shambhala cry, "Ki! Ki! So! So!"

7. An error in the original text gives the Tibetan *cho yu*; it should be *cho ya*, which is a Bön shout for rousing energy.

8. This is Garab Wangchuk.

9. There is a sense here that the wheels have been set in motion, that a time has come when a leader, no matter how powerful or revered, cannot stop the negativity they have spawned.

10. This is spoken sarcastically, as foxes are thought to be cowardly.

11. *dpon gshin rje'i las mkhan mtha' nas bskor*. When people are dying, the lord of death takes away their last breath, but the messengers who come with him also exact amends for misdeeds. Similarly, Gesar has messengers, his warriors, who will demand restitution.

12. The term *yaling* (*ya ling*) is a pun on the name of the sword, "Little Star."

13. The reader will recall that the Seven Siblings are the offspring of Wangjema with each of seven demon spirits. The mu demons arise from ignorance.

14. His name, Shechen Drengyi Yamé, has been contracted, as is common, to Shechen Drenmé.

15. A wrathful form of Padmasambhava, prominent in the previously published volumes of the epic.
16. Nang-ngu has been given Gesar's bow Ragö and his golden-notched arrow, but he is concerned that he is too young and small to manipulate them.
17. Specifically, the Tibetan text lists Tsenkya Bumthub, Tongdü Lenmé, Tongthub Kherkyé, Yenthub Pungring, Drongnak Razung, and so forth.
18. This refers to the fire rings around a wrathful deity that can be seen in thangka depictions.
19. Yuja, or Turquoise Bird, belongs to Trothung's son Dongtsen, but when Gesar revived the horse during the horse race, Dongtsen promised to lend the horse if needed. See Kornman et al., *The Epic of Gesar of Ling*, 496.
20. Although the Tibetan *mnan* literally means "to bury," it also implies a more "black magic" burial intended to curse the enemy.

CHAPTER SEVEN

1. This is Śītavana, a charnel ground situated near Bodhgaya in India.
2. An error in the original text gives the Tibetan *ha khang*, which has no meaning and should be *ha shang*, "Hashang," an area said to be a demon abode.
3. *a ma'i bu bces*. This term translates literally as "mother's cherished boy," but unlike the Western disparaging implication of "a mama's boy," this is a valued quality in Tibetan culture. It refers to a son who has the respect and love of his mother, respects his parents, and is decent and virtuous in his life.
4. An error in the original text gives the Tibetan *'o na*; it should be *'u na* in keeping with the pattern of repeating the beginning song syllables.
5. An error in the original text gives the Tibetan *brgyad*, "eight"; it should be *bco brgyad*, "eighteen," as everywhere else in the text this is given as the eighteen marshlands.
6. "Fivefold" refers to the five buddha families, and "eightfold" to the eight manifestations of Guru Rinpoche.
7. Calling him the "turquoise-haired one" reflects that in the past Yutsé had taken the turquoise hair (*g.yu yi ral pa*) from the body of another māra as a battle trophy.
8. The seven are ruby, sapphire, coral, lapis, emerald, diamond, and pearl.
9. The teurang are associated with dice-playing, and the idea here is that the two maidens called out the numbers of the dice as they rolled them, asking for wishes. There were three dice, six-sided, with a maximum roll of the number eighteen. These were old and fancy dice and the maidens' voices were as beautiful as poetry. Even householders who played dice games never did so inside their homes, afraid that they would attract teurang spirits.
10. Her name refers to the black hammer that teurangs carry, as patrons of blacksmiths, and refers back to her as an emanation of the wrathful protector deity Dorje Lekpa, or Vajrasādhu.
11. This is not the large Khrom River in Tsang in Central Tibet, but a smaller river of the same name in a vast valley in Kham.
12. An error in the original text gives the Tibetan *rnams*, "plural"; it should be *rnam pa*, giving *khong rnam pa*, "him" or "he."
13. Mahākāla Black Eunuch (Dpal ye she gyi gon po ma ning nag po) is one of the foremost protectors of the Nyingma school and of the terma (revealed treasure) tradition.

14. Drong (*'brong*) are wild yak, untamed and dangerous, but the bard seems to use these somewhat interchangeably.

15. An error in the original text gives the Tibetan *sgril*, "roll up"; it should be *sgrib*, "obscure," giving *sgrib med,* "unobstructed."

16. An error in the original text gives the Tibetan *dgongs ya*, which has no meaning and should be *dgongs pa*, "enlightened mind."

17. These are ancient Bön syllables and are analogous to syllables such as "Ala thala," already familiar as the beginning to songs.

18. There is a small flag used in lower practices, but, in this case, it is made of human skin, as it is Amnyé's black magic practice support.

19. The five are hemp, millet, rice, corn, and beans.

20. Also known as Remati, she is a Mahākāli, the sole female of the eight dharmapālas and a protectress in the Geluk tradition. She is the principal protectress of Tibet, a wrathful manifestation of Sarasvatī and the wife of Shinjé, the lord of death.

21. The Tibetan *rdo rje* (Skt. *vajra*) is missing from the Tibetan text, which should read *spras lag la rdo rje bzhag*, "placing the vajra in her hands." This would be a way of subduing and blessing her.

22. An error in the original text gives the Tibetan *srid pa'i mo bon rtsis*; it should be *srid pa'i mo sman rtsis*, giving "diviner," "doctor," or "astrologer." *Bon*, meaning "Bön," gives no clear meaning.

23. The Tibetan *tsha zhang 'den rje bsam grub* gives his full formal name as "Wish-Fulfilling Lord of the Den Clan." We have used his more well-known name of Denma for simplicity.

24. We think that the princess is King Yutsé's daughter, and as she is now installed as the reigning queen of Minyak, this land becomes a gateway for Gesar to access the Düd lands farther north that are currently controlled by Lutsen.

CHAPTER EIGHT

1. An error in the original text gives the Tibetan *rkyang gling*, which has no meaning and should be *rkang gling*, "kangling" or "thighbone trumpet."

2. An error in the original text gives the Tibetan *shog*, meaning "may it happen!"; it should be *thog*, giving *steng shog*, "to the top."

3. *mi ring mi thung mdung mo gang.* This is an expression implying you have a little time to think about all this, but not endless time.

4. An error in the original text gives the Tibetan *'phrod*, "offer"; it should be *srog*, "life force."

5. Some statues are made by blacksmiths, but these were from a mold.

6. They are listed here as: Lhündrub son of Nyiji, Jemé son of Changmo, Ukmik son of Jama, and Norgé son of Khanglé. The Tibetan spelling for these names varies at this point in the text, but for consistency we have kept the spelling as it first appeared.

7. Zorna, Guwu, and Lüngwu (Zor sna, Sgu bu, Rlung bu) are māra people who will reappear in later stories of the epic.

8. A khal (*khal*) is a measure that is given as twenty-five to thirty pounds.

9. A reminder to the reader that this protectress was Manéné who had impersonated Wangjema, and when her spiritual being dissolved into a rainbow, the imposter Wangjema's physical manifestation died simultaneously.

10. An error in the original text gives the Tibetan *sman 'byung gnas*, which has no meaning and should be *padma byung gnas*, "Padmasambhava."

11. A golden bridge or *serzam* (*gser zam*) is the term for a bridge that is made when a river is frozen and people collect many small rocks and recite a heart essence mantra of a longevity deity such as Amitāyus over each rock, blessing it. These rocks are then arranged in many layers from one side of the riverbank to the other. It is called a "golden bridge" although it is made of rock rather than gold.

12. The Tibetan gives this as the Wood Dragon year, but as this is incompatible with other dates given in the text, we have omitted the element and given this simply as the Dragon year.

13. We have chosen to call her by her more familiar name, though the Tibetan here gives her name as Lhamo Drölma (Lha mo sgrol ma).

14. This is an epic style of speaking; by saying that she wishes his hair to turn white in the white helmet, she is expressing the wish that he has longevity but also that he is always worthy of his white helmet.

15. This is the dri that Gesar's mother brought with her from the nāga realm when she came as the nāga princess to the human realm.

16. An error in the original text gives the Tibetan *mkha 'gro ma'i*; it should be *mkha 'gro mas*, giving the instrumental "pure samaya held by the ḍākinīs" rather than "held of the ḍākinīs."

17. Here the text gives his name as Lhasé Dralha Tsegyal (Lha sras dgra lha rtse rgyal), or Prince Victorious Mountain Peak Dralha, but we have chosen not to include the name until later when he is named by Gomchen.

18. An error in the original text gives the Tibetan *bdun*, "seven"; it should be *mdun*, "in front of" or "before."

19. This is a particularly beautiful passage in Tibetan: *byams pa gnyen gyi 'khri shing*, literally "the entwining vine of a loving friend."

20. Because Chipön is an elder of special respect, the vessel itself indicates longevity. This container is filled with tsampa, and on top of it is a design of butter ridges in the four directions with a center moon and sun; it is painted almost like a torma. It is a butter decoration of prosperity and decorated with jewels.

21. Lama Chönam describes an image of babies with protection cords, ornaments, and blessing objects ornamenting their backs, tied onto their chubas just under the collar, and jangling and colorful when the children walk and run. When they have their first haircut at age three or four, the hair lock is tied in a bow.

22. This is a text that explains in detail the biography of a thousand buddhas.

23. These three siblings are Gesar's co-born dralha protectors referenced in the first volume of the Gesar epic, although the Tibetan here gives Thalé Ökar as Thiklé Ötroma (Thig le 'od 'phro ma).

24. The Tibetan gives her name here as Ané Göcham Karmo (A ne rgod lcam dkar mo).

25. An error in the original text gives the Tibetan *ban bun*, "little by little"; it should be *bon bun*, "Bön and monks."

26. He will sing a song detailing the recipients and givers of each gift, but the song is not included in the Tibetan text.

27. The Tibetan text lists attendants by name as Biza Rintsho (Precious Ocean of the Biza family) and Nutünma (Nursemaid Mother).

CHAPTER NINE

1. The Tibetan gives this as the Iron Tiger year, but as this is incompatible with other dates given in the text, we have omitted the element and given this simply as the Tiger year.

2. This refers to Tibetan cosmology in which heaven is seen as having thirteen layers, the highest being the pure land.

3. An error in the original text gives the Tibetan *rma bu*, which has no clear meaning and should be *rma bya*, "peacock," describing the carved peacocks that decorate the base of the throne.

4. The Asura Cave (A su ra'i brag phug) is near Pharping in the Kathmandu Valley. Here, Guru Rinpoche practiced Vajrakīlaya and subdued evil forces.

5. This is an area in Central Tibet, Ütsang; this and the two below are places where there are many herds of sheep and goats.

6. This refers to a nomad land also with the name "Amdo" and is not the more familiar present-day Amdo that makes up most of northeast Tibet.

7. In the Tibetan text, this line is repeated two lines later, we assume, in error.

8. An error in the original text gives the Tibetan *gang*, "everywhere"; it should be *gangs*, "snow mountain."

9. Lutsen comes from the Tibetan, *klu* ("nāga") and *tsen* ("tsen").

10. The Tibetan *dgu zur* is an astrological term that indicates a fragile conjunction of opportunity.

11. Crystal Rock Ocean of Radiance (Shel brag 'od kyi mtsho mo) gives a variation of the name for the Crystal Cave.

12. An error in the original text gives the Tibetan *bum*, "vase"; it should be *'bum*, "Prajñāpāramitā."

13. An error in the original text gives the Tibetan *chos sku*, "dharmakāya"; it should be *chos kyi*, "of the Dharma."

14. An error in the original text gives the Tibetan *phar*, "over there"; it should be *phur*, "fly."

15. These are both more formal names for his aunt Manéné.

16. This is the māra king's wife-to-be. She and Gesar have a previous love connection, and she will help him in his quest to tame the māras. At a feast in the past, the northerners had come, stealing horses and taking with them Meza, who was a young girl at the time.

17. As a young boy, Gesar, along with his mother, had been banished to this valley by the elders of Ling.

18. An error in the original text gives the Tibetan *nang rgyud*, "inner tantra"; it should be *nang bcud*, "inner contents."

19. Recall that on the nineteenth day the moon is only four days past full, so it would still be moonlit after sundown.

20. In Ling, these six songs (*dgu seng drug 'gyur karmo*) have a piercing quality to their melodies.

21. The bard here gives his horn as nineteen armspans in length, presumably making an error, as elsewhere this has been stated as eighteen armspans.

22. An error in the original text gives the Tibetan *gyang*, "magnificence," but *gyang ma* has no real meaning, and all later references are to *g.ya' ma*, "slate."

23. Several other references to this name give it as *Rkyal ba* rather than *Rkyal pa*; we have chosen Kyelwa (*Rkyal ba*) for consistency.

24. This is the first mention of the woman who is the teurang mother. Her full name is Khenpa Genmo (Mkhan pa rgan mo), which we found difficult to translate but clearly refers to an older woman of intellectual repute, and we have settled on "Elder Woman of Knowledge."

25. An error in the original text gives the Tibetan *'phrul*, "magic"; it should be *'khrul*, "unmistaken."

26. "Life force" (*tshe*) here means that according to Buddhist tradition, whether there are one or many sheep, one sheep can be designated so that, from that day on, no harm can come to it. A hole is made in its ear signifying that this sheep is safe as the personal sheep of the one hundred teurang.

27. This is the character who will later be known as Chingön, the main shepherd for the demon māra Lutsen's life-force sheep.

28. An error in the original text gives the Tibetan *glag*, "hawk"; it should be *lag*, "arm."

29. An error in the original text gives the Tibetan *las*, "action"; it should be *la*, "to go."

30. An error in the original text gives the Tibetan *mi 'gyur dal ba ring min*; it should be corrected as the name of the song is always written as *mi 'gyur dal ba ring mo*.

31. This is because the wood of the sandalwood tree is so hard and smooth.

CHAPTER TEN

1. An error in the original text gives the Tibetan *dga'*, "happy"; it should be *dgu*, giving *dgu seng*, which refers to the clear and penetrating beauty of Drukmo's voice.

2. This special bird comes from Mön or a place southwest of Tibet, a tropical place such as Bhutan or Nepal.

3. She is likening Gesar to the wild drong, and his ministers and citizens to the young yaks.

4. Here she is saying that Gesar, being a man, has easily fallen in love and this love has unhesitatingly penetrated his life, whereas she, as a woman, requires that the relationship be nurtured before she can fully trust her feelings.

5. An error in the original text gives the Tibetan *khrung* "liquor"; it should be *khyung*, "garuḍa."

6. An error in the original text gives the Tibetan *phyam*, "ladder," "support"; it should be *phum*, "shield," as elsewhere in the text this name is given to Gesar's shield.

7. An error in the original text gives the Tibetan *bshan*, "butcher"; it should be *bshad*, giving *ris bshad*, "picture design."

8. Metaphorically, this energy is pictured as countless silken banners snapping in the wind.

9. She is describing Atak Lhamo, a powerful archeress with so many special ḍākinī signs that she can't be overlooked, although no one there can figure out who she is.

10. This implies that Atak Lhamo is offering to use them for Gesar, that she is not coming to fight but is giving in to Gesar.

11. These are the same three māras referred to on p. 216 of this text, with slight variations in their Tibetan names.

12. The idea here is that yogurt is a final product—smooth, solid, and without turmoil.

13. These are place names, many of them no longer identifiable. Ayak may be in Ladakh in the "waist" area of Tibet bordering India, and Daryak may be in China.

14. This area, Gyalmo Tshawarong, is in easternmost Kham and has a mild climate with many ravines.

15. An error in the original text gives the Tibetan *ldam ma ldem*, "swaying a bit"; it should be *dem ma sdeb*, "many flavors blended."

16. It is still a tradition in Golok to offer a guest three drinks.

17. The result of reciting the intrinsic awareness mantra (*rig sngags*) is samādhi.

18. An error in the original text gives the Tibetan *ma bun*, which has no meaning and should be *ma bu*, "mother and son."

19. This was previously called Guzi (Dgu zi), but here is Guzé (Dgu ze); we have used Guzi for consistency.

20. We found this term (*rgya tsha*) to refer to a specific double-cross hybrid cow of Nepal, the Indian *mithun*, and also to a county in present-day southeast Tibet, called Gyatsha County (Rgya tsha 'dzong). We have taken it to mean that these cows came from a region outside of northern Tibet where, particularly centuries ago, cows were not common.

21. Here, the Tibetan *shes*, "knowing," could be *shed*, "domestic animals' strength," giving Kyelwa Khashé or Wide-Mouthed Powerful as a Yak. However, later on, in two references, he is called Kyelwa Khadang (Rkyal ba kha gdangs), or Wide-Mouthed Sack, and for consistency we use that name throughout.

22. Reference here is that the enemy is felt to possess all the organs and body parts, represented by different beings. Perhaps this is similar to the sayings in English, "He is the eyes and ears of the president" or "She is the guts of the organization."

23. An error in the original text gives the Tibetan *rjong*, which has no meaning and should be *rdzong* "fortress."

24. An error in the original text gives the Tibetan *bu gsum*, "three children"; it should be *bya gsum*, "three birds."

25. Here the name of this armor is given as *zil ba 'bum rdzong*, in contrast to other versions such as *zil ba 'bum dzoms* or *ze ba 'bum dzoms*. For consistency we have used Zewa Bumdzom.

26. An error in the original text gives the Tibetan *mtho bo ma*, which has no clear grammatical meaning and should be *mtho ba la*, "high up on."

27. An error in the original text gives the Tibetan *mu ne*; it should be *mu le*, giving the correct place name as Mulé, as it was previously.

28. Earlier, this tea was referred to as "hero tea." "Hero" is a reference to Mañjuśrī.

29. An error in the original text gives the Tibetan *chas*, "garments"; it should be *ches*, "very" or "great."

30. Traditionally, Trothung's horse is known as *gug gu rog rdzong* rather than *gug gu rog rdzob* as given here.

31. The cuckoo is famed for its springtime song.

32. An error in the original text gives the Tibetan *phra 'khyil*, which has no meaning; it should be *khra 'khyi*, "pageantry."

33. An error in the original text gives the Tibetan *mi*, "human"; it should be *me*, "fire," giving *me ri*, "blazing mountain."

CHAPTER ELEVEN

1. Meaning "accomplisher of benefit" (*don sgrub*), this is the name that Gesar was known by in the celestial realm before he took a human birth as the boy Joru and then became King Gesar. This is the story that is told in Kornman et al., *The Epic of Gesar of Ling*, 7.

2. An error in the original text gives the Tibetan *brgya*, "one hundred"; it should be *brgyad*, "eight."
3. Bamboo has many joints so the container can have three compartments.
4. This may be an area in Kham.
5. He is speaking to the warriors who are still there in body, although the demon has taken their consciousnesses.
6. Garwa Nakpo is both an attendant and an emanation of Dorje Lekpa. When recalling the purity of the deity and bringing this aspect to mind, the way of riding the goat indicated emptiness, as the goat represents wisdom, and Garwa Nakpo the aspect of method.
7. The Tibetan *sgrib shing* refers to a place where the captured ones (in this case the horses) would be invisible as well as unable to function—a place that is veiled through casting a spell.
8. These are the succession of seven buddhas (*sangs rgyas rab bdun*) ending with Gautama Buddha, the buddha of the current age.
9. Mar me mdzad. Dīpaṃkara is a buddha predating Śākyamuni Buddha.
10. The Tibetan here has "words and arrows" (*tshig dang mda'*), but, traditionally, this proverb is given as *'ja' dang mda'*, "rainbows and arrows" or "arc of a rainbow."
11. These refer back to the story as Manéné advised him to tell it, giving false names for his birthplace and claiming that he is Achung, brother to two māras, Chakchung and Mukchung.
12. He is a reincarnation of an enlightened warrior who was intentionally reborn as a māra in order to be able to help Gesar and is the shepherd of the māra king Lutsen's flock. Gyatsha Zhalkar, Gesar's uncle, and Chingön were brothers in a previous lifetime.
13. These are one-legged beings.
14. An error in the original text gives the Tibetan *ru khra*, which has no meaning; it should be *khra rab*, "Trarab."
15. An error in the original text gives the Tibetan *ma blo*, "wanting particle, mind's desire"; it should be *ma lo*, "dear child."
16. She does not realize she is talking to Joru (Gesar), as he has fooled her into thinking he is Achung.
17. Here, the idea is that there are outer, inner, and secret ways to understand. The physical location of the mountain may be far to the west, but its inner aspect is that of the mountain spirits, and its secret aspect is its bodhisattva nature.
18. *ngan 'gugs.* The idea here is that he has multiple melodies that make the song more lovely.
19. 'Od srung. Kāśyapa is the buddha of the kalpa immediately preceding the time of Śākyamuni.
20. An error in the original text gives the Tibetan *phyug*, "rich"; it should be *phug*, "cave."
21. An error in the original text gives the Tibetan *khu*, which has no meaning here and should be *zhu*, "ask."
22. An error in the original text gives the Tibetan *song*, "went"; it should be *yong*, "come."
23. An error in the original text gives the Tibetan *sa mda'*, "lowlands"; it should be *sa mtha'*; "border region."
24. His family name, Den, was not given as a paternal ending, as Denpa, but a maternal ending, Denma.
25. An error in the original text gives the Tibetan *bcos*, "boil," "fabricate," or "make"; it should be *bcom*, "conquer," "defeat."
26. Here, his name is given formally as Darjé Khyungyal Sengtak (Dar rje khyung rgyal seng stag). We have left it as the more familiar Adom Sengtak.

27. He is saying that, just as sheep cannot defend themselves against wolves, humans cannot defend themselves against him, as he is Miyi Changki (Mi yi spyang ki), "wolf for humans."

28. The Tibetan *rna bar ma 'gro* is, literally, "It did not go to our ears," much as we might say, "We could not get it through our thick skulls."

29. These three lines are intended to convey the idea that the Ling people's problems stem almost coincidentally from the māras, just as, for example, it is not the earth's fault that it is churned up by a crow, but simply the nature of a crow being a crow.

30. This is unusual, as it is said that the snow lion will die if it leaves the snow lands.

31. An error in the original text gives the Tibetan *rta shar*, which has no real meaning and should be *stag shar*, "youth."

32. An error in the original text gives the Tibetan *chu nag*, "black water"; it should be *chas nag*, "black-clothed."

33. An error in the original text gives the Tibetan *ngar*, "fierce"; it should be *ngas*, "by me."

34. The text gives the full names of these warriors (Darphen Dugi Dongpo, Gadé Chökyong Bernak, Tshazhang Denma Jangtra, Darjé Khyungyal Sengtak, and Nyibum Drayi Thowa), but we have chosen to use their simpler common names and put them on one line.

35. *bdud phrug*. This is literally "the demon or māra offspring."

36. The text gives the full names (Gyatsha Zhalkarpo, Gadé Chökyong Kyi Démik, Seng Adom Miyi Changki) of these warriors, but we have chosen to use their simpler, common names and put them on one line.

37. The text gives the full names of these warriors (Gyatsha Zhalkarpo, Yuyi Metok, Nuwo Rongtsha Lhadar, Takrong Nyatsha Aten, and Takrong Anu Zikphen), but we have chosen to use their simpler, common names and put them on one line.

CHAPTER TWELVE

1. They made a tripod, each of them with one knee together and one knee alone.

2. This is a Bön mantra of purification of negative emotions.

3. The Tibetan *su ru* refers to a bush that has very dark leaves and creates deep shade; its wood ignites readily.

4. An error in the original text gives the Tibetan *pham*, "defeat"; it should be *phab*, "bring down" or "let fall."

5. "White and pink" (*gro dkar, gro dmar*) refers to the fact that when examining turquoise, milk is poured over it. If the milk turns pink, this is a sign of superior quality turquoise.

6. An error in the original text gives the Tibetan *sa ma*; it should be *ga ma*, which is the name of a mountain but also describes a mountain stippled but not completely covered with snow.

7. This is somewhat odd as Magyal Pomra is generally portrayed as white, not red.

8. The warrior Gadé is famous for his ability to shoot huge rocks from catapults.

9. In this area of the country are three tribes: the white-, yellow-, and black-helmeted ones.

10. King Gurkar is more powerful than his brothers, Gurnak and Gurser, though they all are kings in Hor.

11. See glossary of terms: "dütsi."

12. This refers to "the seven clotted bloods" (*khrag sha bdun*), but we were not able to clarify "the seven" and have omitted the number.

13. Jowo (Jo bo) is a statue in Lhasa. It is also an honorific term in the ancient Tibetan language and designates the most holy of men, just as "Jomo" would be the most holy of women, Yeshé Tsogyal.
14. The Tibetan for the phrase for "within myself" is *zangs khug kun dga' ba*. Literally *zangs khug* means "copper inside" and refers to his torso and that the inside of his chest and abdominal cavities is a copper-red color; *kun dga' ba* refers to inner beauty like that found inside a shrine room, its complete delight enclosed, and indicates his mature, kindly eloquence.
15. An error in the original text gives the Tibetan *med*, "without"; it should be *shes*, "wisdom."

CHAPTER THIRTEEN

1. An error in the original text gives the Tibetan *kha*; it should be *mkha'*, giving *nam mkha'*, "sky."
2. An error in the original text gives the Tibetan *sdig gcod*, "cutting evil"; it should be *sdig spyod*, "engages with negativity."
3. Padur (pa dur) is the Mongolian term for "warrior," and this would thus be the title given to a warrior in Hor.
4. Although five Hor warrior-ministers are listed here, Dakyen Anga Thebdruk (Mda' skyen a lnga mtheb drug) does not reappear when the action continues later in this chapter.
5. An error in the original text gives the Tibetan Gama Zigo (Ga ma gzig mgo) or Leopard-Head as the horse's name, but Michung's horse is Marchung Dröden (Dmar chung 'gros ldan) or Small Red Steppage.
6. This is something he says out of respect and encouragement to Michung; it is not a put-down.
7. The first line (*rgyab kyi pha ming la ci 'dra zer*) is literally "What is your father's name in back of you?" and, expressed in Tibetan, is quite eloquent. The second (*mdun kyi ma ming la ci 'dra zer*) is literally "What is your mother's name in front of you?"
8. This is Ralo Tönpa of Gok, Gesar's mother Gokmo's stepfather, who cared for her when she, as Yelga Dzeden, came to the human realm from the nāgas.
9. Long ago, before Gesar was born, Shenpa and his brother Kator Shangman had intentionally taken rebirth. Shenpa understands this and actually has good intentions, but he ends up killing Gyatsha later on in a further volume of the epic.
10. An error in the original text gives the Tibetan *rag*, "copper"; it should be *ra*, "goat."
11. It is perilous to contact a scorpion, which here refers to a family that is evil and dangerous. In a more general sense, a scorpion represents the risk of breaking samaya.
12. This is his nickname, much as we might playfully, but endearingly, call someone "pumpkin head." But while animals wear their spots on the outside, humans generally wear their attributes on the inside, and oftentimes, their nicknames point out their inner qualities.
13. This and the line before are one line in the original text, but we have divided them as otherwise the line was too long for poetic meter.
14. An error in the original text gives the Tibetan *rkyang*, "wild ass," "just," or "only"; it should be *lcam*, giving the correct spelling of her name.
15. Wangmo (Dbang mo), "powerful lady" or "queen," emphasizes that she is from the wisdom lineage of Sukhāvatī, the western pure land of Amitābha. Amitābha is the buddha of the western direction, and his enlightened activity is that of magnetizing and compassion. Padmasambhava is an emanation of Amitābha.

16. Minub (Mi nub) was not a place we could identify historically, but it may be a place from which silk came.

17. Palden Lhamo or Makzor Gyalmo (Dmag zor rgyal mo; Skt. Śrī Devi) is the consort of Mahākāla.

18. An error in the original text gives the Tibetan *spungs*, "heap" or pile"; it should be *srung*, "protector."

19. These are different aspects of the same being, although the bard refers to them by two different names.

20. Although she is from the east and therefore dressed like Golok, this is a custom from Lhasa in Central Tibet. There, the lap apron is worn once a woman is married, and whenever something bad occurs or there is a bad omen, the woman would take off the apron and beat it on the ground.

21. The words "cannot rest" (*lhod med*) is in each of these last three lines. The idea here is that he cannot rest in body, speech, or mind.

22. An error in the original text gives the Tibetan *phungs pa*, which has no meaning; it should be *phung pa*, "ruin," "destruction," "disorder."

23. The Tibetan *tshe ring*, literally "long life," is meant sarcastically, as we might say "honey," not meaning it.

24. First, Gesar performs magically, and then his horse does so in order to return Drukmo's horse to Ling.

25. This appears as *bkris*, but one would have to know that the *sh* is hidden and that the syllable is actually a contraction of *bkra shis*, giving "auspicious."

26. The Tibetan text does not include "tiger-skin quiver" here.

27. The Tibetan *ngag 'gugs* is a term for "tune" or "melody" and here reflects that Gesar has multiple harmonies he can access.

28. Although the text only has *sum cu*, this is the Heaven of the Thirty-Three (Sum cu rtsa gsum gyi gnas).

29. An error in the original text gives the Tibetan *kha 'bangs*, "eloquence"; it should be *khu 'bangs*, "snowflake."

30. An error in the original text gives the Tibetan *dung dmar*, "blood-filled conch"; it should be *mdung*, "lance" or "spear."

31. An error in the original text gives the Tibetan *khrab*, "armor"; it should be *rmog*, "helmet."

32. An error in the original text gives the Tibetan *khyi*, "dog"; it should be *khri*, "throne."

33. This is reference to the two rocks, copper and brass-colored, that are so close together as to prevent passage.

34. The Tibetan *smad tshang* is literally "lower parts," taken here to mean the barrel or body of a horse, which includes the torso and internal organs.

35. In Vajrayāna, the three lights refer to the winds, channels, and *bindus*.

36. The qualities of divine sight, divine hearing, recollection of former lives, cognition of the minds of others, capacity for performing miracles, the cognition of the exhaustion of defilements.

37. An error in the original text gives the Tibetan *phyar*, "raise," "brandish"; it should be *phyor mo*, "elegant."

38. An error in the original text gives the Tibetan *zer ba*, "said to be"; it should be *ze ba*, "mane."

39. This count is correct if the sacral vertebrae are considered fused and counted as one.

40. Tibetan transliteration of the Chinese gives *li, khon, dwa, khen, kham, gin, zin, zon*: fire, lake, heaven, wood, water, mountain, earth, thunder.

41. This refers to an invitation sent from the ḍākinīs to great lamas and appears as stretched silk, written upon in five colors. Perhaps this is like the Western expression, "the writing on the wall."

42. An error in the original text gives the Tibetan *gza*, "Rāhula"; it should be *gzi*, "splendor."

43. Tibetans of Amdo heat sand until it is hot and dark and then add barley grain, which pops open, perfectly roasted and not burned. The sand is shaken or sifted out, leaving the roasted barley.

44. This means that a weak man would worry in windstorm that a rock could be carried, but this is a pointless worry; it cannot happen.

45. The bard gives the order as "Dharma, Buddha, and Saṅgha." We have put it in the traditional order.

46. The landscape here is not what is seen by ordinary humans; instead, there is a pure land seen by the divine ones, gods, dralha, and so on. Therefore, although they are in a mountainous inland place, an ocean is seen.

CHAPTER FOURTEEN

1. These are four great guardian kings (*rgyal chen sde bzhi*), each appointed to one of the four cardinal directions: Dhṛtarāṣṭra (east), Virūḍhaka (south), Virūpākṣa (west), Vaiśravaṇa (north).

2. The six sages (*Thub pa drug*) are manifestations of a buddha appointed to each of the six realms of existence (gods, demigods, humans, animals, hungry ghosts, hell beings). For example, Śākyamuni is the buddha of the human realm.

3. See chapter 11, note 8.

4. Dakmema (Bdag med ma) refers to a female bodhisattva.

5. An error in the original text gives the Tibetan rong ma, "farming"; it should be ro ma, "right channel" or "rasanā."

6. An error in the original text gives the Tibetan *bkrugs*, which has no meaning and should be *bkrug*, "commotion."

7. An error in the original text gives the Tibetan *phong ba*, "destitute"; it should be *pha 'ong*, giving *lcags kyi pha 'ong*, "iron boulder."

8. An error in the original text gives the Tibetan *mchid* "discourse"; it should be *mched*, giving *mched pa*, "increase," "intensify."

9. This refers to Gesar and to their childhood love.

10. We switched the order of this line and the one before, for clarity in English.

11. The Tibetan text gives the number of ministers as "sixty," probably a poetic adjustment by the bard who could not fit "three hundred and sixty" into the meter of the line. We have added it for consistency.

12. An error in the original text gives the Tibetan *srog dor*, "sacrifice"; it should be *srog bdag*, "life lord" and here is modified by *dmar*, which means "red" but also "valuable" and emphasizes the importance of the life lord.

13. An error in the original text gives the Tibetan *spog*, "incense"; it should be *srog*, "life force."

14. An error in the original text gives the Tibetan *sne*; it should be *sna*, giving *char sna*, "as the rain is led."

15. Lutsen is saying the fault lies with the ministers who did not work out the situation and Natra acted hastily and arrogantly, bringing punishment down on himself.

CHAPTER FIFTEEN

1. In the Tibetan, this line appears five lines above, but it makes more sense to place it after the geographic description, so we have moved it.

2. The Tibetan *srin tsho 'bar ba* gives this as Sintsho Barwa or Blazing Lake, but we have chosen to keep the previous name of Sintsho Marpo, Cannibal Red Lake, for consistency.

3. An error in the original text gives the Tibetan *'ongs*, which is a future tense indicator; it should be *'ong*, giving *yid du 'ong*, "handsome."

4. An error in the original text gives the Tibetan *shubs*, "quiver"; it should be *shugs*, "strength," "power," or "energy."

5. An error in the original text gives the Tibetan *mdel*, "bullet"; it should be *mda'*, "arrow."

6. An error in the original text gives the Tibetan *skyid*, "happy"; it should be *skyi*, giving *skyi gya'*, "shudder."

7. The three white foods are milk, yogurt, and butter.

8. The Tibetan gives the steed's name as Rakar Dingshé (Rag dkar lding shes), but we have used the previous name of Rakar Tsubshé.

9. This is a wrathful form of Padmasambhava.

10. An error in the original text gives the Tibetan *mtsho*, "lake"; it should be *'tsho*, "nurture."

11. This is somewhat odd, as he is almost always referred to as Ching-ngön.

12. An error in the original text gives the Tibetan *lug mig ngo chod pas phan le min*, "it will do no good to recognize the sheep by its eye"; it should be *lug mgo chod pas phan le min*, "it will do no good to cut off its head," pointing out that that is not the way the sheep will be overcome. Also, the line in error has eight syllables, so does not fit the meter.

CHAPTER SIXTEEN

1. We have added this line, omitted by the bard, which should be here to correspond with the "right horn" line two lines above.

2. In current-day Kham, there is a beautiful lake by this name in the nomadic lands. It is uncertain whether it is the same lake that Lutsen refers to here.

3. These refer back to the image of the six skills of a garuḍa.

4. The implication is that she is a virgin.

5. *sman bu mo'i 'og kha a long yin / a long de la rdzogs rgyu med / a long de la zad rgyu med / pho stag shar 'og 'dzar rgyud pa yin / rgyud pa de la rdzogs rgyu med / rgyud pa de la rul rgyu med.* These six lines are difficult to render in English as beautifully as they are expressed in Tibetan.

6. An error in the original text gives the Tibetan *phyid*, "snow-blindness"; it should be *chen*, "great," giving *gnam mtsho phyid mo*, the consistent name of the lake, Namtsho Chenmo.

7. Usually his horse is called Sinta Phurshé, though here it is referred to as Naktra Phurshé or Mottled Black Flying. We have kept the usual name for simplicity and clarity.

CHAPTER SEVENTEEN

1. See chapter 9, note 4.
2. The idea here is that Gesar will make a model or a diorama, but that it will look life-sized to Lutsen, much as we might make a movie using a miniature set filmed to look realistic.
3. Singmo Thiklé (Sring mo thig le) is another name for Thalé Ökar, used here for consistency.
4. We have reversed the order of these two lines for ease of reading.
5. The exact identity of these areas is unknown, but they are perhaps lands rich in mules and dzo, respectively.
6. See chapter 9, note 6.
7. An error in the original text gives the Tibetan *sman*, "woman"; it should be *mas*, giving "by her," meaning she was the one speaking.
8. This may sound negative, but it is actually a source of pride for the māras.
9. An error in the original text gives the Tibetan *bdud rtse*, which has no meaning and should be *bdud rtsi*, "dütsi" or "amṛta."
10. The Tibetan *chag bzan* refers to a special horse feed that was specially prepared from white and red rice and tsampa, perhaps with tea leaves and butter.
11. Ancient lore has it that when the turquoise dragon ages, it becomes a makara, and when that makara ages, it develops a paisley-like pattern on its head.
12. The original text gives the Tibetan *zam pa*, "bridge," but this list was previously given as *dur*, "charnel ground," and we have changed it for consistency. Again, this variation probably occurred because multiple texts were incorporated in the compilation of the text that we translated.
13. The original text gives the Tibetan *tshang ra*, "hinder part," but this list was previously given as *tshang rul*, "filthy lair," and we have changed it for consistency for the same reason as explained above.
14. The Tibetan here simply says his tiger-skin quiver was on his right, but previously this list was given as the tiger-skin quiver "pinning him down," and we have changed it for consistency.
15. Shelkar Drakphuk (Shel dkar drag phug) is the same as Shelgyi Drubkhang, and we have used its previous name for consistency.
16. She is referring to the nine-square chart of the Mewa (Sme ba) system of Tibetan astrology. It is quite complex, and its full explication is beyond the scope of this text. Suffice it to say that the *mewas* change with each day, month, and year, and at this time in Lutsen's life his mewas are very intense and negative. See Cornu, *Tibetan Astrology*.
17. An error in the original text gives the Tibetan *gyon*, "left"; it should be *gyar*, "borrow."
18. The text says, "Yellow Hat Ones."
19. In the image magically created by Gesar and Manéné, his nostrils were full of flies and coral, but Lutsen sees it here as pus and blood. This is likely another indication that the text has been compiled from multiple bards (see introduction.).
20. The Tibetan *mardo* (*mar do*) means "load of butter," One mardo is about 150 pounds.
21. See chapter 8, note 8.
22. An error in the original text gives the Tibetan *sum brgya drug cu*, "three hundred and sixty," which makes no sense; we assume the bard meant *sum cu*, "thirty."

23. As a reminder to the reader, Achung, also known as Lutsen, is the third brother. At an earlier point in the story, Gesar pretends to be Achung when he goes to meet the teurang mother.

24. Pehar (Pe har) is the guardian deity of the monasteries of Tibet, particularly Samyé.

25. Here Meza gives a different explanation to Gesar regarding where Lutsen has gone rather than saying that he left to check on his spirit sheep, as the bard stated earlier. We assume this is because the text has been compiled from multiple bards, as stated in the translators' introduction.

26. The Tibetan gives this as the Wood Tiger year, but as this is incompatible with other dates given in the text, we have omitted the element and given this simply as the Tiger year.

27. An error in the original text gives the Tibetan *bdun*, "seven"; it should be *gnyis*, "two." This is consistently given elsewhere in the story as two, not seven, copper pots and probably reflects the fact that the story is compiled from multiple bards (see introduction).

28. An error in the original text gives the Tibetan *dkar mo*; it should be *dkar po*. Both mean "white," but his name has always been given Dungkhyung Karpo.

CHAPTER EIGHTEEN

1. An error in the original text gives the Tibetan *bsad*, "kill"; it should be *sad*, "awoke."

2. Her horse was previously given as Kyaka Dingshé (Skya ka lding shes) or Skilled Flying Magpie, and we have kept this name for consistency.

3. An error in the original text gives the Tibetan *phra mo*, "little"; it should be *khra mo*, "sparkling."

4. These refer to three of the twenty-eight *nakṣatras*, gods of the constellations, the fifth resembling the head of an antelope, Lambda Orionis, Alpha Orionis, and Delta Cancri.

5. In Tibetan astrology, those black magic substances sometimes are put inside a bag before they are buried.

6. An error in the original text gives the Tibetan *dgyes*, "pleased"; it should be *rgyas*, "flourish."

7. Shantideva, *A Guide to the Bodhisattva's Way of Life*, 10.55. This verse was added by the translators.

GENEALOGY

1. Although there are many obvious cases of polygamy, polyandry was quite common as well and, although banned by the Chinese, is still said to be practiced in parts of Tibet. Although the topic remains controversial, many scholars consider that it may have developed as a means through which a culture with scarce resources can limit its population growth. See, for instance, Goldstein, "When Brothers Share a Wife."

GLOSSARY OF NAMES

Acham Karmo (A lcam dkar mo). A lasso-wielding demoness and minister of Lutsen.

Achen (A chen). A tribe and a region in the kingdom of Hor.

Akaniṣṭha ('Og min). The highest of the buddhafields, the pure land where bodhisattvas attain buddhahood.

Akhö Tharpa Zorna (Hooked-Nose Tharpa, A khod thar pa'i zor sna). Personal attendant and minister to Trothung.

Akhu Gomchen Tingmé (Profound Great Meditator, A khu sgom chen gting med). A profound meditator and advisor.

Amdo (A mdo). The large area in northeast Tibet.

Amitābha ('Od dpag med). The buddha of the Padma family (one of the five buddha families), who is associated with the western direction and manifests the wisdom of discriminating awareness.

Amnye Machen. See **Magyal Pomra**.

Amoghasiddhi (Don yod grub pa). The buddha of the Karma family (one of the five buddha families), who is associated with the northern direction and manifests the wisdom of all-accomplishing activity.

Anu Paseng of Ombu (Courageous Youthful Lion of Ombu, 'Om bu'i a nu dpa' seng). A minister of the Middle Lineage of Ling of Ombu and one of the four divine heirs.

Atak Lhamo (A stag lha mo). A powerful woman, skilled archer, and one of Lutsen's ministers. She is an emanation of the Lion-Faced One, Siṃhamukha.

Avalokiteśvara (Spyan ras gzigs). A bodhisattva, the embodiment of compassion. He is one of the three principal protectors of this world, the other two being Mañjuśrī and Vajrapāṇi.

Berotsana (Bai ro tsa na, Skt. Vairocana). Greatest of all the Indian translators. Along with Padmasambhava and Vimalamitra, he is responsible for bringing Buddhist teachings to Tibet.

Beu Natra (Spotted-Nose Calf, Beu sna khra). Lutsen's principal minister.

Bloody Tress (Khrag ral ma). The only female and the youngest and most powerful of the Seven Wayward Siblings. She is the daughter of the demoness Wangjema.

Bön (Bon). Held previously to be the indigenous religion of Tibet and now understood as a distinct religion with a long history of mutual exchange with Tibetan Buddhism.

Brahmā (Tshangs pa). (1) The Hindu god of creation. (2) In Buddhist cosmology, the ruler of the gods of the form realm.

Cakrasaṃvara ('Khor lo bde mchog). A fierce tantric deity usually seen in yabyum with Vajravārāhī as a metaphor for bliss-emptiness.

Chakri Tsegu (Nine-Storied Iron Mountain, Lcags ri rtse dgu). The nine-storied māra castle of the Düd king Lutsen; also called Shari Tsegu (Nine-Storied Eastern Mountain, Shar ri rtse dgu), Shari Namdzong (Eastern Mountain Sky Fortress, Shar ri gnam rdzong), or Sharu Namdzong (Staghorn Sky Fortress, Shar ru gnam rdzong).

Chamara (Rnga yab). The island southwest of the continent of Jambudvīpa where the cannibal demons live. It is the abode of Padmasambhava in his wrathful form, Lotus Skull Garland, and generally said to be present-day Sri Lanka.

Chidak. See **Yama.**

Ching-ngön (Ancient Felt, Phying sngon). One of Lutsen's ministers and the shepherd of his life-force sheep. He was turned to the Dharma by Gesar. On one occasion, he refers to himself as Anu Sengtren. He was the brother to Gyatsha Zhalkar, Gesar's uncle, in a previous lifetime.

Chipön Rongtsha Tragen (Spyi dpon rong tsha khra rgan). The chief of the Lesser Lineage, the brother of Senglön, and therefore Gesar's uncle. He was a reincarnation of the mahāsiddha Kukuripa and the Paṇḍita Sergyi Dongchen.

Chölu Buyi Darphen (Chos lu bu yi dar 'phen). One of the Seven Super Warriors and a skilled lancer. He is also often called, simply, Darphen.

Chöphen Nakpo (Chos phan nag po). An ancestral Mukpo clan leader from whom descended the Greater, Middle, and Lesser Lineages of Ling through his marriage to three powerful women, respectively, Serza, Omza, and Changza (or Changmoza) of the Ser (*gser*), Om ('*om*), and Chang (*spyangs*) clans.

Darphen. See **Chölu Buyi Darphen.**

Den ('Dan). A region in Kham.

Denma ('Dan ma). The chief minister of Gesar who is famed as a great archer. His full name is Tshazhang Denma Jangtra (Tsha zhang 'dan ma byang khra), reflecting his homeland. He is considered an emanation of Saraha.

Dokham (Mdo khams). Another name for Kham and Amdo, or eastern Tibet.

Dölpa Nakpo (Gdol pa nag po). Manéné's uncle and the one who provides an army that she disguises in an amulet box when she is impersonating the demoness Wangjema.

Dongtsen Apel (Gdong btsan a dpal). Loyal younger son of Trothung. He accompanies Trothung when he goes to meet with the demon Yutsé.

Dorje Lekpa (Rdo rje legs pa). A wrathful protector deity riding a brown ram and holding the implements of a blacksmith. He is also called Vajrasādhu.

Dralha Tsegyal (Victorious Mountain Peak Dralha, Dgra lha rtse rgyal). The son of Gyatsha and Rakza, born after their first son was snatched away by the demoness Wangjema and her daughter Bloody Tress.

Dri Chu ('Bri chu). The Yangtze River, the longest river in Asia and third longest in the world.

Drukmo (Dragon Woman, 'Brug mo). Gesar's wife and queen and daughter of Tönpa Gyaltsen of Kyalo, said to be the wealthiest man in Tibet. She is also known as Sengcham Drukmo (Lion Sister Dragoness, Seng lcam 'brug mo) because when she was born, a snow lion was seen poised on the mountain. She is an emanation of White Tārā.

Düd (Bdud). (1) The country of māras northwest of Ling. (2) A class of demons.

Duktsho (Poisonous Lake, Dug mtsho). The lake in which the life-force talismans of the gods-demons dwell. This is to the southeast of Ling, south of Nakshö, and somewhere in the vast borderland area of Takrong and Minyak in Yutsé's area of sovereignty. It is also referred to as Duktsho Khölma (Poisonous Boiling Lake, Dug mtsho khol ma) or Duktsho Nakpo (Black Poisonous Lake, Dug mtsho nag po).

Dungkhyung Karpo (White-Conch Garuḍa, Dung khyung dkar po). Gesar's older co-born dralha brother and his personal bodyguard.

Gadé Chökyong Bernak (Ga sde chos skyong ber nag). A leader of the Middle Lineage of Ling, one of the Seven Super Warriors, and an emanation of Mahākāla. He is usually simply called Gadé.

Garab Wangchuk (Dga' rab dbang phyug). The chief māra deity.

Garwa Nakpo (Mgar ba nag po). Both the attendant to and an emanation of Dorje Lekpa. He is depicted as riding a brown ram and holding the implements of a blacksmith.

Gedzo (Ge 'dzo). A mountain spirit, the nyen (*gnyan*) of Mount Gedzo, and a guardian protector for Gesar. He is also called Nyenchen Khulha (Gnyan chen sku lha), a "body protector," and these variations: Nyen Gedzo (Gnyan ge 'dzo), Nyenchen Khula Gedzo (Gnyan chen sku lha ge 'dzo), and Nyenchen Gedzo (Gnyan chen ge 'dzo).

Gesar, king of Ling (Gling rje ge sar). The celestial son born into the human realm as the son of Chief Senglön and Gokmo (Yelga Dzeden), the nāginī princess. He is known by various epithets at different points in the epic. At birth he is known as Joru (Jo ru) and after winning the horse race that brings him the throne of Ling, Padmasambhava confers upon him the name Sengchen Norbu Dradül (Great Lion Jewel Tamer of Enemies, Seng chen nor bu dgra 'dul) or Gesar Norbu Dradül (Jewel Tamer of Enemies, Ge sar nor bu dgra 'dul).

Glorious Copper-Colored Mountain (Zangs mdog dpal ri). A mountain in the mythic subcontinent of Chamara (present-day Sri Lanka), which was inhabited by savage rākṣasas. There, Padmasambhava, Guru Rinpoche, resides in the palace Lotus Light. See chapter 1, note 18.

Göcham Karmo. See **Manéné**.

Gok ('Gog). An area neighboring Ling and home of the Gok tribe whose king, Ralo Tönpa, cared for the nāginī princess, Metok Lhadzé, who would become Gesar's mother.

Gokmo ('Gog mo). Literally, "woman from Gok" and one of the names taken by Gesar's destined mother, the nāginī princess Metok Lhadzé, after she comes to Ling from her sojourn in Gok.

Gokza ('Gog bza'). Literally, "wife from Gok" and one of the names taken by Gesar's destined mother, the nāginī princess Metok Lhadzé, after she comes to Ling from her sojourn in Gok.

Golok (Mgo log). An area of Tibet between Kham and Amdo, and now in the southeastern corner of present-day Qinghai Province in China. Also refers to the nomadic Golok people who live in this area of high-altitude pasturelands.

Gomchen Tingmé. See **Akhu Gomchen Tingmé**.

Gurkar, King (Gur dkar). One of the tribal kings of Hor (the others being Gurnak and Gurser) and a main figure in a later volume of the epic, "The Battle of Hor and Ling," when he captures and holds Drukmo, Gesar's wife.

Gyatsha Zhalkar (Rgya tsha zhal dkar). Literally, "Chinese nephew," the son of Senglön and Gyaza, the elder half brother of Gesar, and nephew of the Chinese emperor. One of the Seven Super Warriors, he is of the Bumpa clan of the Lesser Lineage of Ling.

Gyaza (Rgya bza'). The mother of Gyatsha Zhalkar and the primary wife of Senglön. Her full name is Lhakar Drönma (Divine White Torch, Lha dkar sgron ma).

Hayagrīva (Rta mgrin). A fierce tantric deity, or yidam, and the personal deity of Trothung. He is a wrathful form of Amitābha, most often pictured with the head of a horse.

Hor (Hor). A kingdom to the north and east of Ling, ruled by demons who are enemies of Ling. The Hor are divided into three tribes, each governed by a king: King Gurkar (White Tent), King Gurnak (Black Tent), and King Gurser (Yellow Tent).

Jalak Derchu (Eagle Talon Beak, Bya lag sder mchu). A gatekeeper demoness for the demon king Yutsé.

Jama Jigo (Bat Head, Bya ma byi mgo). A gatekeeper demoness for the demon king Yutsé.

Jambudvīpa ('Dzam bu gling). The southern continent in the cosmology of the Buddhist world system but is an epithet for "the world," roughly equivalent to "planet Earth" in the Western cosmological system, the world populated by human beings. It is named after the *jambu* (rose apple) tree.

Jang ('Jang). A country ruled by King Sadam southwest of Ling in current-day Kham. Gesar conquers it in later volumes of the epic.

Joru (Jo ru). A name given to Gesar when he was a young boy in Ling. See **Gesar**.

Kailash, Mount (Gangs ti se). Located in southwest Tibet, a pilgrimage and sacred site for four religions: Bön, Buddhism, Hinduism, and Jainism. Its 21,778 feet remain unclimbed to this day.

Khergö (Kher rgod). (1) A Ling citizen named Khergö (Solitary Vulture) son of Guru. Guru is known from the previous epic volume as the poorest man in Ling and rode with Gesar in the horse race. (2) A māra named Khergö Mikmar (Joking Red Eye) who is a magician, killed by Gadé in a battle between the māras and the Ling warriors.

Kyalo Tönpa Gyaltsen. See **Tönpa Gyaltsen of Kyalo**.

Kyang Gö (Wild Kyang, Rkyang rgod). Gesar's wondrous horse, who is an emanation of Amitābha. Gesar's horse is not literally a kyang but lived wild among them before he was captured by Drukmo and Gesar's mother, Gokmo.

Lenpa Chögyal (Simpleminded Dharma King, Glen pa chos rgyal). Son of Chipön, who was killed in a battle with Gok. While avenging his death, the Ling warriors come upon the nāginī princess who will become Gesar's mother. This story is told in Kornman et al., *The Epic of Gesar of Ling*, 169–81.

Lhakar Drönma. See **Gyaza**.

Lineage, Elder or **Greater, Middle, Lesser**. The tribal lineages that descend, respectively, from the first, second, and third wives of Chöphen Nakpo, an ancestral leader of Tibet. The terms *Elder* or *Greater Lineage*, *Middle Lineage*, and *Lesser Lineage* are not hierarchical. See genealogy chart.

Ling (Gling). A region within Ma where the epic story takes place. It is often referred to as Tramo Ling (Bkra mo gling), referring to its sunlit striated dark rock and snow-stippled mountainsides. *Upper*, *Middle*, and *Lower* refer to areas in Ling, more or less proximal to the Ma Chu headwaters.

Ludrül Öchung (Nāga Serpent Little Light, Klu sbrul od chung). Gesar's younger dralha brother, one of the magical beings born with him.

Lugön Tongthub Yamé (Unrivaled Nāga Protector Defeats One Thousand, Klu mgon stong thub ya med). One of King Yutsé's ministers, and (the blue) one of the Seven Wayward Siblings.

Lutsen (Klu btsan). The king of Düd, the māra lands northwest of Ling, and an emanation of Trarab Wangchuk.

Ma (Rma). The region of northeastern Tibet (current-day Amdo) surrounding the headwaters and upper course of the Ma River and extending south toward the Dri Chu (Yangtze River). Ling is located within Ma and is Gesar's homeland. *Upper*, *Middle*, and *Lower* Ma refer to the areas that are progressively farther from the headwaters of the Ma Chu (Ma River).

Ma Chu (Rma chu). A river that courses through Tibet and empties into the North Pacific Ocean as the Yellow River with a total length of 3,395 miles.

Magyal Pomra (Rma rgyal spom ra). The name of both the zodor, the guardian spirit, and of the mountain that it guards, Magyal Pomra. The mountain is also known as Amnye Machen and is in the Golok district of present-day Qinghai Province.

Mahākāla (Nag po chen po). Protector deities, typically wrathful, common to Buddhism, Hinduism, and Sikhism.

Manasarovar, Lake (Ma dros pa). A large freshwater lake south of Mount Kailash sacred to those of Buddhist, Hindu, Bön, and Jain faiths.

Manéné (Ma ne ne). Gesar's aunt, guide, and protector. Her full name is Manéné Namen Karmo (Ma ne ne gnam sman dkar mo), and other times she is called Auntie Göcham Karmo (A ne Rgod lcam dkar mo).

Mañjuśrī ('Jam dpal). A bodhisattva, the embodiment of insight and wisdom, and one of the three principal protectors of Tibet, the other two being Avalokiteśvara and Vajrapāṇi.

Margyenma. The Tibetan king Trisong Detsen's wife.

Masang (Ma sang). An ancestral tribe of Ling. It is also used as an epithet for Gesar, "the Masang king."

Meru, Mount (Rgyal mo ri rab). The cosmologic center of the universe common to Buddhism, Hinduism, and Jainism.

Metok Lhadzé (Flower Divine Beauty, Me tog lha mdzes). A nāginī princess, taken from the nāga realm by Padmasambhava to be Gesar's mother.

Meza Bumdrön (Lady of One Hundred Thousand Torches, Me bza' 'bum sgron). The māra king Lutsen's intended wife and an emanation of Red Vajravārāhī. She was taken from her childhood home in Akyi in Ling as a young girl and is living in the māra land, but she had already had a close connection with Gesar and is instrumental in helping him in his quest to defeat Lutsen. She is also referred to as Trishok Meza Bumdron (Khri shog me bza' 'bum sgron).

Michung Khadé (Young Clever Mouth, Mi chung kha bde). A Gok orphan known for his eloquence brought to Chipön's household, who stays in the Hor king's court. He is an emanation of Thangtong Gyalpo.

Mighty Warriors, Thirty. See **Pathül**.

Migö Yamé (Matchless Savage, Mi rgod ya med). One of King Yutsé's ministers and (the yellow) one of the Seven Wayward Siblings. He is a gyalgong emanation.

Minyak (Mi nyag). See **Yutsé, king of Minyak**.

Mön (Mon). Present-day Bhutan, ruled by King Shingtri in Gesar's time.

Mount Kailash. See **Kailash, Mount**.

Mount Meru. See **Meru, Mount**.

Mu clan (Smu or Rmu). A tribe of the Lesser Lineage of Ling. Senglön was descended from the Mu clan through his mother, Muza. It is also called Muchang (Dmu spyang).

Muchang. See **Mu clan.**

Mukpo or **Mukpo Dong** (Smug po gdong). The ancestral lineage of the Mukpo tribe or clan to which Gesar belongs.

Mupa (Mu pa). A clan of the Lesser Lineage.

Nakpo Tongdü Lenmé. See **Tongdü Lenmé.**

Nakshö (Nags shod). The forested lowlands west of Amnye Machen and north of Zima, the territory of Amnyé Bumthub, the ancestral spirit of the māras, and the dark valleys that Gesar must traverse in order to reach the Düd lands.

Namthel, Sathal, Barthel (Gnam thal, Sa thal, and Bar thal). The teurang spirit deities of the sky, earth, and in between.

Namtri Barma (Gnam khri 'bar ma). A mountain pass that forms a southern border of Zima.

Nang-ngu Yutak. See **Yuyi Metok.**

Nang-ngu Yuyi Metok. See **Yuyi Metok.**

Neuchung (Ne'u chung). Drukmo's paternal cousin, childhood friend, and confidante. She is an emanation of Green Tārā. Her full name is Neuchung Lugu Tsharyak (Ne'u chung lu gu tshar yag).

Ngülchu Trodzong (Ormolu Fortress, Dngul chu khro rdzong). Gyatsha and Gyaza's fortress.

Norbu Dradül. See **Gesar.**

Nyatsha Aten (Nya tsha a brtan). One of Trothung's older sons, one of the Thirty Mighty Warriors, and one of the Seven Super Warriors.

Nyenchen Gedzo. See **Gedzo.**

Nyenchen Kulha (Gnyan chen sku lha). See **Gedzo.**

Nyen Gedzo. See **Gedzo.**

Nyentak Marpo (Gnyan stag dmar po). A mountain god and an important dralha.

Nyibum Daryak of Serpa (Gser pa'i nyi 'bum dar yag). The head of the Serpa clan of the Greater Lineage of Ling, one of the Thirty Mighty Warriors, and Falcon, one of the Three Ultimate Warriors.

Nyüljema (Nyul byed ma). Amnye's wife, a black vulture.

Ombu ('Om bu). (1) The clan of the Middle Lineage. (2) An area in northeastern Tibet.

Orgyen Padmasambhava. See **Padmasambhava.**

Padmasambhava (The Lotus Born, Pad ma 'byung gnas). The tantric yogi who was responsible for bringing Vajrayāna Buddhism to Tibet. His name means "Born from a Lotus," which is an indication of his magical origins. He is one of the principal objects of devotion in Tibetan Vajrayāna Buddhism.

Pathül (Dpa' rtul gsum bcu). The thirty chief warriors of Ling, all incarnations of mahāsiddhas. Among them are two groups of warriors of a higher degree: the Seven Super Warriors and the Three Ultimate Warriors.

Phunu (Phu nu sum cu). A contraction of the Tibetan *phu bo* and *nu bo*, meaning, respectively, elder and younger brother. It refers to uncles, cousins, and nephews and also connotes a loyal clan of warriors, many of whom are related to each other through blood or matrimony. Specifically, in this volume of the epic, it refers to a group of thirty great warriors who, in Samten Karmay's words, demonstrate three paradigms: "solidarity, commensality and equality of status." See Karmay, "The Social Organization of Ling."

Porok Nying Dzong (Raven Heart Fortress, Pho rog snying rdzong). Trothung's fortress located in present-day Golok near the confluence of the Ma (Yellow) and Ko Rivers. There are many variations of the name of the fortress, including Sipa Khölmo Rokdzong (Black Bellow Fortress of Existence, Srid pa khol mo'i rog rdzong).

Potala Mountain. The pure land of the bodhisattva of compassion, Avalokiteśvara.

Prajñāpāramitā Sūtra. A twelve-volume collection of Prajñāpāramitā texts kept for centuries by the nāgas before being brought to the human realm by Nāgārjuna. In the epic, the texts are given by the nāgas to Gokmo, Gesar's mother, and hence passed into the common possession of the Ling tribe. It is also known as the *One-Hundred-Thousand-Verse Prajñāpāramitā Sūtra*

protectors of the three families. Also called "lords of the three families," the three bodhisattvas, Mañjuśrī, Vajrapāṇi, and Vajrasattva, who represent the Buddha's wisdom, power, and compassion, respectively.

Queen of Siddhi (Grub pa'i rgyal mo). A goddess invoked in Ling in ceremonies of protection, in particular protecting one's life duration (*tshe*). She is also known as the Sole Mother Queen of Siddhi (Ma gcig grub pa'i rgyal mo).

Rāhu (Sgra gcan). A malevolent heavenly body that causes eclipses by swallowing the moon. He is commonly depicted as either a disembodied head, a head with torso and hands grasping the sun and moon, or with the lower body of a snake.

Rāhula (Holder of Rāhu, Sgra gcan 'dzin). A protector deity that represents a combination of Viṣṇu and Rāhu. He is usually depicted with a snake tail, nine heads crowned by a raven head, a face in his belly, four arms, and a body covered with eyes.

Rakza (Rag bza'). Gyatsha's wife.

Ralo Tönpa Gyaltsen (Ra lo ston pa rgyal mtshan). King of Gok who was requested by Padmasambhava to protect Gokmo (Yelga Dzeden), the nāginī princess, as his own daughter. He was considered an emanation of Thangtong Gyalpo.

Raven Heart Fortress. See **Porok Nying Dzong.**

Rinchen Darlu of Muchang (Smu spyang rin chen dar lu). A minister of the Muchang clan of the Lesser Lineage and one of the four divine heirs.

Rong (Rong). Literally, "farmland valley," but may refer to a land southeast of Ling.

Rongtsha (Rong tsha). Son of Senglön and Rongza. He is also called Rongtsha Marleb and Rongtsha Lhadar and is not to be confused with Chipön Rongtsha Tragen.

Sadam, King (Sa dam). Chieftain of the land of Jang and Gesar's enemy in the saga of the war with Jang.

Samantabhadra (Kun tu bzang po). The primordial dharmakāya buddha, known in Tibetan as Kuntuzangpo, meaning "Ever Excellent."

Sengcham Drukmo. See **Drukmo.**

Sengchen. See **Gesar.**

Sengdruk Taktsé (Lion Dragon Tiger Peak, Seng 'brug stag rtse). Gesar's castle, located in present-day Golok, sometimes called Sengtruk Taktsé (Lion Cub Tiger Peak, Seng 'phrug stag rtse).

Senglön (Lion Minister, Seng blon). The leader of the Thirty Mighty Warriors and the chieftain of all of Ling. He is a brother to both Trothung and Chipön and is Gesar's human father, a son of Chöla Bum of the Lesser Lineage, descending from the Bum tribe. His wife is Gyaza, a Chinese aristocrat named Lhakar Drönma (Divine White Torch, Lha dkar sgron ma), and their son is Gyatsha Zhalkar.

Sengtak Adom (Lion Tiger Youthful Bear, Seng stag a dom). A leader in the Middle Lineage of Ling and one of the Seven Super Warriors.

Serpa (Gser pa). The clan of the Elder or Greater Lineage. The eight Serpa brothers are the principal warriors of Upper Ling.

Sertsho (Golden Lake, Gser mtsho). Trothung's wife, a native of Den, and the daughter of King Khara. Also known as Denza (Dan bza').

Seven Super Warriors (Yang 'thul). A subgroup of the Thirty Mighty Warriors that includes: Gyatsha Zhalkar (Rgya tsha zhal dkar), Sengtak Adom (Seng stag a dom), Tshazhang Denma Jangtra (Tsha zhang 'dan ma byang khra), Anu Zikphen (A nu gzig 'phen), Chökyong Bernak (Chos skyong ber nag), Chölu Buyi Darphen (Chos lu bu yi dar 'phen), and Nyatsha Aten (Nya tsha a rten).

Seven Wayward Siblings (Gdug pa spun bdun). Seven siblings who were born as demons to the demoness Yitrok Wangjema after she copulated with various samaya-violating demons (tsen, māras, rākṣasas, nāgas, mu spirits, teurang, and gongpo spirits). These seven were born from eggs and then took human form. They are blue Lugön, black Tongdü Lenmé, red Tsenkya Bumthub, pale-green Shechen Yamé, yellow Migö Yamé, white Shelgyi Lakring, and the youngest, the female red Trakrelma, Bloody Tress. Their leader was King Minyak Yutsé.

Shari Namdzong. See **Chakri Tsegu**.

Shari Tsegu. See **Chakri Tsegu**.

Sharu Namdzong. See **Chakri Tsegu**.

Shechen Yamé (Unrivaled Great Strength, Shed chen ya med). One of King Yutsé's ministers and (the green) one of the Seven Wayward Siblings.

Sheldrak (Crystal Cave, Shel brag). A treasure cave previously opened by Gesar.

Shelé Lakring (Crystal Long-Arm, Shel las lag ring). One of King Yutsé's ministers, a teurang emanation, and (the white) one of the Seven Wayward Siblings.

Shenpa (Shan pa or Bshan pa). Literally, "butcher," (1) a descriptive name given to the Hor king Gurkar and (2) a name given to one of his ministers, Dikchö Shenpa.

Shingtri, King (Shing khri). King of Mön, one of the kings of the demon lands of the eight directions.

Shinjé. See **Yama**.

Sipa Gangri (Srid pa gangs ri). The snow-mountain range that borders Lutsen's land to the south.

Takphen (Leaping Tiger, Stag 'phen). One of Trothung's sons and one of the Thirty Mighty Warriors.

Takrong (Tiger Valley, Stag rong). A province ruled by Trothung that lies between the Ma Chu (Yellow) and the Dri Chu (Yangtze) Rivers.

Tārā (Sgrol ma). The female counterpart of Avalokiteśvara, the bodhisattva of compassion.

Thalé Ökar (Luminous White Light, Tha le 'od dkar). Gesar's co-born sister, a dralha protector.

Thangtong Gyalpo (Thang stong rgyal po). Literally, "field of emptiness king," a mahāsiddha and the spiritual advisor to the Mukpo tribe and the kingdom of Ling.

Thirty Mighty Warriors. See **Pathül**.

Three Ultimate Warriors (Zhe 'thul gsum). An elite subgroup of the Thirty Mighty Warriors that includes Falcon, Eagle, and Wolf—Nyibum Daryak, Anu Paseng, and Rinchen Darlu, respectively.

Tongdü Lenmé (Unrivaled Thousand Demons, Stong bdud lan med). One of King Yutsé's ministers and the black one of the Seven Wayward Siblings.

Tönpa Gyaltsen of Kyalo (Skya lo ston pa rgyal mtshan). Leader of the wealthy class of Ling and the father of Drukmo, Gesar's bride.

Trakmikma (Bloodshot Eye, Khrag mig ma). The black nāga demon deity of the māras.

Trakrelma (Khrag ral ma). See **Seven Wayward Siblings** and **Bloody Tress**.

Tramo Ling. See **Ling**.

Trishok Meza Bumdrön. See **Meza Bumdrön**.

Trisong Detsen (714–797 C.E., Khri srong lde'u btsan). Ruler of the Tibetan empire four generations after its founder, Songtsen Gampo (Srong btsan sgam po). He brought to Tibet the tantric guru Padmasambhava and the great abbot Śāntarakṣita, the great founders of the Nyingma lineage and the Mahāyāna.

Trogyal (Khro rgyal). Literally, "Wrathful King," another name for Trothung and a reference to the wrathful yidam Hayagrīva, of whom he is an emanation. See **Trothung**.

Trothung (Khro thung). Gesar's uncle, chieftain of the Takrong Province in present-day Golok, and also called Trogyal. He is one of the Thirty Mighty Warriors and Gesar's main foil in the epic such that he is an indispensable part of Gesar's success. Trothung is sometimes considered a reincarnation of Hayagrīva, Trothung's personal yidam.

Tsenkya Bumthub (Pale Tsen Defeats One Hundred Thousand, Btsan skya 'bum thub). One of King Yutsé's ministers and the red one of the Seven Wayward Siblings.

Tshazhang Denma Jangtra. See **Denma**.

Tshazhang Denma. See **Denma**.

Tsukna Rinchen (Precious Jewel at the Crown, Gtsug na rin chen; Skt. Ratnacūṇa). Literally, "Jewel in the Crest," the king of the nāgas and the maternal grandfather of Gesar, pictured as a serpent with a jewel between the eyes.

Turquoise Bird (G.yu bya). Often called Yuja, the horse belonging to Trothung's son Dongtsen.

Ütsang (Dbus gtsang). Central Tibet.

Vairocana (Rnam par snang mdzed). The buddha of the Buddha family (one of the five buddha families), who is associated with the central direction and manifesting the wisdom of space.

Vajradhara (Rdo rje 'chang). Literally, "vajra holder," the primordial buddha of the Kagyü, Sakya, and Gelug schools of Tibetan Buddhism.

Vajrakīlaya (Rdo rje phur pa). Wrathful yidam deity whose practice is used in removing obstacles.

Vajrapāṇi (Phyag na rdo rje). A bodhisattva, the protector and embodiment of the Buddha's power, and one of the three principle protectors of Tibet, the other two being Avalokiteśvara and Mañjuśrī.

Vajrasadhu. See **Dorje Lekpa**.

Vajrasattva (Dorje Sempa, Rdo rje sems dpa'). A bodhisattva of the Mahāyāna and Vajrayāna paths.

Vajravārāhī (Dorje Phagmo, Rdo rje phags mo). A form of the female semi-wrathful buddha, Vajrayoginī. She is the representation of the nature of emptiness and the birthplace of all the buddhas and of phenomenal existence.

Vajrayoginī (Rdo rje rnal 'byor ma). See **Vajravārāhī**.

Wangjema (Hypnotic Ruleress, Yid 'phrog dbang rje ma). Also Yitrok Wangjema, a cannibal blood-drinking demoness and mother of the Seven Wayward Siblings.

Werma Lhadar (Werma Divine Pennant, Wer ma lha dar). An eminent judge in Ling.

Wutaishan (Rgya nag ri bo rtse lnga). The famous five-peaked mountain in the northeast Shanxi Province of China. It is considered the abode of Mañjuśrī, the bodhisattva of wisdom.

Yama Thangchen (Great Slate Pain, Gya' ma thang chen). An area within the great high plateau of northern Tibet, ruled by Lutsen, and the abode of the teurang.

Yama (Gshin rje, Chi bdag). The traditional lord of death in both the Buddhist and Hindu pantheons. He presides over the hell realms.

Yeshé Tsogyal (Wisdom Lake Queen, Ye shes mtsho rgyal). A famous female tantrika, the consort of Padmasambhava and considered the mother of tantra in Tibet.

Yitrok Wangjema. See **Wangjema**.

Yuja. See **Turquoise Bird**.

Yulung Sumdo (Yul lung sum mdo). The unpeopled land near the mountain Magyal Pomra, where Gesar and his mother spent his childhood.

Yutsé, king of Minyak (Mi nyag g.yu rtse rgyal po). The demon king of the land of Minyak that is southeast of Ling.

Yuyi Metok (Turquoise Flower, G.yu yi me tog). The youngest son of Chipön, the youngest among the Thirty Brethren, and one of the Thirteen Cherished Sons. Also called Nang-ngu Yuyi Metok (Snang ngu g.yu yi me tog) and Nang-ngu Yutak (Snang ngu g.yu stag).

Zichim (Zi mchims). An area probably to the southwest of Zima but not historically identifiable.

Zikphen (Leaping Leopard, Gzig 'phen). Trothung's eldest son and one of the Seven Super Warriors.

Zikrong (Gzig rong). The Leopard Valley, an area named for the holdings of Trothung's son Zikphen.

Zima (Zi ma). According to the epic, this was an area close to Ling, now unknown, and nearly inaccessible due to its difficult terrain and bandit inhabitants.

Zi Valley. See **Zima**.

GLOSSARY OF TERMS

amṛta (*bdud rtsi*). A Sanskrit word for nectar or ambrosia. It originally referred to a sacred substance providing immortality but now refers generally to a sacramental liquid used in Vajrayāna meditation practice.

azure firmament (*dgung ngon*). The blue sky above, specifically the "middle sky," that is, the atmosphere as opposed to space.

bodhicitta (*byang chub kyi sems*). Mind that is directed toward clarity and compassion.

bodhisattva (*byang chub sems pa*). One who aspires to attain the state of fully enlightened buddhahood in order to lead all beings to that state. A bodhisattva will consider the needs of others before himself or herself and dedicate his or her life to benefiting beings until saṃsāra is emptied of suffering. A bodhisattva has entered the bhūmis, or levels, and is no longer an ordinary individual subject to karma and passions.

buddha families, five. See **five buddha families**.

buddhafield. See **pure land**.

cakra (*'khor lo*). Literally "wheel," centers of energy along the spinal axis of the human body common to Hindu and Buddhist tantra. In Buddhist tantra, they are most often given as five centers, located at the crown, throat, heart, navel, and genitals.

chang. A general term for liquor but usually referring to beer brewed from barley.

chuba (*phyu pa*). A long, wrapped thick, woolen or sheepskin garment and the traditional dress of Tibetan nomads.

completion stage. See generation and completion stages.

ḍāka (*dpa' bo*). Literally "warrior" or "hero," the male equivalent of ḍākinī, usually wrathful or semi-wrathful.

ḍākinī (*mkha' 'gro*). Literally "sky-goer," female deities who signify the absolute as a messenger principle. They are tricky, playful, magnetizing, motherly, or punishing as they serve the tantric practitioner, bringing messages of enlightenment and guidance. They represent the basic space out of which they manifest to meet the needs of beings in the world.

ḍamaru (*da ma ru*). A small, two-sided drum used in both Hindu and Tibetan Buddhist practices.

damsi (*dam sri*). Powerful oath-breaking demons who began as tantric practitioners and then turned against the Dharma but have power based on their previously accumulated virtue.

Dharma (*chos*). When capitalized, (1) the teachings of the Buddha and when lowercased, (2) phenomena.

dharmadhātu (*chos kyi dbying*). The basic space of phenomena. Phenomena, or dharma (*chos*), refers to all appearances, and dhātu (*dbying*) is expanse or nature, referring to emptiness as the nature of phenomena.

dharmakāya (*chos sku*). See **trikāya**.

dharmapāla (*chos skyong*). Protector principle of the Buddhadharma and its practitioners. In tantra, visualized as wrathful beings.

dohā (*mgur*). A spiritual hymn or spontaneous yogic song sung by a tantric practitioner to express experience in meditation practice. The Bengali mahāsiddhas were famous for these songs, but the form saw its greatest development in the collected songs of the Tibetan yogi Milarepa and his successors.

dön (*gdon*). An evil spirit or obstacle.

dralha (*dgra lha, dgra bla*). Warrior spirits usually portrayed on horseback and represent the strength and physical integrity of a warrior. According to Orgyen Tobgyal Rinpoche, the inner aspect of dralha is connected to the subtle energy system of the body and the secret aspect to the nature of mind. These are also referred to as *werma*, and in fact the two are interchangeable.

drong (*'brong*). A wild yak that runs in herds on the high plains and is never domesticated.

dütsi (*bdud rtsi*). See **amṛta**.

dzo (*mdzo*). A male beast of burden, the result of crossing a yak bull with a female cow, sterile and with horns. They are considered to be the hardiest for merchants' travel and caravans.

dzomo (*mdzo mo*). A female hybrid of a yak bull and a female cow, horned or hornless, fertile, and prized for the richness of its milk and butter.

eight classes (*sde brgyad*). Worldly spirits also referred to as the eight classes of gods-demons (*lha 'dre sde brgyad*), the eight classes of the haughty spirits, or the eight classes of spirits. Although there are other designations, they are commonly given as: māras (*bdud*), mamos (*ma mo*, Skt. *mātṛkā*), nāgas (*klu*), gings (*kiṃkaras*), rāhula (*sgra gcan 'dzin*), tsen (*btsan*), rākṣasa (*srin po*), and yakṣas (*gnod sbyin*).

five buddha families (*sangs rgyas rig lnga*). Buddha, Vajra, Ratna, Padma, and Karma, representing different aspects of confused and enlightened mind. The enlightened aspects are represented by the buddhas of each family, respectively: Vairocana, Akṣobhya, Ratnasambhava, Amitābha, and Amoghasiddhi.

five poisons. See **kleśa**.

gaṇacakra (*tshogs kyi 'khor lo*). A religious feast ceremony.

garuḍa (*khyung*). The mythic king of birds and the representation of a warrior's maturity and fearlessness.

generation and completion stages (*skye rim, rdzogs rim*). Two meditation stages according to Vajrayāna Buddhist practice. In the generation stage, one produces a mental image of a deity and his or her palace. In the completion or fulfillment stage, this visualization is resolved into emptiness and one meditates formlessly without an objective focal point.

gods-demons (*lha 'dre*). This term does not imply duality but rather the dynamic quality of going back and forth. In wisdom deity practice, one must understand the nature of the wisdom deity, otherwise the deity becomes worldly and thence kingly, demonic, and evil.

gongpo (*'gong po*). Shape-shifting sorcerers, spirits who cause mishap.

guru (*gu ru*). Spiritual teacher or lama.

gyalgong (*rgyal 'gong*). Kingly demons born from the union of gyalpo and gongpo spirits.

gyalpo (*rgyal po*). Literally "king," wrathful spirits that travel the skies.

heruka (*khrag 'thung*). Literally, "blood-drinker," a wrathful male yidam that symbolizes the drinking of the blood of ego-clinging and dualistic mind.

hungry ghost (*yi dwags*; Skt. *preta*). Inhabitants of one of the three lower realms among the six realms of rebirth in saṃsāra. They have huge stomachs and tiny mouths and are always hungry and thirsty but never satisfied.

jungpo (*'byung po*). A kind of demon, particularly one that causes the collapse of success.

kāya (*sku*). An honorific term for "body."

ketaka (*ke ta ka*). A precious heirloom water-purifying gem given by Trothung to King Yutsé when they first meet.

kleśa (*nyon mongs*). Conflicting mental states, typically the five negative emotions and their resultant actions: ignorance, aversion, pride, attachment, and envy.

kyang (*rkyang*). The Tibetan wild ass. Unlike Western notions of the ass, this is an exceptionally impressive and noble creature who wanders the high plains and mountains.

lha, lu, and nyen (*lha, klu, gnyan*). The lha, lu, and nyen, are spiritual forces that assist, respectively, energies of space, the divine; energies of the underground, water; and energies of the earth, mountains, trees, and so forth. These forces present themselves on intense occasions and demonstrate the inseparability of one's ordinary mind and enlightened mind. They are referred to numerous times throughout the epic as difficult situations arise.

lhasang (*lha bsangs*). A ceremonial smoke offering, usually of juniper boughs.

lu. See **nāga** and **nāginī**; **lha, lu, and nyen**.

mahāsiddha (*grub thob*). Literally, "great accomplished one," a spiritually accomplished yogi or *yoginī* in both Buddhism and Hinduism. In the Gesar epic, the Thirty Mighty Warriors are considered emanations of thirty of the mahāsiddhas.

MAṆĪ mantra. The six-syllable Sanskrit mantra, repeated as OṂ MAṆI PADME HŪṂ, particularly connected with Avalokiteśvara, Lord of Compassion, and his manifestation Padmasambhava. Translated as "Hail to the Jewel in the Lotus," it indicates the bodhisattva of compassion as well as the indwelling buddha nature that abides as the basic enlightened nature of all living beings. By repeating this mantra, compassionate awareness is stirred to realize that all beings have this enlightened potential and are to be honored and cherished above oneself. Amended as OṂ MAṆI PADME HŪṂ HRĪḤ, the syllable HRĪḤ is Avalokiteśvara's heart essence seed syllable.

māra. A general term for demon or obstructer of virtue but also the entity that challenged the Buddha on the night of his enlightenment. In the epic, it also refers to the demons that inhabited the borderlands of Ling and were Gesar's adversaries. See glossary of names: **Düd**.

menmo (*sman mo*). Female spirits, often wrathful.

mu (*dmu*). A malignant spirit, an evil demon that causes dropsy. This is not to be confused with the mu cord or Mu clan. See glossary of names: **Mu clan**.

mu cord (*rmu thag*). The mu cord is a mythical cord that connects kings and leaders to the space of the heavens. Not to be confused with mu spirits or Mu clan. See **mu**. See glossary of names: **Mu clan**.

myriarchy (*khri skor*). A community of ten thousand under a single ruling leadership or a military force of ten thousand soldiers.

nāga and **nāginī** (*klu, klu mo*). Male and female semi-divine water-dwelling beings with human upper bodies and serpentlike lower bodies; common to Buddhism, Hinduism, and Jainism.

nirmāṇakāya (*sprul sku*). See **trikāya**.

nyen. See **lha, lu, nyen**.

phowa (*'pho ba*). Literally "transference," the ejection of consciousness at the moment of death.

pika (*'bra ba*). An English term, this is a prairie-dog-like rodent that burrows, creating complicated tunnel systems. High pasturage nomads consider them pests, believing that their burrowing activity destroys grasslands, turning the ground into barren "black earth" (*sa nag po*).

prajñā (*shes rab*). Incisive knowledge and the innate quality of the mind's true nature that is capable of discerning with wisdom awareness.

pure land (*zhing khams*). An abode of buddhas and bodhisattvas, also known as a buddhafield.

rākṣasa, rākṣasī (*srin po, srin mo*). Often translated as "cannibal demons," cannibal shape-shifting monsters with magical powers.

realms, six (*'gro ba rigs drug*). The six states of being: the deva or god realm, the asura or jealous god realm, the human realm, the animal realm, the hungry ghost realm, and the hell realm.

sādhana (*sgrub thabs*). A ritual text and liturgy for meditation practice and mantra recitation. It also refers to the meditation practice itself.

samādhi (*ting nge 'dzin*). A state of deep meditative absorption.

samaya (*dam tshig*). Literally, "sacred word," spiritual commitments that generally refer to tantric vows.

sambhogakāya (*longs spyod rdzogs pa'i sku*). See **trikāya**.

saṃsāra (*'khor ba*). Literally, "to circle," a term for the cycle of birth, death, and rebirth that arises out of ignorance and is characterized by suffering.

siddhi (*dngos grub*). Literally, "accomplishment," abilities developed through meditation practice. They are ordinary or supreme: the ordinary siddhis are physical and the supreme siddhi is enlightenment.

six realms. See **realms, six**.

stupa (*chos rten*). Historically a mound and now a less modest monument containing the relics of enlightened beings and representing the nature of enlightened mind.

sugata (*bde bar gshegs pa*). Literally, "gone to bliss," an epithet for the Buddha or a general term for a buddha.

tenma (*bstan ma*). Twelve sisters who were zodors converted by Padmasambhava to protect the land of Tibet and the Buddha's teachings.

terma (*gter ma*). Sacred material objects and texts that were hidden during the lives of Padmasambhava and Yeshé Tsogyal and predicted to be revealed by their designated disciples in future centuries. However, many terma are immaterial, in that the teachings spring forth from the minds of these disciples.

teurang (*the'u rang*). A class of demons.

time periods. The twelve two-hour periods according to the animals of the zodiac in the ancient Chinese system of dividing the twenty-four-hour day. The periods are given as: 11:00 p.m.–1:00 a.m., rat; 1:00 a.m.–3:00 a.m., ox; 3:00 a.m.–5:00 a.m., tiger; 5:00 a.m.–7:00 a.m., rabbit; 7:00 a.m.–9:00 a.m., dragon; 9:00 a.m.–11:00 a.m., snake; 11:00 a.m.–1:00 p.m., horse; 1:00 p.m.–3:00 p.m., goat or sheep; 3:00 p.m.–5:00 p.m., monkey; 5:00 p.m.–7:00 p.m., rooster; 7:00 p.m.–9:00 p.m., dog; 9:00 p.m.–11:00 p.m., pig.

Three Jewels (*dkon mchog gsum*). The objects of refuge: Buddha, Dharma, and Saṅgha.

Three Roots (*rtsa gsum*). Guru, yidam, and ḍākinī.

torma (*gtor ma*). Offering cakes made from roasted barley flour, painted with food dyes, and ornamented with colored wheels of butter.

trikāya (*sku gsum*). The three bodies of the Buddha: dharmakāya, the absolute nature; saṃbhogakāya, the intrinsic nature of reality; and nirmāṇakāya, the physical manifestation as compassion, represented in the present era as Śākyamuni, the buddha of the present age.

tsatsa (*tsa tsa*). A miniature clay image of a deity or of a stupa.

tsen (*btsan*). Literally, "powerful," one of the eight classes of spirits, a nonhuman disease-causing demon.

vajra (*rdo rje*). (1) An ancient Hindu weapon (Indra's thunderbolt). (2) A Buddhist ritual object symbolizing indestructibility.

vajra tent (*rdo rje gur*). A representation of sacredness that guards against negativity of any form. The term *vajra* means "adamantine" or "indestructible," and this term implies a practice or visualization by an accomplished teacher, such as Gesar, that is a protection visualization guarding against mind-based obstacles.

vidyādhara (*rig 'dzin*). Literally, "knowledge holder," an accomplished practitioner of Vajrayāna.

werma (*wer ma*). See **dralha**.

windhorse (*rlung rta*). The inner energy of dignity and confidence that results in good fortune and success when humbly implemented. It is also the term for a representation of a flying horse displayed on pennants that flap in the wind.

yabyum (*yab yum*). Male and female in sexual union, more generally signifying the union of skillful means and wisdom.

yakṣa (*gnod sbyin*). One of the eight classes (see above) and a spirit that can be benevolent or harmful. It is sometimes called the wealth spirit.

yidam (*yi dam*). A meditational deity that is a Vajrayāna practitioner's personal or tutelary deity and a representation of the practitioner's awakened nature.

zodor (*zo dor*). A local guardian spirit of the land. In the epic of Gesar, the zodor, when referred to in the singular, is usually the god of Mount Magyal Pomra.

BIBLIOGRAPHY

Cornu, Philippe. *Tibetan Astrology*. Translated from the French by Hamish Gregor. Boston: Shambhala, 2002.

Goldstein, Melvin C. "When Brothers Share a Wife." *Natural History* (March 1987): 39–48.

Karmay, Samten G. "The Social Organization of Ling and the Term Phu-nu in the Gesar Epic." *Bulletin of the School of Oriental and African Studies* 58, no. 2 (1995): 303–13.

———. "The Theoretical Basis of the Tibetan Epic, with Reference to a 'Chronological Order' of the Various Episodes in the Gesar Epic." *Bulletin of the School of Oriental and African Studies* 56, no. 2 (1993): 234–46.

Kornman, Robin, Sangye Khandro, and Lama Chönam. *The Epic of Gesar of Ling: Gesar's Magical Birth, Early Years, and Coronation as King*. Boston: Shambhala, 2012.

Samuel, Geoffrey. *Civilized Shamans: Buddhism in Tibetan Societies*. Washington, DC: Smithsonian Institute Press, 1993.

Shantideva. *A Guide to the Bodhisattva's Way of Life*. Translated by Stephen Batchelor. Dharamsala: Library of Tibetan Works and Archives, 1979.

Shapiro, David. *Gesar of Ling: A Bardic Tale from the Snow Land of Tibet*. Bloomington, IN: Balboa Press, 2019.

Stein, Rolf. *L'épopée tibétaine dans sa version lamaïque de Ling*. Paris: Presses Universitaires de France, 1956.